Critical reflections on the
Odes of Solomon

JOURNAL FOR THE STUDY OF THE PSEUDEPIGRAPHA SUPPLEMENT SERIES
22

Editors
James H. Charlesworth
Lester L. Grabbe

Sheffield Academic Press

By the same author

Jesus and the Dead Sea Scrolls (Doubleday)

The Odes of Solomon (Clarendon Press)

The Old Testament Pseudepigrapha (2 vols.; Darton, Longman & Todd)

Critical Reflections on the Odes of Solomon

Volume 1: Literary Setting, Textual Studies, Gnosticism, the Dead Sea Scrolls and the Gospel of John

James H. Charlesworth

Journal for the Study of the Pseudepigrapha
Supplement Series 22

The Distinguished Scholars Collection

Copyright © 1998 Sheffield Academic Press

Published by
Sheffield Academic Press Ltd
Mansion House
19 Kingfield Road
Sheffield S11 9AS
England

Typeset by Sheffield Academic Press
and
Printed on acid-free paper in Great Britain
by Bookcraft Ltd
Midsomer Norton, Bath

British Library Cataloguing in Publication Data

A catalogue record for this book is available
from the British Library

ISBN 1-85075-660-0

CONTENTS

PREFACE AND ACKNOWLEDGMENTS

The essays reprinted in this volume appear with corrections and with the original scripts usually now present. Chapters 2, 3, 8, 9 and 10 are revised. Chapters 1, 5, 6 and 7 are rewritten. Chapter 4 is a revised chapter of my PhD dissertation. Appendices to an essay note new insights and draw attention to the most important publications related to the subject discussed in it. I am grateful to Kevin S. Diller for helping me with computer work and showing me how to enter the exotic scripts. He also retyped all these chapters. I am also grateful to Dean Alan Culpepper for allowing me to republish our joint article on the *Odes* and the Fourth Gospel. Casey D. Elledge assisted me in preparing this book. Appreciations also are extended to the periodicals or books in which these essays originally appeared. The reader might appreciate being informed of the original date and location of the essays that have appeared previously:

'The Odes of Solomon: An Overview', *IDBSup* (1976), pp. 637-38 and *ABD*, VI, pp. 114-15.

'Hymns and Odes in Early Judaism', in R.A. Kraft and G.W.E. Nickelsburg (eds.), *Early Judaism and its Modern Interpreters* (Philadelphia: Fortress Press; Atlanta: Scholars Press, 1986).

'Hymns and Odes in Early Christianity', *JJS* [the Yadin Festschrift] 33 (1982), pp. 265-85.

'ܟܬܒܐ in Earliest Christianity', in J.M. Efird (ed.), *The Use of the Old Testament and Other Essays: Studies in Honor of William Franklin Stinespring* (Durham, NC: Duke University Press, 1972), pp. 271-79.

'Paronomasia and Assonance in the Syriac Text of the Odes of Solomon', *Semitics* [Pretoria] 1 (1970), pp. 12-26.

'Haplography and Philology: A Study of the Odes of Solomon', *NTS* 25 (1979), pp. 221-27.

'The Odes of Solomon: Not Gnostic', *CBQ* 31 (1969), pp. 357-69.

'Qumran, John, and the Odes of Solomon', in J.H. Charlesworth (ed.), *John and Qumran* (London: Geoffrey Chapman, 1972; New York: Crossroad, 1991), pp. 107-36.

[with Culpepper] 'The Odes of Solomon and the Gospel of John', *CBQ* 35 (1973), pp. 298-322.

I am most grateful to these periodicals for permission to republish these essays; specifically I wish to extend appreciations for this permission to the following presses: Abingdon, Doubleday, Fortress, Scholars, Cambridge University, Chapman, Crossroad and Duke. I also express appreciations to the Oxford Centre for Postgraduate Studies, the Catholic Biblical Association, and the Studiorum Novi Testamenti Societas. I am also grateful to Sheffield Academic Press for the leadership in sponsoring this important series.

The essays are a record of past study. Hopefully they are more—a stimulus to research on these often amazingly brilliant and insightful *Odes*.

ܒܠܚܝܕ ܐܝܩܪܐ ܠܐܠܗܐ ܐܒܐ ܥܠ ܝܫܘܥ
❖ܡܠܟܐ.

JHC
Princeton
June 1997

ABBREVIATIONS

AB	Anchor Bible
ABD	David Noel Freedman (ed.), *The Anchor Bible Dictionary* (New York: Doubleday, 1992)
AGSU	Arbeiten zur Geschichte des Spätjudentums und Urchristentums
AIPhHOS	Annuaire de l'institut de philologie et d'histoire orientales et slaves
AJSL	*American Journal of Semitic Languages and Literatures*
AJT	*American Journal of Theology*
ALGHJ	Arbeiten zur Literatur und Geschichte des hellenistischen Judentums
ALUOS	Annual of Leeds University Oriental Society
AnBib	Analecta biblica
ANRW	Hildegard Temporini and Wolfgang Haase (eds.), *Aufstieg und Niedergang der römischen Welt: Geschichte und Kultur Roms im Spiegel der neueren Forschung* (Berlin: W. de Gruyter, 1972–)
APOT	R.H. Charles (ed.), *Apocrypha and Pseudepigrapha of the Old Testament in English* (2 vols.; Oxford: Clarendon Press, 1913)
ATDan	Acta Theologica Danica
AusBR	*Australian Biblical Review*
BA	*Biblical Archaeologist*
BASOR	*Bulletin of the American Schools of Oriental Research*
BBB	Bonner biblische Beiträge
BETL	Bibliotheca ephemeridum theologicarum lovaniensium
Bib	*Biblica*
BibB	Biblische Beiträge
BJRL	*Bulletin of the John Rylands University Library of Manchester*
BJS	Brown Judaic Studies
BR	*Bible Review*
BW	*The Biblical World*
BWANT	Beiträge zur Wissenschaft vom Alten und Neuen Testament
BZAW	Beihefte zur *ZAW*
BZNW	Beihefte zur *ZNW*
CAD	Ignace I. Gelb *et al.* (eds.), *The Assyrian Dictionary of the Oriental Institute of the University of Chicago* (Chicago: Oriental Institute, 1964–)

CBQ	*Catholic Biblical Quarterly*
CF	*Ciencia y Fe*
CSCO	Corpus scriptorum christianorum orientalium
DBSup	*Dictionnaire de la Bible, Supplément*
DJD	Discoveries in the Judaean Desert
DL	*Doctrine and Life*
DR	Deutsche Rundschau
DTT	*Dansk teologisk tidsskrift*
EBib	Etudes bibliques
EncIT	*Enciclopedia italiane di scienze, lettere ed arti*
EncJud	*Encyclopaedia Judaica*
EstBíb	*Estudios bíblicos*
Exp	*The Expositor*
ExpTim	*Expository Times*
FRLANT	Forschungen zur Religion und Literatur des Alten und Neuen Testaments
FzB	Forschung zur Bibel
GGA	Göttingische Gelehrte Anzeigen
GThT	*Gereformeerd theologisch tijdschrift*
HeyJ	*Heythrop Journal*
HNT	Handbuch zum Neuen Testament
HSM	Harvard Semitic Monographs
HTR	*Harvard Theological Review*
HTS	Harvard Theological Studies
HUCA	*Hebrew Union College Annual*
ICC	International Critical Commentary
IDB	George Arthur Buttrick (ed.), *The Interpreter's Dictionary of the Bible* (4 vols.; Nashville: Abingdon Press, 1962)
IDBSup	*IDB*, Supplementary Volume
Int	*Interpretation*
IW	*Internationale Wochenschrift für Wissenschaft Kunst und Technik*
JBL	*Journal of Biblical Literature*
JJS	*Journal of Jewish Studies*
JPOS	*Journal of the Palestine Oriental Society*
JQR	*Jewish Quarterly Review*
JSHRZ	Jüdische Schriften aus hellenistisch-römischer Zeit
JSNTSup	*Journal for the Study of the New Testament*, Supplement Series
JSOT	*Journal for the Study of the Old Testament*
JSP	*Journal for the Study of the Pseudepigrapha*
JSS	*Journal of Semitic Studies*
JTC	*Journal for Theology and the Church*
JTS	*Journal of Theological Studies*
KAT	Kommentar zum Alten Testament
KlT	Kleine Texte

MGWJ	*Monatsschrift für Geschichte und Wissenschaft des Judentums*
MPTh	*Monatsschrift für Pastoraltheologie*
Mus	*Le Muséon: Revue des études orientales*
NCB	*New College Bulletin*
NHS	Nag Hammadi Studies
NKZ	*Neue kirchliche Zeitschrift*
NovT	*Novum Testamentum*
NovTSup	*Novum Testamentum, Supplements*
NRSV	New Revised Standard Version
NThT	*Nieuw Theologisch Tijdschrift*
NTOA	Novum Testamentum et orbis antiquus
NTS	*New Testament Studies*
OCA	Orientalia christiana analecta
OLZ	*Orientalistische Literaturzeitung*
OrChr	*Oriens christianus*
OTL	Old Testament Library
OTP	James Charlesworth (ed.), *Old Testament Pseudepigrapha*
PEQ	*Palestine Exploration Quarterly*
PETSE	Papers of the Estonian Theological Society in Exile
PG	J.-P. Migne (ed.), *Patrologia cursus completa ... series graeca* (166 vols.; Paris: Petit-Montrouge, 1857–83)
PTSDSSP	The Princeton Theological Seminary Dead Sea Scrolls Project
RB	*Revue biblique*
RBén	*Revue bénédictine*
RCHL	*Revue critique d'histoire et de littérature*
RechBib	Recherches bibliques
RevQ	*Revue de Qumran*
RevT	*Revue de théologie et des questions religieuses*
RevThom	*Revue thomiste*
RGG	H. Gunkel and L. Zschamack (eds.), *Die Religion in Geschichte und Gegenwart* (Tübingen: J.C.B. Mohr [Paul Siebeck], 3rd edn, 1981).
RocTK	*Roczniki teologiczno-kanoniczne*
RPA	*Revue pratique d'apologétique*
RSR	*Recherches de science religieuse*
RStCST	*Rivista Storico-Critica delle Scienze Teologiche*
RSV	Revised Standard Version
RTP	*Revue de théologie et de philosophie*
SBLDS	SBL Dissertation Series
SBLMS	SBL Monograph Series
SBLSBS	SBL Sources for Biblical Study
SBLSCS	SBL Septuagint and Cognate Studies
SBT	Studies in Biblical Theology
SC	Sources chrétiennes
SE	*Sacris erudiri*

Sem	*Semitica*
SIMSVD	Studia instituti missiogici societatis verbi divini
SJ	Studia judaica
SJLA	Studies in Judaism in Late Antiquity
SNT	Studien zum Neuen Testament
SNTS	*Studiorum Novi Testamenti Societas*
SNTSMS	*Studiorum Novi Testamenti Societas* Monograph Series
ST	*Studia theologica*
STDJ	Studies on the Texts of the Desert of Judah
SUNT	Studien zur Umwelt des Neuen Testaments
SVTP	Studia in Veteris Testamenti pseudepigrapha
TGl	*Theologie und Glaube*
ThSt	*Theologische studiën*
TLZ	*Theologische Literaturzeitung*
TRev	*Theologische Revue*
TS	*Theological Studies*
TSK	*Theologische Studien und Kritiken*
TTod	*Theology Today*
TTZ	*Trierer theologische Zeitschrift*
TU	Texte und Untersuchungen
TZ	*Theologische Zeitschrift*
UNDCSJCA	University of Notre Dame Center for the Study of Judaism and Christianity in Antiquity
VC	*Vigiliae christianae*
VT	*Vetus Testamentum*
VTSup	*Vetus Testamentum*, Supplements
WAT	Wissenschaft vom Alten Testament
WUNT	Wissenschaftliche Untersuchungen zum Neuen Testament
ZAW	*Zeitschrift für die alttestamentliche Wissenschaft*
ZDMG	*Zeitschrift der deutschen morgenländischen Gesellschaft*
ZDPV	*Zeitschrift des deutschen Palästina-Vereins*
ZNW	*Zeitschrift für die neutestamentliche Wissenschaft*

Part I
THE LITERARY SETTING OF THE *ODES*

The *Odes of Solomon*—ܕܫܠܝܡܘܢ ܙܡܝܪ̈ܬܐ—are 42 hymns attributed to Solomon, perhaps because he was known to have composed 1005 songs (1 Kgs 4.32). At least one composition from antiquity attributed to Solomon, or bearing his name, is now lost; it is the Book of the Acts of Solomon mentioned in 1 Kgs 11.41 and 2 Chron. 9.29. Attributed to Solomon are numerous compositions in the Hebrew Bible and in the Old Testament Apocrypha. Only one document in the Old Testament Pseudepigrapha is attributed to him; it is called the *Psalms of Solomon*. This Jewish hymnbook represents the thoughts of Jews similar to the Pharisees. It contains 18 hymns and was composed in Jerusalem just before the rise of Herod the Great (40–4 BCE).

In my judgment, the *Odes of Solomon* are originally Christian, but they are also very Jewish. The Odist writes in a way typical of the authors of the Dead Sea Scrolls. The *Odes* thus are strikingly similar to the hymns found in the *Thanksgiving Hymns*, which was the 'hymn-book' of the Qumran Community. This Community is the one in which some of the Dead Sea Scrolls were composed, and it was most likely the strict or more conservative branch of the Essenes. The author of the *Odes of Solomon* seems to have known other Dead Sea Scrolls. In particular, he knew the most important document of the Community which contains their Qumran rules and guidelines for living; it is now called the *Rule of the Community*. Hence, the speculation arises that the Odist had been an Essene before he 'converted to Christianity', if that is the appropriate choice of words.

To illustrate this point, the Odist seems to know the formula by which the individual compositions in the *Thanksgiving Hymns* customarily begin; that is, he knew the Hodayoth formula which is not found in the Psalter, although they are in the genre of the biblical thanksgiving psalms (the formula is found in Isa. 12.1 and probably developed from the introductory phrases in Pss. 9.2, 111.1 and 138.1). Thus, as the Jew who composed the *Thanksgiving Hymns* begins a hymn with 'I praise you, O Lord, because' (אודכה אדוני כי), the Odist begins *Ode* 5 with 'I praise you, O Lord because' (ܡܘܕܐ ܐܢܐ ܠܟ ܡܪܝ ܡܛܠ). Many other similarities between the *Odes* and the *Thanksgiving Hymns* could be mentioned; only two more examples will suffice. The idea of 'walking in error' (*Ode* 18.14) is similar to 'they who walk in the way that is not good' (1QH 15.18 [Sukenik's numbering]). Likewise, *Ode* 18.6 contains a thought virtually identical to that encountered in 1QS 3.19. In both collections light (ܢܘܗܪܐ = אור) is contrasted to darkness (ܚܫܘܟܐ = חושׁב [N.B. medial consonant in final position]) and falsehood (ܥܘܠܬܐ) or perversity (העול) is antithetical to truth (ܩܘܫܬܐ = האמת).

There is abundant evidence that the original language of the *Odes* is Semitic, probably an early form of Syriac (as in the Old Syriac inscriptions). The date of the composition is most likely some time before 125 CE.[1] Currently, it is impossible to discern the provenience of this pseudepigraphon but it is probably somewhere in Syria (probably western Syria, which would include Galilee).

The striking conceptual and linguistic links between the *Odes* and the Fourth Gospel indicate not that the author of this gospel was somehow dependent upon them (*pace* Bultmann) or that the *Odes* borrowed from the Fourth Gospel. It is most likely that they come to us from the same milieu or community. I have been persuaded that the Odist eventually lived within the Johannine community, which most likely included not only Samaritans but also Essenes who believed that Jesus was the Messiah.[2] These are my own views which have taken shape since the mid-sixties as the reprinted articles in this collection indicate.

The study of the *Odes of Solomon* in this century may be divided into three overlapping, but distinct, periods. First, is the 'Period of Discovery and Excitement' which covers the years from 1909 to 1920. Although in 1812 Bishop F. Münter observed that they were quoted in the *Pistis Sophia* (in Coptic), a manuscript of the *Odes* was not discovered until 1909. In that year J.R. Harris discovered that one of the unexamined Syriac manuscripts in his office contained the long-lost composition known in antiquity as the *Odes of Solomon*. The excite-

---

1. See M. Lattke, 'Dating the Odes of Solomon', in *Antichthon* 27 (1993), pp. 45-59.

2. See J.H. Charlesworth, 'The Dead Sea Scrolls and the Gospel According to John', in R.A. Culpepper and C.C. Black (eds.), *Exploring the Gospel of John* (Louisville, KY: Westminster/John Knox Press, 1991), pp. 43-64.

ment aroused by this discovery attracted the attention of the most distinguished scholars. The following luminaries published something on the *Odes* immediately or soon after Harris's discovery (only the most distinguished scholars and their most significant publication(s) are selected): E.A. Abbott (1912, 1914), B.W. Bacon (1911, 1912), R. Bultmann (1911), J. H. Bernard (1910, 1912, 1913), W. Bousset (1910), C. Brockelmann (1912), A. Büchler (1912), F.C. Burkitt (1912 [*bis*]), R.H. Charles (1910 [*bis*]), F.C. Conybeare (1913), W. Frankenberg (1911), M.D. Gibson (1914 [*bis*]), M. Goguel (1911), E.J. Goodspeed (1910 [*bis*]), H. Gressmann (1911 [many], 1913), H. Grimme (1910, 1911 [many], 1912), C. Guignebert (1911, 1912), H. Gunkel (1910, 1913 [many]), A. Harnack (1910, 1912), J.R. Harris (too many to list), A.C. Headlam (1911), G. Kittel (1913 [*bis*], 1914), J. Labourt (1910, 1911 [many]), M.-J. Lagrange (1910), K. Lake (1911 [*bis*]), J. Lindblom (1911), A. Loisy (1911 [many], 1912), G.R.S. Mead (1909–10, 1910), A. Mingana (1914, 1915), J. Moffatt (1910, 1912), F. Nau (1910, 1911, 1912, 1914), E. Nestle (1910, 1911 [many], 1912 [many]), D. Plooij (1911, 1912 [*bis*], 1913), E. Preuschen (1910, 1913, 1915), A. Reinach (1910 [many], 1911, 1912 [*bis*]), E. Schürer (1910), P. Smith (1915), F. Spitta (1910 [many]), W. Staerk (1910), R.H. Strachan (1910), A. Ungnad and W. Staerk (1910), J. Wellhausen (1910 [*bis*]), T. Zahn (1910), and J. de Zwaan (1911 [*bis*], 1916). Virtually every leading biblical scholar during this period published something on the *Odes of Solomon*.

The period may be characterized as a time of enthusiasm. The *Odes* were deemed to be, if not a first-century composition, at least a second-century writing. The original language was Greek. The *Odes* were seen to have most likely influenced the composition of the Fourth Gospel. They were certainly not a gnostic work.

The second period of research—the 'Period of Denigration'—is from 1920 to 1959. In 1920 Harris and Mingana published the third edition of the *Odes*. In 1959 M. Testuz published the *editio princeps* of the Greek text of *Ode* 11. The importance of the *Odes* seen during the first period led to their inclusion in the second edition of Hennecke's *Neutestamentliche Apokryphen* (1924). Many scholars tend to conclude that the *Odes* are a second-century work, and perhaps late in that century. Some experts judge the original language to be Greek. Frequently, New Testament specialists assume that the Fourth Gospel has influenced the *Odes*. And, most importantly, many scholars contend that the *Odes* are typical of second-century gnostic documents. Representative of this period, to a certain extent, is R. Bultmann's outstanding research. He thought that the *Odes* were an example of Gnosticism, but he claimed that the *Odes* represented the type of early gnostic impulse that shaped the Fourth Gospel. In contrast to the first and second periods, little original research was published on the *Odes*, and they were gradually relegated as relatively insignificant. Perhaps some of the neglect of the *Odes* was due to the world situation, specifically the aftermath following the Great War, the Depression and the Second World War.

The third period may be described as from 1959 to the present. In 1959 Testuz published Bodmer Papyrus XI, which preserved *Ode* 11 in Greek and which was introduced with the following words: ΩΔΗ ΣΟΛΟΜΩΝΤΟΣ (P.Bod. XI of the III Cent.). This is the 'Period of Renewed Interest and Careful Study' of the *Odes*. Although the *Odes* appeared again in Hennecke–Schneemelcher's *Neutestamentliche Apokryphen* of 1964, the effect of the second period in denigrating the *Odes* led to their removal from all subsequent editions of this influential collection.

It seems safe to report that the recovery of the Nag Hammadi Codices and especially the discovery of the Dead Sea Scrolls served as the catalyst for renewed research focused on the *Odes*. For example, Testuz thought that the *Odes* are a Jewish work and perhaps the author was an Essene. He was not the first to make the claim that the *Odes* are a Jewish work. Shortly after their discovery, A. Menzies and B.W. Bacon concluded that the *Odes* are a Jewish work, and Harnack was convinced that the *Odes* were originally Jewish but subsequently edited by a Christian. With the new insights obtained from studying the Dead Sea Scrolls, it is understandable why many scholars now perceive that the *Odes* are influenced by the symbolic theology characteristic of, and at times unique to, the Dead Sea Scrolls. Carmignac and Charlesworth are convinced that the Odist may have been once an Essene but became a Christian. One can conclude that the *Odes* are essentially Jewish and also 'Christian', provided that caveats are articulated clarifying that it is not easy to distinguish between 'Jewish' and 'Christian' documents that were composed in the first two centuries of the Common Era (witness the debates over the character of the *Testaments of the Twelve Patriarchs*).

During this period the date of the *Odes* becomes a topic of major disagreement, with suggestions ranging from the late first to the third century CE. Now, the majority of scholars opt for a date prior to 125 or at least 135 CE (the time of the defeat of Bar Kokhba). Obviously, the *Odes* were composed over numerous years, and perhaps decades, and, like the *Gospel of Thomas,* represent a mixture of early 'Christian' concepts. Like most New Testament documents, they also contain numerous Jewish ideas. Perhaps under the influence of the renewed appreciation of Semitics among New Testament experts, the original language is usually seen to be some form of Semitics, perhaps an early form of Syriac. The *Odes* are seen as important for a study of the Fourth Gospel, but unfortunately they are often ignored in commentaries.

Scholars have not come to a consensus regarding the origins of Gnosticism, yet it is relatively clear that Judaism has significantly influenced some forms of early Gnosticism (see especially the *Apocalypse of Adam* which is gnostic in its present and final form but may derive from Jewish baptist groups). Most experts would agree that the *Odes* are not typical of the late second-century gnostic systems, but they are often similar to the so-called 'gnostic' ideas found in the *Gospel of Thomas* and the *Gospel of Truth.* Note the following examples: *Ode* 38.12 and the *Gospel of Thomas* Log. 28 portray the unrepentant and blind sinners as those who are drunk (ܪܘܝܐ = TOϢЄ [but also see *Ahiqar* (Syriac) 8.31 and *Pss. Sol.* 18.15]). Both in *Ode* 11 and in the *Gos. Truth* 34–36 'fragrance' (ܪܝܚ = CTAЄ) is a key symbolic term; and God, who is the Father (ܐܒܐ [in *Ode* 10.4] = ΠΙΩΤ), is the one who has planted (ܢܨܒ = XO) the righteous (not trees) in paradise (ܦܪܕܝܣܐ = ΠΑΡΑΔΙϹϹΟϹ) which is the place of rest (ܢܝܚ = MTAN). If the *Odes* are to be labeled (certainly not branded) as gnostic, it is the type of thought in the earliest quasi-gnostic works such as the *Hymn of the Pearl.* The *Odes* are obviously not 'gnostic' like the metaphysical systems branded as Gnosticism; that is, they are paradigmatically different from the gnostic myth preserved in the *Secret Book According to John* (the long version). Of course, any discusssion of 'heresy' or 'orthodoxy' in the *Odes* would be simply anachronistic from a historical standpoint.

The *Odes of Solomon* were composed at a time when Gnosticism had not yet developed and when gnosis was a worldwide spiritual way of thinking. They also come to us from a time when Judaism and Christianity had not yet gone their separate ways. They certainly come to us from a mystic who breathed deeply not only from the spirituality of the Essenes but also from the circles in which the Fourth Gospel developed and went through at least two editions. Certainly appealing to the earliest followers of Jesus and to those experts who have devoted their lives to understanding these sometimes breathtakingly beautiful poems are such passages as the following:

> Who can interpret the wonders of the Lord?
> Though the one who interprets will be destroyed,
> Yet that which was interpreted will remain.
>
> For it suffices to perceive and be satisfied,
> For the odists stand in serenity;
>
> Like a river which has an increasingly gushing spring,
> And flows to the relief of those who seek it.
>
> Hallelujah.
>   (*Ode* 26.11-13)

A window into the world of the first believers is provided by sections of these *Odes*. Probably the inebriating excitement of the Jews who felt and experienced the joy of their belief that Jesus was the long-awaited Messiah is preserved in such passages as the following:

> My joy is the Lord and my course is towards him,
> This path of mine is beautiful.
>
> For there is a helper for me, the Lord.
> He has generously shown himself to me in his simplicity,
> Because his kindness has diminished his dreadfulness.
>
> He became like me that I might receive him.
> In form he was considered like me that I might put him on.
>   (*Ode* 7.2-4)
>
> We live in the Lord by his grace,
> And life we receive by his Messiah (ܡܫܝܚܗ) .
>
> For a great day has shined upon us,
> And wonderful is he who has given to us of his glory.
>   (*Ode* 41.3-4)
>
> And his Word (ܘܡܠܬܗ) is with us in all our way,
> The Savior (ܦܪܘܩܐ) who gives life and does not reject us.

The man who humbled himself,
But was exalted because of his own righteousness.

The Son of the Most High appeared
In the Perfection of his father.

And light dawned from the Word (ܡܠܬܐ)
That was before time with him.

The Messiah (ܡܫܝܚܐ) in truth is one.
And he was known before the foundations of the world,
That he might give life to persons for ever by the truth of his name.

A new chant (is) for the Lord from them that love him.
Hallelujah.
   (*Ode* 41.11-16)

Chapter 1

THE *ODES OF SOLOMON*: AN OVERVIEW

The *Odes of Solomon* is an early hymnbook. It is neither pre-Christian and Jewish nor late and gnostic. It reflects the joyful thanksgivings of the early Jewish-Christians and contains metaphorical language characteristic of the Dead Sea Scrolls and the Johannine literature.

Thus, it is evident that some time around or after 100 CE a Christian, heavily influenced by Jewish thought, especially similar to that found in the Jewish apocalypses and within some of the Dead Sea Scrolls, composed 42 Odes. He may even have dedicated them to Solomon.

The *Odes* were listed by Nicephorus and Pseudo-Athanasius. The 11th Ode was found among the Bodmer Papyri in a third-century Greek manuscript (no. 11). Five were translated into Coptic in the fourth century and used to illustrate the *Pistis Sophia* (*Odes* 1, 5, 6, 22 and 25). Also in the fourth century *Ode* 19 was quoted by Lactantius (*Div. Inst.* 4.12.3). In the tenth century a scribe copied the *Odes* in Syriac, but only *Odes* 17.7–42.20 are preserved (British Museum MS Add. 14538). In the fifteenth century another scribe copied them into Syriac, but again the beginning is lost (John Rylands Library Cod. Syr. 9 contains only *Odes* 3.1b–42.20).

In 1812 the *Odes of Solomon* were discovered by a Danish bishop, F. Münter, in the *Pistis Sophia*. In 1909 they were detected by J. Rendell Harris in a manuscript on his shelves. He published the *editio princeps* the same year. In 1912 they were observed by F.C. Burkitt in a manuscript in the British Museum.

During the first decade after the *editio princeps*, there was a flurry of scholarly publications. The consensus emerged that the *Odes* were very early. Harris contended that they were a hymnbook of the first-century church. J.H. Bernard claimed they were written in the last half of the second century. A. Harnack was convinced that the *Odes* antedate and help us understand the origins of the Fourth Gospel.

Since the 1960s scholars have once again been attracted to the *Odes of Solomon*. Many scholars, like K. Rudolph, contend that they are a second-century gnostic work. M. Testuz argued that the author was an Essene who lived sometime in the first century CE. J. Carmignac was convinced that they were composed by a Christian who had been a Qumran Essene and there is ample reason to take seriously that possibility. While some specialists think the *Odes* were composed in Greek (M. Philonenko, A.F.J. Klijn), Syriac scholars such as A. Vööbus, J.A. Emerton, J.H. Charlesworth and L. Abramowski have argued that they were composed in Syriac.

1. *Original Language*

Early arguments for a Greek original were undermined by the recognition of the Semitic quality of the *Odes*, whereupon a Hebrew original was proposed. But there are impressive data to indicate that Syriac (or a mixture of Aramaic and Syriac) may itself be the original language. On the one hand, most of the reasons for a Greek original have lost their persuasiveness: occasional dependence upon the LXX, parallels with gnostic literature, and the style of the extant Greek. On the other hand, the reasons against a Syriac original were suggested early in this century when Syriac was often denigrated and when some scholars anachronistically judged the Syriac poetry of the *Odes* according to the late classical norms of Ephraem Syrus. The most impressive argument for a Syriac original is the intrinsic quality of the Syriac: the play on words, some of which is possible only in Syriac (viz. 19.9), assonance, parallelisms, metrical scheme and rhythm. Numerous variants between the Coptic, Greek and Syriac are evidently explained by a Syriac *Urtext*: e.g. *māryâ* for *mᵉraimâ* in 5.2 and 23.4, and *brk* and *krk* in 22.6.

2. *Date*

Discerning the date of the *Odes* has provoked considerable interest. H.J. Drijvers contends that they are as late as the third century. L. Abramowski places them in the later half of the second century. B. McNeil argued that they are contemporaneous with *4 Ezra*, the *Shepherd of Hermas*, Polycarp, and Valentinus (c. 100 CE). Most scholars date them some time around the middle of the second century; but, if they are heavily influenced by Jewish apocalyptic thought and especially the ideas of the Dead Sea Scrolls, a date long after 100 CE is unlikely. H. Chadwick, Emerton, Charlesworth, and many other scholars are convinced that they must not be labeled 'gnostic' and therefore should not be dated to the late second or third century.

Dating is difficult because the Odist is not quoted by authors during the first two centuries. The Odist also does not refer to historical events. Since the *Odes* are defined by religious experience, they cannot be dated by an examination of the development of dogma. The attempts to place them within the sect that composed the Dead Sea Scrolls have failed to convince specialists, since Christian elements permeate the hymns and are not merely redactional. They cannot be earlier than 30 CE because they are Christian; and, since significant parallels are not with patristic literature but with the Jewish Pseudepigrapha and especially the Dead Sea Scrolls, they are probably not later than 125 CE. The impressive parallels with the Qumran sectarian scrolls and the apparently close but not dependent relationship with the Johannine literature suggest that the most probable date is not far from 100 CE. This date is supported by the *Odes'* joyfulness, strong Jewish nature (the term 'Gentiles' is used negatively, 10.5; 23.15[N]; 29.8) and unrefined and at times almost docetic Christology (note also that two words are used equally for the divine Logos).

3. *Provenience*

Affinities between the *Odes* and the Fourth Gospel make either Ephesus, Antioch, or western Syria a likely place of origin. Antioch, Edessa or western Syria is probable if the original language is Syriac (or Aramaic-Syriac). The *Odes'* relationship with the Johannine literature, parallels to the Dead Sea Scrolls, early date, and affinities with Ignatius support the hypothesis that the *Odes* were composed within or not far from Antioch (which might include Galilee).

4. *Old Testament*

Although the Odist never quoted the Old Testament, he often borrowed a phrase or metaphor (cf. *Ode* 6 and Ezek. 7). *Ode* 41.9 seems dependent upon Prov. 8.22, and *Odes* 8.19, 16.12, and 22.9 are influenced respectively by Isa. 58.8, Gen. 2.2 and Ezek. 37.4-6. The Odist's major literary dependence is upon the Psalms, which he may have known in Hebrew and Greek. *Odes* 7.10 and 9.8-9 are based apparently upon the LXX of Pss. 50.3 [H 51.1] and 20.4 [H 21.3]. In at least two places the Odist seems to have diverged from the LXX; *Odes* 5.8 and 29.10 follow the Hebrew, or Syriac, and not the Greek of Pss. 21.11 and 1.4. As expected in a Christian hymnbook that rejoices in Christ's passion, the most influential psalm is the 22nd (28.14 = Ps. 22.16; 28.18 = Ps. 22.18; 31.8-13 = Ps. 22.16-18).

The Odist probably knew the 'Old Testament' (Hebrew Bible), especially the Davidic Psalter, by heart. Ps. 84.10 ('For a day in your courts is better than a thousand elsewhere') may have been on his mind when he composed *Ode* 4.5 ('For one hour of your faith / Is more excellent than all days and years'). Psalm 1.2 ('And in his Law he will meditate day and night') probably helped him compose *Ode* 41.6:

> And let our faces shine in his light,
> And let our hearts meditate in his love,
> By night and by day.

5. Dead Sea Scrolls
The *Odes* are strikingly similar to many ideas and images found in the Dead Sea Scrolls, especially the *Thanksgiving Hymns* [Sukenik's numbering will be used]. The *Odes* contain a dualism similar to that developed in 1QS 3.13–4.26, notably the paradigm opposing light and truth to darkness and perversity, with hypostatic creatures in polemical confrontation but subordinate to a creator. The *Odes* and the major Qumran sectarian scrolls contain a consciousness of being 'the Way', the dwelling place of the Holy Ones that God has founded upon the rock, and God's planting for his glory. Likewise, both the *Odes* and the Dead Sea Scrolls employ 'knowledge', 'the war', 'crown', 'living water', and 'the sun' as theological symbols. It is difficult to attribute all these similarities to a shared milieu within sectarian Judaism. The *Odes* were most likely influenced by the ideas developed in the Dead Sea Scrolls.

6. New Testament
The documents in the New Testament are not quoted in the *Odes* but the traditions recorded in them are evidently behind many of the Odist's poetic phrases. The traditions that praise Jesus' birth from a virgin, baptism and walking on the water motivate the Odist in *Odes* 19, 24, and 39 respectively. The passion and crucifixion are celebrated in *Ode* 8.5, 27; 28.9-20; 31.8-13; and 42. The tradition behind Mt. 16.18 is reflected in *Ode* 22.12:

> And the foundation of everything is your rock.
> And upon it you have built your kingdom,
> And it became the dwelling place of the Holy Ones.

Scholars tend to agree that the *Odes* and the Fourth Gospel are related, but the explanation of the relationship has not won a strong consensus. Most specialists who have published a detailed comparison conclude that the *Odes* are earlier or contemporaneous with the Gospel of John (see Chapter 10). M. Lattke is correct in pointing out the extreme importance of the *Odes* for studying the origins of the documents in the New Testament. Bernard introduced the claim that the *Odes* were composed by a Christian for baptismal services; and as R. Murray has shown there is reason to take seriously a modified form of that hypothesis. The *Odes* are certainly Christian; and, as Emerton states, the author was probably 'a Jewish Christian' (that is a Christian who was a convert from Judaism).

Of all the literature with which the *Odes* share ideas, the most significant, striking and numerous parallels are between the *Odes* and the Fourth Gospel. It is possible that both come from a community in western Syria that was characterized by a Word Christology and an emphasis on love. These Jewish-Christians may have celebrated eternal life through the drinking of 'living water'.

7. *Gnosticism*

Few scholars would attribute the *Odes* to the fully developed gnostic systems of the second century, but many would place them within proto-Gnosticism or even the earliest gnostic thoughts of Valentinus (cf. the *Gospel of Truth*). The *Odes* seem to be an example of early 'gnosis' and thus a tributary to Gnosticism. Their concept of knowledge is not gnostic, but akin to the Qumran idea that God has made known his mysteries to an elect few who will enjoy a new covenant relationship (cf. 1QpHab 7 and 1QS 1.1-20 with *Odes* 8.8ff. and 9.6ff.).

8. *Theology*

The *Odes'* Christology is related to the concept of the Trinity (cf. 19.2; 23.22), but is not necessarily docetic, as some scholars argue. Passages once considered docetic are better seen as praises of Christ's pre-existence, virginal birth, and victorious death (e.g. 28.17-18), because the *Odes* do not deny that Christ has come in the flesh. The docetism of the *Acts of John* is markedly different from the Christology of the *Odes*.

The most prominent feature of the *Odes* is an expression of joy in the presence of eternal life and love. Salvation is achieved by Christ, through the incarnation (7.1-6) and crucifixion (e.g. 42.1-2, 6-13). Note especially the words attributed to Christ in 31.6-9, 12-13:

> Come forth, you who have been afflicted,
> And receive joy.
>
> And possess yourselves through grace,
> And take unto you immortal life.
>
> And they condemned me when I stood up,
> Me who had not been condemned.
>
> Then they divided my spoil,
> Though nothing was owed them...
>
> And I bore their bitterness because of humility;
> That I might redeem my nation and instruct it.
>
> And that I might not nullify the promises to the patriarchs,
> To whom I was promised for the salvation of their offspring.

These preliminary reflections provide an overview that frames the literary setting of the *Odes*. The next two chapters develop this overview by focusing first upon hymns in Early Judaism and then odes in Early Christianity.

Chapter 2

HYMNS AND ODES IN EARLY JUDAISM

One hundred years ago we knew very little about Jewish hymns, odes and prayers composed during the period of Early Judaism. Since then we have been overwhelmed by the quantity of recovered material and it enables us to recognize that the Jews of this period produced an abundance of liturgical compositions, which provided a contemporary tone and perspective to services wherever Jews would worship collectively or alone. For example, by 1880 only one early Jewish hymnbook had been recovered, the *Psalms of Solomon* (*editio princeps* in 1626). Since then other hymnbooks have been recognized or discovered: the *Hellenistic Synagogal Prayers* (in the *Apostolic Constitutions*), the *Thanksgiving Hymns* (1QH), and the *Odes of Solomon*. No handbook or synthesis is available as an introduction to this area of historical study. Research has been limited almost always to one prayer or one hymnic composition, with only a few references to compositions contemporaneous with it. Certainly we have no comprehensive survey of early Jewish hymns and prayers comparable to J. Heinemann's *Prayer in the Talmud*.[1] S. Talmon has accurately observed that for the most part recent scholarly research on 'institutionalized prayer in Israel' has focused on historical and philological questions 'on the textual criticism of individual prayers and the reconstruction of their original forms'.[2]

Few of the extant early Jewish hymns and prayers have been analyzed and examined with the sophisticated methods developed in the study of the Psalter, and this procedure must precede any synthesis of research

1. J. Heinemann, *Prayer in the Talmud: Forms and Patterns* (SJ, 9; Berlin: W. de Gruyter, 1977).
2. S. Talmon, 'The Emergence of Institutionalized Prayer in Israel in the Light of the Qumran Literature', in M. Delcor (ed.), *Qumrân: Sa piété, sa théologie et son milieu* (BETL, 46; Gembloux: Duculot; Leuven: Leuven University Press, 1978), p. 265.

on them. Hence, we cannot speak of schools of scholars or of chronological phases of research. What can be attempted now is a brief report on the significant developments since 1945 in the study of hymns, prayers, and liturgies in Early Judaism. The first part of this chapter will be a succinct descriptive review; the second will be an evaluative critique.

1. *Review*

Caveats should introduce the report. It is obvious that many of the cardinal distinctions that once were thought to represent the categorical separation of Early Judaism from Early Christianity have eroded. In the light of this recognition, G. Vermes has called for a historical approach to Early Judaism that would abolish 'the age-old distinction between the New Testament and its Jewish background'. He reminds us that the New Testament is 'but a fraction of the literary legacy of first-century Judaism'.[3] There can be no question that early Christians could have (and did) compose hymns and prayers that contained no peculiarly 'Christian' concept or word.[4] We have not yet been able to agree on a definition of 'Judaism' prior to 200 CE.[5] The ambiguity of our categories 'Jewish' and 'Christian' and the recognition that many early Jewish-Christians considered themselves fully Jewish indicate that it is wise to include for consideration compositions by a Christian who was profoundly influenced by Jewish theology and employed Jewish perceptions, expressions, and forms.[6] Hence, among the hymnbooks we have included the *Odes of Solomon*, which, from the time of their discovery until the present, some distinguished scholars have considered to be Jewish.

The vast amount of liturgical material now available from Early Judaism and the new methodology now employed by scholars seriously

---

3. G. Vermes, 'Jewish Studies and New Testament Interpretation', *JJS* 31 (1980), p. 13.

4. See, e.g., R.A. Kraft, 'The Multiform Jewish Heritage of Early Christianity', in J. Neusner (ed.), *Christianity, Judaism and Other Greco-Roman Cults: Studies for Morton Smith at Sixty* (SJLA, 12; Leiden: E.J. Brill, 1975), III, pp. 174-99.

5. See J. Neusner, '"Judaism" after Moore: A Programmatic Statement', *JJS* 31 (1980), pp. 141-56.

6. See Chapter 3 in the present collection.

date almost all attempts at a synthesis. Hence, the works by H.L. Jansen[7] and N.B. Johnson[8] should not be seen as reliable surveys.

Each of the hymnbooks is discussed in the following way: after brief prefatory comments, each is assessed in terms of the debates over the original language, date, and provenience. Subsequently, the characteristic theological features or ideas are summarized.

The Hymnbooks

The movement from private instantaneous prayers to formalized, sometimes cultic, prayers was accompanied both by injunctions not 'to make any prayer a fixed form' (*m. Abot* 2.13) and by the appearance of communal fixed prayers and hymns[9] and even hymnbooks that were apparently intended to supplement—certainly not to replace—the Psalter.[10] Impressive progress has already been made towards the publication of reliable critical texts and translations of these hymnbooks and other documents that contain numerous hymns and prayers. Likewise, significant progress has been made toward a better understanding of the original language, date and, at times, provenience of the respective writings. In particular: (1) Various scholars have published significant studies on each of the aforementioned hymnbooks (1QH, *Pss. Sol.*, *Hell. Syn. Pr.*, *Odes*) and on the 'Supplement' to the Psalter, Pss. 151–55. (2) Christian scholars, especially, have examined intensely the hymns and prayers embedded in the canonical New Testament and have argued for the pre-Christian Jewish character of many of them. (3) Jewish scholars have similarly scrutinized the prayers in rabbinic literature and isolated the existence of some proto-rabbinic prayers.

7.   H.L. Jansen, *Die spätjüdische Psalmendichtung, ihr Entstehungskreis und ihr 'Sitz im Leben': Eine literaturgeschichtlich-soziologische Untersuchung* (Skrifter utgitt av det Norske Videnskaps-Akademi i Oslo, II; Historisk-Filosofisk Klasse, 1937, 3; Oslo: Dybwad).

8.   N.B. Johnson, *Prayer in the Apocrypha and Pseudepigrapha: A Study of the Jewish Concept of God* (SBLMS, 2; Philadelphia: SBL, 1948).

9.   Heinemann, *Prayer in the Talmud*, pp. 14-15.

10.   See, e.g., S. Holm-Nielsen, 'Den gammeltestamentlige salmetradition', *DTT* 18 (1955), pp. 135-48, 193-215; *idem*, 'The Importance of Late Jewish Psalmody for the Understanding of Old Testament Psalmodic Tradition', *ST* 14 (1960), pp. 1-53.

Thanksgiving Hymns

Many hymns and prayers were discovered among the Dead Sea Scrolls.[11] Here only a brief summary of the major consensuses among scholars will suffice; our focus will be solely on the Qumran Community's hymnbook, the *Thanksgiving Hymns,* which was discovered in Cave 1 in the spring of 1947 and was edited with photographs by E.L. Sukenik.[12] This hymnbook is called the *Thanksgiving Hymns* because of the formula 'I thank you, O Lord.' It contains 34[13], 32[14] or 19 hymns or psalms[15]—depending upon how one divides the poetic compositions. The hymnbook must predate the first century BCE because the script of 1QH is Herodian (c. 30 BCE to 70 CE).[16] As a result, the compositions are usually dated from the middle of the second century BCE to the early decades of the first century CE.[17]

Soon after the publication of the *editio princeps,* numerous scholars argued that the founder of the Community, the Righteous Teacher, had composed the hymns.[18] Licht[19] and others[20] rejected this argument.

---

11.   See M. Baillet, 'Psaumes, hymnes, cantiques et prières dans les manuscrits de Qumran', in C. Rabin and Y. Yadin (eds.), *Aspects of the Dead Sea Scrolls* (Scripta Hierosolymitana, 4; Jerusalem: Magnes Press, 1962), pp. 339-405; see also L. Moraldi, *I manoscritti di Qumran* (Turin: Unione Tipografico-Editrice Torinese, 1971), esp. pp. 327-494.

12.   E.L. Sukenik, *The Dead Sea Scrolls of the Hebrew University* (ed. N. Avigad and Y. Yadin; Jerusalem: Hebrew University and Magnes Press, 1978).

13.   G. Morawe, *Aufbau und Abgrenzung der Loblieder von Qumrân: Studien zur gattungsgeschichtlichen Einordnung der Hodajôth* (Theologische Arbeiten, 16; Berlin: Evangelische Verlagsanstalt, 1960).

14.   J. Licht, *The Thanksgiving Scroll* (Jerusalem: Bialik Institute, 1957). A. Dupont-Sommer, *The Essene Writings from Qumran* (trans. G. Vermes; New York: Meridian Books, 1962); M. Mansoor, *The Thanksgiving Hymns* (STDJ, 3; Grand Rapids: Eerdmans, 1961).

15.   S. Holm-Nielsen, *Hodayot: Psalms from Qumran* (ATDan, 2; Aarhus: Universitets-forlaget, 1960).

16.   See S.A. Birnbaum, 'The Date of the Hymns Scroll', *PEQ* 84 (1952), pp. 94-103; see also N. Avigad, 'The Palaeography of the Dead Sea Scrolls and Related Documents', in Rabin and Yadin (eds.), *Aspects of the Dead Sea Scrolls,* pp. 56-87, see esp. pp. 72-73, 76-77.

17.   M. Delcor, *Les Hymnes de Qumran (Hodayot)* (Paris: Letouzey & Ané, 1962), p. 38.

18.   Sukenik, *The Dead Sea Scrolls*; H. Michaud, 'Le Maître de la Justice d'après les hymnes de Qumran', in *Bulletin de la faculté libre de theologie prostestante de Paris,* 19 (1956), pp. 67-77; Dupont-Sommer, *The Essene Writings,* p. 100; *idem,*

In search of the author or authors of these hymns, scholars focused upon the use of the first-person pronoun in the *Thanksgiving Hymns*. S. Holm-Nielsen suggested that the 'I' represents the collective solidarity of the Qumran Community.[21] A. Dupont-Sommer argued that 'I' always represents an individual person, who must be the Righteousness Teacher.[22] It is probable that the 'I' reflects the personal experiences of the Righteous Teacher in some hymns but that in other passages it represents the collective consciousness of the Qumran Community.[23] This insight was researched by G. Morawe, who showed that the *Thanksgiving Hymns* contain more than one *Gattung* and were not composed by one person. This idea was developed by G. Jeremias[24] and P. Schulz[25] with regard to the hymns of the Righteous Teacher, and by J. Becker[26] and H.-W. Kuhn[27] with regard to the hymns of the Community.

The language of the *Thanksgiving Hymns* is heavily influenced by biblical Hebrew, Aramaic, postbiblical Hebrew, and Samaritan Hebrew.[28] Unlike the later *Psalms of Solomon* and *Odes of Solomon*, the poetic forms are a mixture of the Psalter's *parallelismus membrorum*,[29]

Trente années de recherches sur les manuscrits de la mer morte (1947–1977) (Paris: Institut de France, 1977), pp. 15-18.

19.   Licht, *The Thanksgiving Scroll*, pp. 25-26.

20.   Mansoor, *The Thanksgiving Hymns*, p. 45; H. Bardtke, 'Considérations sur les Cantiques de Qumran', *RB* 63 (1956), pp. 220-33; *idem*, 'Das Ich des Meisters in den Hodajoth von Qumran', *Wissenschaftliche Zeitschrift der Karl-Marx-Universität Leipzig* 6 (1956–57), pp. 93-104.

21.   Holm-Nielsen, *Hodayot: Psalms from Qumran*, pp. 329-31.

22.   Dupont-Sommer, *The Essene Writings*, p. 200.

23.   J.T. Milik, *Ten Years of Discovery in the Wilderness of Judaea* (trans. J. Strugnell; SBT, 26; London: SCM Press, 1959), pp. 40, 74.

24.   G. Jeremias, *Der Lehrer der Gerechtigkeit* (SUNT, 2; Göttingen: Vandenhoeck & Ruprecht, 1963).

25.   P. Schulz, *Der Autoritätsanspruch des Lehrers der Gerechtigkeit in Qumran* (Meisenheim am Glan: Hain, 1974).

26.   J. Becker, *Das Heil Gottes: Heils- und Sündenbegriffe in den Qumrantexten und im Neuen Testament* (SUNT, 3; Göttingen: Vandenhoeck & Ruprecht, 1964).

27.   H.-W. Kuhn, *Enderwartung und gegenwärtiges Heil: Untersuchungen zu den Gemeindeliedern von Qumran* (SUNT, 4; Göttingen: Vandenhoeck & Ruprecht, 1966).

28.   Licht, *The Thanksgiving Scroll*; Delcor, *Les Hymnes de Qumran*; Mansoor, *The Thanksgiving Hymns*.

29.   C.F. Kraft, 'Poetical Structure in the Qumran Thanksgiving Psalms', *BR* 2 (1957), pp. 1-18.

usually synonymous,[30] often with extreme disparity in the length of the lines and with no structured meter.[31] Scholars have discerned three *Gattungen* in the *Thanksgiving Hymns:* the Thanksgiving Song (*Danklied*),[32] the Hymn (*hymnischen Bekenntnislied*),[33] and the Didactic Psalm (*Lehrpsalm*).[34] The hymnbook was probably used liturgically in the cult ceremonies at Qumran,[35] certainly as the Community celebrated daily (with the angels) the cosmic dimension of the sanctification of time (1QH 12.3-9)[36] and probably as the Qumranites renewed yearly the covenant (see 1QS 1.16–2.25a).[37] These hymns have been considered 'mystical'.[38] Some scholars stress the fundamental importance of salvation and knowledge.[39] Holm-Nielsen[40] and Delcor[41] have shown cumulatively that the *Thanksgiving Hymns* are frequently similar to other compositions, especially the Lucan hymns, the Five More 'Davidic' Psalms, the *Psalms of Solomon* and the *Odes of Solomon*. Parallels with the *Odes* are impressive.[42] Both hymnbooks celebrate the present

30.   Licht, *The Thanksgiving Scroll*; Mansoor, *The Thanksgiving Hymns*, pp. 23-25.

31.   Licht, *The Thanksgiving Scroll*; Kraft, 'Poetical Structure'; Mansoor, *The Thanksgiving Hymns*; Holm-Nielsen, *Hodayot: Psalms from Qumran*. But on prosody in the *Thanksgiving Hymns* see J. Arlis Ehlen, 'The Poetic Structure of a Hodayah from Qumran: An Analysis of Grammatical, Semantic, and Auditory Correspondence in 1QH 3.19-36' (Dissertation, Harvard University, 1970; summarized in *HTR* 63 [1970], p. 516).

32.   S. Mowinckel, 'Some Remarks on Thanksgiving Hymns 39 (V, 5-20)', *JBL* 75 (1956), pp. 265-76; Morawe, *Aufbau und Abgrenzung*; Delcor, *Les Hymnes de Qumran*; Schulz, *Der Autoritätsanspruch*.

33.   Morawe, *Aufbau und Abgrenzung*; Schulz, *Der Autoritätsanspruch*.

34.   Schulz, *Der Autoritätsanspruch*, p. 3.

35.   Holm-Nielsen, *Hodayot: Psalms from Qumran*, pp. 332-48; Kuhn, *Enderwartung und gegenwärtiges Heil*; D.E. Aune, *The Cultic Setting of Realized Eschatology in Early Christianity* (NovTSup, 28; Leiden: E.J. Brill, 1972).

36.   See Mansoor, *The Thanksgiving Hymns*, p. 49.

37.   J. Murphy-O'Connor, 'La genèse littéraire de la Règle de la Communauté', *RB* 76 (1969), pp. 528-49.

38.   Dupont-Sommer, *The Essene Writings*, p. 199; *idem*, *Trente années de recherches*, p. 7.

39.   G. Vermes with P. Vermes, *The Dead Sea Scrolls: Qumran in Perspective* (Cleveland, OH: Collins, 1978), p. 56.

40.   Holm-Nielsen, *Hodayot: Psalms from Qumran*.

41.   Delcor, *Les Hymnes de Qumran*.

42.   See Chapter 9 in the present volume.

experience of a realizing eschatology[43] and frequently employ the paradise motif (as in the *Psalms of Solomon*) to express the conception that the eschatological end (*Endzeit*) is portrayed in light of the beginning of time (*Urzeit*) as a restored creation (*restitutio principii*).[44]

Considerable progress has been made in the attempt to understand the *Thanksgiving Hymns*. Some issues debated in the study of other hymnbooks are impressively solved. First, there can be no doubt that the *Thanksgiving Hymns* were composed originally in their extant language, Hebrew. Second, they predate the destruction of the temple in 70 CE Third, they were all—or almost all—composed at Qumran. Fourth, the *Thanksgiving Hymns* contain numerous ideas, some of which probably express the personal sufferings of the founder of the Qumran Community when he was persecuted by the Wicked Priest and forced to live exiled in the desert, and others of which preserve the Community's collective consciousness of being the elect and Holy Ones who live near the end of time.

The Supplement to the Psalter: Five More 'Davidic' Psalms
In Hebrew the Davidic Psalter contains 150 psalms; in Greek (and in some Syriac manuscripts) it has 151. Almost one hundred years ago W. Wright drew attention to and translated five 'apocryphal' psalms in Syriac (now called Pss. 151–55).[45] The significance and early date of these psalms became clear with the discovery of three (Pss. 151a–151b; 154; 155) in the Dead Sea Psalms Scroll (11QPsª).[46] These three psalms are certainly earlier than the Qumran Psalms Scroll, which dates from the first half of the first century CE.[47] Some specialists claim that one or

---

43.   Clearly demonstrated for 1QH by Kuhn, *Enderwartung und gegenwärtiges Heil*; see also G.W.E. Nickelsburg Jr, *Resurrection, Immortality, and Eternal Life in Intertestamental Judaism* (HTS, 26; Cambridge, MA: Harvard University Press, 1972).

44.   See Aune, *The Cultic Setting of Realized Eschatology*, pp. 37-42.

45.   W. Wright, 'Some Apocryphal Psalms in Syriac', *Proceedings of the Society of Biblical Archaeology* 9 (1887), pp. 257-66.

46.   See J.A. Sanders, *The Psalms Scroll of Qumrân Cave 11 (11QPsª)* (DJD, 4; Oxford: Clarendon Press, 1965); see also *idem*, *The Dead Sea Psalms Scroll* (Ithaca, NY: Cornell University Press, 1967).

47.   Sanders, *The Psalms Scroll*; J. Strugnell, 'More Psalms of David', *CBQ* 27 (1965), pp. 207-16.

more of these psalms were composed by the Essenes.[48] Others argue that the evidence will not support this identification.[49] M. Hengel links these psalms with the Hasidim.[50]

The style is clearly imitative of the Psalter. In contrast to the *Thanksgiving Hymns* but similar to the *Odes of Solomon*, the parallel lines are of roughly uniform length and usually constructed in synonymous parallelism. The appearance of 'apocryphal' psalms within the Davidic Psalter suggested to M.H. Goshen-Gottstein[51] and P. Skehan[52] that the Dead Sea Psalms Scroll is a sectarian version of the canonical Psalter; but this phenomenon seems to reveal that (at least in some Jewish circles) the Psalter was not set, closed, and canonized prior to the first century CE.[53]

The original language of Psalms 151a–151b, 154 and 155 is certainly Hebrew;[54] the original language of Psalm 152 is possibly Hebrew,[55] and that of Psalm 153 is perhaps Hebrew.[56] The date of these compositions varies. Psalm 151 may date from as early as the third century BCE.[57] Psalms 154 and 155 apparently date from the second century BCE to the

---

48.   M. Philonenko, 'L'origine essénienne des cinq psaumes syriaques de David', *Sem* 9 (1959), pp. 35-48; Delcor, *Les Hymnes de Qumran*; A. Dupont-Sommer, 'Le psaume CLI dans 11QPsᵃ et la problème de son origine essénienne', *Semeia* 14 (1964), pp. 25-62.

49.   Sanders, *The Dead Sea Psalms Scroll*, p. 108; A.S. van der Woude, *Die fünf syrischen Psalmen* (JSHRZ, 4.1; Gütersloh: Gerd Mohn, 1974), p. 35.

50.   M. Hengel, *Judaism and Hellenism: Studies in their Encounter in Palestine during the Early Hellenistic Period* (2 vols.; trans. J. Bowden; Philadelphia: Fortress Press, 1974), I, pp. 176-78.

51.   M.H. Goshen-Gottstein, 'The Psalms Scroll (11QPsᵃ): A Problem of Canon and Text', *Textus* 5 (1966), pp. 22-33.

52.   P. Skehan, 'A Liturgical Complex in 11QPsᵃ', *CBQ* 35 (1973), pp. 195-205.

53.   Sanders, *The Psalms Scroll*; idem, *The Dead Sea Psalms Scroll*. Sanders's hypothesis is now confirmed by the research of P. Flint.

54.   J. Strugnell, 'Notes on the Text and Transmission of the Apocryphal Psalms 151, 154 (= Syr. II) and 155 (= Syr. III)', *HTR* 59 (1966), pp. 257-81; J.H. Charlesworth with J.A. Sanders, 'More Psalms of David', *OTP*, II, pp. 609-24.

55.   Strugnell, 'Notes on the Text and Transmission', p. 259; Charlesworth with Sanders, 'More Psalms of David'.

56.   Charlesworth with Sanders, 'More Psalms of David'. Contrast Strugnell, 'Notes on the Text and Transmission', p. 259.

57.   F.M. Cross, 'David, Orpheus, and Psalm 151.3-4', *BASOR* 231 (1978), p. 70.

early first century CE. Psalms 152 and 153 are difficult to date.[58] The provenience of composition for these hymns is uncertain, but it is clear that all were not composed at Qumran—and perhaps none were written there. Psalms 151a–151b, 152 and 153 are pseudepigraphically composed with David in mind and celebrate how he rendered glory to the Lord (151a), defeated the Philistine (151b), the lion, and the wolf (152; 153). Psalm 154, anonymous in Hebrew but attributed to Hezekiah in the Syriac, is a hymn of praise to God. Psalm 155 is a petition and praise for deliverance.

Note that in the autobiographical aside in the Qumran Psalms Scroll David is celebrated as wise:

> And David, the son of Jesse, was wise, a light like the light
> of the sun, literate, and discerning even perfect in all his ways
> before God and humans. And the Lord gave him a discerning
> and enlightened spirit (11QPs^a).

Thus, in many early Jewish circles David, and not only Solomon, was revered for his wisdom.

Psalms of Solomon

The *Psalms of Solomon* consist of eighteen hymns (or psalms) composed and presumably recited by Jews around the turn of the Common Era. Near the beginning of this century, there was a consensus that these hymns are pharisaic.[59] Some scholars today continue to affirm a pharisaic origin;[60] others correctly warn that they should not be linked with the Pharisees,[61] the Essenes[62] or any particular sectarian group.[63]

58.　Charlesworth with Sanders, 'More Psalms of David'.

59.　J. Wellhausen, *Die Pharisäer und die Sadducäer: Eine Untersuchung zur inneren jüdischen Geschichte* (Greifswald: Bamberg, 1874), pp. 112-20; H.E. Ryle and M.R. James, *Psalmoi Solomôntos: Psalms of the Pharisees Commonly Called the Psalms of Solomon* (Cambridge: Cambridge University Press, 1891), pp. xliv-lii; G.B. Gray, 'The Psalms of Solomon', *APOT* 2 (1913), p. 630.

60.　M. Black, 'Pharisees', *IDB* 3 (1962), p. 777; J. Schüpphaus, *Die Psalmen Salomos* (ALGHJ, 7; Leiden: E.J. Brill, 1977), p. 158.

61.　J. O'Dell, 'The Religious Background of the Psalms of Solomon (Reevaluated in the Light of the Qumran Texts)', *RevQ* 3 (1961), pp. 241-57; R.B. Wright, 'The Psalms of Solomon, the Pharisees and the Essenes', in R.A. Kraft (ed.), *1972 Proceedings: International Organization for Septuagint and Cognate Studies and the Society of Biblical Literature Pseudepigrapha Seminar* (SBLSCS, 2; Missoula, MT: SBL, 1972), pp. 136-54; E.P. Sanders, *Paul and Palestinian Judaism: A Comparison of Patterns of Religion* (Philadelphia: Fortress Press, 1977), p. 388.

The Greek and Syriac derive ultimately from Hebrew, which is certainly the original language.[64] Trafton has shown that the Syriac and the Greek texts are important and that in some passages the Syriac may derive directly from the lost Hebrew.[65] There is wide agreement that they date from the middle or latter half of the first century CE.[66] The provenience of these psalms is Palestinian; they were probably composed in or near Jerusalem.[67]

Like the *Odes of Solomon*, but in contrast to the *Thanksgiving Hymns*, they are composed in the style of the Psalter and continue the poetic norm of *parallelismus membrorum*, transforming some of the older *Gattungen*.[68] Schüpphaus has argued that the theme of these psalms is the righteousness of God and his help in difficulties and that they reflect the pharisaic divine service of Jerusalem synagogues near the end of the first century BCE.[69] Other characteristics of these psalms should be mentioned: the belief in the resurrection for those who fear God (3.16; 13.9),[70] the pervasive claim that Israel is in covenant with God (9.16-19; 10.5; 17.7),[71] the celebration over the death of Pompey (2.24-35)[72] and a

62. S. Holm-Nielsen, 'Salomos Salmer', in E. Hammershaimb *et al.* (eds.), *De Gammeltestamentlige Pseudepigrapher* (Copenhagen: G.E.C. Gad, 1970), V, pp. 548-95.

63. P. Winter, 'Psalms of Solomon', *IDB* 3 (1962), pp. 958-60; U. Rappaport, 'Solomon, Psalms of', *EncJud* 15 (1971), pp. 115-16.

64. Wellhausen, *Die Pharisäer und die Sadducäer*; Ryle and James, *Psalmoi Solomôntos*; Gray, 'The Psalms of Solomon'; K.G. Kuhn, *Die älteste Textgestalt der Psalmen Salomos insbesondere auf Grund der syrischen Übersetzung neu untersucht, Mit einer Bearbeitung und Übersetzung der Psalmen Salomos 13–27* (BWANT, 4.21; Stuttgart: W. Kohlhammer, 1937); M. Delcor, 'Psaumes de Salomon', *DBSup* 48 (1973), cols. 221-25; Holm-Nielsen, 'Salomos Salmer'.

65. J.L. Trafton, *The Syriac Version of the Psalms of Solomon: A Critical Evaluation* (SBLSCS, 11; Atlanta, CA: Scholars Press, 1985).

66.

67. A.-M. Denis, *Introduction aux pseudépigraphes grecs d'Ancien Testament* (SVTP, 1; Leiden: E.J. Brill, 1970), pp. 60-69; Wright, 'The Psalms of Solomon', p. 150; Schüpphaus, *Die Psalmen Salomos*, p .158.

68. Jansen, *Die spätjüdische Psalmendichtung*; Delcor, 'Psaumes de Salomon', cols. 228-29.

69. Schüpphaus, *Die Psalmen Salomos*, pp. 154-58.

70. See Nickelsburg, *Resurrection, Immortality and Eternal Life*, pp. 131-34.

71. A. Jaubert, *La notion d'alliance dans le judaïsme aux abords de l'ère chrétienne* (Patristica Sorbonensia, 6; Paris: Seuil, 1963), p. 256; Sanders, *Paul and Palestinian Judaism*, pp. 387-409.

locus classicus for Jewish messianism (17.4-51; 18.1-14).[73] Striking parallels between the *Psalms of Solomon* and the hymns in the first two chapters of the Gospel of Luke have been discussed by Ryle and James[74] and also by Viteau.[75]

Hellenistic Synagogal Prayers
The other hymnbooks discussed in this section have received more attention than the *Hellenistic Synagogal Prayers*, which are unknown to many scholars, even to specialists in Early Judaism. Yet, scattered throughout the Christian liturgy of books 7 and 8 of the Apostolic Constitutions are at least 16 prayers that are most likely originally Jewish.[76]

The first scholar to publicize the existence of remnants of Jewish synagogal prayers in this major Christian writing was K. Kohler.[77] Apparently unfamiliar with Kohler's insight, W. Bousset claimed that the *Apostolic Constitutions* preserved Jewish prayers derived from Diaspora Judaism.[78] Less than a decade later, Kohler, unfamiliar with Bousset's publication—a phenomenon all too prevalent in the study of the hymns and prayers of Early Judaism—developed his idea that the *Apostolic Constitutions* incorporated originally Jewish 'Essene prayers' that were 'Christianized by verbal changes or additions'.[79] Although ignorant of Kohler's pioneering publications, E.R. Goodenough was introduced to Bousset's study by A.D. Nock. Goodenough became

72. Gray, 'The Psalms of Solomon', pp. 627-30; Delcor, 'Psaumes de Salomon', cols. 233-35.

73. See J.H. Charlesworth, 'The Concept of the Messiah in the Pseudepigrapha', *ANRW* II.19.1, pp. 188-218.

74. Ryle and James, *Psalmoi Solomôntos*.

75. J. Viteau, *Les Psaumes de Salomon* (Paris: Letouzey & Ané, 1911).

76. D.A. Fiensy, *Prayers Alleged to be Jewish: An Examination of the Constitutiones Apostolorum* (BJS, 65; Chico, CA: Scholars Press, 1985).

77. K. Kohler, 'Über die Ursprünge und Grundformen der synagogalen Liturgie: Eine Studie', *MGWJ* 37 (1893), pp. 441-51, 489-97; *idem*, 'Didascalia', in *The Jewish Encyclopedia* (New York: Funk & Wagnalls, 1903), IV, pp. 588-95.

78. W. Bousset, 'Eine jüdische Gebetssammlung im siebenten Buch der apostolischen Konstitutionen' (1915) (reprinted in *Religionsgeschichtliche Studien: Aufsätze zur Religionsgeschichte des hellenistischen Zeitalters* [NovTSup, 50; Leiden: E.J. Brill, 1979], pp. 231-86).

79. K. Kohler, 'The Essene Version of the Seven Benedictions as Preserved in the VII Book of the Apostolic Constitutions', *HUCA* 1 (1924), p. 410.

thoroughly persuaded by Bousset's arguments and utilized these Jewish prayers to demonstrate the existence of a 'mystic Judaism' that is similar and prior to the thought of Philo of Alexandria who can be understood only in light of this 'Jewish Mystery.'[80] Although Kohler's theory of Essene origin should now be rejected in light of our vastly increased knowledge of the Essenes (thanks to the recovery of the Dead Sea Scrolls), and although Goodenough's hypothesis should be isolated for separate examination,[81] it is becoming increasingly apparent[82] that Jewish prayers, now interpolated and redacted (with deletions) by Christians, are incorporated in books 7 and 8 of the *Apostolic Constitutions*.

Research on these allegedly Jewish prayers is in its infancy. Their number, provenience, and date have not yet been adequately examined. The publication by Darnell and the monograph by Fiensy will direct scholars' attention to these Jewish prayers, which are frequently similar to the Seven Benedictions and to the *Kiddush* for Sabbath Eve.[83] This and subsequent research will help us better understand their origin, character and form (which seems to be another example of development of the Psalter's synonymous and synthetic parallelism).

Odes of Solomon

This hymnbook originally contained 42 hymns (or odes). All are preserved, except for the second and portions of the third and perhaps the first. These odes are Christian,[84] although some scholars[85] claim that

80.   E.R. Goodenough, *By Light, Light: The Mystic Gospel of Hellenistic Judaism.* (New Haven: Yale University Press, 1935).

81.   See S. Sandmel, 'Goodenough on Philo', in *Philo of Alexandria: An Introduction* (New York: Oxford University Press, 1979), pp. 140-41.

82.   See J.H. Charlesworth, 'Christian and Jewish Self-Definition in Light of the Christian Additions to the Apocryphal Writings', in E.P. Sanders and A.I. Baumgarten (eds.), *Judaism from the Maccabees to the Mid-Third Century* (Philadelphia: Fortress Press, 1980); D.A. Fiensy and D. Darnell, 'Hellenistic Synagogal Prayers', *OTP*, II, pp. 671-97; Fiensy, *Prayers Alleged to be Jewish.*

83.   P. Birnbaum, *Daily Prayer Book: Ha-Siddur Ha-Shalem* (New York: Hebrew Publishing Company, 1949), pp. 189-90.

84.   J.A. Emerton, 'Notes on Some Passages in the Odes of Solomon', *JTS* NS 28 (1977), pp. 507-19; H. Chadwick, 'Some Reflections on the Character and Theology of the Odes of Solomon', in P. Granfield and J.A. Jungmann (eds.), *Kyriakon* (Festschrift Johannes Quasten; 2 vols.; Münster: Aschendorff, 1970), pp. 266-70; T. Baarda, '"Het Uitbreiden van mijn Handen is zijn Teken": Enkele notities bij de

they are Jewish (an old view, which goes back to Harnack, and Menzies).[86] They are closely aligned with many of the early Jewish hymns already mentioned, and the Christian (or Jewish-Christian) who composed them was probably influenced by the images and thoughts contained in the Dead Sea Scrolls, especially the *Thanksgiving Hymns*.[87] Three positions recently have been defended regarding the original language of the *Odes*: Hebrew,[88] Greek[89] and Syriac.[90] The *Odes* were most likely composed near 100 CE[91] or in the early second century,[92]

gebedshounding in de Oden van Salomo', in *Loven en Geloven* (Festschrift N.H. Ridderbos; Amsterdam: Bolland, 1975), pp. 245-59; R. Murray, *Symbols of Church and Kingdom: A Study in Early Syriac Tradition* (Cambridge: Cambridge University Press, 1975).

85. M. Testuz (ed.), *Papyrus Bodmer VII–IX*, (Cologne: Bibliothèque Bodmer, 1959); see also I. Gruenwald, 'Knowledge and Vision: Towards a Clarification of Two "Gnostic" Concepts in the Light of their Alleged Origins', *Israel Oriental Studies* 3 (1973), pp. 63-107.

86. A. von Harnack (ed.), *Ein jüdisch-christliches Psalmbuch aus dem ersten Jahrhundert* (trans. Johannes Flemming; TU, 35.4; Leipzig: J.C. Hinrichs, 1910); A. Menzies, 'The Odes of Solomon', *Interpreter* [London] 7 (1910), pp. 7-22.

87. J. Carmignac, 'Les affinités qumrâniennes de la onzième Ode de Salomon', *RevQ* 3 (1961), pp. 71-102; *idem*, 'Un qumrânien converti au christianisme: L'auteur des Odes de Salomon', in H. Bardtke (ed.), *Qumran-Probleme* (Deutsche Akademie der Wissenschaften zu Berlin, 42; Berlin: Akademie Verlag, 1963), pp. 75-108; J.H. Charlesworth, 'Les Odes de Salomon et les manuscrits de la mer morte', *RB* 77 (1970), pp. 522-49; *idem*, 'Qumran, John and the Odes of Solomon', in *idem* (ed.), *John and Qumran* (London: Geoffrey Chapman, 1972; New York: Crossroad, 1991); Licht, 'Solomon, Odes of', *EncJud* 15 (1971), pp. 114-15; Gruenwald, 'Knowledge and Vision'.

88. Carmignac, 'Un qumrânien converti au christianisme'.

89. Testuz (ed.), *Papyrus Bodmer VII–IX*, p. 57; A.F.J. Klijn, 'The Influence of Jewish Theology on the Odes of Solomon and the Acts of Thomas', in *Aspects du judéo-christianisme: Colloque de Strasbourg 23–25 avril 1964* (Paris: Presses universitaires de France, 1965); M. Philonenko, 'Conjecture sur un verset de la onzième Ode de Salomon', *ZNW* 53 (1962), p. 264.

90. A. Vööbus, 'Neues Licht zur Frage der Originalsprache der Oden Salomos', *Mus* 75 (1962), pp. 275-90; J.C.L. Gibson, 'From Qumran to Edessa: Or the Aramaic Speaking Church before and after 70 A.D.', *NCB* 2 (1965), pp. 9-19 (reprinted in ALUOS 5 [1963–65], pp. 24-39); J.A. Emerton, 'Some Problems of Text and Language in the Odes of Solomon', *JTS* NS 18 (1967), pp. 372-406.

91. J.H. Charlesworth, *The Pseudepigrapha and Modern Research* (SBLSCS, 7; Missoula, MT: Scholars Press, 1976).

but surely not as late as the first half of the third century.[93] Although they may come from within or near Antioch,[94] their provenience is not clear.

The Odist's thoughts and images are strikingly similar to those of the author and editors of the Gospel of John.[95] They are not gnostic[96] but contain ideas, images and emphases that were systematically developed and redefined by Gnostics. As stated above, the *Odes* continue the style of the Psalter, and the thought is presented in parallel lines. These hymns were most likely used in public services[97]—perhaps even in the community (or 'school') in which the Gospel of John was written and edited.[98] The pervasive tone is jubilant because of the present experience of salvation, eternal life (as at Qumran and in the *Psalms of*

92.   B. Ehlers, 'Kann das Thomasevangelium aus Edessa Stammen? Ein Beitrag zur Frühgeschichte des Christentums in Edessa', *NovT* 12 (1970), pp. 284-317. A. Vööbus, 'Solomon, Odes of', *Encylopaedia Britannica* 20 (1971), p. 878.

93.   H.J.W. Drijvers, 'Die Oden Salomos und die Polemik mit den Markioniten im Syrischen Christentum', in R. Lavenant (ed.), *Symposium Syriacum* (OCA, 205; Rome: Pontificium Institutum Orientalium Studiorum, 1978), pp. 39-55; *idem*, 'Kerygma und Logos in den Oden Salomos dargestellt am Beispiel der 23. Ode', in A.M. Ritter (ed.), *Kerygma und Logos* (Festschrift Carl Andresen; Göttingen: Vandenhoeck & Ruprecht, 1979).

94.   J.R. Harris and A. Mingana, *The Odes and Psalms of Solomon* (2 vols.; Manchester: University Press; London: Longmans, Green, 1916–20), II, p. 69. Charlesworth, *The Pseudepigrapha and Modern Research*; *idem*, *Odes of Solomon*, *IDBSup* (1976), pp. 637-38.

95.   R. Bultmann, *The Gospel of John: A Commentary* (trans. G.R. Beasley-Murray; Oxford: Blackwell, 1971). B.M. Metzger, 'Odes of Solomon', in L.A. Loetscher (ed.), *Twentieth Century Encyclopedia of Religious Knowledge: Supplement* (Grand Rapids: Baker Book House, 1955), II, pp. 811-12; Charlesworth, 'Qumran, John and the Odes of Solomon'; J.H. Charlesworth and R.A. Culpepper 'The Odes of Solomon and the Gospel of John', *CBQ* 35 (1973), pp. 298-322. Contrast C.K. Barrett, *The Gospel According to St John: An Introduction with Commentary and Notes on the Greek Text* (Philadelphia: Westminster Press, 2nd edn, 1978), see esp. pp. 65, 112-13, 507.

96.   See Chapter 8 in the present collection. Chadwick, 'Some Reflections'; Vööbus, 'Solomon, Odes of'; Murray, *Symbols of Church and Kingdom*. Contrast K. Rudolph, 'War der Verfasser der Oden Salomos ein "Qumran-Christ"? Ein Beitrag zur Diskussion um die Anfänge der Gnosis', *RevQ* 4 (1964), pp. 523-55.

97.   Charlesworth, *Odes of Solomon*; J.H. Charlesworth, 'Haplography and Philology: A Study of Ode of Solomon 16.8', *NTS* 25 (1978–79), pp. 221-27.

98.   See Charlesworth and Culpepper, 'The Odes of Solomon and the Gospel of John'.

Solomon expressed through the paradise motif) and divine love.[99] The thesis of J.H. Bernard[100] that the *Odes* were used in baptismal services has been accepted in a modified form by some scholars.[101]

Possibly Jewish Prayers and Hymns in the New Testament

Significant developments in the study of the New Testament will be discussed in the third volume of this trilogy.[102] Our attention here will be solely upon Jewish hymns and prayers inherited by early Christians and incorporated into the New Testament.[103] Hence, the pre-Pauline christological hymns, for example, in Colossians (1.15-20) and Philippians (2.6-11) will not be discussed, although Paul, who is clearly a Christian, still considered himself a Jew (Gal. 2.15; Rom. 11.1-2; 2 Cor. 11.22).

Most important, of course, is the Jewish prayer that Jesus of Nazareth reputedly taught to his disciples (Lk. 11.1; cf. Mt. 5.1), which 'displays all of the characteristics of Jewish private prayer'.[104] Although we do not possess the prayer supposedly taught by John the Baptist to his disciples (see Lk. 11.1), we do have three distinct versions of the Lord's Prayer (Lk. 11.1-4; Mt. 6.9-13; *Did.* 8). Some have claimed that the evangelists

---

99. See Charlesworth, *Odes of Solomon*; R. Terzoli, 'Le Odi di Salomone', in *Il Tema delta Beatitudine nei Patri Siri* (Rome: Morcelliana, 1972); Aune, *The Cultic Setting*, pp. 166-94.

100. J.H. Bernard, *The Odes of Solomon* (TS, 8.3; Cambridge: Cambridge University Press, 1912).

101. G. Schille, *Frühchristliche Hymnen* (Berlin: Evangelische Verlagsanstalt, 1965); Murray, *Symbols of Church and Kingdom*.

102. See also J.H. Charlesworth, 'A Prolegomenon to a New Study of the Jewish Background of the Hymns and Prayers in the New Testament', in G. Vermes and J. Neusner (eds.), *Essays in Honor of Yagael Yadin* (Oxford, 1983).

103. See R. Deichgräber, *Gotteshymnus und Christushymnus in der frühen Chistenheit: Untersuchungen zu Form, Sprache und Stil der frühchristlichen Hymnen* (SUNT, 5; Göttingen: Vandenhoeck & Ruprecht, 1967); Schille, *Frühchristliche Hymnen*; M. Rese, 'Formeln und Lieder im Neuen Testament: Einige notwendige Anmerkungen', *Verkündigung und Forschung* (Beihefte zu *Evangelische Theologie*), 15 (1970), pp. 75-95; J.T. Sanders, *The New Testament Christological Hymns: Their Historical Religious Background* (SNTSMS, 15; Cambridge: Cambridge University Press, 1971); K. Wengst, *Christologische Formeln und Lieder des Urchristentums* (SNT, 7; Gütersloh: Gerd Mohn, 1972).

104. J. Heinemann, 'The Background of Jesus' Prayer in the Jewish Liturgical Tradition', in J.J. Petuchowski and M. Brocke (eds.), *The Lord's Prayer and Jewish Liturgy* (New York: Seabury, 1978), pp. 81-89, see esp. p. 88.

created this prayer,[105] but most scholars have been persuaded—and I think correctly—that it (or most of it) is genuine Jesus tradition.[106] J. Jeremias has argued that generally Luke preserves the original length, and Matthew the original wording.[107] Jesus' prayer was certainly spoken and perhaps first composed in Aramaic.[108] The prayer is constructed especially in Matthew according to *parallelismus membrorum*. It is frequently similar to other early Jewish prayers in Aramaic especially the *Qaddish*, and in Hebrew, notably Psalm 155 (esp. vv. 11-12). According to *Did.* 8.3, the prayer was to be said 'three times a day'; the parallel to the other Jewish 'prayers', especially the *Shema*[109] and Eighteen Benedictions,[110] is impressive. As with these 'prayers', the Lord's Prayer was soon included in worship services, first probably as a model for prayer (see Mt. 6.9) and then as a prayer with an added conclusion. Our earliest clear evidence for the liturgical use of the Lord's Prayer is either the *Didache* (c. early second century) or the 24th catechetical lecture by Cyril of Jerusalem (c. 315–86).

Other pre-Christian Jewish prayers may be preserved in the New Testament. Numerous specialists, especially Winter,[111] have argued that the *Magnificat*, the *Benedictus*, the *Gloria in Excelsis* and the *Nunc Dimittis* preserved in the first two chapters of Luke are totally or in part

105. S. van Tilborg, 'A Form-Criticism of the Lord's Prayer', *NovT* 14 (1972), pp. 94-105. M.D. Goulder, 'The Composition of the Lord's Prayer', *JTS* NS 14 (1963), pp. 32-45; *idem, Midrash and Lection in Matthew* (London: SPCK, 1974).

106. J. Carmignac, *Recherches sur le 'Notre Père'* (Paris: Letouzey & Ané, 1969); J. Jeremias, *The Prayers of Jesus* (SBT, 2/6; London: SCM Press, 1967; Philadelphia: Fortress Press, 1978); R.E. Brown, 'The Pater Noster as an Eschatological Prayer', in *New Testament Essays* (New York: Doubleday, 1965); B. Noack, *Om Fadervor* (Copenhagen: G.E.C. Gad, 1969); P.B. Harner, *Understanding the Lord's Prayer* (Philadelphia: Fortress Press, 1975).

107. Jeremias, *The Prayers of Jesus*.

108. Jeremias, *The Prayers of Jesus*, p. 93.

109. See Harner, *Understanding the Lord's Prayer*, pp. 69-70.

110. K.G. Kuhn, *Achtzehngebet und Vaterunser und der Reim* (Tübingen: J.C.B. Mohr, 1950).

111. P. Winter, 'Magnificat and Benedictus: Maccabean Psalms?', *BJRL* 37 (1954–55), pp. 328-47. See also earlier scholars such as K. Bornhäuser, H. Gunkel, S. Mowinckel and F. Spitta; contrast, e.g., P. Benoit, 'L'enfance de Jean-Baptiste selon Luc I', *NTS* 3 (1956–57), pp. 169-94; and R.E. Brown, *The Birth of the Messiah: A Commentary on the Infancy Narratives in Matthew and Luke* (Garden City, NY: Doubleday, 1977).

originally Jewish. Ryle and James[112] and Viteau[113] pointed to numerous significant parallels between the *Magnificat* and *Benedictus* and the *Psalms of Solomon*.

Bultmann argued that behind Jn 1.1-18 lies an originally Jewish hymn, which is strikingly similar to the *Odes of Solomon*.[114] His arguments have been challenged or rejected by many scholars.[115] The hymns in Revelation are seen as originally Jewish by J.M. Ford,[116] but a more persuasive case for Christian authorship has been presented in a detailed study by K.P. Jörns.[117]

Proto-Rabbinic Prayers
L. Finkelstein demonstrated to many scholars that parts of the Passover Haggadah antedated the present era and are possibly 'pre-Maccabean' documents.[118] I. Elbogen,[119] E. Schürer,[120] G.F. Moore,[121] J. Neusner,[122]

112. Ryle and James, *Psalmoi Solomôntos*, pp. xci-xcii.

113. Viteau, *Les Psaumes de Salomon*, pp. 146-48.

114. R. Bultmann, 'Der religionsgeschichtliche Hintergrund des Prologs zum Johannes-Evangelium', in H. Schmidt (ed.), *Eucharisterion* (Festschrift Hermann Gunkel; FRLANT, 36.2; Göttingen: Vandenhoeck & Ruprecht, 1923), II, pp. 1-26; Bultmann, *The Gospel of John: A Commentary*.

115. See esp. S. de Ausejo, 'Es un himno a Christo el prologo de San Juan?' *EstBíb* 15 (1956), pp. 223-77, 381-427. J. Schattenmann, *Studien zum neutestamentlichen Prosahymnus* (Munich: Beck, 1965), p. 29; R.E. Brown, *The Gospel According to John* (2 vols.; AB, 29, 29A; Garden City, NY: Doubleday, 1966, 1970), I, p. 20; Sanders, *The New Testament Christological Hymns*.

116. J.M. Ford, *Revelation* (AB, 38; Garden City, NY: Doubleday, 1975), pp. 21, 79-80, 316.

117. See also G. Delling, 'Zum gottesdienstlichen Stil der Johannesapokalypse', *NovT* 3 (1959), pp. 107-37 (reprinted in F. Hahn, T. Holtz and N. Walter [eds.], *Studien zum Neuen Testament und zum hellenistischen Judentum: Gesammelle Aufsätze 1950–68* [Göttingen: Vandenhoeck & Ruprecht, 1970], pp. 425-50; Deichgräber, *Gotteshymnus und Christushymnus*. J. Kroll, *Die christliche Hymnodik bis zu Klemens von Alexandreia* (Darmstadt: Wissenschaftliche Buchgesellschaft, 2nd edn, 1968); Wengst, *Christologische Formeln*.

118. L. Finkelstein, 'The Oldest Midrash: Pre-Rabbinic Ideals and Teachings in the Passover Haggadah', *HTR* 31 (1938), pp. 291-317 (reprinted in L. Finkelstein, *Pharisaism in the Making: Selected Essays* [New York: Ktav, 1972]); also, L. Finkelstein, 'Pre-Maccabean Documents in the Passover Haggadah', *HTR* 35 (1942), pp. 291-332; and *HTR* 36 (1943), pp. 1-38 (reprinted in Finkelstein, *Pharisaism in the Making*).

119. I. Elbogen, *Der jüdische Gottesdienst in seiner geschichtlichen Entwicklung* (Frankfurt: J. Kauffmann, 3rd edn, 1931).

E.E. Urbach,[123] J. Heinemann and J.J. Petuchowski,[124] L.A. Hoffman,[125] and other scholars have shown that the *Shema* (Deut. 6.4; the liturgy included the reading of Deut 6.4-9; 11.13-21; Num. 15.37-41, plus beginning and closing benedictions), although not a prayer in the strict sense because 'it is God's word addressed to man',[126] was liturgically recited long before the fall of Jerusalem. Before the beginning of the present era, Jews religiously recited the *Shema* in the evening and in the morning (*m. Ber.* 1.1–3.5); the houses of Hillel and Shammai debated the proper way to recite it.[127]

Recently specialists in rabbinics have been more concerned than their forebears about the date of rabbinic traditions. J. Neusner[128] has certainly been the most prominent leader and the most prolific writer in this endeavor, and J. Heinemann[129] has demonstrated the importance of approaching Jewish liturgy using form-critical analysis.[130] At least five prayers are very early, certainly proto-rabbinic: the Grace after Meals, the *'Ahabah Rabbah* (With Abounding Love), the *'Alenu*

120. E. Schürer, *A History of the Jewish People in the Time of Jesus Christ* (trans. J. MacPherson, S. Taylor and P. Christie; 6 vols.; Edinburgh: T. & T. Clark, 1897–98).

121. G.F. Moore, *Judaism in the First Centuries of the Christian Era: The Age of the Tannaim* (3 vols.; Cambridge, MA: Harvard University Press, 1927–30).

122. J. Neusner, *The Rabbinic Traditions about the Pharisees before 70* (3 vols.; Leiden: E.J. Brill, 1971), II, pp. 41, 49; *idem*, *From Politics to Piety: The Emergence of Pharisaic Judaism* (New York: Ktav, 2nd edn, 1979), pp. 111-13.

123. E.E. Urbach, *The Sages: Their Concepts and Beliefs* (trans. I. Abrahams; 2 vols.; Jerusalem: Magnes Press, 1975), I, pp. 400-402.

124. J. Heinemann and J.J. Petuchowski (eds.), *Literature of the Synagogue* (New York: Behrman, 1975), pp. 15-28.

125. L.A. Hoffman, *The Canonization of the Synagogue Service* (UNDCSJCA, 4; Notre Dame: University of Notre Dame Press, 1979).

126. J.J. Petuchowski, 'The Liturgy of the Synagogue', in Petuchowski and Brocke (eds.), *The Lord's Prayer and Jewish Liturgy*, pp. 45-57, see esp. p. 48.

127. See Neusner, *The Rabbinic Traditions*, II, pp. 41, 49.

128. E.g., Neusner, *The Rabbinic Traditions*.

129. Heinemann, *Prayer in the Talmud*.

130. See also A. Spanier, 'Zur Formengeschichte des altjüdischen Gebetes', *MGWJ* 77 (1934), pp. 438-47; *idem*, 'Stilkritisches zum jüdischen Gebet', *MGWJ* 80 (1936), pp. 339-50; *idem*, 'Die erste Benediktion des Achtzehngebets', *MGWJ* 81 (1937), pp. 71-76; *idem*, 'Dubletten in Gebetstexten', *MGWJ* 83 (1939), pp. 142-49. L. Finkelstein, 'The Development of the Amidah', *JQR* NS 16 (1925–26), pp. 1-43, 127-70.

lesabbeah Prayer (It is our duty to praise), the *Qaddish* (Magnified and sanctified), and the *Tefillah* (*Shemoneh 'Esreh* or Eighteen Benedictions).

The Hebrew text and English translation of the *'Amidah* (עמידה) are presented conveniently by Heinemann,[131] who asserts that its original form(s) 'goes back to the ancient *hᵃbûrah* meals'.[132] This liturgical formula for grace after meals clearly predates the fall of Jerusalem in 70 CE;[133] moreover, grace is mentioned in *Jub.* 22.6 and *Letter of Aristeas* 184–185 (see also *m. Ber.* 3.4; 6.5).

The Hebrew text and English translation of the *'Ahabah Rabbah* are found in P. Birnbaum.[134] Heinemann[135] traces the original form(s) of this benediction to the period before the destruction of Jerusalem; it was recited by the priests (see *m. Tam.* 5.1).

The Hebrew text and English translation of the *'Alenu lᵉšabbeah* (עלינו לשבח) are printed in P. Birnbaum.[136] This prayer clearly predates 70 CE since it 'was composed against the background of the Temple service'.[137] Heinemann has demonstrated that this prayer has 'all the formal elements of the Bêt Midras pattern' and should be considered a *Bêt-midras* prayer.[138]

The Hebrew text and English translation of the *Qaddish* (קדיש) are published in P. Birnbaum.[139] The simple form of the eschatological hopes for the establishment of the kingdom of God and the absence of any allusion to the destruction of the Temple may indicate that this prayer predates 70 CE.[140] However, the *Qaddish* was probably not 'a part of the congregational service during the Mishnaic period'.[141] It was

131. Heinemann, *Prayer in the Talmud*, pp. 70-72, 288-89.

132. Heinemann, *Prayer in the Talmud*, p. 3.

133. See Heinemann and Petuchowski (eds.), *Literature of the Synagogue*, pp. 89-90.

134. Birnbaum, *Daily Prayer Book*, pp. 73-74.

135. Heinemann, *Prayer in the Talmud*, pp. 129, 174.

136. Birnbaum, *Daily Prayer Book*, pp. 135-38; see also Heinemann, *Prayer in the Talmud*, p. 271.

137. Heinemann, *Prayer in the Talmud*, p. 273. So also *EncJud* 2, col. 557.

138. Heinemann, *Prayer in the Talmud*, pp. 270-73.

139. Birnbaum, *Daily Prayer Book*, pp. 45-48; see also Heinemann and Petuchowski (eds.), *Literature of the Synagogue*, pp. 81-84.

140. 'Kaddish', *EncJud* 10, col. 661.

141. Heinemann, *Prayer in the Talmud*, p. 25.

originally recited at the conclusion of the public sermon.[142] Like the *ʿAlenu lešabbeah,* it is another classic example of the *Bêt-midraš* prayers.[143] It is strikingly similar to the Lord's Prayer,[144] and both may 'spring from the same source and are at home in one and the same world of belief'.[145]

The most famous of the proto-rabbinic prayers ('the Prayer' in Talmudic sources), of course, is the Eighteen Benedictions (the *Tefillah* or *Shemoneh ʿEsreh*). The common Hebrew text and translation are found in P. Birnbaum;[146] Schechter's English translation of the Cairo Genizah fragment (which is the old Palestinian rite) is reprinted in Heinemann.[147] There is little doubt that this prayer *par excellence,* which according to the Mishnah is to be recited in the morning, afternoon and evening (*m. Ber.* 2.4–5.5), was redacted at Jamnia (Yavneh) under the direction of Rabban Gamaliel II and that the original forms (it circulated orally in more than one form) antedate 'the destruction of the Temple by a considerable period of time'.[148] The Eighteen Benedictions is similar in numerous ways to the Lord's Prayer.[149] In support of Elbogen's[150] and Spanier's[151] argument that with liturgical texts that once circulated orally it is unwise to search for an 'original' text, Heinemann[152] rejects Finkelstein's,[153] Grant's[154] and K.G. Kuhn's[155]

142. Heinemann, *Prayer in the Talmud,* pp. 25, 266, 301.

143. Heinemann, *Prayer in the Talmud,* pp. 256-75, 280.

144. D. de Sola Pool, *The Kaddish* (Jerusalem: Sivan Press, 3rd edn, 1964), p. 112.

145. B. Graubard, 'The Kaddish Prayer', in Petuchowski and Brocke (eds.), *The Lord's Prayer and Jewish Liturgy,* pp. 59-72, 62.

146. Birnbaum, *Daily Prayer Book,* pp. 81-98.

147. Heinemann, *Prayer in the Talmud,* pp. 26-29; see also Heinemann and Petuchowski (eds.), *Literature of the Synagogue,* pp. 33-36.

148. Heinemann, *Prayer in the Talmud,* p. 22; Heinemann, 'Amidah', *EncJud* 2, cols. 838-45; R. Le Déaut, A. Jaubert and K. Hruby, *The Spirituality of Judaism* (trans. P. Barrett; Religious Experience Series, 11; St Meinrad, IN: Abbey Press. 1977), p. 37; Elbogen, *Der jüdische Gottesdienst,* pp. 28-29; I. Elbogen, 'Studies in Jewish Liturgy', pp. 1-51, K. Kohler, 'The Origin and Composition of the Eighteen Benedictions', pp. 52-90, L. Finkelstein, 'The Development of the Amidah', pp. 91-177, in J.J. Petuchowski (ed.), *Contributions to the Scientific Study of Jewish Liturgy* (New York: Ktav, 1970).

149. Heinemann, 'The Background of Jesus' Prayer', p. 86.

150. Elbogen, *Der jüdische Gottesdienst,* pp. 41-42.

151. Spanier, 'Dubletten in Gebetstexten', *MGWJ* 83 (1939), pp. 142-49.

152. Heinemann, *Prayer in the Talmud,* pp. 43-44.

claim or assumption that the Eighteen Benedictions originally existed in one standard text. Heinemann amasses impressive evidence to support the claim that this prayer, as well as others, originally did not receive standardization.[156]

Urbach[157] argues against the consensus date for the insertion of the *Birkat ha-Minim* ('Let the Christians and *mynym* perish in a moment...') to the 12th benediction of the *Tefillah*, which—according to most recent publications[158]—is attributed to the time of Rabban Gamaliel II (c. 85 CE). Urbach claims that this benediction prior to 70 contained a curse against the *pryshym*, those leaving the community, and that this curse later was directed against the *mynym*, which did not include the Christians but denoted the heretics. Eventually, after the Bar Kokhba revolt, Christians were included in the curse, 'and to emphasize their inclusion the נוצרים are mentioned explicitly'.[159]

Summary

This brief report attempts to survey the results of the most fruitful recent research regarding the early hymnbooks, the possibly Jewish prayers and hymns in the New Testament, and the proto-rabbinic prayers. The progress and quality of analytical research are impressive, and the origins of these hymns and prayers have been clarified considerably.

If one is to speak of a scholarly consensus, it would seem to be the growing recognition of the importance of such hymns and prayers not only as a significant witness to forms of Jewish piety and liturgy around the turn of the era but also as a major source for understanding Jesus and his earliest followers, as well as the nomenclature, style, and form of the earliest Christian hymns and prayers now preserved in the New

153. Finkelstein, 'The Development of the Amidah'.
154. F.C. Grant, 'Modern Study of the Jewish Liturgy', *ZAW* 65 (1953), pp. 59-77.
155. Kuhn, *Achtzehngebet und Vaterunser und der Reim*.
156. Heinemann, *Prayer in the Talmud*, pp. 45-52.
157. E.E. Urbach, 'Self-Isolation or Self-Affirmation in Judaism: Theory and Practice in the First Three Centuries', in Sanders and Baumgarten (eds.), *Judaism from the Maccabees to the Mid-Third Century*.
158. E.g. W.D. Davies, *The Setting of the Sermon on the Mount* (Cambridge: Cambridge University Press, 1966), pp. 272-77.
159. Urbach, 'Self-Isolation or Self-Affirmation'; see also *idem*, *The Sages*, I, p. 401.

Testament and related literature. Grant argued convincingly that 'the study of the ancient Jewish liturgy is of paramount importance' for 'the proper understanding of the New Testament'.[160] There is also a growing consensus today that research on these compositions must be freed from the attempt to align them with the Essenes, the Pharisees, or any other sectarian group;[161] from the misleading and anachronistic attempt to separate them into Hellenistic or Palestinian proveniences; and from the assumption that Early Judaism was ordered by a dominant orthodoxy.

It is clear that from the earliest times emphasis was on personal and instantaneous prayer.[162] Although an emphasis on the spontaneous nature of authentic prayer continued after 70 (see *m. Ber.* 4.4 and *m. Abot* 2.13), fixed prayers did begin to develop prior to the destruction of the Temple and during the period of Early Judaism.[163] Talmon focuses upon this development, but he correctly cautions that we do not presently know the 'precise beginning of institutionalized prayer in Judaism'.[164] The development is clear, but unfortunately it has been discussed with little, if any, reference to the hymnbooks described above.

Critique

Research into early Jewish hymns, odes, and prayers has been characteristically analytical, focusing generally on manuscript study and the higher critical issues of language, date, and provenience. Relatively little, if any, research has been directed to the questions of genre, form criticism, the relation of a composition's poetic style (*parallelismus membrorum*, rhythm, meter) to the Davidic Psalter, the similarities among the numerous hymns, odes, and prayers, and their use and function in the cult, synagogue *ḥᵃbûrâ* meals, *Bêt-midraš*, and even the

---

160. Grant, 'Modern Study of the Jewish Liturgy', p. 60.

161. E.g. M. Smith, 'Palestinian Judaism in the First Century', in M. Davis (ed.), *Israel: Its Role in Civilization* (New York: Harper & Brothers, 1956), pp. 67-81.

162. Heinemann, *Prayer in the Talmud*, pp. 37-51; Le Déaut, Jaubert and Hruby, *The Spirituality of Judaism*, pp. 69-70.

163. Heinemann, *Prayer in the Talmud*, p. 15; Heinemann and Petuchowski (eds.), *Literature of the Synagogue*, p. 31; Le Déaut, Jaubert and Hruby, *The Spirituality of Judaism*.

164. Talmon, 'The Emergence of Institutionalized Prayer', pp. 265-84.

Temple. Heinemann's monumental publication[165] is a singular exception.

We remain ignorant of the social and religious settings of most of the extant hymns and prayers.[166] We do not know why some hymns and prayers are in prose (e.g. Bar. 1.15–3.8) and others in poetry (e.g. *Psalms of Solomon*), and why and to what extent wisdom motifs are dominant in late hymns and prayers (e.g. the poem in praise of Wisdom in Bar. 3.9–4.4).[167] We need to know more about the historical background of these compositions and to explore the theology of the shared themes. We need to examine why many of the Jewish apocalypses are intermittently punctuated by hymns and prayers.

Publications have tended to be atomistic. Focus has customarily been narrowed to one (or a few) hymn(s) or a single hymnbook with scarcely any attention to the other extant data. For example, too frequently an article titled 'Qumran Hymns' will discuss only the *Thanksgiving Hymns*, and another article similarly titled will barely mention this collection. Jansen's monograph of 1937[168] is seriously out-dated and includes only the following early Jewish documents: 1, 2, 3 Maccabees, Tobit, Judith, *Prayer of Manasseh*, *Prayer of Azariah*, *Song of the Three Young Men*, Esther, Baruch, Ben Sira, Wisdom of Solomon, *Psalms of Solomon*, and *2 Baruch*. No one has yet attempted to write the history of liturgy in Early Judaism.

To assist preparations for this desideratum—and with the hope that some scholar may report its existence and receptions—the following prolegomenous comments are offered. The Jewish hymns and prayers need to be discussed in the context of the history of religions. G.F. Moore correctly noted that Jewish prayers are unique in that they do not request material possessions or luxuries.[169] Certainly the documents discussed herein will prove to be classified within B. Taylor's[170] 'higher' levels of culture. If the 'true nature of a religion is most clearly revealed

165. Heinemann, *Prayer in the Talmud*.

166. See Jansen, *Die spätjüdische Psalmendichtung*.

167. See C.A. Moore, *Daniel, Esther, and Jeremiah: The Additions. A New Translation with Introduction and Commentary* (AB, 44; Garden City, NY: Doubleday, 1977), pp. 295-304.

168. Jansen, *Die spätjüdische Psalmendichtung*.

169. Moore, *Judaism in the First Centuries of the Christian Era*; see also B. Martin, *Prayer in Judaism* (New York: Basic Books, 1968), pp. 14-23.

170. E.B. Taylor, *Religion in Primitive Culture* (Primitive Culture, 11; New York: Harper & Brothers, 1958), pp. 455-56.

by what men seek from God in it',[171] then it is clear that the early Jews neither created an efficacious God (*pace* L. Feuerbach) nor evidenced tendencies toward a *deus ex machina.* Rather they often adhered to traditions regardless of rewards or punishments (see Dan. 3.18; 2 Macc. 6.27-28). Some later Jews, however, using these and other early traditions, attempted to manipulate God through magical formulas.[172]

Although early Jewish writers emphasized the remoteness of God, they habitually punctuated their compositions with prayers in which God's presence is affirmed (see the list below). He hears prayers and answers them (*T. XII Patr.*, esp. *T. Jos.* 10.1-2; *2 Bar.* 48.25-43, esp. v. 26; *Par. Jer.* 6.15; cf. *LAB* 51; Sir. 35.17; *m. Ber.* 4.4; and the 15th of the Eighteen Benedictions). The responsiveness of God is illustrated in the well-known traditions regarding the 'heroes of prayer': Akiba, Hanina ben Dosa and Honi. God's historical acts demonstrated the valid assumption of his continuing mercy (see *Prayer of Manasseh*[173]). There is abundant evidence to warrant the conclusion that many Jews, rejoicing in God's benevolence and the joy of the Law, felt constrained—even in amazingly trying periods—at all times to praise the creator and covenanter (see *Letter of Aristeas* 197; Tob. 4.19; 1QS 10.9-17; cf. *Odes* 16). The cosmic and calendrical dimension of praise is palpable (see *Jubilees, 1 Enoch,* 1QH). According to the late and Christian portions of the *Ascension of Isaiah,* the quality of angelic singing improves as one ascends, and according to the (Christian?) *Testament of Adam,* the hours of the day and night are filled with praises to God by all his creatures.

Within many of the pseudepigrapha there are hundreds of hymns and prayers. For example, Pseudo-Philo obviously felt impelled—for reasons still unknown to us—to rewrite 'the Bible',[174] so that the narrative was expanded with poetic compositions. He added at least four psalms (Lament of Seila, *LAB* 40.5-7; Psalms of David, *LAB* 59.4; 60.2-3; Hymn of Deborah, *LAB* 32.1-17) and 12 prayers (of Moses, *LAB*

171. Moore, *Judaism in the First Centuries of the Christian Era,* II, p. 213.

172. M. Simon, *Verus Israel: Etude sur les relations entre chrétiens et juifs dans l'empire romain (135–425)* (Paris: Boccard, 1966 [1948]), pp. 399-404; E.R. Goodenough, *Jewish Symbols in the Greco-Roman Period* (Princeton: Princeton University Press, 1953), II, p. 161; Urbach, *The Sages,* pp. 97-134.

173. J.H. Charlesworth, 'Prayer of Manasseh', *OTP*, II, pp. 625-37.

174. See D.J. Harrington, J. Cazeaux, C. Perrot and P.-M. Bogaert (eds.), *Pseudo-Philon: Les Antiquités Bibliques* (2 vols.; SC, 229, 230; Paris: Cerf, 1976).

12.8-9; 19.8-9, 14-16; of Joshua, *LAB* 21.2-5; of Kenaz, *LAB* 25.6; 27.7; 28.5; of Jael, *LAB* 31.5, 7; of 'the people', *LAB* 39.7; of Samson's parents, *LAB* 42.2, 5; of Anna, *LAB* 50.4; 51.3-6).

Recognizing that many early Jewish hymns and prayers are now lost (see *T. Job* 49.3; 50.3), we should include in a survey of them *at least* the following compositions:

A. *Early Jewish Hymns*
   1. Hymns of Joshua ben Sira (Sir. 51.1-12, 13-30; 39.12-35)
   2. The psalms in 1 Maccabees (3.50-53)
   3. Psalms 151–155 (Supplement to the Psalter)
   4. Qumran non-Masoretic Psalms (11QPs^{a-e})
   5. *Thanksgiving Hymns* (Qumran hymnbook)
   6. Other Qumran hymns (1QS 10–11; 1QM 10.8–12.16; 13.7–14.1)
   7. Hymns from Qumran, probably not Essene (e.g. 4QShirShabb)
   8. Psalm in Baruch (1.15–3.8)
   9. The *Song of the Three Young Men*
   10. Judith's Song of Thanksgiving (Jdt. 16.1-17)
   11. Hymn to Wisdom (Wis. 7.22–8.1)
   12. *Psalms of Solomon* (hymnbook)
   13. Psalms in *Pseudo-Philo* (see above)
   14. Hymns in the *Testament of Job* (25.1-7b; 32.la-12c; 43.2b-13b; 53.lb-4)
   15. Psalm of Taxo (*T. Mos.* 10.1-10)
   16. Psalms in *2 Baruch* (10.6-19; 11.1-7; 14.8-10; 35.2-5; 75.1-8)

B. *Early Nonrabbinic Jewish Prayers*
   1. Prayer of Joshua ben Sira (Sir. 36.1-17)
   2. Prayer of Enoch (*1 En.* 84.1-6)
   3. Prayer of Judas Maccabeus and the Priests (1 Macc. 4.30-33)
   4. Prayers in 2 Maccabees (1.24-29; 15.22-24)
   5. Prayers in *3 Maccabees* (2.2-20; 6.2-15)
   6. Prayers in *Jubilees* (1.19-21; 5.24-26; 12.2-5; 15.6-8; *et passim*)
   7. *Prayer of Azariah*
   8. Prayers in Tobit (3.2-6; 3.11-15a; 8.5-8; 13.1-18).
   9. Prayer of Judith (Jdt. 9.2-14)
   10. Prayers of Esther and Mordecai (Add Est. 13.9-19; 14.3-19)
   11. *Prayer of Manasseh*
   12. Prayer of Solomon (Wis. 9.1-18)

13. Prayer of Jesus (Mt. 6; Lk. 11; *Did.* 8)
14. Prayers in *Pseudo-Philo* (see above)
15. Prayer of Asenath (*Jos. Asen.* 12–13)
16. Laments and Prayers of Ezra (esp. Confessio Esdrae, *4 Ezra* 8.20-36)
17. Prayers in *2 Baruch* (38.1-4: 48.2-24; 54.1-22)
18. Prayers in *Paraleipomena Jeremiou* (esp. 6.6-10, 12-14; 9.3-6)
19. *Prayer of Joseph*
20. *Prayer of Jacob*
21. Zephaniah's Prayers (*Apoc. Zeph.* 9.1-10; 12.5-10)
22. *Hellenistic Synagogal Prayers (Apos. Const.* 7–8, a hymnbook)
23. Prayers in the Targumim e.g. Tamar (Gen. 38.25), Moses (Deut. 32–50), Abraham (Gen. 22)

C. *Proto-Rabbinic Prayers and Synagogue Litanies*
   1. *'Amîdah* (Standing Prayer)
   2. *Shemoneh 'Esreh* or *Tefillah* (Eighteen Benedictions)
   3. *'Ahabah Rabbah* (With Abounding Love)
   4. *'Alenu lᵉšabbeah* (It is our duty to praise)
   5. *Qaddish* (Magnified and sanctified)
   6. Grace after Meals

D. *Other Early Possibly Jewish or Jewish-Christian Hymns and Prayers*
   1. *Magnificat, Benedictus, Gloria in Excelsis, Nunc Dimittis* (Lk. 1–2)
   2. Hymns in Paul (Col. 1.15-20; Phil. 2.6-11)
   3. Hymns in Revelation
   4. Jn 1.1-18
   5. *Odes of Solomon* (hymnbook)
   6. Hymn in Ignatius (Eph. 19.2-3)
   7. *Hymn of the Pearl* (*Acts Thom.* 108–113)
   8. Hermes' Hymn of Rebirth (*C.H.* XIII)
   9. Hermetic Prayer of Thanksgiving (CG VI, 7)
   10. Hymn of the First Stele of Seth (CG VII, 5)
   11. *The Mandean Hymnbook* (late)
   12. *The Manichaean Psalmbook* (late)

Conclusion

These hymns and prayers need to be examined in light of the psalms and prayers in the late canonical documents, namely, the psalm in Dan. 2.20-23 and Psalm 110, and the prayers in Dan. 2.4-19, Ezra 9.6-15 and Neh 1.5-11. The abundance of the data should be evaluated in light of the fact that the earliest prayers were not written down, following the principle that 'they who write down prayers are as they who burn the Torah' (*b. Šab.* 115b[175]).

New Testament scholars must put aside the old view that Jewish liturgy in Jesus' time was cold and concretized. Schürer was in error when he claimed that in early Judaism prayer 'was bound in the fetters of a rigid mechanism' and that the *Shema* and *Shemoneh 'Esreh* were 'degraded to an external function'.[176] The editors of the 'New Schürer' have wisely rewritten this section 'from a historical rather than a theological vantage point'.[177] Jewish prayers and hymns were frequently warm, alive, and personal. Even for the apocalypticists, prayers and hymns provided intimate interlocution with God. Codified laws for *some* Jews did lead to a myopic, legalistic religion; to others they ordered time and cosmos, regularizing stimuli for prayer praise, and the experience of God's presence in creation.[178]

175. See I. Elbogen, 'Studies in Jewish Liturgy', in Petuchowski (ed.), *Contributions to the Scientific Study of Jewish Liturgy*, pp. 1-51.

176. Schürer, *A History of the Jewish People*, II.2, pp. 115-25.

177. E. Schürer (ed.), *A History of the Jewish People*, II.2 (1979), p. 464.

178. See, e.g., M. Kadushin, *The Rabbinic Mind* (appendix by S. Greenberg; New York: Bloch Publishing Co., 3rd edn, 1972); see also Sanders, *Paul and Palestinian Judaism*.

Chapter 3

HYMNS AND ODES IN EARLY CHRISTIANITY

Jesus was a Jew; his earliest followers were Jews. He and they inherited the prayers developed by common folk, and perhaps occasionally by priests, that structured the day[1] through the statutory public prayers, recited in the morning, afternoon, and evening (cf. Dan. 6.11 [10 in ET]).[2] Gathering together either informally or within the more structured settings of the *hᵃbûrah* meals, the Synagogue, *Bêt midraš*, and especially the Temple, Jews would recite hymns and prayers which only in the Second Temple period had become fixed. Emphasis continued to

---

1.　See the popular article by J. Jeremias titled, 'Daily Prayer in the Life of Jesus and the Primitive Church', in *idem, The Prayers of Jesus.* Jews also participated in the ordering of the cosmos through calendrical observances, especially new moons and sabbaths, and evening and morning prayers, which as we learn from 4Q *Morgen und Abendgebete,* helped prepare for or dispel the darkness. The crisis caused by the observance of two paradigmatically different calendars, the solar and lunar calendars, was a profound theological, even cosmological, issue in Early Judaism, especially during the second century BCE. A devout Jew would have been horrified to learn that his calendar was not identical with God's own; what a catastrophe to observe the sabbath on the wrong day, or to celebrate in song or prayer out of synchronization with the celestial hosts (cf. *Jubilees, Ascension of Isaiah, Testament of Adam*). Y. Yadin has once again served us well by acquiring, and recording with notes and photographs the opening of tefillin from their capsules. These tefillin are dated to the first half of the first century CE and may be from Qumran (Y. Yadin, *Tefillin from Qumran [XQPhyl 1–4]* [Jerusalem: Israel Exploration Society and Shrine of the Book, 1969]).

2.　See the classical discussions of this phenomenon in Elbogen, *Der jüdische Gottesdienst* and in Heinemann, *Prayer in the Talmud.* As J. Neusner states, 'Life under the law means praying—morning, noon, night, and at meals—both routinely and when something unusual happens. To be a Jew...one lives...constantly aware of the presence of God and always ready to praise and bless God. The way of Torah is the way of perpetual devotion to God.' See J. Neusner, *The Way of Torah: An Introduction to Judaism* (Belmont, CA: Wadsworth, 1993), p. 53.

be placed on the necessity of personal, spontaneous prayer, but this ancient practice was now accompanied by the recognition of fixed prayers and of statutory prayers. As J. Heinemann demonstrated, the 'institution of fixed, communal prayer' was a 'radical innovation of the Second Temple period'. 'Fixed prayer, in and of itself constituting the entirety of the divine service, was a startling innovation in the ancient world, which both Christianity and Islam inherited from Judaism.'[3]

It was obvious to historians that as the Jews who followed Jesus became gradually more separated from other Jews, and eventually Judaism itself, they took with them into the movement soon to be called Christian not only the tradition of personal, spontaneous prayer, but also some revered fixed liturgies.[4] The latter probably included hymns and prayers[5] cherished through experience and regardless of their original *Sitz im Leben* and of their relation within, or to, the evolving canon of the so-called Old Testament. As I will attempt to show, this process of borrowing and reappropriating in a redefined manner early Jewish hymns and prayers stretches from the earliest phases of Christianity until at least[6] the fourth century and the Council of Nicea in 325.

In this chapter I shall present a prolegomenon for assessing the importance of the Jewish hymns and prayers for a better understanding of the hymns and prayers contained in the New Testament. After a few comments regarding methodology, the major research on the Jewish data will be summarized briefly, and the abundance of such data outlined. Subsequently, the research on the hymns and prayers in the

3.   Heinemann, *Prayers in the Talmud*, pp. 14-15.

4.   Christian literature did not absorb the standard Jewish fixed prayers. Only a myopic and synchronic reading of Christian writings would hesitate to acknowledge the borrowing mentioned above; moreover, we must be sensitive to the sociological situations behind the writings themselves and the palpably apologetic, reactionary tone of the early Christian literature. Literature is at best an imperfect mirror of historical phenomena.

5.   Numerous publications have attempted to demonstrate the differences between hymns and prayers. Although forms do reveal functions, the differences should not be exaggerated. We should remember that hymns and psalms became prayers in the standard Jewish hymnbooks or prayer-books.

6.   On the fringes of the Roman Empire and beyond the spheres of the controlling Church, the living influence of Judaism continued into the Middle Ages— and indeed continues today. We must resist the popular and reigning claim that after Jamnia, or at least Bar Kokhba, Judaism never again influenced Christianity. This egregious perception is shattered by the following discussion.

New Testament will be sketched and evaluated. After three generic considerations, the *Hellenistic Synagogal Prayers* will be utilized to illustrate the preceding discussion. This research and these reflections are offered with thanksgiving to a distinguished scholar of Second Temple Judaism, Yigael Yadin, in celebration of his 65th birthday.

Methodology

Over the last few centuries biblical scholars and historians of Early Judaism and Earliest Christianity have become painfully aware of the need constantly to refine the presuppositions and methods used in studying the sources available. As so many distinguished scholars have pointed out frequently over the last few decades, much earlier 'erudite and careful' research is now seen as misleading because of the delimiting and distorting methods employed. At the outset, therefore, I think it would be wise to reflect on the proper methodological approach to the study of the Jewish hymns and prayers for a better understanding of similar compositions in earliest Christianity.

1. *Canon*
A historian of earliest Christianity must not approach 'non-canonical' texts with a theological bias or with methods different from those employed in the study of 'canonical' writings. Many hymns and prayers that were eventually not included in the Jewish or Christian canons were often used authoritatively in Jewish services prior to, and during, the time of Jesus. This fact applies to many hymns and prayers that were sectarian, such as two early Jewish hymnbooks—the *Thanksgiving Hymns* and the *Psalms of Solomon*—as well as to those that were used in more than one sect or group and appear to have been part of widespread Jewish religious custom around the time of Jesus.

Many scholars[7] who attempted to study the early Jewish 'non-canonical' hymns and prayers, including those codified in the Mishnah and Talmudim, regarded them as second-rate, inferior compositions and as

---

7.   E. Schürer misrepresented Jewish prayer life and falsely claimed that since Jewish prayer 'was bound in the fetters of a rigid mechanism, vital piety could scarcely be any longer spoken of', *A History of the Jewish People*, II.2, p. 115). This absurdity is now corrected in 'the new Schürer': G. Vermes, F. Millar, M. Black and P. Vermes (eds.), *The History of the Jewish People in the Age of Jesus Christ (175 B.C.– A.D. 135)* (Edinburgh: T. & T. Clark, 1979), II, p. 481.

literature degenerate in relation to the Davidic canon. As S. Holm-Nielsen warned over 20 years ago,

> This implies an unspoken value judgment which—perhaps under the influence of the old dogma of inspiration, of which research has hardly ever been able to rid itself completely—regards the canonical books as 'sacred', while everything else is of secondary importance.[8]

While the historian should not wish to diminish the importance of the canonical psalms, and while the theologian certainly has the right to elevate in importance hymns, psalms, and prayers historically meaningful in one's own tradition, it is unwise to label as 'not sacred' or 'unauthoritative' (especially in the period when the Jewish and Christian canons were not yet fixed) compositions that for early Jews and Christians effectively created sacred space and bridged the distance between God and humankind, evoking meaningful discourse and communication between human beings and God.

2. *Experience*

The above comments lead to the recognition that the compositions with which we are concerned here are not necessarily 'apocryphal' because they were not rejected as unworthy, but 'extra-canonical'. Outside the Jewish canon is an abundance of hymns and prayers that were memorized and recited as sacred by Jews, not only from the period when the canon began to take shape, but also through the centuries when the text of the *Biblia Hebraica* was becoming canonized, and even up to the present. When historians look into the first century CE, they often see Jews and Christians (especially before 85 and the Council of Jamnia [Yavneh]) worshipping together and reciting the *Shema*, Eighteen Benedictions, and other prayers. The importance of distinguishing between 'apocryphal' and 'non-canonical' works is necessary here; only the latter non-judgmental concept accurately describes the early Jewish hymns and prayers.[9] As L.A. Hoffman has emphasized, we need to recognize that running alongside of, and eventually subsequent to, the canonization of scripture is the 'canonization' of liturgy.[10]

---

8.   Holm-Nielsen, 'The Importance of Late Jewish Psalmody', p. 2.

9.   'Apocryphal' often denotes something false or spurious; 'non-canonical' merely indicates something not within a group (or canon).

10. Hoffman, *The Canonization of the Synagogue Service*.

A major distinction, however, must be drawn between the hymns and prayers used liturgically by most religious Jews and the hymns and prayers composed by the authors (and redactors) of the non-canonical writings, especially the so-called Apocrypha and Pseudepigrapha. The former (e.g. the *Shema)* infused life with meaning and kept alive the covenantal relationship with God; the latter (e.g. the hymns in the *Testament of Job)* often punctuated a theological point and clarified the relationships in the story. The former were becoming fixed from ancient traditions but still had the verve of an oral life; the latter were frequently written *de novo* to embellish the literary genre.[11] Allowing for this caveat and paradigmatic distinction, we must attempt to perceive the phenomenon of reciting hymns and prayers in Early Judaism and the possible effects of this tradition on Early Christianity.

3. *Jews and Christians*

The early relationship between Jews and Christians has been portrayed customarily—but incorrectly[12]—as follows: a mutual, albeit tense, kinship existed until the war of 66–74; this connection was shattered permanently by a falling-out during the beginning of the first war, by the results of the Council at Jamnia (Yavneh) in 85—especially the addition of the *Birkath ha-Minim* ('Let the Christians and *mynym* perish in a moment') to the 12th of the Eighteen Benedictions—by the growing anti-Jewish tendencies and Gentile character of Christianity, and by the caustic charges and counter-charges made during the second war under Bar Kokhba (Bar Kosiba) in 132–135. These phenomena are well documented, and these polemics are reflected, for example, in Matthew's passion narrative, in Justin's *Dialogue with Trypho,* and in the Christian apocalyptic depictions of Jews suffering in hell (cf. *Apocalypse of Paul, Apocalypse of the Virgin);* yet the relationships between Jews and Christians must not be so neatly categorized. Indeed a less short-sighted and more sensitive portrayal of Jewish–Christian relationships is emerging.

E.E. Urbach has seriously challenged the well-known and popular claim[13] that the *Birkath ha-Minim* was introduced at Jamnia in order to

11. I leave open for future study the possibility that some of the hymns and prayers in the Apocrypha and Pseudepigrapha prior to their written form had enjoyed a liturgical life.

12. See n. 6.

13. See esp. J.L. Martyn, *History and Theology in the Fourth Gospel* (Nashville: Abingdon Press, 2nd edn, 1979).

prohibit Jewish Christians from reciting the Eighteen Benedictions.[14] The Early Fathers, notably Origen (c. 185–c. 254)[15] and Jerome (342–420),[16] learned much from contemporary Jews, and were influenced by Jewish sources (many non-canonical and now lost)[17] and by Jewish interpretation of scripture.[18] The anti-Semitic John Chrysostom (c. 347–407) clearly, but unintentionally, disclosed that Christians continued to frequent Jewish services: 'And many who belong to us and say that they believe in our teaching, attend their festivals, and even share in their celebrations and join in their fasts' (*Hom. adv. Jud.* 1.1; *PG* 48.844).[19] It is not clear how widespread (geographically and chronologically) was this practice which Chrysostom wished 'to drive from the church' (*PG* 48.844); but it is certain that in Antioch in the fourth century and the early fifth century Christians frequented the synagogue and participated in Jewish festivals. In addition to this literary evidence is the archaeological data that suggests 'far more contact between the two communities—Jewish and Christian—than ordinarily has been assumed possible'.[20] We must acknowledge the possibility—indeed probability—that

14. Urbach, *The Sages*, I, pp. 400-401; *idem*, 'Self-Isolation or Self-Affirmation', *The Sages*, I, pp. 269-98, see esp. p. 288.

15. See now especially H. Bietenhard, *Caesarea, Origines und die Juden* (Stuttgart: W. Kohlhammer, 1974); L. Levine, *Caesarea under Roman Rule* (SJLA, 7; Leiden: E.J. Brill, 1975); and N.R.M. De Lange, *Origen and the Jews: Studies in Jewish-Christian Relations in Third-Century Palestine* (University of Cambridge Oriental Publications, 25; London: Cambridge University Press, 1976).

16. I know of no recent, full-scale treatment of Jerome's relationship with the Jews, but see M. Rahmer, *Die hebräischen Traditionen in den Werken des Hieronymus. I. Die 'Quaestiones in Genesin'* (Breslau: Schlatter, 1861).

17. *OTP*, II, pp. 773-918, concludes with a massive Supplement that contains fragments of lost Jewish documents quoted by the Fathers, especially Eusebius and Clement of Alexandria.

18. De Lange (*Origen*, p. 7), for example, can report: 'Much of what Origen says cannot be understood without a knowledge of the Rabbis, and some of the arguments which have been produced by modern scholars crumble to dust when the evidence of the rabbinic writings is adduced.' De Lange (pp. 13, 15-17) continues to stress Origen's dependence also upon 'extrabiblical Jewish legends'.

19. W.A. Meeks and R.L. Wilken, *Jews and Christians in Antioch in the First Four Centuries of the Common Era* (SBLSBS, 13; Missoula, MT: Scholars Press, 1978), p. 86.

20. E.M. Meyers and J.F. Strange, *Archaeology, the Rabbis and Early Christianity: The Social and Historical Setting of Palestinian Judaism and Christianity* (Nashville: Abingdon Press, 1981), p. 10.

the influence of Jewish liturgy on Early Christianity does not end in the late first century but continues—at least in some religious settings.[21]

4. *History*

In attempting to comprehend the impact of Judaism on Earliest Christianity, especially the New Testament, the historian must recognize that to a certain extent many New Testament writings fit better within the history of Judaism than within the history of the Church. This opinion may sound wildly revolutionary to some New Testament scholars. They would claim, correctly, that it is the Church, following the lead of local churches, that officially collected and canonized the New Testament writings. Collectively, the New Testament writings are the product of the Church; but individually they are almost without exception compositions by Jews[22] who perceived themselves and their claims, not as something new and unparalleled, but as the continuation, indeed fulfillment, of very old sacred traditions. As Paul said, from the beginning until his time, the good news reflects a history 'through faith for faith' (Rom. 1.17; cf. Heb. 11).

Placing the New Testament, however, solely either within the history of Judaism or within the history of the Church fails to acknowledge that neither in Judaism nor in the Church do we have writings appreciatively similar to them. Jews produced testaments, expansions of the biblical record, Targums and wisdom tracts; but no document in the New Testament collection is classified like one of these.[23] Jews did not produce gospels or acts; and the Jewish letters and apocalypses are usually distinguishable from similar 'genres' in the New Testament. Post-New Testament Christians did complete gospels, acts, letters and apocalypses, but these are almost always characteristically different from the 'canonical' models, derivative from them, and are intermittently marked by perspectives and institutional concerns representative of a period later than most of the New Testament writings.

21. See especially the discussion below of the *Hellenistic Synagogal Prayers*.

22. E.E. Ellis has argued persuasively that Luke, the author of the Third Gospel, was not a Gentile but 'a Jewish Christian who followed a Greek life-style and was comparatively lax in ritual observances'. See Ellis, 'Luke, Saint', *Encyclopaedia Britannica* (15th edn, 1974), XI, p. 178; and Ellis, 'The Circumcision Party and the Early Christian Mission', in *Prophecy and Hermeneutic* (WUNT, 16; Tübingen: J.C.B. Mohr, 1978), pp. 116-28.

23. These types of documents, of course, did shape some passages in the New Testament.

Having granted that the New Testament fits neatly neither within Jewish history nor within Church history, we should also admit that we are confronted here by issues of degree not of kind. Jews did compose apocalypses (viz. *1 En.* 37–71)[24] and ethical tracts (viz. *Testaments of the Twelve Patriarchs*)[25] that are virtually indistinguishable from related Christian writings (respectively Revelation and the *Didache*). Likewise, the post-New Testament period does contain gospels, acts, letters and apocalypses.

The historian subsequently should acknowledge that the historical study of the New Testament is unique; the discipline belongs to a certain extent in both the history of Judaism and the history of the Church. Many New Testament writings were composed by Jews; hence the historical study of the New Testament belongs within the fringes of Judaism; but these authors were obviously 'Christians'[26] who saw in the Jesus-event a paradigmatic shift in the history of God's dealings with 'Israel'[27] and their writings were eventually canonized; hence the discipline belongs also within the history of the Church. For our present purposes, it is not so important to recognize the foreground as it is to identify the background. At least to a certain extent most New Testament writings are part of, or contiguous to, the history of first-century Judaism.[28]

5. *Extant Works*
While we cannot speak about the Jewish and early Christian hymns and prayers that are no longer extant, at least we should be aware that we do not possess all that was written during the early centuries and that what

24. During the *SNTS* Pseudepigrapha Seminars, the specialists agreed that *1 Enoch* 37–71 was Jewish; cf. J.H. Charlesworth, 'The SNTS Pseudepigrapha Seminars at Tübingen and Paris on the Books of Enoch', *NTS* 25 (1979), pp. 315-23.

25. J.H. Charlesworth, 'Reflections on the SNTS Pseudepigrapha Seminar at Duke on the Testaments of the Twelve Patriarchs', *NTS* 23 (1977), pp. 296-304.

26. I put this noun within quotation marks because its precise meaning is *sub iudice*, and because later doctrinal definitions must be resisted.

27. Again, the quotation marks warn that the nation was redefined already by the first generation of Jesus' followers.

28. I have not put Judaism within quotation marks; I assume it to be clear that I have been talking about Early Judaism, which was richly variegated, and not Judaism after 200 CE. J. Neusner rightly and judiciously warns against employing the term 'Judaism' for a religion that covers everything 'Jewish' from 200 BCE to 600 CE. See Neusner's extremely important *Judaism: The Evidence of the Mishnah* (Chicago: University of Chicago Press, 1981), see esp. p. 8.

has survived often is only the remnant of earlier writings, since it is the end-result of a process first of oral transmission and then of editing and re-editing. It follows that some hymns and prayers in the New Testament are remnants of, or modeled on, earlier Jewish compositions now lost except for the evolved excerpts. In particular, it is probable that the hymn fragment preserved in Eph. 5.14 is a Christian pastiche of earlier Jewish compositions ('Awake, O sleeper, and arise from the dead, and Christ shall give you life' RSV). Years ago, K.G. Kuhn[29] drew attention to the parallels between this hymn fragment and the *Psalms of Solomon* (16.1-4) and the *Thanksgiving Hymns* (3.19f.).

6. *Definitions*

The preceding comments bring to mind the repeated warnings of the best scholars over the last century that we must not approach Christian origins with the misleading categories and false contraries such as Palestinian Judaism versus Hellenistic Judaism, normative Judaism versus Sectarian Judaism, and 'orthodoxy' versus 'heresy'.[30] As demonstrated above, we must be very careful in using the adjectives 'canonical', 'extra-canonical' and 'apocryphal', and recognize the dual process of canonization of scripture and 'canonization' of liturgy. We must be sensitive to the problems in defining the nouns 'Judaism' and 'Christianity' and the related adjectives 'Jewish' and 'Christian'. It is clear that it is not easy to answer the question of whether some documents are 'Jewish' or 'Christian'. Most notable among such documents that have been difficult to categorize are *1 Enoch* 37–71, *Testaments of the Twelve Patriarchs*, *2 Enoch*, *Apocalypse of Abraham*, James, Hebrews, Revelation and the *Odes of Solomon*, although I am persuaded that the first four are Jewish, or fundamentally Jewish (with Christian expansions in *Testaments of the Twelve Patriarchs*, *2 Enoch*, and *Apocalypse of Abraham*), and that the final four are Christian (with sections more characteristic of Judaism than of the Church). Nevertheless, the tortuous attempt to

29. K.G. Kuhn, 'The Epistle to the Ephesians in the Light of the Qumran Texts', *NTS* 7 (1960–61), pp. 334-46 (repr. in J. Murphy-O'Connor and J.H. Charlesworth [eds.], *Paul and the Dead Sea Scrolls* [New York: Crossroad, 1990], pp. 115-31).

30. See esp. W. Bauer, *Orthodoxy and Heresy in Earliest Christianity* (appendices by G. Strecker, trans. R.A. Kraft and G. Krodel; Philadelphia: Fortress Press, 1971). See also H.E.W. Turner, *The Pattern of Christian Truth: A Study in the Relations between Orthodoxy and Heresy in the Early Church* (Bampton Lectures 1954; London: Mowbrays, 1954).

3. Hymns and Odes in Early Christianity

separate Jewish and Christian writings brings forward our major insight: the palpable kinship of Jewish and earliest Christian literature.

Research on the Jewish Data

During this century, an overview of early Jewish hymns and prayers has been advanced significantly by three major publications, of which the first depended on, and the third eventually superseded, the work of L. Zunz and S.D. Luzzatto.[31] I. Elbogen's *Der jüdische Gottesdienst in seiner geschichtlichen Entwicklung* saw three editions (1913, 1924, 1931), plus a Hebrew version,[32] and focused on the historical development of *rabbinic* prayers, while presupposing with Zunz an evolution from simple to complex form. Elbogen did not, however, include in his survey the hymns, hymnbooks and prayers preserved in the Apocrypha and Pseudepigrapha.[33] This desideratum was only partially supplied by H.L.

---

31. My comments here, of course, are merely intended as a brief summary. For a brilliant, fresh and insightful review of research on Jewish liturgy from Zunz's *Die gottesdienstlichen Vorträge der Juden* in 1832 to Heinemann's *Ha-tefillah bitequfat hatanna' im weha' amora' im* in 1964 (and 1966 with an ET in 1977), with astute input from the methodological foundations laid by H. Gunkel (on the Old Testament Psalms) and M. Dibelius (on the traditions in the gospels), see R.S. Sarason, 'On the Use of Method in the Modern Study of Jewish Liturgy', in W.S. Green (ed.), *Approaches to Ancient Judaism: Theory and Practice* (BJS, 1; Missoula, MT: Scholars Press, 1978), pp. 97-172. I have not included in this rapid survey the publications by K. Kohler, L. Finkelstein, L.J. Liebreich, and Z. Karl; these works are important, but the misleading presuppositions and methodologies in them prohibit me from including them among those that have significantly advanced research. For further discussion, see J.H. Charlesworth, 'Jewish Liturgies: Hymns and Prayers (c. 167 B.C.E.–135 C.E.)', in R.A. Kraft and G.W.E. Nickelsburg (eds.), *Early Post-Biblical Judaism and its Modern Interpreters* (SBL Centennial Publications Series, 2; Chico, CA: Scholars Press, 1986).

32. The Hebrew version was updated under the editorship of Heinemann: J. Heinemann (ed.), *Hat-tefillah be-Yisra'el* (Tel-Aviv: Diver, 1972).

33. Almost every publication on early Jewish liturgy ignores the hymns and prayers not found in the rabbinic corpus; even Sarason's superb review is myopic in this sense. An examination of Jewish liturgy of the intertestamental period must not be reduced to a study of Jewish liturgy that survived within rabbinic Judaism. Besides many other points that could be emphasized, suffice it to state now only that our ignorance of the origin of the synagogue, our recognition of the multiplicity and types of synagogues—certainly at least dozens in Jerusalem itself—and our awareness of other settings for Jewish liturgies besides the synagogue, should render absurd and thoroughly tendentious any attempt to state definitively that

Jansen in his *Die spätjüdische Psalmendichtung* in 1937. In this monograph, Jansen excluded the rabbinic evidence and included for discussion only the hymns in Sirach, the late 'canonical' psalms (he is influenced by Gunkel and Mowinckel) and scattered (but important) references to the following intertestamental writings: Wisdom of Solomon; 1, 2, and 3 *Maccabees*; Tobit; Judith; *Prayer of Manasseh*; *Prayer of Azariah*; *Song of the Three Young Men*; Esther; Baruch; *Psalms of Solomon*; *2 Baruch*. More recently,[34] J. Heinemann in his *Prayer in the Talmud: Forms and Patterns*, which saw two Hebrew versions (1964, 1966) and an English translation (1977), demonstrated that 'form-criticism can be a useful supplement to the historical-philological method' (p. 6). He applied this method, however, only to the prayers in the Talmud, as the title indicates.

During this century, therefore, the approach to early Jewish hymns and prayers has advanced markedly, but it has been fragmented and analytical. We are still far off from a definitive summary; the most distinguished publications have focused on individual collections, such as the two early hymnbooks,[35] the *Thanksgiving Hymns*[36] and *Psalms of Solomon*,[37] and the Talmud.

only rabbinic hymns and prayers defined early Jewish liturgy. Furthermore, we must also include in our study the traditions about prayers, including those of the ancient Hasidim and charismatics; cf. G. Vermes, *Jesus the Jew: A Historian's Reading of the Gospels* (London: Collins, 1973; Philadelphia: Fortress Press, 1981), pp. 69-72, 210-13.

34. I have excluded the authoritative publications by E.D. Goldschmidt because they are not directly on Jewish hymns and prayers, but on the related and indeed ancient Passover Haggadah (for a good review of Goldschmidt and bibliographical data, see Sarason, 'On the Use of Method', pp. 124-27, 161-63). Despite its title, N.B. Johnson's monograph, *Prayer in the Apocrypha and Pseudepigrapha: A Study of the Jewish Concept of God* (SBLMS, 2; Philadelphia: SBL, 1948), is selective and, as the subtitle indicates, really a theological study.

35. To label these documents 'sectarian' hymnbooks does not condone a tendency by some scholars to judge them insignificant and esoteric.

36. See esp. Licht, *The Thanksgiving Scroll*; Holm-Nielsen, *Hodayot: Psalms from Qumran*; Mansoor, *The Thanksgiving Hymns*.

37. For a bibliography on and brief introductions to the *Psalms of Solomon*, see J.H. Charlesworth, *The Pseudepigrapha and Modern Research with a Supplement* (SBLCS, 7S; Chico, CA: Scholars Press, 1981), pp. 195-97, 303-304.

An Abundance of Unexamined Data

A full-scale examination of the importance of Jewish hymns and prayers for similar writings in earliest Christianity is impossible at the present time. There are too many desiderata; we must polish the methodological approach to this literature and we must complete an examination, and then obtain a synthesis, of *all* the Jewish evidence now extant. This synthesis must recognize that many early Jewish hymns and prayers are now lost and must include at least the following works:

A. *Jewish Hymns that predate 70 CE and Mark* (see also the catalogue in Chapter 2)

1. Hymns of Joshua ben Sira (Ecclus. 51.1-12; 51.13-30; 39.12-35)
2. The psalms in 1 Maccabees (viz. 3.50-53)
3. Psalms 151–155 (Supplement to the Psalter)
4. Qumran non-Masoretic Psalms (11QPs^{a-e})
5. *Thanksgiving Hymns* (Qumran hymnbook)
6. Other Qumran hymns (viz. 1QS 10f.; 1QM 10.8–12.16; 13.7–14.1)
7. Qumran hymns probably not Essene (e.g. 4QShirShabb)
8. Psalm in Baruch (1.15–3.8)
9. The *Song of the Three Young Men*
10. Judith's Song of Thanksgiving (Jdt. 16.1-17)
11. Hymn to Wisdom (Wis. 7.22–8.1)
12. *Psalms of Solomon* (hymnbook)
13. Psalms in Pseudo-Philo
14. Hymns in the *Testament of Job* (25.1-7b; 32.la-12c; 43.2b-13b; 53.lb-4)
15. Psalm of Taxo (*T. Mos.* 10.1-10)[38]

---

38. Other early Jewish hymns and prayers will be discovered; for example Greenfield has probably recovered a Jewish psalm embedded in the Mandaic liturgies. See J.C. Greenfield, 'A Mandaic "Targum" of Psalm 114', in F. Fleischer and J.J. Petuchowski (eds.), *Studies in Aggadah, Targum and Jewish Liturgy in Memory of Joseph Heinemann* (Jerusalem: Magnes Press, 1981), pp. 23-31. Other Jewish poetic compositions should be kept on the fringes of the synthesis, among them the fragments of the 'pseudepigraphical' poetical works, especially Philo the Epic Poet, Theodotus, Ezekiel the Tragedian and the Jewish Orphica. See also *OTP*, II, pp. 773-918.

B. *Jewish hymns that date from 70–100 CE*

    1.   Psalms in *2 Baruch* (viz. 10.6-19; 11.1-7; 14.8-10; 35.2-5; 75.1-8)

C. *Nonrabbinic Jewish prayers that predate 70 CE and Mark*

    1. Prayer of Joshua ben Sira (Eccl. 36.1-17)
    2. Prayer of Enoch (*1 En.* 84.1-6)
    3. Prayer of Judas Maccabeus and the Priests (1 Macc. 4.30-33)
    4. Prayers in 2 Maccabees (1.24-29; 15.22-24)
    5. Prayers in *3 Maccabees* (viz. 2.2-20)
    6. Prayers in *Jubilees* (viz. 1.19-21; 5.24-26; 12.2-5; 15.6-8; *et passim*)
    7. Prayer of Azariah
    8. Prayers in Tobit (Tob. 3.2-6; 3.11-15a; 8.5-8; 13.1-18).
    9. Prayer of Judith (Jdt. 9.2-14)
    10. Prayers of Esther and Mordecai (Add Est. 14.3-19; 13.9-19)
    11. *Prayer of Manasseh*
    12. Prayer of Solomon (Wis. 9.1-18)
    13. Prayer of Eleazar (*3 Macc.* 6.2-15)
    14. Prayers in *Pseudo-Philo*

D. *Proto-rabbinic prayers and Synagogue litanies*

    1.   *'Amîdah* (Standing Prayer)
    2.   *Semôneh 'Esreh* or *Tefillah* (Eighteen Benedictions)
    3.   *'Ahabah Rabbah* (With Abounding Love)
    4.   *'Alenu lešabbeah* (It is our duty to praise)
    5.   *Qaddîs* (Magnified and sanctified)
    6.   Grace after Meals

E. *Nonrabbinic Jewish prayers that postdate 70 CE and are roughly contemporaneous with the gospels*

    1.   Prayer of Asenath (*Jos. Asen.* 12f.)
    2.   Laments and Prayers of Ezra (esp. *Confessio Esdrae*, 4 Ezra 8.20-26)
    3.   Prayers in *2 Baruch* (viz. 38.1-4; 48.2-24; 54.1-22)
    4.   Prayers in *4 Baruch* (esp. 6.6-10; 6.12-14; 9.3-6)

E. *Nonrabbinic Jewish prayers that are also early*

1. *Prayer of Joseph*
2. *Prayer of Jacob*
3. Zephaniah's Prayers (*Apoc. Zeph.* 9.1-10; 12.5-10)
4. *Hellenistic Synagogal Prayers* (*Apos. Const.* 7–8; a remnant of a Jewish hymnbook?)
5. Prayers in the Targumim; e.g. Tamar (Gen. 38.25); Moses (Deut. 32.50); Abraham (Gen. 22)

E. *Other early possibly Jewish but probably Jewish-Christian, Christian or Christian-related hymns and prayers*

1. Hymns in Paul (esp. Col. 1.15-20; Phil. 2.6-11)
2. *Magnificat, Benedictus, Gloria in Excelsis, Nunc Dimittis* (Luke 1–2)
3. Hymns in Revelation
4. Jn 1.1-18
5. *Odes of Solomon* (hymnbook)
6. Hymn in Ignatius (Eph. 19.2-3)[39]
7. *Hymn of the Pearl* (*Acts Thom.* 108–113)
8. Hermes' Hymn of Rebirth (*C.H.* XIII)
9. Hermetic Prayer of Thanksgiving (CG VI, 7)
10. Hymn of the First Stele of Seth (CG VII, 5)

E. *Later Hymnbooks related to the early Jewish and Jewish-Christian hymns*

1. *The Manichaean Psalmbook*
2. *The Mandean Hymnbook*

The abundance of extant early Jewish hymns and prayers and other similar compositions profoundly influenced by them is impressive; in fact, their volume can seem overwhelming. Here, these hymns and prayers are brought together for the first time, and I confess that the best I can do at present is to attempt a prolegomenous outline for a synthesis. We need a synthesis of this data. We need to explore the relationships of shared themes, perspectives, symbols, and metaphors. We need to explore the possibility of a development of the ancient

---

39. It is possible that *1 Clement* (c. 95 CE) preserves, albeit in a form redacted by a Christian, older Jewish prayers (cf. esp. 59.3–61.1).

forms of Semitic poetry, rhythm, and rhyme. We need to clarify the social setting of the compositions, and to explore whether there is a significant relation between the prayers composed by the apocalypticists and the statutory prayers of the Synagogue, *Bêt midraš*, and other liturgically formalized Jewish settings. Especially, we need to probe the possible kinship among those that phenomenologically had a life within some liturgical setting. In terms of these concerns, the above outlined data is a promised land without maps.

Research on the Hymns and Prayers in the New Testament

In contrast to this territory for future research, the hymns and prayers contained in the New Testament have received abundant and distinguished scholarly attention.[40] The publication of synthetic studies has been voluminous, especially since the middle sixties. One should mention at least the books by G. Schille (1965), J. Schattenmann (1965), R. Deichgräber (1967), J. Kroll (1968), J.T. Sanders (1971) and K. Wengst (1972).[41] These studies have tended to focus on the form and style of the earliest Christian hymns, their theology and Christology, and only partly on the possible Jewish background.[42]

Unfortunately, research on the New Testament data has proceeded unaware of the dire need of a synthesis of the early Jewish hymns and prayers. When we possess this synthesis, it will be possible to organize

40. We should expect the New Testament to be thoroughly researched; the collection of documents has been known and deemed highly significant by a large body of people (often characterized by an interest in study) ever since the fourth century. The Jewish data is paradigmatically different; some of it is only now being drawn to the attention of the public. Some documents have been recovered (or recognized) only in the past few decades, and it is too early to judge whether the new collections will be considered worthy of intensive research.

41. Schille, *Frühchristliche Hymnen*; Schattenmann, *Studien zum neutestamentlichen Prosahymnus*; Deichgräber, *Gotteshymnus und Christushymnus*; Kroll, *Die christliche Hymnodik*; Sanders, *The New Testament Christological Hymns*; Wengst, *Christologische Formeln*.

42. The exception would be Sanders' study; he does seek to discover 'the pre-Christian religious circles' behind the New Testament hymns. But he appears uninformed about much of the Jewish data, is preoccupied with trying to prove the pre-Christian date of the so-called redeemer myth, and focuses on only three works, the *Odes of Solomon*, the *Gospel of Truth* and the *Apocalypse of Adam*. Of these three, only the *Apocalypse of Adam* may perhaps be an edited form of a Jewish work that predates Christian influence; and it, of course, is neither a hymn nor a prayer.

the New Testament hymns and prayers into categories according to their ties with Palestinian Judaism. An organization might eventually look somewhat similar to the following four divisions of published scholarly conclusions.

First, some New Testament hymns have no Palestinian Jewish background but come from non-Palestinian communities, especially those in the eastern half of the Roman Empire. Into this category would be placed the view of E. Käsemann and others[43] that Col. 1.15-20, after two additions are removed, is a pre-Christian Hellenistic hymn.

Second, some New Testament hymns and prayers seem to be originally and thoroughly Christian, although under the influence of Jewish traditions. Under this division would go the arguments by M. Dibelius and H. Greevan and others, including W.G. Kümmel,[44] that Col. 1.15-20 was composed by the epistle's author, who used Jewish traditions. Likewise included here would be the claim by G. Delling and K.-P. Jörns[45] that the numerous hymns in Revelation were composed by the author of the Apocalypse himself, who was thoroughly indebted to Jewish traditions. Finally, under this second category would also be placed the almost universal consensus that in Phil. 2.6-11 Paul quotes from an early Christian hymn that may have incorporated some Jewish traditions.[46]

---

43. Käsemann claimed that Col. 1.15-20 is a pre-Christian gnostic hymn that is influenced by 'Hellenistic Judaism'. See Käsemann, 'A Primitive Christian Baptismal Liturgy', first published in the Bultmann Festschrift of 1949, now conveniently translated and collected in *Essays on New Testament Themes* (trans. W.J. Montague; SBT, 41; London: SCM Press, 1964), pp. 149-68. Deichgräber (*Gotteshymnus und Christushymnus*, p. 154) and E. Lohse (*Colossians and Philemon* [trans. W.R. Poehlmann and R.J. Karris; Hermeneia; Philadelphia: Fortress Press, 1971], p. 45) eschew the hypothesis of a gnostic background and trace the hymn back to 'Hellenistic Judaism'. It is important to observe that the best scholars see behind all the New Testament hymns traces of Judaism, even if this influence is via some type of early Gnosticism.

44. Dibelius and Greeven, *An die Kolosser, Epheser, an Philemon* (HNT, 12; Tübingen: J.C.B. Mohr, 3rd edn, 1953). C.F.D. Moule, C. Mauer, and A. Feuillet also defend this interpretation; for a bibliography see Kümmel, *Introduction to the New Testament* (trans. H.C. Kee; Nashville: Abingdon Press, 1975), p. 343.

45. Delling, 'Zum gottesdienstlichen Stil'; K.-P. Jörns, *Das hymnische Evangelium: Untersuchungen zu Aufbau, Funktion und Herkunft der hymnischen Stücke in der Johannesoffenbarung* (SNT, 5; Gütersloh: Gerd Mohn, 1971), esp. pp. 178-79.

46. Lohmeyer deserves credit for this penetrating insight. See E. Lohmeyer, *Die Briefe an die Philipper, an die Kolosser und an Philemon* (Göttingen: Vandenhoeck &

Third, scholars have judged many hymns and prayers in the New Testament to be Christian redactions of Jewish originals.[47] This group would include J.M. Ford's (incredible) suggestion that the hymns in Revelation 4–11 'emanate from the circle of John the Baptist and his followers',[48] and also the famous claim by R. Bultmann and others[49] that Jn 1.1-18 was once 'a cultic community hymn' revered by the followers of John the Baptist, and that it was interpolated and redacted by the Evangelist.

Fourth, some New Testament hymns may be Jewish compositions with little Christian editing, although they were significantly re-interpreted. Within this group would belong the intriguing and well-known arguments of K. Bornhäuser, H. Gunkel, E. Klostermann, S. Mowinckel, F. Spitta, and P. Winter[50] to the effect that the famous hymns in Luke's infancy narrative were Jewish in origin. Winter even

---

Ruprecht, 1930), p. 91; see also R.P. Martin, *Carmen Christi: Philippians 2.5-11 in Recent Interpretation and in the Setting of Early Christian Worship* (SNTSMS, 4; London: Cambridge University Press, 1967); and Deichgräber, *Gotteshymnus und Christushymnus*, pp. 118-33. Lohmeyer (see note 47) sees the influence of the Jewish celebrations of Yom Kippur behind the hymn in Col. 1.13-20; these are more likely to be behind the hymn in Phil. 2.6-11 (which is also strikingly similar to the *Odes of Solomon*).

47. Lohmeyer claimed that Col. 1.13-20 reflects the Jewish cultic confessions and celebrations on the Day of Atonement. See Lohmeyer, *Die Briefe an die Philipper, an die Kolosser und an Philemon*, pp. 41-47. See also S. Lyonnet, 'L'hymne christologique de l'Epître aux Colossiens et la fête juive du Nouvel An', *RSR* 48 (1960), pp. 92-100.

48. Ford, *Revelation*, p. 3, cf. pp. 21, 316.

49. Bultmann, *The Gospel of John*, pp. 17-18. While the connection with the circles of John the Baptist is attractive but speculative, it seems clear that the Evangelist has borrowed a Jewish or Jewish-Christian hymn on the Logos. Bultmann's hypothesis has been accepted *mutatis mutandis* by S. Schultz, H.H. Schaeder, H. Thyen, R. Macuch, and E. Stauffer. See the review of scholarly opinions in Brown, *The Gospel According to John*, I, pp. 19-37; and in R. Schnackenburg, *The Gospel According to St John* (trans. K. Smyth; London: Burns; New York: Herder & Herder, 1968), pp. 229-30.

50. For a full bibliography see Brown, *The Birth of the Messiah*, esp. pp. 346-66. Brown himself advocates a pre-Lucan origin for the canticles; Luke borrowed them from Jewish-Christian circles; they 'have their closest parallel in the Jewish hymns and psalms attested in the literature from 200 B.C. to A.D. 100, e.g., in I Maccabees, Judith, II Baruch, IV Ezra, the Qumran *Hodayoth* (Thanksgiving Psalms), and the Qumran War Scroll' (p. 349).

argued that the *Benedictus* (Lk. 1.67-79) and *Magnificat* (1.46-55) were Maccabean battle hymns.

Obviously, scholars are currently far from a consensus on many key issues. We do not know the exact length of most of the hymns quoted in the New Testament, whether they are complete or fragmentary, or whether they originate with the author, his community, or with an earlier anonymous Jew or Christian. We are convinced that many—if not most—of the hymns and prayers have been expanded or interpolated, but the extent of such editorial activity is not clear. We have no refined sieve with which to isolate and remove a quoted hymn.[51] Most importantly—as one should expect from the opening comments—when a hymn or prayer is isolated as a source borrowed by the author of a New Testament document, we have no clear-cut paradigm or set of categories with which to judge if it is originally Jewish or Jewish-Christian. Considerable debate continues on whether the following compositions are merely poetic passages, disguised hymns, confessions, or confessional hymns: 1 Tim. 3.16; Heb. 1.3; Eph. 1.3ff.; 2.14-16, 19ff.; 1 Pet. 2.6-8, 2.21-25; 3.18-22.

Generic Considerations

1. *Parallels in Style*
Above the confusing debates over the background of the hymns and prayers quoted in the New Testament arise three generic features. First, it is undeniable that there are impressive parallels in poetic style between the Christian (or Christian redacted or interpreted) hymns and prayers and the earlier (or contemporaneous) Jewish compositions; in particular, it is worth noting the shared expanded use (often with mixed forms) of *parallelismus membrorum*, the repetitive use of key-words, and the utilization of rhythm (which is lost somewhat in translation from Semitic languages into Greek).[52] Likewise, it is obvious that there are impressive ideological and theological parallels; these should not be explored only in search of literary dependences.

A good example of this first generic relationship is the 'cultic hymn' in Jn 1.1-18 (or possibly v. 16), especially vv. 1-11. Whether it was

---

51 See the attempts at a refined methodology by Schille, *Frühchristliche Hymnen*, pp. 11-23.

52. Here it is pertinent to emphasize once again the importance of the Syriac recension of the New Testament.

composed by a Jew and subsequently redacted by the Evangelist, or whether by a person who may have been a Jew converted to Christianity (and then perhaps redacted by the Evangelist), it is apparent, despite some claims to the contrary, that the first three strophes of the hymn are structured according to step parallelism (*parallelismus membrorum*) as found in the New Testament, for example, in Mk 9.37 (Mt. 18.5, Lk. 9.48), Mt. 10.40, Jn 8.32 and 10.11. Moreover, it is probable that behind this hymn lies Jewish reflections on 'the Word', 'Wisdom' (*Sophia*), and perhaps other divine (hypostatic) figures. The step parallelism of three strophes, characterized by verses of two *stichoi*, can be recovered and isolated:

First Strophe

1.   In the beginning *was the Word,*
     And *the Word was* with God.

Second Strophe[53]

3.   Everything through *him was made,*
     And apart from *him was made* nothing which was made.
4.   In him *was*[54] *life,*
     And the *life was the light* of men.
5.   And *the light* shines[55] in *the darkness,*
     And *the darkness* did not overcome it.

Third Strophe[56]

10. He was in *the World,*[57]
     And *the world* was made through him.[58]

53.   Jn 1.1b-2 linguistically (the anarthrous use of *theos*) and structurally (no *parallelismus membrorum*) seems intrusive and may be redactional, possibly revealing a Christian desire to stress the divine attributes of *ho logos*.

54.   I have not translated slavishly, e.g. 'life was', because of the freedom regarding the placing of the verb in poetic forms. The verb's position does not shatter the step parallelism.

55.   See note 54.

56.   Jn 1.6-9 is redactional, stressing in polemical Johannine fashion that John the Baptist was not 'the true light', the Messiah.

57.   See note 54.

58.   Jn 1.10b seems redactional and brings out the Johannine emphasis that the world (a technical word in John) did not know (another Johannine technical word) him (Jesus).

11. He came to *his own*,[59]
     And *his own* did not receive him.

In the arrangement and selection of these verses, I am influenced by various insights by Bultmann, Brown, and R. Schnackenburg.[60] The 'pearl within this Gospel', as Brown describes it,[61] has parallels that shoot off into two directions: they draw us back historically into the Jewish milieu out of which the author and school[62] of John came; and they draw us forward literarily to the cosmic dimensions of the salvific Christology and to the step parallelisms elsewhere in John (esp. 8.32 and 10.11).

2. *Shared Theological Emphases*

Second, in addition to the striking literary parallels between the Jewish hymns and prayers and the New Testament excerpts, there is an impressive kinship of shared phenomenological and theological perceptions. Both portray in similar language the conception that the human needs God and addresses to him petitions, laments and wishes, and perhaps most important of all that, as *homo religiosus*, he needs to praise the Creator, and desires to offer thanksgiving to him.[63]

Many Jewish and New Testament hymns and prayers express utter dependence on God; only God can make one righteous. This emphasis, usually incorrectly associated only with Paul's soteriology, is clearly

---

59. See note 54.

60. Bultmann does not employ the *terminus technicus* 'step parallelism', but he observed it: 'In each sentence two words normally carry the emphasis, and the second of these stressed words often recurs as the first word emphasized in the next sentence' (Bultmann, *The Gospel of John*, p. 15). Schnackenburg (*The Gospel According to St John*, I, pp. 226, 232) judges that the Evangelist derived the hymn from early Christian liturgy. Brown (*The Gospel of John*, I, pp. 20-21) thinks that the Evangelist redacted 'a hymn composed in the Johannine church' (p. 21).

61. Brown, *The Gospel of John*, I, p. 18.

62. See R.A. Culpepper, *The Johannine School* (SBLDS, 26; Missoula, MT: Scholars Press, 1975).

63. From the viewpoint of the history of religions, it must be stressed that the hymns and prayers with which we are interested transcend the false dichotomy of recited history versus cosmic consciousness—praise was both, often at the same time, a celebration of *Heilsgeschichte* and an indwelling of the forces of the cosmos and the divine natural rhythms (viz. in *Jubilees*, *1 Enoch*, *Psalms of Solomon*, *Testament of Adam*, *Ascension of Isaiah*, 1QH, Col. 1, Jn 1, Phil. 2, *Odes of Solomon* and the hymns in Revelation).

present in some Jewish hymns, notably the *Thanksgiving Hymns* (esp.
1QH 4.27f.; 7.28f.; cf. the hymn in 1QS 11.9f.) and the *Prayer of
Manasseh*. A development of concepts found in the Prophets and
Psalms, this idea shows the New Testament hymns to be anchored in
the Jewish hymns:

> Yet Thou bringest all the sons of Thy truth
>   in forgiveness before Thee,
>
> [to cleanse] them of their faults
>   through Thy great goodness,
>
> and to establish them before Thee
>   through the multitude of Thy mercies
>   for ever and ever. (1QH 15[*olim* 7].28-29)[64]

3. A Continuum of Expressed Needs and Praises

Third, in addition to the comments regarding stylistic parallels and
shared theological sensitivities, a study of the Jewish hymns and prayers
which may lie behind many of the New Testament passages reveals
something profound: a continuum of expressions of need and of praise,
and also a history of a long period when Jewish liturgy profoundly
influenced Christian liturgy.[65] The best example of fruitful research into
this relationship is found in publications on a rarely recognized extra-
canonical writing, the *Hellenistic Synagogal Prayers*. We now turn to an
examination of this document which illustrates much of what has been
argued above.

---

64. Translation by G. Vermes in *The Complete Dead Sea Scrolls in English* (New
York: Penguin, 1997), p. 277.

65. Bouyer rightly laments a tendency in some erudite and intuitive scholars to
avoid grasping the Jewish roots of Christian liturgy. See L. Bouyer, 'Jewish Liturgy
and Christian Liturgy', in *Eucharist: Theology and Spirituality of the Eucharistic
Prayer* (trans. C.U. Quinn; Notre Dame: University of Notre Dame Press, 1968), pp.
15-28. Of course, as Christian liturgy developed it was successively influenced by
non-Jewish elements. Earlier in this century, Oesterley attempted 'to show that the
Jewish liturgy has left many marks of its influence, both in thought and word, on
early forms of Christian worship, and, therefore, ultimately on the Christian Liturgy
itself' (p. 5). We are not yet able to assess the extent or duration of that obvious
influence. See W.O.E. Oesterley, *The Jewish Background of the Christian Liturgy*
(Oxford: Clarendon Press, 1925). The influence of Jewish hymns and prayers on
early Christian cultic worship is examined in terms of a selection of documents by
Aune in *The Cultic Setting of Realized Eschatology*.

The Hellenistic Synagogal Prayers

The compiler of the *Apostolic Constitutions* collected and expanded at least three major sources: the *Didascalia* (*Apos. Const.* 1–6), the *Didache* (*Apos. Const.* 7.1-32) and the *Hellenistic Synagogal Prayers* (*Apos. Const.* 7.33-38). This last collection was taken from Jewish prayers (perhaps a prayer-book) that were modeled on the Seven Benedictions for Sabbath and festivals (the first three, last three, and middle benediction for the sanctification of the day in the Eighteen Benedictions).

Immediately after quoting the *Didache*, the compiler of the *Apostolic Constitutions* presented a series of prayers whose themes and allusions to the Old Testament are in the same order as those in the Seven Benedictions. This sequence is especially impressive in the first six prayers both in the *Apostolic Constitutions* and in the Seven Benedictions. Moreover, there are significant parallels in the order of words and even phrases. As K. Kohler[66] claimed long ago, and as D.A. Fiensy[67] has attempted to demonstrate recently, the compiler of the *Apostolic Constitutions* has preserved a collection of *Hellenistic Synagogal Prayers*. The Jewish nature of these prayers was perceived correctly by W. Bousset, E.R. Goodenough, A. Baumstark, M. Simon, and Bouyer.[68]

Apparently, some time in the early centuries, a Christian, perhaps a convert from Judaism, introduced into the liturgy of his community Jewish prayers modeled on the Seven Benedictions. It is clear, as some of the undeniable Christian interpolations reveal, that he (or another Christian) re-interpreted the original Jewish prayers. Although it is difficult to date their author or the compiler of the *Apostolic Constitutions*, it is certain that long after the New Testament period ended, Jewish hymns and prayers continued to influence Christians and be recited by them. Furthermore, the *Apostolic Constitutions* contain not only original Jewish, but also Christian prayers; hence we can view in

66. Kohler, 'Über die Ursprünge', pp. 441-51, 489-97; among his other publications see also *The Origins of the Synagogue and the Church* (New York: Macmillan, 1927).

67. D.A. Fiensy, 'A Redactional Examination of Prayers Alleged to be Jewish in the Constitutiones Apostolorum' (PhD dissertation, Duke University, 1980).

68. Bousset, 'Eine jüdische Gebetssammlung', pp. 438-85; Goodenough, *By Light, Light*; Baumstark, 'Trishagion und Qeduscha', *Jahrbuch für Liturgiewissenschaft* 3 (1923), pp. 18-32; Simon, *Verus Israel*, pp. 8, 52, 74-82; Bouyer, *Eucharist*, pp. 119-35.

one text the evidence of a continuum and of a transition from Jewish to Christian prayers.

An example of Jewish composition with Christian redaction, and finally Christian expansion, may be found in *Hellenistic Synagogal Hymn* 5.1-7 (*Apos. Const.* 7.36.1f.; clearly Christian material is in italics):

> O Lord, Almighty One,
> You created [the] cosmos *through Christ*,
> and marked out a Sabbath-day for a remembrance of this;
> because on it you rested from the works [of creation],
> in order to give attention to your own laws.
> And you appointed festivals for [the] gladdening of our souls,
> so that we may come into remembrance of the Wisdom created by you:
> > *how for us he submitted to birth, that [birth] through a woman;*
> > *[how] he appeared in [this] life, having demonstrated himself in [his]*
> > *baptism;*
> > *how he who appeared is God and man;*
> > *[how] he suffered for us with your consent,*
> > *and [how] he died and arose by your strength.*
> > *Therefore, celebrating the resurrection festival on the Lord's Day,*
> > *we rejoice over the one who indeed conquered death,*
> > *having brought to light life and immortality.*[69]

The Christian redactor has clarified for a new liturgical *Sitz im Leben* the means by which God has created the cosmos, identifies Wisdom with Christ, and rehearses the economy of salvation.

Non-Conclusive Observations

A prolegomenon such as this one cannot have a conclusion. It is obvious from the above brief programmatic discussion that many significant issues—historical, sociological, and theological—are related to the study of the importance of the Jewish hymns and prayers for a better understanding of the New Testament hymns and prayers. The authors of the New Testament books obviously were influenced, not only by the Psalter, but also by some 'non-canonical' hymns and prayers. While we are far from a consensus on the major issues related to the understanding of the early Christian hymns and prayers, we are relatively close to

69. Translation by D.R. Darnell, 'Hellenistic Synagogal Prayers', in *OTP*, II, pp. 682-83. For other examples of reasons for Christian interpolations, see Charlesworth, 'Christian and Jewish Self-Definition', pp. 27-55.

an agreement on the proper methodological approach to the study of their possible Jewish background. Certainly, we are far closer to the compiler of the *Apostolic Constitutions,* who affirmed the beauty and grandeur of Jewish prayers, than to Jerome, who spoke so disparagingly about them (*In Amos* 5.23). Finally, it is sane to recall that one of the most beautiful Jewish models for prayer was composed by Jesus of Nazareth, and that 'the Lord's Prayer' (Mt. 6.9-13; Lk. 11.1-4; *Did.* 8) 'displays all of the characteristics of Jewish private prayer', as Heinemann perceived.[70] In terms of our present concerns, it is well to note that Jesus' prayer is constructed in *parallelismus membrorum* and is frequently similar to the *Qaddish* (the doxology to the liturgy of the synagogue) and Psalm 155.[71]

70. Heinemann, 'The Background of Jesus' Prayer', p. 88. Some scholars (notably S. van Tilborg and M.D. Goulder) have claimed that 'the Lord's Prayer' is the product of the Church; it seems relatively certain (as J. Carmignac, J. Jeremias, R.E. Brown, B. Noack and P.B. Harner have shown) that at least most of it derives ultimately from Jesus himself.

71. See also J.H. Charlesworth, *et al.* (eds.), *The Lord's Prayer and Other Prayer Texts from the Greco-Roman Era* (Valley Forge, PA: Trinity Press International, 1994).

Chapter 4

THE ORIGINAL LANGUAGE OF THE *ODES OF SOLOMON*

Arguments for a Greek Original

Bibliographical Introduction

Following Harris's discovery of MS H, a heated controversy arose concerning the original language of the *Odes of Solomon*. Scholarly debates revealed two alternatives: either the original language was Syriac (or a similar Semitic language), or the original language was Greek. In the *editio princeps* Harris argued that both the Syriac and the Coptic had been translated from a Greek text.[1] His position was quickly supported by the conclusions of J. Wellhausen,[2] E. Buonaiuti,[3] F. Schulthess,[4] H. Gunkel,[5] A. Wabnitz,[6] and E.J. Goodspeed.[7] In 1911 the hypothesis

---

1.   *Editio princeps*, pp. 36-37, 46-47. He maintained this same opinion in his second edition. See J.R. Harris, *The Odes and Psalms of Solomon: Published from the Syriac Edition* (Cambridge: Cambridge University Press, 2nd edn, 1911), pp. 46-47.

2.   'Die Oden Salomos sind ebenfalls aus dem Griechischen übersetzt, welches hier wohl auch die ursprache war', J. Wellhausen, review of *The Odes and Psalms of Solomon*, by J.R. Harris, in *GGA* 172 (1910), pp. 629-641 (631). See his review of *Ein jüdisch-christliches Psalmbuch aus dem ersten Jahrhundert* (TU, 35.4; Leipzig: J.C. Hinrichs, 1910), by A. Harnack and J. Flemming, in *GGA* 172 (1910), pp. 641-42.

3.   E. Buonaiuti, 'Il più antico Innario cristiano', *RStCST* 6 (Marzo, 1910), p. 194.

4.   F. Schulthess, 'Textkritische Bemerkungen zu den syrischen Oden Salomos', *ZNW* 11 (1910), p. 251.

5.   'Das Griechische aber ist, wie auch Schulthess und Wellhausen annehmen für das Original zu halten' (H. Gunkel, 'Die Oden Salomos', *ZNW* 11 [1910], p. 292).

6.   A. Wabnitz, 'Un Psautier judéo-chrétien du 1er siècle', *RevT* 19 (1910), p. 251.

7.   E.J. Goodspeed, review of *The Odes of Solomon*, by J.R. Harris, in *BW* 36 (August, 1910), p. 142.

of a Greek original was strengthened by the researches of W. Franken-
berg,[8] R. Bultmann,[9] H. Gressmann,[10] A. De Boysson,[11] H. Hansen,[12]
A.J. Wensinck,[13] A. d'Alès,[14] P. Kleinert,[15] and J. Labourt and
P. Batiffol.[16]

W. Frankenberg was so convinced that the original language was
Greek that he translated *Odes* 3–42 into Greek. Others apparently
shared his assurance, for the following year F.C. Burkitt declared: 'No
theory of the origin of these Odes is satisfactory, which regards the
Syriac translation that we possess otherwise than as an exotic.'[17]
A. Loisy, although critical of Frankenberg's interpretations, appears to
have accepted his retroversion into Greek: 'Les Odes ayant été, selon
toute vraisemblance, composées en grec, M. Frankenberg a pris à tâche
d'en reconstituer le texte primitif.'[18] In the same year F. Perles obviously agreed with Burkitt and Loisy for he remarked, 'Dass der vorliegende syrische Text aus dem Griechischen übersetzt ist, was für

8.   W. Frankenberg, *Das Verständnis der Oden Salomos* (BZAW, 21; Giessen:
Alfred Töpelmann, 1911), pp. 1 *et passim*.

9.   Although Bultmann was not primarily concerned with the higher critical
problems, he asserted that we possess the certain knowledge ('sichere Erkenntnis'),
'dass unser syrischer Text (ebenso wie der koptische der Pistis Sophia) auf einen
griechischen zurückgeht...'. R. Bultmann, 'Ein jüdisch-christiliches Psalmbuch aus
dem ersten Jahrhundert', *MPTh* 7 (October 1910–September 1911), p. 24.

10.   H. Gressmann, 'Die Oden Salomos', *IW* 5.29 (July, 1911), pp. 900-901.

11.   A. De Boysson, 'Les Odes de Salomon', *RPA* 12 (1911), p. 499.

12.   H. Hansen, *Die Oden Salomos in deutschen Nachdichtungen* (Gütersloh:
C. Bertelsmann, 1911), p. 1.

13.   A.J. Wensinck wrote that 'onze psalmbundel uit het Grieksch vertaald is'
('De Oden van Salomo, een oud-christelijk psalmboek', *ThSt* 29 [1911], pp. 54-55).

14.   A. d'Alès, 'Les Odes de Salomon', *Études* 129 (December, 1911), pp. 755-56.

15.   'Aber beide Übersetzungen der Oden, sowohl das syrische Korpus wie die
koptischen Stücke gehen offenbar auf eine griechische Vorlage zurück'. P. Kleinert,
'Zur religionsgeschichtlichen Stellung der Oden Salomos', *TSK* 84 (1911), p. 574.

16.   J. Labourt and P. Batiffol, *Les Odes de Salomon: Une oeuvre chrétienne des
environs de l'an 100–120* (Paris: Librairie Lecoffre, 1911), p. 2.

17.   F.C. Burkitt, 'A New MS of the Odes of Solomon', *JTS* 13 (April 1912), pp.
373-74.

18.   'The Odes were, in all probability, composed in Greek, M. Frankenberg having taken on the task of reconstructing its original text.' A. Loisy, review of *Les Odes
de Salomon*, by J. Labourt and P. Batiffol, and *Das Verständnis der Oden Salomos*, by
W. Frankenberg, in *RCHL* 74 (1912), p. 344.

jedem Kenner sofort klar.'[19] In the next three years six other scholars shared this conclusion: G. Kittel,[20] R.H. Connolly,[21] G. Beer,[22] L. Tondelli,[23] P. Smith,[24] and E. Preuschen.[25] G. Kittel argued that both MS H and MS N were not only translations, but translations from the same Greek text.[26]

In the first half of the second decade of this century scholars were so convinced the *Odes of Solomon* were originally written in Greek that D.J. de Puriet could state that, though there was scholarly dissension regarding the *Odes*, at least one fact was certain: the original language was Greek, 'Il paraît acquis en tout cas que le texte qui n'existe plus qu'en syriaque était écrit d'original en grec.'[27] Although the tide of scholarly consensus regarding the original language of the *Odes* began to turn around 1913 from the Greek to the Semitic hypothesis, biblical scholars until the present have intermittently advocated and presented new evidence that the *Urtext* is Greek.

19. 'That the present Syriac text is translated from the Greek, is at once clear to any scholar.' F. Perles, review of *Die Oden Salomos* (Neue Studien zur Geschichte der Theologie und der Kirche, 9; Berlin: Trowitzsch, 1911), by G. Diettrich, in *OLZ* 15 (January 1912), p. 26.

20. G. Kittel, 'Eine zweite Handschrift der Oden Salomos', *ZNW* 14 (1913), pp. 79-93.

21. R.H. Connolly, 'Greek the Original Language of the Odes of Solomon', *JTS* 14 (1913), pp. 530-38; *idem*, 'The Original Language of the Odes of Solomon', *JTS* 15 (1914), pp. 45-47; *idem*, Review of *The Odes and Psalms of Solomon*, by R. Harris and A. Mingana, in *JTS* 22 (October 1920), pp. 80-82.

22. G. Beer, 'Pseudepigraphen des A.T.s', in E.A. Hauck (ed.), *Realencyklopädie für protestantische Theologie und Kirche* (Leipzig: J.C. Hinrichs, 3rd edn, 1913), pp. xxiv, 375-79.

23. 'Gli argomenti addotti tendono a provare che non solo il siriaco e stato formato su un testo greco, ma che il greco è l'originale: essi si aggiungeranno altre prove della origine ellenica delle Odi'. L. Tondelli, *Le Odi di Salomone: Cantici Christiani degli inizi del II Secolo* (prefazione del Angelo Mercati; Rome: Francesco Ferrari, 1914), p. 49.

24. P. Smith, 'The Disciples of John and the Odes of Solomon', *The Monist* 25 (April 1915), pp. 168-69.

25. E. Preuschen, 'Ein Übersetzungsfehler in den Oden Salomos', *ZNW* 16 (1915), pp. 233-35.

26. G. Kittel, 'Eine zweite Handschrift', pp. 80, 92.

27. 'It seems well established, however, that the text which now only exists in Syriac was written originally in Greek.' D.J. De Puriet, review of *Les Odes de Salomon*, by J. Labourt and P. Batiffol, *RBén* 28 (1911), pp. 449-50.

In the second edition of E. Hennecke's *Neutestamentliche Apokryphen* of 1924, H. Gressmann reaffirmed his earlier conclusion with the categorical statement, 'Der Urtext war griechisch.'[28] In the thirties J.M. Bover reported to the Spanish-speaking world that the consensus of critical scholarship concluded, 'la lengua original de las Odas de Salomón fué el griego',[29] and in Germany H. Gunkel and W. Bauer contended,[30] 'Die Grundsprache der S.-O. ist das Griechische'.[31] In 1935 G. Bardy also opted for the Greek hypothesis.[32] Similarly, in the forties A. Omodeo,[33] B. Steidle,[34] and H.E. Del Medico[35] argued that the original language was indubitably Greek.

An exciting discovery was made in the fifties: a Greek miscellany from the third century was found in which the 11th *Ode of Solomon* was extant. The editor of the miscellany, M. Testuz, remarked that we now possess an ode in the original language.[36] Two years after Testuz's publication J. Daniélou echoed these sentiments: 'C'est en effet la première

---

28. H. Gressman, 'Die Oden Salomos', in E. Hennecke (ed.), *Neutestamentliche Apokryphen* (Tübingen: J.C.B. Mohr, 2nd edn, 1924), pp. 437-72 (437).

29. 'The original language of the Odes of Solomon was Greek.' J.M. Bover, 'La Mariologia en las Odas de Salomon', *Estudios Eclesiasticos* 10 (1931), p. 349.

30. W. Bauer, *Die Oden Salomos* (KlT, 64; Berlin: W. de Gruyter, 1933) (reprinted with an expanded note in E. Hennecke and W. Schneemelcher [eds.], *Neutestamentliche Apokryphen* [Tübingen: J.C.B. Mohr, 1964], II).

31. 'The original language of the O[des of]S[olomon] is Greek.' H. Gunkel, 'Salomo Oden', *RGG*, V, p. 87.

32. G. Bardy, 'Les Odes de Salomon', in *La vie spirituelle: D'après les Pères des trois premiers siècles* (Paris: Bloud & Gay, 1935), p. 95.

33. He argued that all critics considered the Syriac MS was a translation from a Greek original. Not only does he seem unaware of the existence of the other extant versions of the *Odes*, but also uninformed regarding the numerous critics who contend the original language is Syriac (*vide infra*). Omodeo wrote: 'Tutto fa ritenere che questo testo siriaco sia la versione di un originale greco: lo attestano sopra tutto le citazioni dell'Antico Testamento secondo la versione dei LXX.' See A. Omodeo, 'Le Odi di Salomone', *La Parola del Passato: Rivista di Studi Calssici* 1 (1946), p. 91.

34. B. Steidle, 'Die Oden Salomons', *Erbe und Auftrag* 24 (1948), p. 241.

35. H.E. Del Medico, 'La Lamelle Virolleaud', Παγκάρπεια: *Mélanges Henri Grégoire* (AIPhHOS, 9; Brussels: De Meester Wetteren, 1949), pp. 179-92.

36. 'C'est l'unique exemplaire existant en langue originale...'. M. Testuz (ed.), *Papyrus Bodmer X–XII* (Cologne: Bibliothèque Bodmer, 1959), p. 3. H.J.W. Drijvers followed Testuz's belief that the Greek of *Ode* 11 'proves superior to the Syriac'. H.J.W. Drijvers, *Bardaisan of Edessa* (trans. G.E. Von Baaren-Pape; Studia Semitical Neerlandica, 6; Assen: Van Gorcum, 1966), p. 209.

fois que nous avons en grec, c'est-à-dire dans le texte original, une partie de cet ouvrage.'[37] The next year M. Philonenko attempted to show that by a comparison of the extant Greek and Syriac versions the Syriac proved to be inferior and to be translated from another Greek text.[38] The same year, 1962, J. Quasten[39] and A.F.J. Klijn[40] assumed the original language was Greek. Klijn argued that a comparison of the extant Greek ode with the Syriac MS H leads to a certain conclusion ('duidelijk dat vrijwel zeker') that the *Odes* were originally composed in Greek.[41] Finally, in conclusion to this bibliographical introduction, W. Bauer recently reaffirmed his earlier contention by claiming, 'Die Grundsprache der Oden ist wohl sicher das Griechische.'[42]

Facts and Observations Supporting the Greek Hypothesis with Critical Observations
It is difficult to present convincing proof either for a Semitic or for a Greek original of a text which was written in the first or second century CE. This difficulty appears because the geographical and linguistic barriers that preserved the purity of the Semitic and Greek languages had been destroyed. The geographical barrier was finally removed when Alexander the Great invaded Palestine (332 BCE) and popularized the Greek language in that region.[43] The linguistic barrier crumbled when

37. 'It is, in fact, the first time that we have in Greek, that is to say the original text, of a portion of this work.' J. Daniélou, 'Histoire des origines chrétiennes', *RSR* 49 (1961), p. 576. In 1964 Daniélou remarked that 'the original was certainly in Greek' (*The Theology of Jewish Christianity* [trans. J.A. Baker; The Development of Christian Doctrine before the Council of Nicaea; London: Darton, Longman & Todd, 1964], I, p. 31).

38. For a discussion of his attempt, *vide infra*. M. Philonenko, 'Conjecture sur un verset'.

39. J. Quasten, *Patrology: The Beginnings of Patristic Literature* (Westminster, MD: Newman, 1951; Utrecht: Spectrum, 1962), I, p. 161.

40. A.F.J. Klijn, *The Acts of Thomas* (SNT, 5; Leiden: E.J. Brill, 1962), p. 46.

41. A.F.J. Klijn, *Edessa, De Stad van de Apostel Thomas: Het oudste Christendom in Syrië* (Baarn: Bosch & Keuning, 1962), p. 44.

42. 'The original language of the Odes is almost certainly Greek.' Bauer, 'Die Oden Salomos', in Hennecke and Schneemelcher (eds.), *Neutestamentliche Apokryphen*, II, p. 577.

43. Archaeological discoveries indubitably prove that there were Greek influences in Palestine before the conquest of Alexander. Such infiltration can be traced as early as the tenth century BCE since fragments of pottery made in Greece around 925 BCE have been unearthed at Tell Abu Hawam, which is situated on the northern

subsequently the Greek and Semitic languages both borrowed and loaned idioms and vocabulary. An example of Semitic Greek from the first or second century CE is select portions of the Greek New Testament. Examples of Hellenistic Syriac are found in the works of Ephraem Syrus.[44]

Archaeological discoveries have proved that Palestine in the first and second centuries CE was quadrilingual: Greek, Aramaic, Latin,[45] and Hebrew were frequently used, and probably in that order of frequency. Two recent excavations prove this formerly debated contention. On Mt Olivet ossuaries were unearthed which predate the Jewish War (66–73 CE). These numerous ossuaries were written in Greek, Aramaic, and Hebrew.[46] Second, Y. Yadin in the spring of 1960 in a cave in the Nahal Hever near the Dead Sea discovered 15 letters written in the time of the Bar Kokhba revolt (132–35 CE). Two of the letters were written in Greek, nine in Aramaic, and four in Hebrew.[47] It is important to note that these letters were written by Palestinian Jews to other Palestinian Jews; moreover, they were not composed in Gentile areas distant from Jerusalem, for example in the Decapolis, but in the southern Palestine

point of Mt Carmel. See D. Auscher, 'Les relations entre la Grèce et la Palestine avant la conquête d'Alexandre', *VT* 17 (1967), pp. 8-30.

44. I choose the language of Ephraem Syrus to exemplify the fact that Syriac had borrowed from Greek because, although Ephraem Syrus was erudite in Syriac, he did not know Greek. For example, Sozomen wrote: ' Ἰδὼν δὲ Ἐφραὶμ καίπερ Ἑλλενικῆς παιδείας ἄμοιρος...' Sozomen, ΕΚΚΛΗΣΙΑΣΤΙΚΗΣ ΙΣΤΟΡΙΑΣ (PG, 67; Paris: Migne, 1864), pp. 4, 16. Consequently the possibility that we are dealing with translation Syriac is uniquely absent. An example of the Greek loan words Ephraem Syrus was fond of were ܪܘܚܐ (διαθήκη), ܪܡܣܐܠ (τύπος), ܟܝܢܬܐ (κῆρυξ), and ܐܪܓܠ (πεῖσαι). See Ephraem Syrus, *Hymnen de Virginitate* (ed. E. Beck; CSCO, 223; Scriptores Syri, 94; Louvain: Secretariat de Corpus SCO, 1962).

45. Latin was not only the language of the Roman soldiers who occupied Palestine but also the language in which political and legal documents were customarily written. Moreover, as M. Black has suggested (*An Aramaic Approach to the Gospels and Acts* [Oxford: Clarendon Press, 3rd edn, 1967], p. 13), the Latin borrowings in Aramaic suggest that at least on a minor scale Latin was occasionally used in commercial transactions.

46. See P.B. Bagatti and J.T. Milik, *Gli Scavi del 'Dominus Flevit'. I. La Necropoli del Periodo Romano* (Pubblicazioni dello Studium Biblicum Franciscanum, 13; Jerusalem: Tipografia dei PP. Francescani, 1958), pp. 70-109.

47. Y. Yadin, 'More on the Letters of Bar Kochba', *BA* 24 (September 1961), p. 86.

between Engedi and Masada. Consequently the *Odes of Solomon*, which were certainly composed before 135 CE, took shape during an epoch that was permeated by syncretistic languages.[48]

The foregoing statements, however, should not be taken to mean that a manuscript originally written in Hellenistic Syriac cannot be distinguished from a Greek translation of the self-same manuscript: it can. A distinction can be made precisely because a Hellenistic Syriac original is only influenced by the Greek language; it is not written in it. The degree is the important factor: the moment we can distinguish more Semitic than Greek qualities in a Greek manuscript we may conclude that we are probably dealing not with an original but rather with a translation. With this brief methodological background, we may now examine the factors that lead scholars to argue that the original language is Greek.

In 1909 J.R. Harris concluded that the original language is Greek both because the Coptic is a direct translation from the Greek and because retroversion into Greek often explains unintelligible passages in both the Coptic and Syriac versions. He argued that τῇ παρέσει αὐτῶν or τῇ παραλύσει αὐτῶν ('They gave them strength for their paralysis') probably lies behind *Ode* 6.17.[49] With this conjecture Harris claimed to have explained the reason for a fault which he thought was in the Syriac text. In essence he speculated that the Syriac ܝܗܘܒܬܐܠ ܚܝܠ ܝܗܒܘ ('They gave strength to their coming') was corrupt.

Similarly he suggested the ܚܝܠ ܐܠ ('without corruption')[50] translates ἄφθαρτος ('uncorrupted'), and ἀφθαρσία ('incorruption'). A good example of this translation, he contends, is in *Ode* 9.4:

extant Syriac	ܘܕܠܐ ܚܒܠܐ ܗܝ ܓܡܝܪܘܬܟܘܢ
translation	And without corruption is your perfection.
conjectured Greek	καὶ ἐν ἀφθαρσίᾳ τὸ τέλος ὑμῶν
translation	And your end is immortality.

Moreover, he argued that ܚܣܡ ܐܠ stands for ἄφθονος ('without envy') and ἀφθόνως ('abundantly').[51]

Harris's first point should be eliminated. The five Coptic odes are translated from a Greek *Grundschrift*, which scholars agree (*vide supra*)

---

48. Since the *Odes* were written either in the first or second century CE, no conclusion is presupposed by the above statement.

49. *Editio princeps*, p. 36.

50. Harris's translation; ܚܝܠ ܐܠ may also be translated 'incorrupted', 'incorruptible', 'immortal' and 'incorruption'.

51. Harris, *The Odes and Psalms of Solomon* (2nd edn, 1911), p. 47.

formed a part of the *Urschrift* of the *Pistis Sophia*. Evidences of a Greek text behind the Coptic Odes, therefore, show that they have been translated, but their Greek qualities are probably due to the original language of the *Pistis Sophia*.

In answer to his second point, it appears that he later rejected the idea that the Syriac was corrupt since in 1920 he defended the following translation:

> They gave strength to their coming
> And light to their eyes.

His contention that ܚܝܠܐ ܐܠ translates ἄφθαρτος and ἀφθαρσία in a *Grundschrift* is devoid of any convincing force. Most Syriac lexicons show that ܚܝܠܐ ܐܠ[52] means exactly what Harris's conjectured restoration reads.[53] Likewise, ܣܘܡ ܐܠ itself means 'generous', or 'ungrudging'.[54]

In 1910 J. Wellhausen made an observation which was immediately adopted by subsequent scholars who believed the original language is Greek. He claimed that what appeared to be Semitic qualities in the *Odes* were actually biblical qualities: 'Von Semitismen habe ich nichts entdecken können, nur von Biblizismen; die biblische Sprache war ja aber auch und sogar vorzugsweise christlich.'[55] (Unfortunately he neither illustrates nor elaborates this generalization.) P. Batiffol accepted Wellhausen's distinction between 'Semitisms' and 'Biblicisms', claimed it was ingenious, and contended that such a perspective proved the dependence of the odist on the LXX.[56]

While a complete answer to Wellhausen's general statement will be given in the second half of the present chapter, it is difficult to overlook the beautiful Semitisms (paronomasia, parallelism) in the following verse (*Ode* 33.2):

---

52. Greek, Syriac, Coptic, and Hebrew are preserved in their own scripts; they are transliterated occasionally in order to clarify poetry, such as alliteration and the sounds that unify concepts.

53. See, for example, R. Payne Smith, *Thesaurus Syriacus* (Oxford: Clarendon Press, 1879), I, col. 1179.

54. Payne Smith, *Thesaurus Syriacus*, I, col. 1333.

55. Wellhausen, review of Harnack and Flemming, p. 642.

56. Labourt and Batiffol, *Les Odes de Salomon*, p. 2.

ܘܐܘܒܕ ܠܚܒܠܐ ܡܢ ܩܕܡܘܗܝ
ܘܚܒܠ ܠܟܠ ܬܩܢܘܬܗ

> And he destroyed the destruction from before him
> And corrupted all his preparation.

One should also note that the 'Corrupter' (33.1 ܡܚܒܠܐ) is the one who 'corrupts' (ܚܒܠ), and hence the two Syriac words are etymologically related. Here is an impresive instance of Semitic paronomasia.

Wellhausen, a year after he contended there were no 'Semitisms' in the *Odes*, argued in his *Einleitung in die drei ersten Evangelien* that an important Semitism was the initial position of the verb: 'Das mutet semitisch an und nicht griechisch.'[57] Perhaps if he had re-examined the *Odes* he would have reconsidered his conclusion because the verb is almost always placed first. Therefore in light of the Semitic paronomasia and word order, we may answer Wellhausen's often-quoted dictum: there are Semitisms in the *Odes*.

While G. Diettrich remarked he was not prepared to answer the question regarding the original language, he made one observation which was subsequently used *afferre argumenta* by the advocates for a Greek original. He claimed that the description of 'truth' as a virgin in *Ode* 33.5 is not good Syriac.[58] It seems that his argument rests on the contention that the original language must be one in which the noun 'truth' is feminine so that the author can refer to her as a 'virgin'. In verse five we read:

ܐܠܐ ܩܡܬ ܒܬܘܠܬܐ ܓܡܝܪܬܐ

> But a perfect virgin stood.

One should admit that 'truth' (ἡ ἀλήθεια) and 'virgin' (ἡ παρθένος) are both feminine in Greek, but that in Syriac 'truth' is masculine.[59] However, a further observation must be made: ܩܘܫܬܐ ('truth') does not appear as a subject in this ode. The Syriac noun ܩܘܫܬܐ appears only once, and it is the object of a preposition: 'in ways of truth' (33.8, ܒܐܘܪ̈ܚܬܗ ܕܩܘܫܬܐ). In the extant Syriac versions 'truth' is not described

---

57. 'It strikes one as Semitic and not Greek.' J. Wellhausen, *Einleitung in die drei ersten Evangelien* (Berlin: Georg Reimer, 2nd edn, 1911), p. 10.

58. Diettrich, *Die Oden Salomos*, p. xi.

59. E.g. *Ode* 38.10: 'And I asked the Truth, who are these? And he said (ܘܐܡܪ)...'

as a virgin, though it is possible the 'virgin' uttered wisdom sayings. Hence Diettrich's observation is not persuasive.

H. Gressmann argued not only that MS H is translated from the Greek, but also that 'griechisch, nicht hebräisch, war auch die Original-sprache der Oden.'[60] He claimed that one is certain ('zweifellos') the Syriac is a translation because of the 'particularly inaccurate or abso-lutely false renderings'. Moreover, one can be certain that Greek is the original language because of the 'Einheitlichkeit und dem gnostischen Ursprunge der Lieder'.[61] In addition to the reasons already mentioned he argued that the original language must be Greek because the dis-cernible technical terms are Greek and not Semitic.[62]

In answering Gressmann we may make three observations. First, one would like to know what he considers are the false renderings in the Syriac; indeed it is unfortunate that he has not illustrated any of his conclusions with specific examples. Second, if the *Odes* are gnostic, which seems to be unlikely, this conclusion does not weaken the Syriac hypothesis. It is clear that Gnosticism was strong in Syria and some forms of Gnosticism most likely originated there. Finally, in answer to his last point, it is now obvious that some Greek 'technical terms' were early borrowed by Syriac-speaking Christians.

Although F.C. Burkitt, perhaps the father of critical research on primitive Christianity in Syria, presented no specific reasons why the original language is Greek, he made a general proclamation. He announced that the Syriac of the *Odes* was neither 'graceful' nor 'flexible', but was rather 'stiff' and lacked any 'really characteristic native idiom'.[63] These contentions will be examined in the second half of this chapter.

R.H. Connolly, the resolute champion of the Greek hypothesis, pre-sented four arguments that convinced him, and others, that the original language is Greek. Each demands full consideration.

60. 'Greek, not Hebrew, was the original language of the Odes.'
61. '...unity and the gnostic origin of the songs.' H. Gressmann, 'Die Oden Salomos', *IW* 5.29 (1911), p. 900.
62. Gressmann, 'Die Oden Salomos', pp. 900-901.
63. F.C. Burkitt, 'A New MS of the Odes of Solomon', *JTS* 13 (1912), p. 373.

Argument 1. He claims that there is 'almost conclusive evidence that our present Syriac text is a translation from Greek' in *Ode* 41.15:

ܐܝܬܘܗܝ ܡܫܝܚܐ ܚܕ ܗܘ
ܘܐܬܝܕܥ ܡܢ ܩܕܡ ܬܘܩܢܗ ܕܥܠܡܐ

The Messiah is truly one;
And He was known before the constitution of the world.

Connolly claims that 'from before the constitution of the world' is a translation of the Greek: ἀπὸ (or πρὸ) καταβολῆς κόσμου. Seven out of ten times the Peshitta New Testament translates καταβολή with ܬܘܩܢܐ, but this feminine noun never appears in the Peshitta Old Testament. Since ܬܘܩܢܐ is a comparatively rare word outside the Peshitta New Testament, Connolly ruled that it must have come into the *Odes* 'as a Syriac translation of πρὸ καταβολῆς κόσμου by one who was familiar with the usual Pesh. Version of this phrase'.[64]

Criticism of Argument 1. Connolly's first argument suffers from four perspectives. First, to contend that one noun in this Syriac Ode presents 'conclusive evidence' of a Greek original reflects that he has searched diligently to prove a hypothesis that has been grasped prior to the investigation. Furthermore, if the Ode is translated from a Greek *Grundschrift*, why are there not more traces of the supposed underlying Greek?

Second, is it not possible, even probable, that the factors that led the translator of the Peshitta to use this word were also operative in the mind of the Odist? Since translators do not usually intentionally choose their words but rather passively accept a word that is inherited, is it not probable that the noun 'constitution' derives not from a Greek *Grundschrift* but from the milieu that the translator of the Peshitta and the Odist shared? That might suggest that the *Odes* were composed in Syriac. Indeed, it is very precarious to argue that this noun could appear in the *Odes* only via a translation of a conjectured Greek original. Any argument regarding the original language of the *Odes* is is weakened by the observation that there are few Syriac texts from the first or early second century CE.

64. R.H. Connolly, Review of *Light on the Gospel from an Ancient Poet* (Diatessarica, 9; Cambridge: Cambridge University Press, 1912), by E.A. Abbott, in *JTS* 14 (1913), p. 316.

Third, the Syriac noun ܬܐܪܝܬܐ has various meanings; hence one is assuming too much to conclude that in *Ode* 41.15 it must have the same meaning it possessed 70 per cent of the time in the Peshiṭta New Testament. Moreover, is not Connolly's argument for a Greek original weakened by the recognition that ܬܐܪܝܬܐ means primarily 'a foundation', and not 'constitution'? Finally, the possibility must be left open that the author of the Peshiṭta borrowed ܬܐܪܝܬܐ from the Odist or some other earlier Syriac composition or the Syriac-speaking Christians.

Argument 2. Connolly argues that retroversion into Greek clarifies an ambiguous verse in *Ode* 7.3:

ܐܘܕܥܝ, ܢܦܫܗ ܕܠܐ ܚܣܡ ܒܚܡܝܡܘܬܗ
ܕܢܗܘܬ ܠܥ ܡܣܓܝܐܘܬܗ ܐܝܪܬ.

> He caused me to know Himself without envy
>   in (or by) His simplicity;
> For His kindness made His greatness little.[65]

Following Harris's suggestion given above, that 'without envy' stands for ἀφθόνως, Connolly turns to another problem in this verse. He points out that 'in His simplicity' (ܒܚܡܝܡܘܬܗ) is a meaningless and confused expression. The Greek word for 'simplicity' is ἡ ἁπλότης. But when this noun is preceded by the preposition ἐν and subsequently put into the dative case an idiom appears: ἐν τῇ ἁπλότητι αὐτοῦ means 'in his bounty' (cf. 2 Cor. 8.2; 9.11, 13). The verse is thereby not only meaningful to Connolly, but ostensibly restored to its original sense:

> He caused me to know himself without envy in his bounty;
> For his kindness made His greatness little.[66]

Likewise Connolly emends *Ode* 34.1:

> No way is hard where there is a *simple* heart;
> Nor is there any wound in right thoughts [italics mine].

Following the method explained above, Connolly translates:

> No way is hard where there is a *generous* heart;
> Nor is there any dismay in right thoughts [italics mine].

---

65. Connolly's translation.
66. Connolly, 'Greek the Original Language', p. 531.

Criticism of Argument 2. This argument is not convincing because the Syriac noun ܦܫܝܛܘܬܐ itself also means 'generosity' or 'liberality'. For example in 2 Cor. 9.11 'in all liberality' (εἰς πᾶσαν ἁπλότητα) is rendered in the Peshiṭta by ܒܟܠ ܦܫܝܛܘܬܐ. Hence those who think Connolly's translation is demanded by the context and is more original may obtain it without assuming the existence of a Greek *Grundschrift*. The Syriac may be translated thus:

> He has generously shown Himself to me through His liberality;
> Because His kindness has reduced His magnitude.

Argument 3. Finally,[67] Connolly claims to have found an important clue to the Greek original by the anomalous use of the possessive particle ܕܝܠ. He remarks that, 'Strictly speaking ܕܝܠ should not be used in cases where a possessive suffix is grammatically possible except to give some sort of prominence to the possessor or to emphasize the fact of possession.'[68]

In translations from Greek ܕܝܠ is often used to translate the possessive pronouns when the pronominal suffixes would have been more appropriate in Syriac. Moreover, Connolly remarks that the best Syriac writers use it only to express an emphatic possessive such as 'my', 'mine' or 'my own'. He lists eight examples of an unidiomatic use of ܕܝܠ in the *Odes*:

8.20 [=18]	ܘܡܢ ܝܡܝܢܐ ܕܝܠ	and at my right hand
11.18	ܒܐܪܥܐ ܕܝܠܟ	in your land
12.4	ܕܫܘܦܪܟ ܕܝܠܟ[69]	of your beauty
17.12 [=13]	ܒܚܘܒܐ ܕܝܠ	in my love
17.14 [=15]	ܒܘܪܟܬܐ ܕܝܠ	my blessing
25.2	ܘܡܥܕܪܢܐ ܕܝܠ	and my helper
26.2	ܙܡܝܪܬܐ ܩܕܝܫܬܐ ܕܝܠܗ	his holy song
28.10 [=11]	ܘܛܠܘܡܝܐ ܕܝܢ ܕܝܠ	by my (suffering of) wrong[70]

Criticism of Argument 3. Argument 3 presents convincing evidence for the Greek hypothesis if it can be proved that the Syriac writer used ܕܝܠ anomalously and in obvious neglect of the customary pronominal

---

67. Connolly presents other arguments for the Greek hypothesis but we have omitted them here not only because they are too conjectural but also because Connolly seems to have felt they were inferior in force to those selected.

68. Connolly, 'Greek the Original Language', p. 537.

69. He has erred in this citation because MS H preserves ܕܝܠܗ.

70. Connolly, 'Greek the Original Language', p. 537.

suffix. In favor of Connolly's argument is the observation that Ephraem Syrus rarely uses ܕܝܠ while the Odist is quite fond of it.[71]

Connolly assumes that occasionally the 'Syriac translator' inadvertently followed the Greek word order and translated a pronominal genitive in the predicative position by ܕܝܠ. For example, he might translate ὁ πατὴρ ἐμοῦ as ܐܒܐ ܕܝܠܝ when he should have written ܐܒܝ. In analyzing the weight of this argument, one should remember that the conjectured Greek could also have read ὁ ἐμὸς πατήρ, and consequently the order of the words, on which Connolly depends so heavily, would be reversed.

Four observations must be presented. First, it is questionable that a Syriac scribe in the early centuries of the Christian era so closely distinguished between the meaning of a pronoun attached to ܕܝܠ and a pronominal suffix. Unfortunately there is no evidence to inform us what was the custom in the first two centuries, when Syriac was so closely aligned with Aramaic.

Second, with Connolly's argument in mind a comparison must be made of the Greek and Syriac of *Ode* 11. First, however, it must be noted that *Ode* 11.18 in MS H does not read ܒܐܪܥܐ ܕܝܠܟ, as Connolly might expect, but ܒܐܪܥܟ. Furthermore, in the Syriac of *Ode* 11 there are three occurrences of ܕܝܠ which Connolly may have failed to note:

11.20	ܠܒܣܝܡܘܬܐ ܕܝܠܟ	to your pleasantness
11.21	ܒܐܪܥܐ ܕܝܠܟ	in your land
11.22	ܐܝܟ ܥܘܗܕܢܐ ܕܝܠܟ	like a reminder of yourself

Of these three examples only the first two, according to Connolly's definition of the customary use of ܕܝܠ, are unidiomatic. Now let us compare these two with the respective portions of the Greek Ode that was recovered after Connolly's work:

| 11.20 | ΕΙΣ ΧΡΗΣΤΟΤΗΤΑ | to kindness |
| 11.21 | ΕΝ ΤΗ ΓΗ ΣΟΥ | in your land |

In the first incident the Greek does not record a possessive pronoun, but in the second we find a possessive pronoun in the predicative position as Connolly would have suggested. However, before we should conclude that Connolly may be correct we should note that there are 27 other possessive pronouns in this Ode that could have been written with ܕܝܠ; but they were not.

---

71. See, for example, Ephraem Syrus, *Hymnen de Virginitate*.

Finally, the use of ܕܝܠ to modify a substantive may be due to the analogy of the Greek predicative position of the pronominal genitive as Connolly has suggested, but such analogy need not come only from a supposed *Grundschrift*. It might be traced to a bilinguist such as Bardaiṣan[72] or to a province in which Syriac and Greek were both spoken. Moreover, we should not forget what T. Nöldeke observed after his critical examination of numerous Syriac manuscripts: 'No doubt even the best original writings in Syriac give evidence of the strong influence of Greek Syntax; but, on the other hand, everything is not immediately to be regarded as a Graecism, which looks like one.'[73]

Argument 4. In 1920, when Harris changed his position and concluded that the original language is Syriac, Connolly published new evidence which he contended tipped the scales in favor of the Greek hypothesis. He argued that *Ode* 7.10 virtually quotes the LXX of Ps. 51.1. It is necessary to juxtapose these two verses:

Ode 7.10	ܡܛܠ ܗܢܐ ܪܚܡ ܥܠܝ ܒܚܘܣܢܗ ܣܓܝܐܐ
	Therefore he had mercy on me in His abundant mercy[74]
LXX of Ps. 51.1	Ἐλέησόν με, ὁ θεός, κατὰ τὸ μέγα ἔλεος σου[75]

Connolly claimed the Odist was working from the LXX on the basis of three observations. First, the verb and noun are cognate in the LXX but not so related in either the Peshitta or the Hebrew. Second, ܚܣܢ and ܚܘ usually render respectively ἔλεος and ἐλεεῖν in the Peshitta. Third, the adjective 'abundant', or 'much' appears neither in the Hebrew nor in the Greek, but appears only in the LXX.[76]

Criticism of Argument 4. What Connolly refers to as 'cognate' noun and verb is actually a well-attested Semitic quality called either *schema etymologicum, figura etymologica*[77] or simply paronomasia. We are not

---

72. Epiphanius of Salamis (c. 316–403) records that Bardaiṣan knew both Greek and Syriac: λόγους τις ὢν ἐν ταῖς δυσὶ γλώσσαις, Ἑλληνικῇ τε διαλέκτῳ καὶ τῇ τῶν Σύρων φωνῇ. See *Panarion* 56. Drijvers, *Bardaisan of Edessa*, p. 177.

73. T. Nöldeke, *Compendious Syriac Grammar* (trans. J.A. Crichton; London: Williams & Norgate, 1904), pp. ix-x.

74. Connolly's translation.

75. In the LXX it is Ps. 50.1.

76. Connolly, review of Harris and Mingana, p. 80.

77. See Gesenius, *Hebrew Grammar* (re-edited and rev. E. Kautsch; trans. A.E.

suggesting that paronomasia should be taken alone as evidence of a Semitic original, but it is certainly no *via* through which to prove the existence of a Greek *Urtext*. Nevertheless, suppose the *Odes* was influenced by the LXX, would such an observation prove that the *Odes* were written in Greek? It is clear that many scholars in Syria, especially in the famous school in Edessa, read Greek with ease; and sometimes their own compositions showed influence from the LXX. Would not Connolly's argument first have to assume that a Syriac composer was either ignorant of Greek or composing somewhere completely isolated from all influences of the LXX? And just where could one suggest that the erudite odist would have been so free of LXX influences?[78]

Recent discoveries help us answer this question. In Cave 4 at Qumran three fragments of the LXX were recovered (two copies of Leviticus and one of Numbers)[79] and in Cave 7 two other fragments were discovered (a copy of Exodus, and a copy of Jeremiah).[80] With the observation that the LXX was occasionally consulted by the conservative Semitic Community at Qumran, we are led to believe that it was not only read by Diaspora Jews, as earlier held, but also by Palestinian Jews. Consequently, since the Odist was an erudite scholar, he would probably have been acquainted with the LXX variants. Thus, indirect allusions to the LXX in the *Odes of Solomon* are no longer grounds upon which to base an argument for a Greek original.

In the last 20 years advocates of the Greek hypothesis have found two new grounds upon which to base their contention. The first of these arguments is presented by H.E. Del Medico. He claims that a recently

Cowley; Oxford: Clarendon Press, 2nd edn, 1960), section 117p.

78. Other arguments for the Greek hypothesis have been published, but I have not reviewed them here because I do not believe they warrant critical examination. Moreover, I have not discussed the five arguments for a Greek original presented in Harris's 1920 edition of *The Odes and Psalms of Solomon*, II (see pp. 138-58). The reason for this omission is twofold: they are presented and *refuted* by a scholar who contended the original language is Syriac, and the presuppositions on which many of the arguments depended have been proved false by subsequent biblical scholarship and archaeological discoveries.

79. See P.W. Skehan, 'The Qumran Manuscripts and Textual Criticism', in J.A. Emerton *et al.* (eds.), *Volume du Congrès* (VTSup, 4; Leiden: E.J. Brill, 1957), pp. 155-60.

80. See M. Baillet, J.T. Milik and R. De Vaux (eds.), *Discoveries in the Judaean Desert of Jordan: Les 'petites Grottes' de Qumrân* (Oxford: Clarendon Press, 1962), III, pp. 142-43.

discovered Aramaic silver amulet, which he dates between 364 and 380 CE, proves the original language of the *Odes of Solomon* is Greek: 'Par elle, nous avons la certitude que les Odes de Salomon remontent à un original grec'.[81] Before we can intelligently discuss Del Medico's argument, it is necessary to present the text and an English translation of his translation of this amulet:

1.	‏+ ואו . בר תאון . רבא‏	+ et AΩ (is) Son of God, the Savior
2.	‏חסינא . קדיש אילא‏	(He is) powerful, the Holy God.
3.	‏חן יד . תלתא . קימן . בה‏	Being one, the three (the Trinity) dwell in him
4.	‏גברתא . רבתא . דאוקין‏	The strength of the (All)-Powerful is made of the oce-
5.	‏וס . ומדברין . מיא . וע‏	an and of the deserts, of the sea and of the uni-
6.	‏למא . במעברתא . דע‏	verse. During the crossing of the uni-
7.	‏למא . ומום מיא ובך‏	verse, and (if there is no blemish (in you) and (if) in you
8.	‏וד בו ואקים ׀ באותו‏	(is) assurance in him and the Saints, -ǀ- in the sign and
9.	‏פרקי וטרף סדך ו‏	(in) my Savior, and (when) your raft is about to be dashed to pieces, then,
10.	‏דיו או אנדר וכותך‏	God AΩ, the Light and your companion, (who is):
11.	‏ו או ובר ותאון ואילא ו‏	and AΩ, and the Son, and God, (who is): and God and
12.	‏אר ׀ מוכך ורבון ואק‏	the Light, -[- (if you humble yourself and (before) Our Lord and (before) the Sa
13.	‏ים ׀ באות ופרק וטרף ס‏	ints, -ǀ- by the Sign and the Savior and (when) your raft is about to break up,
14.	‏דך ו . דיו או תלטא זמן‏ ‏איטי + אטיר‏	then, God, AΩ will curb the sea (Thus) it will be + (Thus) it will be.
15.	‏דמול . לך ובנקותא‏	The Sun which is in your presence and (which) with (its) purity
16.	‏יליך‏	envelopes... ... ...

Del Medico contended the source of inspiration for lines four through fourteen was unquestionably the 39th *Ode of Solomon*. The parallelism between them is so striking that three passages are borrowed almost word for word ('presque mot-à-mot'):

81. 'Through it, we have the certainty that the Odes of Solomon go back to a Greek original.' Del Medico, Παγκάρπεια, p. 189.

Amulet 4-5a   גברתא רבתא דאוקינוס
The power of the (All)-Powerful is the ocean

Ode 39.1a   ܢܗܪ̈ܘܬܐ ܬܩܝܦܐ ܐܢܝܢ ܚܝܠܗ ܕܡܪܝܐ
Mighty rivers are the power of the Lord

Amulet 6–8   במעברתא...ומום מיא
ובך וד בו

During the crossing…and (if) there is no blemish
(in you) and (if) in you is the assurance in him

Ode 39.5-6   ܘܗܢܘܢ ܕܥܒܪܝܢ ܠܗܘܢ ܒܗܝܡܢܘܬܐ
ܠܐ ܡܬܬܙܝܥܝܢ

And those who cross them…in faith
And those who walk on them…without blemish

Amulet 8–9   באות ופרקי
in the sign and (in) my Savior

Ode 39.7   ܡܛܠ ܕܐܬܐ ܕܒܗܘܢ ܐܝܬܘܗܝ ܗܘ
For the sign in them is the Lord

Del Medico argued that the difference in vocabulary of the two versions and the large number of Greek terms employed by the redactor of the amulet permit one to suppose that here is an independent translation of the *Odes* from a Greek text. He suggested the following points: where the original read ὠκεανός, as evidenced by the amulet, the Syriac scribe translated *nhrwt' 'šyn*;[82] the Greek θάλαττα of the amulet corresponds to the Syriac *hww gll'*; the *prq* of the amulet and the *mšyh'* of the Syriac are both translations of σωτήρ; and the *rbt'* of the amulet and the *mrym'* of the Syriac are both probably translations of παντοκράτωρ.

Now let us examine each of these four points successively in order to see what strength they give to the contention that the *Odes of Solomon* were originally written in Greek. The first point is not supported by manuscript evidence. On the contrary, it is highly unlikely that a Syriac scribe would have related ὠκεανός, with ܢܗܪ̈ܘܬܐ ܥܫܝ̈ܢܐ, which means 'raging rivers'. While in Homer's day ὠκεανός could have meant 'a great river' (see *Iliad* 18.399, *Odyssey* 20.65), in later times, when the

82. Either Del Medico or the publisher erred and produced '*nrhwt' 'šyn*'.

Odes were composed, 'ocean' tended to be used for the name of 'the great Outward Sea', the Atlantic, in contrast to the 'great Inward Sea', the Mediterranean.

The second point is also dubious. A Syriac scribe would most likely have translated θάλασσα by ܝܡܐ, as suggested by the Peshiṭta in Mt. 4.13, 18 *et saepe*. His third point is stronger than the previous two since ܦܪܘܩܐ translates σωτήρ in Lk. 2.11. However, the second half of this argument would also force us to assume the conjectured translator would have also intentionally altered his text, since ܡܫܝܚܐ represents the cognomen χρίστος (see, for example, the memorable passages in Lk. 9.20 and Jn 20.31). Finally, Del Medico's argument appears unpersuasive when we are forced to follow him and assume that a feminine adjective meaning 'great' (רבתא) and a masculine emphatic pael passive participle meaning 'the Most High' (ܡܪܝܡܐ) must go back to the same Greek word, least of all παντοκράτωρ. Does it not weaken Del Medico's argument when we note that παντοκράτωρ never translates either of these two substantives, but rather the noun is very common in the LXX for either צְבָאוֹת or שַׁדַּי?[83]

Second, even Del Medico, it appears, would not suggest the respective verses from which רבתא and ܡܪܝܡܐ are taken are parallel as his argument would demand. Third, manuscript evidence shows that these two words are not parallelistic, but have distinctly different meanings and functions. In conclusion, to accept Del Medico's arguments above would necessitate both conjecturing an original Greek and assuming the conjectured Syriac translator of the *Odes* not only misunderstood the supposed Greek but also deliberately altered it. Since there are no grounds for these numerous conjectures and because the respective contexts in the *Odes* do not make them logical, we are led to conclude that they are unpersuasive.

There are three further reasons why we must reject Del Medico's contention that the amulet proves the original language of the *Odes of Solomon* is Greek. First, the amulet contains not only Greek words but also Latin and Aramaic words. Once, in the first line, the author appears to have written the Greek word for God (θεός) in Aramaic characters (תאון). In line 14 he seems to have written the Greek word for sea (θάλαττα) and again in Aramaic characters (תלטא). Twice he applies the Latin word for God (deus): דיו, lines 10 and 14, and once

---

83. See G. Kittel (ed.), *Theological Dictionary of the New Testament* (trans. G.W. Bromiley; Grand Rapids: Eerdmans, 1965), III, pp. 914-15.

he uses the Aramaic word for God: אירלא, in line 2. Hence it does not appear that this amulet was translated from a Greek *Grundschrift*, as Del Medico suggests. The author of the amulet was a trilinguist who was freely composing a magical charm to protect himself from danger when traveling on land or sea. A suitable text, which he had remembered, was select verses of the 39th Ode.

Second, while we agree with Del Medico that the amulet appears to have been influenced by the thought and expressions of the 39th Ode, we doubt his conclusion that verses 1, 5-6, and 7 were borrowed almost word for word. The great difference between vocabulary of the respective parallel sections of the amulet and the 39th Ode is to be explained, argues Del Medico, by the fact that both were independently translated from a Greek text. A more likely possibility is that the author of the amulet was composing a charm not by copying directly from the text of the *Odes of Solomon*, but, as was often the case in the composition of an amulet,[84] was freely composing from his memory. Third, one should note that he gives no evidence that the present Syriac recensions were translated from a Greek original. Consequently, we conclude that this amulet does not provide evidence for a Greek original of the *Odes of Solomon*. If one were to conclude that the amulet depends on a Greek text of the Ode, that only assumes that the *Odes* were extant in Greek by that time—and we have proof of that fact in Bodmer Papyrus XI to which we now turn our attention.

The second of the two recent discoveries, which advocates of the Greek hypothesis claim have proved their contention, is the recovery of the 11th Ode in Greek. M. Testuz, the editor of this Greek Ode, concluded the original language was Greek on the basis of three observations. First, although he remarked the Ode was characterized by paronomasia, a style he admitted was very frequently found in Semitic languages but not in Greek, he held this style was only a resemblance of form. Second, he accepted Wellhausen's dictum that there were not real 'Semitisms' in the *Odes*, for such characteristics were actually only 'Biblicisms'. Third, and this argument seems to be not only his own but

---

84. Schrire reports that the craftsmen, who were not learned in Talmudic and Kabbalistic lore, called in more learned scribes to write the desired formulae. Moreover, the craftsmen, either because of a personal error or the difficulty encountered when trying to etch the cursive Hebrew script into a metallic surface, frequently miscopied. See T. Schrire, *Hebrew Amulets: Their Decipherment and Interpretation* (London: Routledge & Kegan Paul, 1966), pp. 23-24, 42-43.

the one that has convinced him, he believed the Ode had been composed in Greek because of the resemblance of form with certain poetic texts in the New Testament (e.g. Eph. 1.3-14).

In answer to Testuz's first two points, one should see the respective discussions in the above pages. Regarding his third point, he suggests that in both Eph. 1.3-14 and the 11th Ode there is a predilection for final -OY and -Ω, and that this assonance is easily discernible to the ear. This observation is correct, but it does not prove—or even intimate— that the 11th Ode was originally written in Greek. Rather, in many lines there is no rhyme and in others the attempt to obtain this assonance is often forced. These facts suggest that either the author was a very poor poet or the translator of a Syriac manuscript struggling to make the endings rhyme. An example of such forced construction is found in v. 6b. This line in Syriac describes the origin of the 'speaking waters' and how they 'drew near'. The line in Greek appears to serve the same function, but when the writer came to the adverb that modified the verb ΗΓΓΙ[ΣΕ he attempted to arrange the line so as to rhyme with the MOY of line 6a. Hence he chose the prepositional phrase: EN ΑΦΘΟΝΙΑ ΑΥΤΟΥ, which translates 'in its abundance', obtaining the rhyme but resorting to crude Greek. The Greek would be improved had he written the adverb ἀφθόνως, which means 'abundantly', an improvement represented by the extant Syriac, ܢܘܡ ܪܠܢ. Thus, it appears that assonance was more important than good construction, and that the Greek of Bodmer Papyrus XI was translated from Syriac (or some Semitic langauge). In conclusion, Testuz's arguments do not strengthen the case for the Greek hypothesis.

More recently, M. Philonenko has renewed Testuz's arguments in the attempt to prove the Greek hypothesis. He compares the Greek and Syriac of v. 21b (22a in Syriac) and concludes that the Syriac is corrupt. Before further discussion, it is necessary to juxtapose these two recensions:

ΚΑΙ ΓΕΙΝΕΤΕ ΤΑ ΠΑΝΤΑ	And all occurs
ΩΣ ΤΟ ΘΕΛΗΜΑ ΣΟΥ	according to your will
ܐܝܟ ܠܥܘܢܝ ܗܘܐܘ	all has become as a
ܐܢܝܬ ܕ.ܠܝܘ	remembrance of yourself

The difference between these two recensions is clearly in the two nouns ΘΕΛΗΜΑ and ܐܢܝܬ. Philonenko correctly reports that ܐܢܝܬ translates κατάλειμμα, ἐγκατάλειμμα, ὑπόλειμμα, λείψανον and finally λεῖμμα.[85] To explain the textual variant he suggests the Syriac results from a Greek text that possessed λεῖμμα as a corruption of ΘΕΛΗΜΑ. He concludes by stating that if this conjecture is accepted, 'on admettra volontiers que le texte syriaque de l'Ode est une traduction du grec.'[86]

One must thank Philonenko for this ingenious conjecture, and agree with him that if the explanation is adopted one could admit the Syriac text is a translation of a Greek *Grundschrift*. The acceptance or rejection of this conjecture obviously begins with the decisions as to whether or not the Syriac variant is corrupt.

While comparing these two variants one observes that they come from two strikingly different contexts.

21b   ΚΑΙ ΓΕΙΝΕΤΕ ΤΑ ΠΑΝΤΑ ΩΣ ΤΟ ΘΕΛΗΜΑ ΣΟΥ

22a   ΕΥΛΟΓΗΜΕΝΟΙ ΟΙ ΔΡΩΣΤΗΣ ΓΩΝΥΔΑ[Δ]ΤΩΝ ΣΟΥ

And everything occurs according to your will
Blessed are the workers of your waters[87]

22a   ܘܗܘܐ ܟܠܡܕܡ ܐܝܟ ܥܘܗܕܢ ܕܢܦܫܟ

22b   ܘܕܘܟܪܢܐ ܕܠܥܠܡ ܕܡܫܡܫܢܝܟ ܡܗܝܡܢܐ

And everything became as a remembrance of yourself,
And an eternal reminder for your faithful servants.[88]

When one sees the beautiful parallelism of the Syriac version, and the close harmony with the context, one tends to reject both Philonenko's translation of v. 22a: 'Et tout est devenu comme un reste de toi', and his contention that this verse 'est bien énigmatique'.[89] His conjecture seems consequently shorn of its foundation. Moreover, his conjecture presupposes at least three stages of text transmission and such is unlikely.

Conclusion

In the preceding pages we have chronologically discussed and criticized the intermittent arguments presented to prove that the original

85. Payne Smith, *Thesaurus Syriacus*, II, cols. 4332-33.

86. Philonenko, 'Conjecture sur un verset', p. 264.

87. For a defense of this translation, *vide supra*.

88. J.R. Harris (1920) translated, 'And a memorial for ever of thy faithful servants'. The above translation is presented because it better represents the Semitic parallelism. The first dalath shows that ܕܠܥܠܡ in ܘܕܘܟܪܢܐ ܕܠܥܠܡ ܕܡܫܡܫܢܝܟ is an attributive adjective, which means 'eternal'. The second dalath shows that 'faithful servants' is genitival, hence it represents 'of', 'by', 'about', 'for', 'against' and 'on account of'.

89. 'And everything has become a reminder of you...' 'is quite enigmatic'.

language is Greek. Each of these points has been found deficient and subsequently rejected. Two presuppositions seem to have been implicit behind the belief that the original language is Greek. The first assumption is that the *Odes* are of too high a poetic and theological quality to have been written in any language except Greek. This position was represented in 1910 by J.A. Montgomery: 'The manuscript is written in Syriac, which is not a very promising language from which to expect much of oriental worth.'[90] Since this statement was written, insightful, detailed research of such Semitic scholars as A. Meyer, G. Dalman, A.J. Wensinck, C.C. Torrey, J. Jeremias, M. Black, J.A. Fitzmyer, A. Vööbus, and others has proved that Syriac (or Aramaic, since the two names may be used interchangeably) is a language from which to expect rich, original insights.

The second assumption concerns the conntention by most scholars that the *Odes* and the Fourth Gospel are ideologically related. A cursory examination of the issue, however, shows that the vast majority of critics who hold the Greek hypothesis wrote at a time when critical consensus affirmed Johannine theology could not originate in a Semitic environment. Further research, aided by the insights afforded by subsequent archaeological discoveries, however, has led most contemporary scholars to believe that the provenience of this tradition is somewhere in Syria or Palestine.[91]

When we began this discussion the following four conclusions seemed possible: (1) the language of the autograph is Greek and the extant Syriac, Coptic, and Greek MSS are from this original; (2) the original is Greek but the extant Greek MS is translated from a Semitic translation; (3) the original is Syriac but all the extant MSS are taken from a Greek translation; (4) the original is Syriac and the extant MSS derive either directly or indirectly from this text. We have gradually discovered that these possibilities are listed in an ascending order of probability. Indeed, the first two possibilities have been eliminated:

90. J.A. Montgomery, 'The Recently Discovered Odes of Solomon', *BW* 36 (August 1910), p. 93.

91. 'I detect a growing readiness to recognize that...there is no compelling need to let our gaze wander very far, either in space or in time, beyond a fairly limited area of southern Palestine in the fairly limited interval between the Crucifixion and the fall of Jerusalem.' J.A.T. Robinson, *Twelve New Testament Studies* (London: SCM Press, 1962), pp. 98-99.

there is no convincing evidence of a Greek *Urtext*. It is now necessary to turn our attention to the evidence of a Semitic *Urtext*.

Arguments for a Semitic Original

Bibliographical Introduction

Although the arguments for the Greek hypothesis were published first, and won the acclaim of almost all the critics, dissenting voices gradually began to be heard. A. Harnack, J.A. Montgomery, and H. Grimme were the first scholars to question the validity of the Greek hypothesis. Harnack argued because of the Semitic quality of the *Odes*, 'dass die Oden hebräisch (aramäisch?) abgefasst werden'.[92] J.A. Montgomery suggested that, by analogy with the history of the *Psalms of Solomon*, Hebrew is probably the original language. He presented two observations to substantiate his position: the character of the *Odes* is evidently Semitic, and some faults in the construction of the tenses can best be explained from a hypothetical Hebrew original.[93]

H. Grimme argued that when one translated the extant *Odes* into Hebrew, the beginning of the *Odes* forms an alphabetical pattern, many ambiguous passages are clarified, and a correct biblical poetic meter appears.[94] The following year, 1911, when W. Frankenberg translated the *Odes* into Greek, Grimme was so convinced his theory was correct that he translated the 41 extant *Odes* into Hebrew.[95] In the same year he attempted to strengthen his arguments for a Hebrew *Urtext* by examining *Ode* 19.[96]

C. Bruston appears to be the first critic to argue that Syriac is the original language. In 1911, after a critical comparison of the Coptic and Syriac, he confidently asserted, 'qu'elles furent écrites en *syriaque*, et non en grec, comme on l'a généralement supposé jusqu'ici'.[97] The

92. '...that the Odes were composed in Hebrew (Aramaic?).' Harnack and Flemming, *Ein jüdisch-christliches Psalmbuch*, p. 105.

93. Montgomery, 'The Recently Discovered Odes of Solomon', p. 94.

94. H. Grimme, review of *Die Oden Salomos*, by A. Ungnad and W. Staerk, in *TRev* 9 (1910), p. 547.

95. H. Grimme, *Die Oden Salomos: Syrisch–Hebräisch–Deutsch* (Heidelberg: Carl Winter, 1911).

96. H. Grimme, 'Die 19. Ode Salomos', *TGl* 3 (1911), pp. 11-19.

97. '...that they were written in Syriac and not in Greek, as has been up till now generally supposed.' C. Bruston, 'Les plus anciens cantiques chrétiens: Les Odes de Salomon', *RTP* 44 (1911), p. 488.

following year he defended the Syriac hypothesis in two articles[98] and a book.[99] It is also important to note that he did *not* argue, erroneously, as do some subsequent pro-Syriac critics, that the extant Syriac is translated from a Greek text.

Although in his first two articles on the *Odes* J.H. Bernard took no position regarding the original language,[100] he suggested in 1912 that the original may be Aramaic or even Syriac. While he was critical of Grimme's arguments that the original language must be biblical Hebrew, he stated that 'Grimme's arguments tend to support the theory of a Semitic original for the *Odes*'.[101]

In 1912, 1913, and 1914 E.A. Abbott successively published several arguments for the Semitic hypothesis, concluding that the original language is Hebrew. First, he noticed that almost all the words in the *Odes* are to be found in the Syriac Bible and that since the Peshiṭta was translated from Hebrew, 'the Odes, too, might have proceeded from a Hebrew original.'[102] Second, after examining Harris's attempts to show the original language is Greek, he came to the provisional conclusion that 'there is no proof that our Syriac comes to us as a translation of a Greek original.'[103]

In 1913 Abbott confronted two of Connolly's arguments for a Greek original. He correctly showed, using observations similar to those we employed, that 'from before the constitution of the world' in *Ode* 41.15 is not necessarily a Syriac translation of πρὸ καταβολῆς. Furthermore, he rejects Connolly's argument that 'it was set in the midst' in *Ode* 30.6 derives from ἐς τὸ μέσον τιθέναι with the observations that such a phrase is not only uncommon in Greek but contains two Hebraisms. He concludes that this prepositional phrase may point to a Hebrew original.[104]

---

98. C. Bruston, 'La seconde édition du text des Odes de Salomon', *RevT* 21 (1912), p. 150; *idem*, 'Quelques observations sur les Odes de Salomon', *ZNW* 13 (1912), p. 113.

99. C. Bruston, *Les plus anciens cantiques chrétiens* (Paris: Librairie Fischbacher, 1912), pp. 30-36.

100. J.H. Bernard, 'The Odes of Solomon', *The Spectator* 105 (22 October, 1910), p. 637; *idem*, 'The Odes of Solomon', *JTS* 12 (1910), pp. 1-31.

101. Bernard, *The Odes of Solomon*, p. 10.

102. Abbott, *Light on the Gospel*, p. ix.

103. Abbott, *Light on the Gospel*, p. xxiv.

104. E.A. Abbott, 'The Original Language of the Odes of Solomon', *JTS* 14 (1913), p. 443.

In 1914 he correctly showed that Connolly's argument for a Greek *Grundschrift* behind the Syriac of *Ode* 20.6 was based on an ignorance of the presence of a beth in both MS H and MS N.[105] Both manuscripts preserve ܕܡܐܒ, 'with blood' (or 'be like'). In his book *The Fourfold Gospel. II. The Beginning*, published in the same year, he systematically rejected Connolly's arguments, and concluded that the *Odes* must have been originally written in Hebrew because of the Hebrew conceptions and expressions, and the dependence on Jewish traditions.[106] It is surprising that his arguments reflect the erroneous belief that there are only two possibilities, viz. that the *Odes* were composed in either Greek or Hebrew.

The same year A. Mingana, the sensitive, erudite Syriac scholar who was later to share with Harris in the edition of the *Odes* in 1916–20, entered the debate regarding the original language. This debate had by 1914 become quite heated as one can easily surmise from the personal words exchanging between Connolly and Abbott. With contrastingly calm, seemingly disinterested observations, Mingana argued that the original language is Aramaic or Syriac. Moreover, he is the first critic to suggest the specific dialect of the *Odes*: 'Et cette langue est l'araméo-syriaque, ou la langue presque syriaque classique, parlée en Palestine au temps de Notre Seigneur, et langue que les juifs avaient apprise dans leur exil en Babylonie.'[107] He concluded that the style of the *Odes* is distinct from the Edessan Syriac but similar to the Palestinian Syriac.[108] In the following pages we will critically examine his insights. In this introductory section, however, suffice it to report that time and further research strengthened his conviction.[109] Finally, one should note that he was influential in reversing the position of the father of research on the *Odes of Solomon*, J.R. Harris.

---

105. E.A. Abbott, 'The Original Language of the Odes of Solomon', *JTS* 15 (1914), p. 45.

106. E.A. Abbott, 'The Interpretation of Early Christian Poetry', in *The Fourfold Gospel. II. The Beginning* (Cambridge: Cambridge University Press, 1914), pp. 372-456.

107. '...and this language is Aramaic/Syriac, or a language close to classical Syriac, spoken in Palestine at the time of our Lord and the language that the Jews acquired during the Babylonian exile.' A. Mingana, 'Quelques mots sur les Odes de Salomon. I', *ZNW* 15 (1914), p. 248.

108. Mingana, 'Quelques mots sur les Odes de Salomon. I', pp. 248-49.

109. A. Mingana, 'Quelques mots sur les Odes de Salomon. II (Schluss)', *ZNW* 16 (1915), p. 167.

In 1916, after examining the arguments of Harris, Schulthess, Plooij, and Mingana, F.W. Grosheide advised both that the probabilities are greatest for the Syriac hypothesis. Nevertheless, he thought one should remain open to the possibility that the *Odes* were written originally in Greek. His position is represented by the words, 'Veel pleit voor Syrië en het Syrisch.'[110]

Before Harris co-edited the *Odes* with Mingana, he independently became convinced that at least one of the *Odes* had been composed in Aramaic. In July 1911, in contrast to his position in the second edition of *The Odes and Psalms of Solomon*, he concluded a detailed examination of the 38th Ode with the conviction 'that the Ode was in Aramaic and not in Greek'.[111] In the third edition of *The Odes and Psalms of Solomon* in 1920 he concluded the discussion regarding the original language with some hesitancy: 'We suggest tentatively that the Syriac of the *Odes* is the original language in which they were composed.'[112]

In 1921 all hesitancy was removed. In 1920 he had mentioned that the decisive factor in the solution of the argument regarding the original language is the possible dependence of the Odist on the Targumim.[113] In the following year he claimed, 'If our *Odes* suggest anything it is the use of a written Targum.'[114] Claiming to have proved the Odist depended upon both the Targum and the Peshitta, Harris concluded that the language of the Odist was 'Syro-Aramaic'.[115] We shall soon critically examine his arguments that the Odist depended on the Targumim.

In 1937 J. De Zwaan[116] argued for the Syriac hypothesis. He

110. '…much evidence points to Syria and the Syriac language.' F.W. Grosheide, 'De Oden van Salomo', *GThT* (1916), p. 131.

111. J.R. Harris, 'The Thirty-Eighth Ode of Solomon', *Exp* 8.2 (July 1911), p. 37.

112. Harris and Mingana, *The Odes and Psalms of Solomon*, II, p. 165. On p. 170 of this volume Harris is less hesitant but still not absolutely convinced: 'With the reserve in question which comes under the formula *exceptis excipiendis*, we affirm the Aramaic origin of the Odes.' By the 'reserve in question' he means 'the possible bilingualism of the author'.

113. Harris and Mingana, *The Odes and Psalms of Solomon*, p. 170.

114. J.R. Harris, 'The Odes of Solomon and the Biblical Targums', *Exp* 8.21 (April 1921), p. 290.

115. Harris, 'The Odes of Solomon and the Biblical Targums', p. 287.

116. J. de Zwaan, 'The Edessene Origin of the Odes of Solomon', in R.P. Casey *et al.* (eds.), *Quantulacumque: Studies Presented to Krisopp Lake by Pupils, Colleagues and Friends* (London: Christophers, 1937), p. 288.

contended that the vague metrical scheme, the rhythm and the style of the poetry were so fundamentally Syriac that 'to my view there is no presumption at all that can hold for a non-Semitic original.'[117]

In the forties M. Mar Yosip argued that these 'hymns were written by a member of the Aramaic-speaking church'.[118] He contended that the Aramaic of the *Odes* is 'akin to', but not identical with, the Aramaic of Palestine in the days of Jesus Christ. Examinations of his other arguments reveal that he is referring to the dialect of Edessa, for he quotes F.C. Burkitt's statement that 'the inhabitants of the city [Edessa] and the district spoke a dialect of Aramaic akin to, but not identical with, that spoken in Palestine by our Lord and His apostles.'[119] It is important to note that he disagrees with Mingana's opinion that the dialect of the *Odes* is closer to Palestinian than Edessan Syriac.

In the fifties W. Baumgartner, A. Vööbus, and F.M. Braun assumed that the original language is Semitic. W. Baumgartner believed, however, that the extant Syriac manuscripts do not derive from the Semitic original but are translations of a Greek text.[120] Vööbus wrote that he had no doubt the *Odes* were a product of the ancient Syrian Christian community: 'Their Semitic character in style and rhythm is obvious and does not allow one to accept the view presented by Harris, that originally the Odes were written in Greek.'[121] Vööbus correctly recognized the Semitic quality of the *Odes* but fails to notice that Harris reversed his position concerning the original language. F.M. Braun

117. De Zwaan, 'The Edessene Origin of the Odes of Solomon'.

118. M. Mar Yosip, *The Oldest Christian Hymn-Book* (foreword by M. Sprengling; Temple, TX: M. Mar Yosip, 1948), pp. 11-12.

119. F.C. Burkitt, *Early Eastern Christianity: Lectures on the Syriac-Speaking Church* (New York: E.P. Dutton, 1904), p. 7.

120. W. Baumgartner, 'Das trennende Schwert Oden Salomos 28.4', in W. Baumgartner, O. Eissfeldt, K. Elliger and L. Rost (eds.), *Festschrift Alfred Bertholet zum 80. Geburstag* (Tübingen: J.C.B. Mohr, 1950), p. 50. Schulz shared Baumgartner's opinion: 'Sehr wahrscheinlich geht der jetzt vorliegende syr. Text auf ein griech. Original zurück, dem vielleicht ein semitisches zugrunde liegt.' S. Schulz, 'Salomo-Oden', *RGG*, V, 3rd edn, pp. 1339-42.

121. A. Vööbus, *Celibacy: A Requirement for Admission to Baptism in the Early Syrian Church* (PETSE, 1; Stockholm: The Estonian Theological Society in Exile, 1951), p. 21. In 1958 he wrote, 'These poems reflect a Syriac cast everywhere we look', (*History of Asceticism in the Syrian Orient* [CSCO, 14; Belgium: Louvain-Heverle, 1958], p. 63).

shared Vööbus's feelings when he remarked that 'l'auteur était un sémite, marqué par le génie de sa race.'[122]

In the sixties, four Semitic scholars concluded that the original language is Semitic (A. Adam, A. Vööbus, J. Carmignac, J.C.L. Gibson). A. Adam, in 1961, after critically comparing the Syriac with both the Greek and Coptic variants, concluded that they pointed to a Semitic original: 'Diese Beobachtungen lassen die Annahme, dass die ursprüngliche Sprache der Salomo-Oden nicht griechisch, sondern semitisch ist, also begründet erscheinen.'[123] Finally, although he does not offer any reasons for his conjecture regarding the dialect of the extant Syriac, he seems to agree more with Mar Yosip than Mingana: 'Als ursprüngliche Sprache der Salomo-Oden ist ein Aramäisch anzunehmen, das dem edessenischen Syrisch nahesteht.'[124]

The next year A. Vööbus turned his attention to a critical examination of the 'Original language of the *Odes of Solomon*' ('Originalsprache der Oden Salomos'). After a year of concentrated study he concluded that the language of the autograph is Syriac:

> I have personally examined the language (which no one would consider refined), the poetic form, the play on words, the various parallelisms, prosody, the dependence upon the Peshitta and Targumim, the characteristic conceptions, and also the source of errors in the translation which could originate only in a Syriac original. These examinations lead me to conclude that we are dealing in the Odes with *einer Originalschrift*.[125]

After comparing Bodmer Papyrus XI with MS N he correctly reports: 'Ihm gegenüber erscheint der Grieche also die zweite Version, die die

---

122. '...the author was a semite distinguished by the genius of his race.' F.M. Braun, 'L'énigme des Odes de Salomon', *RT* 58 (1957), p. 598 (reprinted in *idem, Jean le théologien et son evangile dans l'église ancienne* [3 vols.; Paris: Librairie Lecoffre, 1959–66], pp. 224-59).

123. 'Thus these observations appear to allow the hypothesis to be established that the original language of the Odes of Solomon was not Greek, but rather Semitic'. A. Adam, 'Die ursprungliche Sprache der Salomo-Oden', *ZNW* 52 (1961), p. 155.

124. 'As the original language of the Odes of Solomon is an imported Aramaic which is closely allied to Edessene Syriac.' Adam, 'Die ursprungliche Sprache der Salomo-Oden', p. 156.

125. Vööbus, 'Neues Licht', pp. 278-79. (This passage is presented in English translation for purposes of clarification.)

ursprüngliche Stärke verloren hat.'[126] A second observation which verifies the Syriac hypothesis is that, while 'der syrische Text metrisch verfasst ist', the Greek text is both imperfect and lacks the vitality and freshness an original should have.[127] Furthermore, 'ἀνεζωοποίησεν in 11.11 is a confusion of the extant ܐܝܚܝܢ which cannot be explained from the Greek but only from the Syriac since ܢܚܐ ('he will give life') is frequently confused with the similar appearance of the verb 'to give rest': ܐܢܝܚ.[128] A. Vööbus's explanation is not only based on sound methodology but is probably correct. Furthermore, his observations confirm our earlier arguments that Bodmer Papyrus XI can only be explained as a translation of a Syriac *Grundschrift*.[129]

The most convincing argument for a Hebrew original was presented by J. Carmignac in 1961. He raised the following question: If the *Odes* were originally written in Syriac or Greek, then why did the author maintain Hebrew techniques in the place of the usual Syriac or Greek? In the attempt to prove that the original language is Hebrew, he translated the 11th Ode into Hebrew. Subsequently, he argued that four observations established a serious probability for a Hebrew original: (a) 19 times there are rhymes, assonances, and word-play in the translated Hebrew; (b) three or four times confusion in the extant Syriac and Greek are resolved by the Hebrew; (c) four times the Odist quoted the Hebrew Old Testament; and (d) twice one ascertains the Hebrew waw consecutive imperfect is translated by a participle. Consequently, he argued that the Hebrew translation both appeared in better poetic form and clarified ambiguities in both the extant Greek and Syriac. He argued that since neither the Syriac nor the Greek of this Ode is consistently preferable, neither can be traced back to the other. 'Dans ces conditions, une seule hypothèse rests plausible: le grec et le syriaque sont des versions indépendantes provenant d'un original hébreu.'[130]

---

126. 'Hence, contrary to him, the Greek appears to be the secondary version, which has lost the vigor of the original…' Vööbus, 'Neues Licht', p. 281.

127. '[T]he Syriac text is metrically composed.' Vööbus, 'Neues Licht'.

128. Vööbus, 'Neues Licht', p. 282.

129. These arguments are strengthened by the observations presented under the heading 'Arguments from Variants'. *Vide infra.*

130. '[U]nder these conditions, only one hypothesis remains plausible: the Greek and Syriac are independent versions stemming from a Hebrew original.' Carmignac, 'Les affinités qumrâniennes'.

Two years later he disagreed with A. Adam and A. Vööbus's contention that the original language is Syriac: 'j'envisageais plutôt une origine hébraïque.'[131] At the same time he rejected M. Philonenko's conjecture that the variant in 11.21 is caused by a confusion of TO ΘΕΛΗΜΑ and TO ΛΕΙΜΜΑ in the original Greek. He discarded this explanation in favor of the hypothesis of a Hebrew original in which שארית and שרירות were confused. He also attempted to explain some of the variants between the Coptic and Syriac by means of a Hebrew hypothesis. We will critically examine these arguments in the following pages.

K. Rudolph compared the *Odes of Solomon* with the Mandean hymns and concluded there was a close relationship. He claimed both hymns were characteristic of a type of Semitic *parallelismus membrorum* in which each verse was usually divided into two parts of three-beat rhythm. This close relationship strengthens the probability that the original language is Aramaic.[132]

In 1965 J.C.L. Gibson entered this discussion. Following the advice of A. Adam and A. Vööbus, he correctly remarked that if the Bodmer Papyrus is a sample of the original, 'then its Greek author was as bad a poet as its Syriac translator was a good one'. He also presented the valid judgment that the free rhythm of the Syriac *Odes*, which is dissimilar to later Syriac poetry, is strikingly similar to the Qumran hymns. His conclusion is clear: 'the Odes were written by a Syriac-speaking Jewish Christian when ties with Palestine were still being maintained.'[133]

In concluding the latter half of the biographical statement of critics debating the original language of the *Odes of Solomon*, it is necessary to classify the researchers as to the hypothesis defended and the date(s) of their publication(s). Such a list is essential at this point in our discussion since one probably has forgotten that J. Daniélou, M. Philonenko, J. Quasten, A.F.J. Klijn, and W. Bauer have published *in the sixties* their judgment that the original language is Greek.

131. 'I would envisage, rather, a Hebrew original.' Carmignac, 'Recherches sur la langue originelle des Odes de Salomon', *RevQ* 4 (1963), pp. 429-32 [429].

132. K. Rudolph, 'War der Verfasser der Oden Salomos ein "Qumran-Christ"?', *RQ* 4 (1964), p. 536.

133. J.C.L. Gibson, 'From Qumran to Edessa', *NCB* 2 (1965), p. 16.

Semitic Original				Greek Original	
Syriac		*Hebrew*			
				J.R. Harris	1909
		A. Harnack?	1910	J. Wellhausen	1910
		J.A. Montgomery	1910	E. Buonaiuti	1910
C. Bruston	1911	H. Grimme	1911	F. Schulthess	1910
	1912	E.A. Abbott	1913,	H. Gunkel	1910
J.H. Bernard	1912,		1914	A. Wabnitz	1910
	1920,	J. Carmignac	1961,	E.J. Goodspeed	1910
	1921		1963	W. Frankenberg	1911
A. Mingana	1914,			R. Bultmann	1911
	1915,			J.D. Puriet	1911
	1921			H. Gressmann	1911,
F.M. Grosheide	1916				1924
J.R. Harris	1911,			H. Hansen	1911
	1920,			A.J. Wensinck	1911
	1921			A. d'Alès	1911
J. De Zwaan	1937			J. Labourt and	
M. Mar Yosip	1948			P. Batiffol	1911
A. Vööbus	1951,			F.C. Burkitt	1912
	1958,			A. Loisy	1912
	1962			F. Perles	1912
A. Adam	1961			G. Kittel	1913,
K. Rudolph	1964				1914
J.C.L. Gibson	1965			R.H. Connolly	1913,
					1914,
					1920
				G. Beer	1913
				L. Tondelli	1914
				E. Preuschen	1915
				P. Smith	1915
				J.M. Bover	1931
				W. Bauer	1933,
					1964
				G. Bardy	1935
				A. Omodeo	1946
				B. Steidle	1948
H.E. Del Medico 1949				M. Testuz	1959
				J. Daniélou	1961,
					1964
				M. Philonenko	1962
				J. Quasten	1962
				A.F.J. Klijn	1962,
					1965

Finally, our biographical discussions would be incomplete if we failed to mention that A. Menzies,[134] E. Nestle,[135] R. Abramowski,[136] E.E. Fabbri,[137] and H.J.W. Drijvers[138] have argued that it is impossible to determine with certainty what the original language is because of the paucity of sources and the ambiguity of the extant sources. Very recently H.J.W. Drijvers, after mentioning that the discovery of Bodmer Papyrus XI, which he believed 'proves superior to the Syriac', shines a new light on the problem of the *Odes*, wrote: 'It is true it is not possible to decide in which language the *Odes* were originally written.'[139] We now turn our attention to an examination of the Semitic hypothesis.

Methodological Observations

In the previous section, as I criticized the Greek hypothesis, it was not necessary to develop a methodology since each argument usually dictated the method. In the following pages, however, I shall not only present the reasons for a Semitic original, but defend some of them; such intentions require a sound procedure. Methodologies that have heretofore been developed for testing a translation hypothesis have been based on an extant Greek. Since we are primarily dealing with an extant Syriac, the situation calls for a revised methodology. One can, however, profit from previous discussions; thus, in the following pages I have been influenced by the principles developed by M. Burrows.[140] In the following discussion, therefore, I shall suggest a methodology for determining the language of an autograph written in the first two Christian centuries.

134. A. Menzies, 'The Odes of Solomon', *Int* 7 (1910), p. 10.

135. E. Nestle, review of *Ein jüdisch-christliches Psalmbuch aus dem ersten Jahrhundert*, by Harnack and Flemming, and *Die Oden Salomos*, by Diettrich, in *TLZ* 36 (1911), p. 588.

136. R. Abramowski misunderstood Harris and Mingana's position, for he wrote 'Harris-Minganas Annahme des Ursprungs aus syrisch-griechischem Sprachgebiet, in dem die Frage der Originalsprache offen bleibt, ohne als Problem empfunden zu werden, empfiehlt sich am ehesten' ('Der Christus der Salmooden', *ZNW* 35 [1936], p. 49).

137. 'No es posible determinar con exactitud su lengua original.' E.E. Fabbri, 'El tema del Cristo vivificante en las Odas de Salomon', *CF* 14 (1958), p. 484.

138. Drijvers, *Bardaisan of Edessa*, pp. 209-10.

139. Drijvers, *Bardaisan of Edessa*, p. 209.

140. M. Burrows, 'Principles for Testing the Translation Hypothesis in the Gospels', *JBL* 53 (1934), pp. 13-30.

1. The first prerequisite is a disinterested approach. While pure objectivity is chimerical, we should be true to our text and not distort an examination by prejudices for or against Semitic culture or an a priori *Vorverständnis* regarding the original language.

2. The language of the manuscript discussed should be assumed to be the language of the autograph until convincing evidence is presented to the contrary.

3. The nature of the problem may be so complex that only varying degrees of probability are possible. Hence suggestive evidence must be distinguished from conclusive facts.

4. Although the accumulation of unconvincing evidence does not increase the probabilities of a conjectured original, each successive possibility increases the probability of a previous suggestion by decreasing the incidence of chance and coincidence.

5. Successive examinations must proceed critically and with the awareness that each new discovery may reverse the suggestiveness of antecedent possibilities. Of course, this principle would not apply where antecedent probabilities were conclusive.

6. If the provenience and date of composition are known, the linguist must be aware of what language would be most probable in such a milieu for the respective manuscripts.

7. Arguments that prove the dependence of a writer on the LXX alone or on the Peshiṭta and Targumim alone increase the possibility that the original language is respectively Greek or Aramaic-Syriac. However, one must always allow for the possibility that a translator would be influenced by his native version.

8. Evidence that a particular manuscript reflects a LXX variant is not convincing proof of a Greek original since a Semitic scholar would probably have known Greek as it was the lingua franca in almost all of the provinces.

9. Evidence of dependence on either a Peshiṭta or Targum variant is evidence that presents a strong probability for a Semitic original (especially for Syriac or Aramaic). Such evidence is probable since one cannot assume that a Greek scholar could read Semitic manuscripts.

10.   An extant Greek manuscript, which is conjectured to be a translation from a Semitic original, might contain numerous mistranslations. This is especially obvious when one recognizes that an unpointed Semitic manuscript contains only consonants. Moreover, these consonants are frequently similar in appearance and hence easily confused.

11.   The test of a conjectured mistranslation is not so much the cause of the error as the degree to which a retroversion resolves the difficulty. Such a restoration must not only restore meaning but also parallelism and rhythm if the particular section is composed in a style using these characteristics of Semitic poetry.

12.   If variants between two manuscripts of different languages can be explained to originate with only one of the languages, then that language is probably the original. For example, if the variants between C and H obviously could originate in a Syriac manuscript, but at the same time *cannot* originate in a Greek, then Syriac is probably the original language.

13.   If the tacit qualities of a manuscript convince an authority in the respective language that there are no signs of translation, and that the composition flows evenly and in good style, then the probability is high that the manuscript is in the same language as the autograph. Nevertheless, there always remains the possibility that the translator was a better phenomenological linguist than the author. Fortunately this possibility is usually remote, yet it does occur; for example, the English masterpiece known widely as the *Ruba'iyat of Omar Khayyam* is the result of Edward Fitzgerald's poetic improvement of the Classical Persian composition.

14.   Finally, when analyzing a particular historical phenomenon one must be conservative in applying general principles. The goal must always be to let the source tell its own story.

Rejection of the Hebrew Hypothesis
A critical examination of the Hebrew hypothesis should begin with H. Grimme's attempt to translate the Syriac *Odes* into classical Hebrew in 1911, and conclude with J. Carmignac's observations published in 1961 and 1963.

Grimme asserted that three observations showed the language of the autograph to be biblical Hebrew ('und zwar biblisch-hebräischer Sprachform abgefasst'). First, he claimed that when one translates the Syriac into Hebrew an alphabetic acrostic appears. The acrostic resulting from his reconstruction appears in the following order.[141]

1.	א	12.	ה	23a.	מ	33.	שׁ
2.	lost	13.	ה	23b.	מ	34.	א
3.	lost	14.	כ	24.	נ	35.	ר
4.	א	15.	כ	25.	נ	36.	נ
5.	א	16.	כ	26.	נ	37.	פ
6.	ב	17.	כ	27.	ס	38.	ע
7.	ב	18.	ה	28.	כ	39.	נ
8.	ג	19.	כ	29.	שׁ	40.	כ
9.	ג	20.	כ	30.	שׁ	41.	י
10.	ה	21.	כ	31.	שׁ	42.	פ
11.	ה	22.	מ	32.	שׁ		

Recognizing that this conjectured acrostic was insufficient evidence of a Hebrew *Urschrift*, he admitted that a similar acrostic could appear in Aramaic since both languages share the same alphabet. Moreover, he confessed the failure to construct an acrostic beyond *Ode* 33. In the attempt to establish his belief in a Hebrew original he turned to another approach.

Second, he declared that many oddities and incomprehensible passages in the Syriac are resolved when one recognizes that the confusion is due to a misunderstanding of characteristics peculiar to Hebrew. Since most Hebrew nouns have more than one specific meaning, some of the confusion in the Syriac is probably due to a translator's poor choice. For example, he suggested that ܐܚܘܗܘܢ in *Ode* 28.17 ('And I did not perish, for I was not *their brother*') probably mistranslated אחיהם which means not only 'their brother' but also 'their equal', of 'their likeness'.

Third, he claimed that when one translates the *Odes* from Syriac into Hebrew the rhythmic-metric-strophic form of biblical Hebrew poetry appears, and the linguistic structure is changed from prose to correct poetry.[142] He concluded his lengthy examination with the affirmation that there is now proof the *Urschrift* is probably Hebrew: 'dass keine

141. See Grimme, *Die Oden Salomos*, pp. 109-10.
142. Grimme, *Die Oden Salomos*, pp. 108-18.

andere Sprache als die biblisch-hebräische von ihrem Autor bei der Abfassung verwendet worden ist'.[143]

It is now necessary to evaluate Grimme's three points. First, one notices that his conjectured acrostic is both imperfect and forced. It is imperfect because: (a) it ends abruptly with *Ode* 33; (b) consonants ד, ו, ז, ח, ט, י, ל, ס, ע, צ, ק, ר and ת are not present; (c) the consonants that are represented are repeated as many as seven times; and (d) ה, כ and שׁ respectively interrupt the acrostic in *Odes* 18, 28 and 32. The acrostic is forced because of improbable translations. For example it is unlikely that a Syriac translator would have translated a putative Hebrew כ with the Syriac ܐܝܟ which begins *Odes* 6 and 7, since ܐܝܟ ('as', 'as if', 'almost') usually translates כאשׁר ('as', 'when') or כ ('like', 'according to') as his retroversion shows in *Ode* 14. Likewise it is dubious that a Syriac scribe would have thought כף ('palm', 'hand', 'sole', 'spoon') meant a putative Aramaic-Hebrew דרעא ('arms') as Grimme's translation demands at *Ode* 21. Moreover, an important weakness in Grimme's method is the presupposition that a conjectured translator misunderstood a conjectured Hebrew original. P. Dhorme has correctly remarked that if the Syriac text is so faulty how can one proceed from it to a hypothetical Hebrew?[144] Indeed the task of seeking to discern the original language of the *Odes of Solomon* is too delicate for such blunt conjectures. Having found no evidence or even probability of a Hebrew *Grundschrift* on the basis of the first point, we turn to his second.

Although he presented numerous examples in the attempt to prove his assumption that passages become meaningful when translated into Hebrew, none of these retroversions are convincing. For example, one of the more impressive explanations is the instance in *Ode* 28.16, which we have discussed above. Yet this example loses its force after three observations. First, both ܐܚܐ and אח primarily mean 'brother'. Second, ܐܚܐ also means 'kinsman', 'friend', 'neighbor' and 'colleague.' Finally, the sentence is meaningful and clear as it stands in the Syriac.[145]

With the last observation we move into the area covered by his third point. We are led to reject this final point because the *Odes* in Syriac

143. Grimme, *Die Oden Salomos*, p. 118.

144. P. Dhorme, 'Les Odes de Salomon', *RB* 21 (1912), p. 465.

145. Other criticisms of both Grimme's translation and his arguments for the Hebrew hypothesis are presented by A. Mingana. See Mingana, 'Quelques mots sur les Odes de Salomon', pp. 235-37.

represent good Semitic poetic form and that retroversion into Hebrew does not improve the poetry. In the following pages we shall show how beautifully conceived is the poetic structure: there are numerous word-plays, paronomasiae, parallelisms, assonances, and an aesthetic rhythm, and metrical scheme. Grimme's arguments for a Hebrew original are not convincing. We now must examine the recent observations of J. Carmignac.

Carmignac's arguments, in contrast to Grimme's claims, raise a serious probability for the Hebrew hypothesis. His first argument, however, that the *Odes* could not have been written in Syriac because they are composed in the style of Hebrew poetry is not convincing. This argument incorrectly presupposes that when the *Odes* were written Syriac poetry was distinct from Hebrew poetry. However, since classical Syriac poetics begin with Ephraem (c. 306–73),[146] and since the *Odes* were composed before Ephraem, they could not have been written in classical Syriac style.

It is necessary to present another observation. It has been suggested by others that the earliest Syriac was quite similar to Palestinian Aramaic,[147] yet no one seems to have noticed that the rhythm and parallelism of the *Odes* is closer to some of the words of Jesus than they are to the five- or six-syllable verse that probably was characteristic of Bardaiṣan,[148] the father of hymnology in Edessa, or the six-syllable verse of the two gnostic hymns in the *Acts of Thomas* (The Soul's Wedding and The Hymn of the Soul). Compare, for example, the similarity of the following rhythm and synonymous parallelisms.[149]

Ode 11.11	And the Lord		renewed me		in his raiment,
			And possessed me		by his light.
Jn 4.36	He that reapeth		receiveth		wages
			And gathereth		fruit unto life eternal.

146. For a discussion of Syriac poetry see M. Sprengling, 'Antonius Rhetor on Versification with an Introduction and Two Appendices', *AJSL* 32 (April 1916), pp. 145-216.

147. J.C. James, *The Language of Palestine and Adjacent Regions* (Edinburgh: T. & T. Clark, 1920), p. 102.

148. The only extant poetry by Bardaiṣan is quoted by Philoxenus and Ephraem Syrus. For a translation of these fragments, see Sprengling, 'Antonius Rhetor', pp. 196-98.

149. I have been influenced by C.F. Burney's dicussion regarding the style of Jesus' discourses. See his *The Poetry of Our Lord* (Oxford: Clarendon Press, 1925).

Ode 11.10	And I forsook		the folly cast away		over the earth,
	And I stripped it		and cast it		from me.
	off				
Mt. 7.6	Give not		the holy thing		to the dogs
	And cast not		your pearls		before swine.

Also note the identical rhythm (three beats to a line) of the following synthetic parallelisms:

Ode 11.12	And from above		he gave me rest		without corruption;
	And I became		like the land		and rejoices in
			which blossoms		its fruits.
Lk. 12.49	Fire		I came to cast		upon the earth;
	And would		if it already		it were kindled!
	But a baptism		I have		to be baptized with;
	And how		I am constrained		until it is completed.

How different the *Odes* are from the following hymn of Bardaiṣan which Ephraem Syrus quotes:

> Let her who comes I after thee
> To me I be a daughter
> A sister I to thee.[150]

The purpose of this important observation is to show that the *Odes* are probably closer to early Aramaic-Syriac poetry than later Syriac poetry, and that Aramaic (early Syriac) poetry is characterized by the same types of parallelism and rhythm that are found in the Psalter. Hebrew had no monopoly on this Semitic style as J. Carmignac's argument suggests. Hence Carmignac's first argument is unpersuasive.

Of Carmignac's four observations regarding an original Hebrew, only three are relevant to our present discussion since the observation that the Odist quoted the Hebrew Old Testament is an argument directed only against the Greek hypothesis. His first observation, that there are 19 instances of rhyme, assonance, or word-play in the translated Hebrew, seems impressive. Upon critical examination, however, we discover that many of his statements are misleading. For example, in *Ode* 11.2 there is no assonance between a putative Hebrew עליון and כליותי for they would not be in parallel columns; and they certainly are not assonant. Note also that in 11.2 there is no play on words since

---

150. F.J.A. Hort's translation. See his article 'Bardaisan', in W. Smith and H. Wace (eds.), *A Dictionary of Christian Biography, Literature, Sects and Doctrines* (London: William Clowes, 1877), I, p. 253.

a conjectured מלל ('he circumcised') and מלא ('he filled') are not
assonant. The accent in the piel imperfect under the influence of a
prefixed waw consecutive does *not* shift to the penultima, because of the
closed syllable and short vowel, but remains on the ultima. In 11.3 his
translation completely eliminates the beautiful assonance found in the
Syriac:

ܐܬܘܬܐ ܒܐܠܟܣ
ܐܬܘܬܐ ܕܢܗܪܐ

In 11.5 Carmignac's translation preserves the paronomasia found in the
Syriac, but a niphal followed by a feminine noun from the same root
fails to preserve the linguistic beauty of an ethpaal followed by a noun
derived from a pael of the same root. Moreover, the Hebrew (ואאמן
על סלע אמונה) is comparatively harsh since it fails to ring with
the assonance caused by the sonorous *shin* in the Syriac. ܘܐܫܬܪܪܬ
ܥܠ ܫܘܥܐ ܕܩܘܫܬܐ.

Carmignac claims the Hebrew has paronomasia (*n'm*), assonance
(between ותנעם and נשמתי) and rhyme (פני and אדוני) in 11.15.
However, when the text is pointed, on the one hand the necessary
vowels destroy the assonance (וְתִנְעַם and נִשְׁמָתִי), but, on the other
hand, פני and אדוני would probably have rhymed. Nevertheless, these
arguments for a Hebrew original are not persuasive, because the Syriac
has not only paronomasia (ܒܣܡ) but also assonance in 15a and 15b:

ܐܬܒܣܡܬ ܢܦܫܝ,
ܒܚܘܒܗ ܒܣܝܡܐ ܕܡܪܝܐ

These examples demonstrate that the translation into Hebrew, aided
by thesaurus, lexicon, grammar, and other tools of higher criticism,
does not always improve the Semitic poetry of the *Odes of Solomon*.
Generally speaking, the Syriac flows freely and is characterized by freshness, but the translated Hebrew moves mechanically and is often aca-
demically stale.

We now turn to Carmignac's second point, that difficulties in the
Syriac or Greek are resolved by translation into Hebrew. Only one of
the instances he indicates appertains to our discussion since the others
are found in the six verses that are extant only in Greek. This instance
occurs in *Ode* 11.12 and is based on a theoretical confusion of a supposed ending in a conjectured Hebrew original.

Finally, his argument that two waw consecutives in the Hebrew
(11.17 and 11.19b) are translated by a participle does not apply to the

Syriac text. The two verbs referred to (וישׁנו and וידהפכו) are represented respectively in the Syriac by a pael perfect third masculine plural (ܫܢܝܘ) and aphel perfect third masculine plural (ܐܣܦܟܘ). On the basis of these critical observations, the probabilities of a Hebrew original are not as strong as we first imagined.

We now turn our attention to J. Carmignac's arguments for the Hebrew hypothesis which were published in 1963. First, he suggested that the variant in *Ode* 11.21 between the noun 'will' (ΘΕΛΗΜΑ) and the noun 'remnant' (ܫܪܟܐ) may result from a confusion of two Hebrew nouns. The idea of 'remnant' was probably expressed by שְׁאֵרִית, and that noun is very similar to שְׁרִירוּת, which Carmignac claimed 'means "will"'.

In objection to Carmignac's conjecture, however, it is only remotely possible palaeographically that an א would be confused with a ר and a י. A more serious objection to his conjecture is admitted by Carmignac himself. Both in the Qumran literature and in the Old Testament (or Hebrew Bible) שְׁרִירוּת means 'firmness', and is usually joined with לֵב to denote 'hardness of heart'. In summation, there is no evidence that שרירות meant 'will'. There is no convincing evidence, consequently, of a Hebrew original behind the Syriac manuscripts of the *Odes of Solomon*. In all fairness to this fine scholar, we must note that he presented this conjecture primarily to refute Philonenko's speculation for a Greek original.

Carmignac argued, moreover, that some of the variants between the Coptic and Syriac probably originated with a Hebrew manuscript. In *Ode* 22.12 the Syriac reads: 'that your rock may be the foundation of everything'. In contrast, the Coptic reads: 'that your light may be the foundation for all of them'. Carmignac traces **OYOEIN** in the Coptic back through a conjectured φῶς to a postulated אוֹר. Likewise, he speculates the Syriac ܟܐܦ goes back to צוּר.

This idea is ingenious, and the two Hebrew nouns in the conjectured original are almost identical; the only visible difference is the bottom of the א and צ. This minute difference is easily lost in an early cursive manuscript. Another fact in favor of his conjecture is the observation that precedents, e.g. Gen. 1.3, reveal that if אוֹר had been in a text it would have probably been translated by φῶς, which in turn would have probably been translated by **OYOEIN** ('light'). However, it is also possible that the corruption originated in the Coptic as **ⲰⲚⲈ** ('stone') and **OYOEIN** may be confused since they can be pronounced in a similar way. Another observation reduces the force of his conjecture: צוּר is usually translated by ܛܝܢܐ (e.g. Ps. 78.15, 20), while כַּף is usually translated by ܟܐܦܐ.

Finally, Carmignac suggests that the variant in *Ode* 22.2 between the Syriac ('and throws to me') and the Coptic ('and taught me') is caused by a double meaning in the original Hebrew. The Hebrew verb ירה means both 'to throw' and 'to teach' (in the hiphil).

This suggestion is also ingenious since neither the Syriac ܪܡܐ nor the Coptic **TCABO** possesses both meanings. One must admit this point increases the probability of a Hebrew *Grundschrift*. However, there are at least two facts that reduce the force of the conjecture: ܪܡܐ usually corresponds to the Hebrew verb רמה ('to cast'). Second, the extant Syriac form is a peal active masculine participle but the conjectured Hebrew must be in the hiphil. The probability of correlation decreases since the Hebrew hiphil usually corresponds to the Syriac aphel, and hardly ever translates a peal active participle.

In conclusion, the data force us to reject the Hebrew hypothesis both because the above conjectures are not convincing and because the following discussion[151] reveals that the Syriac hypothesis is the most probable.

Advocacy of the Syriac-Aramaic Hypothesis

Direct Dependence on the Targumim: Denial
J.R. Harris argued that the *Odes of Solomon* borrowed from the Targumim.[152] The force of his argument was weakened by the a priori assumption that some Targumim had been committed to writing when the poet composed the *Odes*.[153] This presupposition has been proved by subsequent discoveries. In Qumran Cave 11 a fragment of a lost Targum to Job was found,[154] and in Cave 4 fragments of a Targum to

---

151. *Vide infra*, in particular the section headed 'Arguments from Variants'.

152. Harris and Mingana, *The Odes and Psalms of Solomon*, pp. 85-91; Harris, 'The Odes of Solomon and the Biblical Targums', pp. 271-91.

153. Although J.R. Harris claimed that direct borrowing is possible if the Targumim were still in the oral stage when the *Odes* were composed, the foundation of his argument is that they had already been written.

154. F.M. Cross Jr, *The Ancient Library of Qumran and Modern Biblical Studies* (rev. edn; New York: Anchor Books, 1961), p. 34.

Leviticus (16.12-15, 18-21) were discovered.[155] These discoveries led to the insight that 'indeed by the time of Jesus it is clear that there were written Targums.'[156] Harris's thesis may now be unexpectedly supported; it must now be re-examined. If Harris's position is correct the probability of a Syriac original is strengthened.[157]

Harris argued that the Odist borrowed not only the language of the Targumim but also the verses. Attempting to prove this contention, he compared *Ode* 1 with Psalm 1, and claimed that upon examination 'the act of borrowing was undeniable.'

First, he argued that 'a crown of unwithering and blossoming and fruit-bearing branches in the Odes' was 'clearly the duplicate of the tree whose branches hang over the first Psalm [*sic*], whose leaf never withers and which brings forth its fruit in its season'.[158] From this 'coincidence in theme' Harris seemed to assume that the Odist was working from the first psalm.

Next he wonders if the Odist borrowed from the first psalm the following statement: 'All that he might do shall prosper'[159] (וְכֹל אֲשֶׁר־יַעֲשֶׂה יַצְלִיחַ).[160] He claims that the Odist is directly dependent on this verse, but has referred the action of the verb not to the human agent but to the trees, which represent the believer metaphorically. Hence the odist wrote:

155. Milik, *Ten Years of Discovery*, p. 31.

156. O. Eissfeldt, *The Old Testament: An Introduction* (trans. P.R. Ackroyd; New York: Harper & Row, 1965), p. 696. See also W.O.E. Oesterley and G.A. Box, *A Short Survey of the Literature of Rabbinical and Mediaeval Judaism* (London: SPCK, 1920), p. 44.

157. Harris, 'The Thirty-Eighth Ode', p. 276.

158. Harris, 'The Thirty-Eighth Ode'.

159. Most scholars agree that this verse 'speaks of the godly man and therefore does not belong any more to the picture of the tree: if it were otherwise, it would mean an inappropriate repetition.' A. Weiser, *The Psalms: A Commentary* (OTL; Philadelphia: Westminster Press, 1962), p. 105.

160. R. Kittel (ed.), תורה נביאים וכתובים: *Biblia Hebraica* (Textum Masoreticum curavit, P. Kahle; rev. and ed. Alt and O. Eissfeldt; Stuttgart: Wurttembergische Bibelanstalt, 1962), p. 977. It is important to note that the editors of this edition of the Hebrew Bible propose the deletion of this clause. R. Kittel remarked that this clause, '...stört etwas die Symmetrie, fällt augleich aus dem Belde; viell. Zusatz'. R. Kittel, *Die Psalmen* (KAT, 13; Leipzig: Deichert, 5th and 6th edns, 1929), p. 1.

ⲚⲈⲔⲔⲀⲢⲠⲞⲤ ⲤⲈⲘⲈϨ ⲀⲨⲰ ⲤⲈⲬⲎⲔ
ⲈⲨⲘⲈϨ ⲈⲂⲞⲖ ϨⲘ̄ ⲠⲈⲔⲞⲨⲬⲀⲒ̈

Your fruits are full grown and perfect,
They are full of your salvation.

An examination of the Targum on the first psalm reveals that the Meturgeman has also referred the action of the verb not to the agent but to the tree:

וכל לובלבוי דמלבלב מגרגר ומצלח.[161]

Every germ that germinates ripens and prospers.[162]

Harris believed this coincidence shows the Odist borrowed from the Targum. Furthermore, he compared the Targum on the psalm with the Ode in search of further coincidences of thought and expression. It is now necessary to juxtapose this Psalm and Ode:

Psalm 1 (Targum)	*Ode 1*
Blessed, etc.	The *Lord* is upon my head
But his delight is in the Law	like a crown;
(νόμος) of the *Lord*, and in	And I shall not be without
his law doth he meditate day	him (it).[163]
and night;	The crown of truth was woven
And he *shall* be like a tree *of*	for me;
life (or living tree) that is	And it caused your branches to
planted by the streams of water,	*germinate* in me.
whose *fruit* ripens in its season,	For it is not like a withered
and its leaves do not	crown that buddeth not.
fall, and every germ that	But you *live* upon my head;
it *germinates* swells like	And you have blossomed upon my
a berry and prospers.[164]	head.
	Your *fruits* are full-grown and
	perfect;

---

161. Paulus de Lagarde (ed.), תרגום כתובים: *Hagiographa Chaldaice* (Leipzig: Teubner, 1873), p. 2. See also P. Churgin's, כתובים תרגום: *The Targum to Hagiographa* (New York: Shulsinger Bros, 1945), esp. pp. 17-62.

162. Harris's translation; published in 'The Thirty-Eighth Ode', pp. 277-78.

163. The masculine possessive adjective (ⲠⲈϤ) can refer either to the crown (ⲔⲖⲞⲘ) or Lord (ⲬⲞⲈⲒⲤ) since both are masculine nouns.

164. Harris's translation; published in 'The Thirty-Eighth Ode', pp. 277-78.

They are full of your salvation.

Hallelujah.

[italics mine]

טוביה דגבר דלא הליך במלכת רשיעין ובאורדת חייבין לא קם
ובסועת ממיקני לא איסתהר: אילהן בנמוסא דיהוה רעותיה
ובאוריתיה מרנין יומם ולילי: ויהי כאילן היי דנציב על טוררפי
מוי די אינביה מבשל בעידניה ואטרפוי לא נתרין וכל לובלבוי
דמלבלב מגרגר ומצלח: לא היכנא רשיעי אילהין כמוזא
די תשקפיניה עלעולא: מטול היכנא לא יזכון רשיעי ביומא רבא
וחייבין בסיעת צדיקיא: מטול דגלי קדם יהוה אורח צדיקיא
ואורחתהון דרשיעי תהובד.[165]

П.ХОЄIC ?IХN ТААПЄ N̄ΘЄ N̄OYΚΛOM· AYш N̄-
†NAPПЄЧΒΟΛ AN ·

AYшшNT̄ NAΪ MПЄΚΛOM N̄TAΛΗΘIA· AYш AЧTPЄ
NЄΚΚΛAΔOC †OYш ?PAΪ N̄?HT·

ХЄ ЄЧЄINЄ AN N̄OYΚΛOM ЄЧшOYшOY ЄMЄЧ†-
OYш· AΛΛA KON? ?IХN ТААПЄ· AYш AΚ†OYш ?PAΪ
?IХшΪ·

NЄΚΚAPПOC CЄMЄ?· AYш CЄХΗΚ· ЄYMЄ? ЄΒΟΛ
?M ПЄΚΟYХAΪ·[166]

After placing the Ode and Psalm in juxtaposition and without further elucidation, he claims, 'The coincidences are open and palpable'.[167] But are they? Where is there open and palpable coincidence? One must carefully note to whom the fruit belongs in the Psalm and to whom the fruit belongs in the Ode. In the Psalm the fruit comes from the tree, which is a simile for the faithful servant, but in the Ode the fruit is the Lord's (**NЄΚΚAPПOC**). Failure to observe this distinction led Harris to err and to translate 'your fruits' as 'my fruits'. Moreover, the motif of the tree is not clear in the Ode, although the Greek loan words **ΚΛAΔOC** ('branch') and **ΚAPПOC** ('fruit') usually refer to a tree.[168] The desire to link this Ode with the first Psalm is immediately confronted with the difficulty of explaining the origin of the most

165. De Lagarde (ed.), תרגום כתובים, p. 2.

166. C. Schmidt (ed.), *Pistis Sophia* (Coptica, 2; Copenhagen: Glypdendalske Boghandel-Nordisk Forlag, 1925), p. 117.

167. Harris, 'The Thirty-Eighth Ode', p. 278.

168. See H.G. Liddell and R. Scott (eds.), *A Greek–English Lexicon*, p. 879b; W. Bauer, *A Greek–English Lexicon of the New Testament and Other Early Christian Literature* (trans. W.F. Arndt and F.W. Gingrich; Chicago: The University of Chicago Press, 4th edn, 1952), pp. 405b-406a.

important simile in the Ode: the crown. Moreover, Harris's contention that the Odist is copying from the Targum of Psalm 1 is based upon the presupposition that the Odist is working from the first Psalm, a presupposition certainly open to doubt.[169] Moreover, the date of the extant Targum on the Psalms is far too late to establish any literary relation between it and the *Odes*.

Furthermore, if it could be proved that the Ode was dependent on the first Psalm, two other possibilities would have to be overcome before it would be probable that the Odist was working from the Targum. The first possibility is that the coincidence could be attributed to the milieu[170] and traditions that the Targumist and Odist shared. For example, *Psalm of Solomon* 14 would probably have been known to the Meturgeman and Odist since it antedates both. In *Psalm of Solomon* 14 we find in v. 2 an idea that is similar to both the first Ode and the first Psalm:

ὅσιοι κυρίου ζήσονται ἐν αὐτῷ
εἰς τὸν αἰῶνα ὁ παράδεισος
τοῦ κυρίου, τὰ ξύλα τῆς
ζωῆς, ὅσιοι αὐτοῦ.[171]

The pious ones of the Lord shall live with him for ever;
The paradise of the Lord [and] the trees of life [are] his pious ones.[172]

The metaphorical designation of the human as a tree seems to have been widespread in the first centuries of the Christian era as shown by two examples: Mt. 12.33-35 ('the tree is known by its fruit... The good man out of his good treasure brings forth good.') And *Odes* 11.18 ('And I said, blessed, O Lord are they / That are planted in your land, / And that have a place in your Paradise.')

The second possibility is that the Odist was dependent on the Syriac translation of the Psalter since the verb that translates the Hebrew

---

169. Not only is the 'coincidence in theme' dubious, but it is questionable that the Targum on the Psalter (at least the extant version) antedates or is contemporaneous with the *Odes*.

170. So J.H. Bernard, review of *The Odes and Psalms of Solomon*, by Harris and Mingana, in *Theology* 1 (November 1920), p. 293.

171. J. Viteau and F. Martin, *Les Psaumes de Salomon* (Paris: Letouzey et Ane, 1911), p. 324.

172. The translation presupposes a Hebrew original.

יַצְלִיחַ[173] can be pointed to refer either to the tree or to the human:

ܟܠ ܕܝܗܒ ܡܨܠܚ[174]

All that it bears is prospering.

Later in his discussion Harris contended that the opening of the first Ode has been borrowed from the Targum on Isa. 28.5-6a:

בעדנא ההוא יהי משיחא
דיוי צבאות לכליל דחדוא
לכתר דתשבחא
לשארא דעמיה
ולמימר קשוט.[175]

In that time the Messiah of the Lord of Hosts shall be for a crown of joy and for a diadem of praise for the remnant of the people, for the word of truth, etc.[176]

From this Targum Harris made three observations. First, he claimed the word for 'crown' (ܟܠܝܠ) was the same in both the Psalm and Ode. Unfortunately, he had forgotten that the first Ode is not extant in Syriac. The Coptic word for 'crown' which is used in *Ode* 1 is ΚΛΟΜ. Second, the Meturgeman translated 'diadem' (צְפִירַת) with an uncommon word (כתר), which means 'garland' or 'crown'. This noun is a derivative of the verbal root כתר, which is usually used in the pael to mean 'to turn around' or 'to wait for'. Third, Harris used the Peshitta to support his contention, for he seems to have assumed the scribe of the Peshitta to support his contention, assuming further that the scribe of the Peshitta translated צפערת with the peal passive participle of ܨܕܝ: ܨܕܝܠܐ, which means 'to be interweaved'. However, there is no ܝ between the ܕ and ܠ in the Peshitta.[177] Rather it preserves the noun ܨܕܠܐ which when combined with ܡܗܝܡܢܐ means 'a wreath or crown of

173. From the verbal root צלח which in the hiphil imperfect means 'shall carry a thing through to success'.

174. See W.E. Barnes (ed.), *The Peshitta Psalter According to the West Syrian Text* (Cambridge: Cambridge University Press, 1904); C. Tunmer (ed.), *Biblia Sacra: Juxta Versionem simplicem quae dicitur Pschitta* (3 vols.; Beirut: Typis Typographiae Catholicae, 1951). This section of the Peshitta probably dates around the beginning of the second century CE.

175. A Sperber (ed.), *The Bible in Aramaic: The Latter Prophets According to Targum Jonathan* (Leiden: E.J. Brill, 1962), III, p. 52.

176. Translated by Harris, 'The Thirty-Eighth Ode', p. 278.

177. Tunmer (ed.), *Biblia Sacra*.

glory'. Consequently, Harris's translation ('The crown of truth was woven for me') of the Syriac phrase, ܚܠܠܬܐ ܝܣܝܪܐ ܟܠܝܠܐܕ ܩܘܫܬܐ, appears inaccurate.[178] After his examination, which we have expanded, Harris claims: 'Thus there is no doubt that the opening verses of the Ode are also Targumic in origin.'[179]

This conclusion should be rejected. To clinch his argument Harris left the Targum and referred to the Syriac translation. Moreover, the concepts and expressions through which he attempted to link the Ode with *Targ. Isa.* 28.5 are also in the Hebrew, the Syriac, and the Greek. For example, 'Lord of Hosts' is found in each of these versions (צְבָאוֹת יְהוָה, ܣܒܠܘܬ ܚܝܠܐ, κύριος σαβαωθ), 'a crown of beauty and a diadem of glory' is also found, if one recognizes the license of the translator, in each (לַעֲטֶרֶת צְבִי וְלִצְפִירַת תִּפְאָרָה, ܚܫܒܐ ܠܚܠܠܐ ܕܚܝܢܐ ܘܟܠܝܠܐ, στέφανος τῆς ἐλπίδος ὁ πλακεὶς τῆς δόξης).[180] Nevertheless, there appears to be one similarity peculiar to *Targ. Isa.* 28.5-6a and the first two verses of the Ode: both contain the word for truth. The Meturgeman translated the Hebrew 'for a spirit of justice' (וּלְרוּחַ מִשְׁפָּט) as 'for the word of truth' (וּלְמֵימַר קְשׁוֹט). In *Ode* 1.2a we find the expression 'the crown of truth' (ⲔⲖⲞⲘ ⲚⲦⲀⲖⲎⲐⲒⲀ). Certainly this coincidence cannot support the conclusion that 'the opening verses of the Ode are also Targumic in origin'. Consequently, there appears to be no convincing evidence that the Odist quoted from the Targum. However, before we conclude this discussion we should examine the possibility that the *Odes* were strongly influenced by the Targumim.

Anyone who has worked on the Targumim immediately notices the habitual attempt to alter the Hebrew in line with a doctrine of divine transcendence. Especially characteristic of the Targumim is the desire to remove all anthropomorphisms.

Let us turn to the *Odes* to see if there is a constant attempt to avoid anthropomorphic theological expressions. Our examination has provided information in three categories: expressions referred to Jesus Christ, to 'the Lord', and to God. Under the first category are arranged

---

178. J.R. Harris's translation; published in 'The Thirty-Eighth Ode', p. 278. A better translation is 'a crown of strength and a wreath of glory'.

179. Harris, 'The Thirty-Eighth Ode', p. 278.

180. See Kittel (ed.), *Biblia Hebraica*; Tunmer (ed.), *Biblia Sacra*; A. Rahlfs (ed.), *Septuaginta* (Stuttgart: Privilegierte Wurttembergische Bibelanstalt, 5th edn, 1952).

those sayings that were obviously composed with Christ as speaker.[181] As one might anticipate, these sayings contain anthropomorphic reflex utterances. In *Ode* 8.14-20 Christ refers to 'my eyes', 'my own breasts', and 'my own right hand'. In *Ode* 28.15 he refers to 'my right hand'. In *Ode* 26.7 'my mouth' and 'my heart' are written. And in *Ode* 42, vv. 13, 14 and 19, 'Christ' respectively refers to his 'face', 'lips', and 'heart'. On this evidence alone, however, it is still possible to accept Harris's belief that the Odist was a converted Meturgeman, since Christ is depicted referring to himself. That is not exactly the same thing as the Targumic avoidance of metaphorical expressions attributed to God.

As we examine the expressions that are attributed to 'the Lord', it becomes extremely difficult to maintain the idea that the *Odes* are influenced by the Targumim. In *Ode* 12.3 we read about the 'mouth of the Lord'. In *Odes* 14, 17 and 18 we find respectively the following anthropomorphisms: 'your right hand', 'by his hands', and 'your right hand'. In *Ode* 22 the Lord's 'hand' is referred to twice and his 'face' is mentioned once. In *Ode* 30.5 the Odist wrote 'lips of the Lord', and 'heart of the Lord'. In *Ode* 31 the Lord is mentioned in terms of 'his mouth' and 'his voice'. In *Ode* 38 we again read 'the hand of the Lord'. And finally in *Ode* 39 the following three anthropomorphisms are attributed to the 'Lord': 'and he walked and crossed them on foot', 'his footsteps', and 'the footsteps of our Lord Messiah' (again the latter instance may not be against the Targumic circumlocutions).

Under the third category we discovered that five odes speak of God or the Lord in anthropomorphic terms. In *Ode* 19.4 the Odist mentions 'the two breasts of the Father'. In *Ode* 23.21 he uses the expression 'the finger of God.' In *Ode* 25.9 he ascribed to God a 'right hand'. In *Ode* 28.19 he mentions that the 'Most High' has a 'heart'. In *Ode* 41.10 he has 'Christ' speak of the 'heart' of the 'Father of Truth'.

The contention that these are not anthropomorphisms should be eliminated. These passages can be interpreted as mere metaphors only by habitually violating the action of the accompanying verb and overlooking the precedent that many of these nouns (e.g. 'breasts' and 'fingers') are not mere metaphors in the extant texts. Consequently, the above evidence is conclusive: the *Odes* are not influenced by the deanthropomorphic tendencies of the Targumim. A Meturgeman would

181. The texts do not arrange these sayings under the caption 'Christ Speaks'. Rather this heading comes from the interpretation demanded by the context, and should be placed within parentheses.

have been displeased, as most of us are, by the idea that God has 'breasts'.

Before we conclude this discussion of the possible Targumic features in the *Odes* a further possible dependence must be examined. Another characteristic feature of the Targumim is the frequent circumlocutions of the divine names, such as 'Lord' being repeatedly translated 'the word of the Lord'. For example, the beginning of Psalm 31 is altered from 'In you, O Lord', בך יהוה, to 'In your word, O Lord', במימרך יהוה. Moreover, Ps. 31.23 'before your eyes', מנגד עיניך, is changed to 'opposite your honor', מקביל יקרך. In the *Odes* we find similar circumlocutions. The Odist does not write that 'the Lord will go before you'; he periphrastically writes: 'And his glory shall go before you' (*Ode* 20.9). A good example of this tendency is the Odist's belief that the Lord's action must be circumlocutory: 'The Lord has directed my mouth by his word: / And he has opened my heart by his light' (*Ode* 10.1). However, it appears that this coincidence of theological expression is not caused by the Odist's literary dependence on the Targumim: it most likely originates in the milieu that the two shared.

The conclusion to this examination is twofold. First, there is no convincing evidence that the *Odes of Solomon* are literarily dependent on or influenced by the Targumim.[182] Second, the Syriac hypothesis is only partly strengthened by a comparison with the Targumim.

182. This conclusion should not be construed to mean the New Testament was not influenced by the Targumim, for such seems to be likely. Elsewhere Harris argued that the New Testament was influenced by the Targumim; however, his criterion for such borrowing was the presence of a deanthropomorphized quotation from the Old Testament (see J.R. Harris, 'Traces of Targumism in the New Testament', *ExpT* 32 [1920–21], pp. 373-76). This criterion is too weak to support the conclusions Harris defended; the Targumim had no monopoly on deanthropomorphisms. Any student of Second Temple Judaism knows that deanthropomorphic theological emphases developed in postexilic times, as evidenced by Gen. 1.1-24. Moreover, the LXX also occasionally avoided anthropomorphisms, e.g. in Exod. 16.3 ביד יהוה ('by the hand of the Lord') is translated ὑπὸ κυρίου ('by the Lord'). Consequently, deanthropomorphisms are not unique to the Targumim. Therefore, the dependence of the New Testament on the Targumim cannot be proved through deanthropomorphic similarities alone. Perhaps the only valid criterion for a New Testament passage's dependence on the Targumim is a direct biblical quotation that contains a variant or idiosyncrasy that is shared with the Targum but with no other version. Using this criterion, H. Kosmala has presented a convincing argument that Mt. 26.52 is dependent on the Targum to Isa. 50.11. See his 'Matthew xxvi 52: A Quotation from the Targum', *NovT* 4 (October, 1960),

Arguments from Variants

Many of the variants between the Coptic, Greek, and Syriac are readily and easily traceable to a Syriac *Urtext*. For example, the variant in 5.2 is probably due to a confusion in the Syriac ܡܪܐ (Lord) for the extant ܡܪܝܡܐ ('Most High'). Thereby the Coptic variant, **ⲬⲞⲈⲒⲤ** ('Lord'), is explained. Furthermore, ܡܪܝܡܐ and ܡܪܐ represent a variant between MS H and MS N at 23.4 revealing that Syriac scribes often confused these two nouns. While this confusion is possible in Syriac, it is virtually impossible in Hebrew since אדן ('Lord') and עֶלְיוֹן ('Most High') are readily distinguishable. The probability, therefore, that the original language is Syriac has been greatly increased by an examination of variants.

The variant between the Coptic and Syriac (MS H) in *Ode* 22.6 is readily explained by a Syriac *Urtext*. In Syriac the Coptic variant, 'it surrounded', would be expressed by the triliteral root ܟܪܟ. This root is almost identical with the extant reading of MS H, 'a blessing', which is expressed by the triliteral root ܒܪܟ. Moreover, kaph and beth are readily and frequently confused in Syriac manuscripts. It appears, therefore, that the Coptic scribe was working from a Syriac manuscript that contained ܟܪܟ; and in confirmation of our conjecture, MS N preserves just this reading.

Likewise, in *Ode* 25.8 the variant between the Coptic ('mercy') and Syriac ('spirit') may be explained by a Syriac *Grundschrift* behind the extant Coptic. In Syriac ܪܚܡܬ ('mercy') and ܪܘܚܐ ('spirit') are similar; hence, they can be easily confused.

Similarly the variant in *Ode* 22.9 can only be explained by an assumed Syriac original. The Coptic preserves the singular while the Syriac preserves the plural of the noun 'body'. In the Syriac the distinction between the singular, ܦܓܪܐ, and the plural, ܦܓܪܐ, was not noted in early Estrangela manuscripts, but in Greek (σῶμα, and σώματα), Coptic (**ⲞⲨⲤⲰⲘⲀ** and **ⲤⲈⲚⲤⲰⲘⲀ**) and Hebrew (גְּוִיָּה, and גְּוִיּוֹת) the distinction is easily recognized.

The variant between the Greek and Syriac in 11.5 is easily traced to a

---

pp. 3-5. One should also see T.W. Manson's enlightening comment that the quotation in Mk 4.12 agrees with the Targum of Isa. 6.9-10. T.W. Manson, *The Teaching of Jesus: Studies of its Form and Content* (Cambridge: Cambridge University Press, 1931), pp. 77-80. Finally, see also R. Le Déaut, *Liturgie juive et Nouveau Testament: Le témoignage des versions araméennes* (Scripta Pontificii Instituti Biblici, 115; Rome: Pontifical Biblical Institute, 1965).

Syriac *Grundschrift*. The Greek noun στερέος ('firm', 'solid') appears to be a mistranslation of the extant Syriac, ܪܬܝܫ, since the Syriac noun means both 'firm' or 'solid' and 'truth'. Furthermore, it is important to note that Carmignac's Hebrew translation, אמונה, cannot claim this double meaning. The Syriac (or Aramaic) original becomes more probable.

In *Ode* 11.20 the variant in the Greek, 'kindness', can clearly be traced to the extant Syriac noun ܒܣܝܡܘܬܐ. The Syriac noun means not only 'pleasantness', but also 'kindness' and 'gentleness'. Consequently, we discover that the Greek translator chose one of the meanings of the Syriac noun, but one which does not conveniently fit into the context. Again it is enlightening to note that Carmignac's Hebrew translation, נועם, does not have the polyvalent menings of the Syriac; it can mean only 'delightfulness' or 'pleasantness'. The variant cannot arise from a Hebrew *Grundschrift*, but it can easily originate with a Syriac (or Aramaic) manuscript.

On the basis of these observations alone it becomes extremely probable that the original language is Syriac (or Aramaic).

Intrinsic Qualities
The most convincing argument for the Syriac-Aramaic hypothesis is the intrinsic qualities of the *Odes* in Syriac. Not only are Hebraisms and Grecisms relatively rare, but the Syriac flows evenly and rhythmically, and conveys such a spirit of fresh spontaneity that it is difficult to avoid the *Sprachgefühl*. The following discussion of the intrinsic qualities of the Syriac is divided into four categories: (1) paronomasia, (2) assonance, (3) word-play and (4) rhythm and parallelism.

1.   The *Odes* are permeated by Semitic paronomasiae. For example in *Ode* 20.1-2 we find paronomasiae on ܟܗܢ and ܩܪܒ:

> I am a priest of the Lord,
> And to him I do priestly service;
> And to him I offer the offering of his thought.

Two other examples of paronomasia are *Ode* 28.4a: 'Blessing, he has blessed me', and *Ode* 36.4:

> For I was most glorified among the glorified ones;
> And I was greatest among the great ones.

This paronomasia is typical of Semitic poetry, appearing before the

Odes in the *Hymn to the Creator* (11QPsᵃ 26.9), 'the holiest of the Holy Ones' (קדוש קדושים) and after the *Odes* in *Ma'aseh Merkavah* (Par 548 11 [In MS M22 only], 'Magnificent over all the Magnificent Ones').[183] These two examples obviously refer to God.

Finally, perhaps the most striking example of paronomasia in the *Odes* is the fivefold paronomasiae in *Ode* 38.9:

> And I continually saw the corruptor (ܡܚܒܠܢܘܬܐ) of
> corruption (ܚܒܠܐ)
> When the bride who was being corrupted (ܕܡܬܚܒܠܐ)
> was adorned,
> And also the bridegroom who was both corrupting (ܡܚܒܠ)
> and being corrupted (ܘܡܬܚܒܠ).

These excerpts are but examples, for almost every ode abounds with Semitic paronomasia.

2.   The *Odes* exhibit numerous cases of assonance. For example, in *Ode* 34.1a ('There is no hard way where there is a simple heart') one finds an appealing assonance between *q^eŝîthâ* and *p^eŝîṭâ'*: ܐܝܬ ܐܘܪܚܐ ܟܕ ܩܫܝܬܐ ܐܝܟܐ ܕܠܒܐ ܦܫܝܛܐ (using transliterations that bring out phonetics). Especially pleasing is the difference between between *q^eŝîthâ* and *p^eŝîṭâ'* since in the first adjective the emphatic consonant comes at the end of the word, thereby closing both the syllable and the line by its force. Another excellent example of assonance in the *Odes* is found in *Ode* 35.4b, 5.[184] In these two verses we are confronted with assonance caused by a clever word-play on four roots: *ṭalēl* ('to shade'), *ṭ^elē* ('a child'), *ṭ^e'ēn* ('to carry') and *ṭal* ('dew'). This clever use of Syriac may be attributed to an ingenious Syriac translator, but it is most likely evidence of a poet who composed the poem in Syriac. The passage is translated:

> More than shadow (ܛܠܠ) was he to me, and more than support.
> And I was carried (ܡܛܥܢ ܗܘܝܬ) as a child (ܛܠܝܐ) by its mother;
> And he gave me milk, the dew (ܛܠܗ ܕܡܪܝܐ) of the Lord.

3.   This last examination leads us into the frequent play on words by the Odist. An ingenious play on the root *ḥyā'* is found in *Ode* 19.9:

183. See M.D. Swartz, *Mystical Prayer in Ancient Judaism: An Analysis of Ma'aseh Merkavah* (Texte und Studien zum Antiken Judentum, 28; Tübingen: J.C.B. Mohr [Paul Siebeck], 1992), p. 228.

184. Harris and Mingana, *The Odes and Psalms of Solomon*, pp. 380-81.

'And he did not need a midwife (*ḥaitâ'*) because he caused her to give life (*deʿaḥyāh*).' This play on words is possible only in Syriac (or Aramaic). In Hebrew, for example, 'midwife' would probably be the piel feminine participle of ילד: מְיַלֶּדֶת, but the verb would be from the root *ḥāyāh*. The weight that this coincidence in the extant Syriac manuscripts gives to the probability that the original language is Syriac (or Aramaic) led A. Mingana to state: 'Cette coincidence est capitale et péremptoire, car le mot *sage-femme* ne signifie vivificatrice, et ne provient du verbe ܐܚܝ qu'en syriaque. Cette seule phrase donc suffirait peut-être à trancher la question.'[185]

Another example of the recurring word-play in the *Odes* is found in *Ode* 25.8b, 9a: 'And I removed (*weʿarīmēth*) from me the raiment of skins; / For your right hand lifted me up (*ʿarīmtani*).' This careful construction looks like the work of the Odist, and not the clever skill of a translator.

4.   The final intrinsic quality of the language of the *Odes of Solomon* that indicates that the original language is Syriac (or Aramaic) is the rhythm and parallelism in the extant Syriac. For example, *Ode* 24.1-4 is composed in *parallelismus membrorum*:

The dove	flew	over the Messiah[186]
Because the head	he was	to (for) her;
And she sang	over him,	
And her voice	was heard.	
And the dwellers	were afraid,	
And the foreigners	were troubled.	
The bird	let loose	her wings[187]
And all creeping things	died	in their holes.

The parallelisms seem to be respectively synthetic, synthetic, synonymous, and synthetic.

In *Ode* 26.11 there is paronomasia, parallelism, rhythm, and asso-

185. A. Mingana, 'Quelques mots sur les Odes de Salomon. I', p. 239.

186. MS N preserves the following variant: 'The dove flew over the head of our Lord the Messiah.' It seems that this fuller reading is not original but is an addition by a later Christian who wanted to harmonize this passage with Mt. 3.16, Mk 1.10, Lk. 3.22 and Jn 1.32. This conjecture explains why it is not found in MS H and accounts for the disruption of the three-beat rhythm.

187. Both Harris and Mingana, *The Odes and Psalms of Solomon, ad loc.*, and M. Mar Yosip translated this line as follows: 'The birds took to flight.' This translation is incorrect because the noun, verb and pronominal suffix are *all* singular.

nance. This verse is also constructed according to *parallelismus mem-brorum*:

Who is able	to interpret	the wonders of the Lord?
Though	he who interprets	would be destroyed,[188]
Yet	that which was interpreted	will remain.

Again we find parallelism arranged in a three-beat rhythm. Furthermore, there is not only paronomasia on the root *targem*, but resonant assonance which sews the threads of the verse together: *dantargem, damtargem, d^emethtargam*.

The above selections from the *Odes* are not isolated examples. They are representative portions of the poetic strain that runs through the *Odes*. The data have been critically examined: the original language is probably Syriac (Syriac-Aramaic).

Aliae animadversiones

Three other observations reinforce this judgment. MS N was discovered in Egypt. Since the lingua franca of Egypt in the first few centuries of the Christian era was Greek, is it not more likely that an original Syriac composition would have been preferred to a 'translation Syriac', of a 'Greek original'? Second, both Syriac manuscripts are superior to either the extant Greek or the Coptic. Is it not improbable, consequently, that a 'translation' would be less corrupt than an extant portion in the 'original' language? Third, we have noticed how similar are the two Syriac manuscripts. Is it not more probable that they are so similar because they are copies in the original language than it is to suppose that two independent translations would have repeatedly chosen the same expressions, roots, and conjugations?

One final comment. If the Christian quality and early date of the *Odes* could be demonstrated, as I am convinced it can, then it is obvious that the Palestinian-Aramaic-speaking Church would have composed their hymnbook in their own language. Hence, the Syraic-Aramaic hypothesis is the most probable one.

---

188. This verb has been incorrectly pointed. Harris and Mingana in 1920 pointed it with the vowels of the ethpeel which means 'would be dissolved'. The correct vocalization is that of the ethpaal: *neštara*, which means 'would be destroyed'. (My edition of the *Odes of Solomon* needs to be corrected at this point also.)

Conclusion

In this chapter the question regarding the language of the autograph has been systematically and critically examined. It soon became apparent that the Greek hypothesis is no longer tenable. Moreover, while the Semitic quality of the *Odes* became increasingly manifest, the Hebrew hypothesis, in contrast to the Syriac-Aramaic, slowly waned in probability. Numerous phenomena strengthened the probability of a Syriac (or Aramaic) original, of which the most noteworthy are the following three observations: the Odist and the Meturgeman shared the same milieu; many textual variants can be directly traced to confusion originating only in or with a Syriac-Aramaic manuscript; and the intrinsic qualities of the extant Syriac *Odes* witness to original, spontaneous expressions (*afflatus*) and to carefully crafted expressions. Furthermore, there are data regarding the dialect of this document which have heretofore been completely overlooked. In *Ode* 17.13 we find the following line:

ܘܩܢܝܬܗ، ܣܘܡܐ ܕ.ܠ

Harris and Mingana's dubiety concerning the meaning of this line is reflected in their equivocal translation of the verse: 'And I imparted my knowledge without grudging; / And their request to me with my love.' It is important to note that they appended the following note: 'The sense is very doubtful.'[189] The translations presented by M. Mar Yosip,[190] J.H. Bernard,[191] and W. Bauer[192] are also ambiguous.

C.C. Torrey, however, speculated that ܣܘܡܐ was employed by the Aramaic-speaking Christians for '*their* great "triumph", the resurrection of Jesus, and for the day which commemorated it; then also for "the resurrection" in general'.[193] When this meaning is applied to the verse the following translation appears: 'And I imparted my knowledge without grudging, / And my resurrection through my love.' This translation is not only lucid but beautifully parallels v. 10: 'And nothing appeared closed to me, / Because I was the door of everything.'

189. Harris and Mingana, *The Odes and Psalms of Solomon*, p. 291.

190. Mar Yosip, *The Oldest Christian Hymn-Book*, p. 62.

191. Bernard, *The Odes of Solomon*, p. 85.

192. Bauer, *Die Oden Salomos*, p. 37.

193. C.C. Torrey, *Documents of the Primitive Church* (New York: Harper & Brothers, 1941), p. 261.

Moreover, the ones to whom Christ offers his resurrection (in this context) are those who are bound in Hell as v. 11 denotes: 'And I went towards all of them who were barred[194] in order to free them'

The important observation to be made here is that ܪܕ܈ܐ meant 'resurrection' only in Palestinian Syriac-Aramaic.[195] Moreover, there is another intrinsic quality that causes one to believe that the *Odes* were originally written in Palestinian Syriac-Aramaic. In *Ode* 17, vv. 4c-9a are begun with waw; that is ten consecutive redundant 'ands'. These superfluous 'ands' are characteristic of the *Odes* (e.g. *Ode* 19.3: 'Because His breasts were full, / *And* it was not desirable that his milk should be fruitlessly spilt' [italics mine]).

Torrey also speculated that the superfluous use of 'and' is characteristic of Palestinian Aramaic, preserved only in the earliest Christian scriptures.[196] For example, in the oldest extant Syriac-Aramaic version of the Four Gospels, the Sinaitic Palimpsest (which may have been written around Antioch and reflects the Palestinian dialect),[197] one reads in Lk. 7.12: 'When he drew near to the gate of the city, *and* behold (ܘܗܐ), they were bringing out a dead man' [italics mine]. Furthermore, it is important to note that the younger version of the *Evangelion Da-Mepharreshe*, eponymously called Curetonianus, and the even more recent Peshitta customarily omit these superfluous 'ands'.[198]

These observations, coupled with the above examination (especially the observation that the poetic form is similar to Jesus' words and A. Mingana's contention that the dialect of the *Odes* is Palestinian Syriac)[199] and other observations (viz. the surrogate 'Power' for the

---

194. The same passive participle of the same root is used in the Peshitta of *3 Pet.* 3.19 to render the spirits 'who were shut up in the lower regions'.

195. Torrey, *Documents of the Primitive Church*, p. 261.

196. C.C. Torrey, *Our Translated Gospels* (New York: Harper & Brothers, 1936) pp. 64-73.

197. A.S. Lewis (ed.), *The Old Syriac Gospels or Evangelion Da-Mapharreshê* (London: Williams & Norgate, 1910), p. xiii. Torrey, *Our Translated Gospels*, pp. 64-65.

198. F.C. Burkitt (ed.), *Evangelion Da-Mepharreshe* (2 vols.; Cambridge: Cambridge University Press, 1904). See Torrey's discussion in his *Our Translated Gospels*, pp. 70-71.

199. From an unexpected source our conjecture has been strengthened. R. Bultmann claimed that the style of the Johannine 'Revelation-discourses' is that of 'Semitic poetry such as is known to us from the Odes of Solomon...' (*Theology of*

divine name may be a North Palestinian idiom) prompt one to specu-
late that the original language may be either Christian Palestinian
Aramaic,[200] to use the nomenclature of F. Schulthess,[201] or Syriac-
Aramaic. Furthermore, it is possible that the *Odes* were originally com-
posed in the Aramaic square characters that antedate the so-called
Syriac script. It is even conceivable that the original language was
Palestinian Jewish Aramaic,[202] similar to that of the recently discovered
Genesis Apocryphon. For convenience, however, we shall subsequently
refer to the original language of the *Odes* as an early form of Syriac.

APPENDIX

This previously unpublished chapter was completed in 1967 as part of a PhD
dissertation defended in September 1967 at Duke University. The conclusion that
the *Odes of Solomon* were originally composed in an early form of Syriac was also
defended by J.A. Emerton in 'Some Problems of Text and Language'. E. Azar is
convinced that the Odist composed his masterpiece in Syriac; see Azar, *Les Odes de
Salomon* (Sagesses Chrétiennes; Paris: Cerf, 1996), p. 50. V. Tsakonas concludes
that the *Odes* were composed συριαστί. See V.G. Tsakonas, Αι Ωδαι Σολομωντος
(Athens, 1974), p. 11. A. Peral and X. Alegre also lean towards a Syriac original; see
their 'Odas de Salomon', in A. Diez Macho, *et al.* (eds.), *Apocrifos del Antiguo
Testamento* (Madrid: Ediciones Cristiandad, 1982), III, p. 62. Obviously, 30 years
later I would write this chapter quite differently, stressing, *inter alia*, that the form
of Syriac was very early when Aramaic was shaping it (as witnessed, for example, in
the so-called Old Syriac inscriptions, which are quasi-Aramaic).

B.D. Fanourgakis is convinced that the original language of the *Odes* is Greek.
See his important ΑΙ ΩΔΑΙ ΣΟΛΟΜΩΝΤΟΣ (Analekta Vlatadon, 29; Thessalonika:
Patriarchal Institute for Patristic Studies, 1979), p. 137, ῾Η ἀρχικὴ γλῶσσα τῶν
᾽Ωδῶν Σολομῶντος ἦτο ἡ ἑλληνική.' He also admits that this is his personal opin-
ion and that the issue remains undecided. M. Lattke also judges that the question of
the original language of the *Odes of Solomon* remains still unanswered. Of course,

the *New Testament* [trans. K. Grobel; New York: Charles Scribner's Sons, 1955], II,
p. 10). See also Bultmann, *The Gospel of John*, pp. 14-15, 29-31.

200. One should not be confused by a semantic problem; generally speaking the
only major distinguishable characteristic between the square Aramaic script and the
various Syriac scripts.

201. F. Schulthess, *Grammatik des christlich-palästinischen Aramäisch* (Tübingen:
J.C.B. Mohr, 1924). The form of the alphabet used by Schulthess is the Jacobite
script. Both MS H and MS N were written in this script.

202. As described by W.B. Stevenson, *Grammar of Palestinian Jewish Aramaic*
(Oxford: Clarendon Press, 2nd edn, 1962).

Lattke and Fanourgakis have not seen the previous research. See Lattke, *Odes Salomos* (Fontes Christiani 19; Freiburg: Herder, 1995), pp. 16-18.

This whole area of research needs to be continued, especially in light of possible Essene influences on the Odist and the recognition that the Aramaic documents found in the 11 Qumran caves most likely come from Essenes or Essene-like Jews who lived in Palestine but in the non-Qumran Essene camps.

Part II

TEXTUAL STUDIES

Chapter 5

ܒܥܘܬܐ IN EARLIEST CHRISTIANITY

Almost 30 years ago Professor W.F. Stinespring's mentor, C.C. Torrey, speculated on the meaning of בעותא among the earliest Aramaic-speaking Christians. His conjecture has been subsequently ignored both by Semitists and historians. Recent discoveries of Aramaic manuscripts and contemporary research on related subjects show that a reassessment of Torrey's speculation is opportune.

In the present essay we shall discuss the following: the definition of בעותא customarily held by Semitists today; Torrey's position; the meaning of this noun in an apocryphal Syriac psalm; the use of ܒܥܘܬܐ[1] in the Sinaitic Palimpsest; the derivation of the Arabic word bâ'ûth; and finally the probable meaning of ܒܥܘܬܐ in the earliest Christian hymnbook, the so-called *Odes of Solomon*.

The denotation of בעותא that is usually given is 'petition', and this meaning is said to derive etymologically from the familiar verb בעא ('to ask', 'to pray'). There is no question that this definition is supported by the expression in Dan. 6.14 [13]: בעא בעותא 'petitioning his petition'. The meaning 'petition' for בעותא, however, does not apply in some later texts, viz. the Sinaitic Palimpsest and the *Odes of Solomon*, as we shall see.

Professor Torrey's speculation regarding the meaning of this noun was that בעותא also meant 'resurrection', but that this meaning was peculiar to the earliest Aramaic-speaking Christians.[2] He obtained this meaning from the use of ܒܥܘܬܐ in the Sinaitic Palimpsest, a variant reading found also in Aphraates, and from an etymological examination of the Arabic word bâ'ûth. In the following pages we shall attempt

---

1. In this improved version the Syriac is no longer in square characters.

2. *Documents of the Primitive Church* (New York: Harper & Brothers, 1941), pp. 257-62.

to revive Torrey's inference. At the outset it is important to observe that he did not challenge the meaning of this noun in Jewish circles.

While בעותא is not found in the *Genesis Apocryphon*, it is present in the five apocryphal Syriac psalms[3] described by M. Delcor as 'Cinq Psaumes Syriaques Esséniens'.[4] We are in agreement with Delcor's judgment 'que ces cinq psaumes trouvent leur explication normale sinon dans le milieu essénien proprement dit, du moins dans un milieu essénisant'.[5]

Our attention is drawn to the third psalm, the fifth line of which is as follows:

ܒܥܘܬܝ ܠܐ ܬܟܠܐ ܡܢܝ

My ܒܥܘܬܐ do not withhold from me.

What is the denotation of ܒܥܘܬܐ in this line? The answer is clarified by the corresponding word in the first line of the synonymous parallelism: ܫܐܠܬܝ ('my request').[6] The meaning of this stich, therefore, is as follows:

And give me my request,
My petition withhold not from me.

Consequently, as in Dan. 6.14 [13] so in this Jewish, Syriac Psalm, ܒܥܘܬܐ signifies 'petition'. The denotation is precisely the one Torrey would expect since the Psalm is not Christian. For example, see line 11, ܒܥܘܬܗܘܢ, and lines 37-38:

3. These psalms have been known to Western scholars since Assemani's publication in 1759 (*Bibliothecae Apostolicae Vaticanae Codicum Manuscriptorum Catalogus* [1759], I, §3, pp. 385-86). For a succinct bibliographical statement regarding the extant manuscripts of these psalms, see Delcor, *Les Hymnes de Qumran*, p. 299. For a translation of these psalms see Charlesworth with J.A. Sanders, 'More Psalms of David', *OTP*, II, pp. 609-24.

4. Delcor, *Les Hymnes de Qumran*, p. 299.

5. '...that these five psalms find their natural explanation, if not within an Essene milieu properly speaking, at least within an Essene-like environment.' Delcor, *Les Hymnes de Qumran*, pp. 299-300. An important parallel between these hymns and Qumran ideology is the emphasis that praise is more important than cultic sacrifices (Ps. 2, lines 17-21). Also of importance is the meaning of the communal meal (Ps. 2, lines 24-25) and the intermittent use of words that have an Essene connotation (see Delcor, *Les Hymnes de Qumran*, p. 303).

6. M. Noth brought out this meaning through his translation of the line into Hebrew: תְּחִנָּתִי ('my supplication for favor'). See Noth's important study 'Die fünfsyrisch überlieferten apokryphen Psalmen', *ZAW* 47 (1930), pp. 1-23.

ܦܪܘܩܘ ܠܫܝܘܠ ܟܦܢܝ
ܘܠܒܥܘܬܐ ܢܚܘܒ ܒܣܝܪܝ

When we turn to the early Christian, Syriac literature, we discover that another meaning is given to this noun.

In the earliest Syriac recension of the gospels, the Sinaitic Palimpsest (Syr[s]), we find the following unusual uses of ܒܥܘܬܐ (juxtaposed with the parallel passages in the Greek and the Peshiṭta):

Luke 2.25

προσδεχόμενος παράκλησιν τοῦ Ἰσραήλ,	GK
ܘܡܣܟܠ ܗܘܐ ܒܥܘܬܐ ܕܐܝܣܪܝܠ	Syr[s]
ܘܡܣܟܐ ܗܘܐ ܠܒܘܝܐܗ ܕܐܝܣܪܝܠ	Peshiṭta
waiting for the consolation of Israel,	NRSV

Luke 6.24

Πλὴν οὐαὶ ὑμῖν τοῖς πλουσίοις, ὅτι ἀπέχετε τὴν παράκλησιν ὑμῶν.	GK
ܒܪܡ ܘܝ ܠܟܘܢ ܥܬܝܪܐ ܕܩܒܠܬܘܢ ܒܥܘܬܟܘܢ	Syr[s]
ܒܪܡ ܘܝ ܠܟܘܢ ܥܬܝܪܐ ܕܩܒܠܬܘܢ ܒܘܝܐܟܘܢ	Peshiṭta
But woe to you who are rich, for you have (already) received your comfort.	NRSV

It is important to note that the Peshiṭta follows the Greek and that the Sinaitic Palimpsest alone attests to this use of ܒܥܘܬܐ (the Curetonian version has neither passage).

In attempting to understand the meaning of this noun, it is first necessary to note that in the Sinaitic Palimpsest it translates (or corresponds to) παράκλησις, which means 'summons, imploring, invocation, request, exhortation, consolation' (Liddell–Scott–Jones–McKenzie). In the New Testament it is conceptually linked with παράκλητος, 'the helper, intercessor'. The latter Greek noun is used only by John (four times); the former is peculiar to Luke (twice in the Gospel, four times in Acts) and Paul (twenty times).[7] The two passages cited above, consequently, are the only ones in the gospels in which we find the noun παράκλησις. In both passages it means 'consolation'. The translator of the Sinaitic Palimpsest would have rendered παράκλησις, if this noun was in his *Vorlage* and all the evidence leads to that presupposition, with a Syriac noun of similar meaning. Hence בעותא

7. R. Morgenthaler, *Statistik des neutestamentlichen Wortschatzes* (Zürich: Gotthelf Verlag, 1958).

in early western, Christian Aramaic[8] probably obtained the meaning 'consolation'.

It should be observed that the Greek noun means both 'petition' and 'consolation'. In Jewish Aramaic and Edessene Syriac ‎ܦܪܩܠܛܐ means only 'petition'. Of the numerous Aramaic and Syriac lexicons only those by R. Köbert[9] and C. Brockelmann[10] record the meaning *solatium* for ‎ܦܪܩܠܛܐ. Brockelmann alone cites textual evidence; he lists the two passages in the Sinaitic Palimpsest given above.

What is the relationship between παράκλησις in the Greek New Testament and ‎ܦܪܩܠܛܐ in the Sinaitic Palimpsest? There are three reasonable possibilities. The first is that the Syriac translator chose ‎ܦܪܩܠܛܐ because it corresponded to one meaning of the Greek word, viz. 'petition'. This possibility is highly unlikely. It would demand the unfounded presupposition that the translator of the Sinaitic Palimpsest was unskillful. The second possibility is that ‎ܦܪܩܠܛܐ obtained a new meaning from παράκλησις, viz. 'consolation'. This possibility seems unlikely because there were Aramaic and Syriac words that meant 'consolation,' for example, נֶחָמָה (a Hebrew loan-word, it is frequently

---

8.   C.C. Torrey was convinced that the Sinaitic Palimpsest was written 'at or near Antioch, early in the second century' (*Documents of the Primitive Church*, p. 275). See also A.S. Lewis's comments in *The Old Syriac Gospels* or *Evangelion da-Mepharreshê* (London: Williams & Norgate, 1910), pp. v, xiii. P.E. Kahle 'fully' agreed with Torrey's conclusions regarding the date of the Old Syriac Gospels (OSG) but changed 'in the region of Antioch' to 'in Adiabene' (*The Cairo Geniza* [Oxford: Basil Blackwell, 2nd edn, 1959], pp. 287-88). Cf. A. Vööbus, *Studies in the History of the Gospel Text in Syriac* (Louvain: Imprimerie Orientaliste, 1951), pp. 26ff. Kahle rightly sees the weaknesses in Torrey's comment about Antioch, but his own conjecture about Adiabene is burdened with more difficulties. M. Black's discussion of the sources and antiquity of the OSG raises the possibility that a Palestinian Aramaic Gospel or gospel tradition influenced the OSG; for example, the Sinaitic Syriac alone retains in Jn 10.12 a paronomasia characteristic of Jesus (*sakhir shaqqar*). While Black stated that Torrey's conclusion goes beyond the evidence, he nonetheless amasses data to support the suggestion that the OSG were directly influenced by Palestinian Aramaic. We are in total agreement with his comment that 'it is certainly difficult to believe...that in bilingual Antioch the Gospels were not translated in Syriac early in the second century' (*An Aramaic Approach*, pp. 262-70).

9.   R. Köbert, *Vocabularium Syriacum* (Rome: Pontificium Institutum Biblicum, 1956), p. 23.

10.   C. Brockelmann, *Lexicon Syriacum* (Berlin: Reuther & Reichard, 1895; Göttingen: Niemeyer, 1928), p. 83.

used as a verb in the *Thanksgiving Hymns*; e.g. 5.3; 6.7; 9.13 [*bis*]; 11.32; 16.17) and בּוּיָאא (not found in the *Genesis Apocryphon* but used in the Peshiṭta at Lk. 2.25 and 6.24).[11] The third possibility is that ܒܥܘܬܐ in the Sinaitic Palimpsest goes behind the Greek to the self-same word in Palestinian Aramaic.

This suggestion would demand that בעותא in Palestinian Aramaic during the first Christian century meant both 'petition' and 'consolation'. The possibility seems conjectural, but the following discussion tends to confirm it. For the moment, suffice it to state that new ideologies usually coin new words and infuse old words with new meanings. Certainly the earliest Christians used old words in new ways. Unfortunately, we cannot presently prove the third possibility since the earliest Christian Aramaic documents have not been preserved. However, the meaning of the noun בעותא in the extant manuscripts from earliest Aramaic-(Syriac-)speaking Christianity, the Sinaitic Palimpsest and the *Odes of Solomon*, does reinforce the third possibility, as we shall soon see.

Professor Torrey argued that among the earliest Aramaic-speaking Christians בעותא acquired the meaning 'resurrection'. The distance from 'petition' to 'resurrection' is extreme; the separation from 'consolation' to 'resurrection' is much less, but the two nouns are not exactly synonymous. They are not far from being synonyms, however, when one realizes that the 'consolation' Simeon was looking for was certainly the 'salvation' of Israel. 'Salvation' and 'resurrection' were metonyms for the early Christians, as Professor Torrey clearly demonstrated (p. 259; see also Jn 11.25 in the Sinaitic Palimpsest). Likewise, if one could push aside the veil of history, *et hoc genus omne*, that separates us from the earliest Palestinian Christians, and ask them what was their consolation, or what was their salvation, the answer would probably be the same, viz. the resurrection of the Messiah. The deduction is that for them בעותא denoted 'consolation' and connoted 'resurrection'. The following two observations, one concerning an Arabic word and the other about the use of ܒܥܘܬܐ in the *Odes of Solomon*, certainly go a long way to substantiate this inference.

As we turn to Arabic for possible elucidation on this point, we note that two scholars besides Professor Torrey have argued that *bâ'ûth* is a

---

11. It is highly unlikely that ܒܥܘܬܐ is a corruption of בּוּיָאא. The second and fourth consonants in each word are too dissimilar. Likewise, it is improbable that the supposed error would be repeated precisely the same way four chapters later.

Syriac loan-word. Both scholars note that the meaning of the Arabic word is connected with Easter. The first, S. Fraenkel, could not etymologically diagnose the origin of this meaning in Arabic, 'Wieso aber gerade das Osterfest speciell das "Gebet" genannt wurde, weiss ich nicht zu sagen.'[12] The second, Adrien Barthélemy, reported that the Arabic word meant 'prières du lundi de Pâques', and that it derives etymologically from the Syriac ܒܥܘܬܐ, which comes from the root ܒܥܐ, 'to demand, to pray'.[13] The problem with Barthélemy's explanation, however, is that *bâ'ûth* does have the meaning he suggests, but primarily means 'Easter', and it is difficult to see how that meaning came from the verb 'to demand'.

The attempt to explain the Arabic noun on the basis of the Arabic verb *ba'atha* ('to revive'—a dead person) has been suggested,[14] but to represent the noun *Easter* requires the additional word *yôm*, which means in Arabic 'the day of resurrection'. There is no need to show that this latter derivation is different from the Syriac loan-word which by itself means 'Easter'. Suffice it to say that *B'Th* in Arabic means 'to revive', but the self-same root in Syriac means 'to be formidable'.

Perhaps some light will be shed on a solution if we follow Torrey's lead and turn to a previously unmentioned Aramaic root, namely בוע, which means 'to swell, burst forth, rejoice'. The derivative בועתא means 'rejoicing'. It is easy to see how *Easter* could have derived from *rejoicing*, but the waw is in the wrong place. The Targum to Ps. 43.4, however, has the waw after the 'ayin: בעותי, as does the Targum to Ps. 42.5: בעותא. It is possible that the first Aramaic-speaking Palestinian Jewish-Christian circles used this noun to signify their Easter, the time of rejoicing, because of the resurrection of their Lord. It is clear why בעותא did not have this meaning for later Syriac-speaking Christians: בוע as a verb with this meaning is found neither in biblical Aramaic nor Edessene Syriac.[15] Moreover, it seems relatively certain that the

12. 'But exactly why Easter in particular would be called "Prayer", I really cannot say.' *Die aramäischen Fremdwörter im Arabischen* (Leiden: E.J. Brill, 1886), p. 277.

13. *Dictionnaire arabe–français* (Paris: Librairie Orientaliste Paul Geuthner, 1935), p. 51.

14. R. Blachtère, M. Chouémi and C. Denizeau (eds.), *Dictionnaire arabe–français–anglais* (Paris: G.-P. Maisonneuve et Larose, 1967–), pp. 697-99.

15. In Syriac another verb has the same radicals (ܒܘܥ), but is found only in participial forms: ܒܘܥܐ. R. Payne Smith reported that the verb signifies *cessavit, tempus trivit* (*Thesaurus Syriacus*, I, *ad loc*).

peculiarly western portions of the Old Syriac Gospels were edited out by Edessene Christians. The evidence, therefore, clearly points in one direction. The Arabic word *bâ'ûth*, which means Easter, is a Syriac loan-word that (a) goes back to the Syriac noun ܒܘܬܐ; (b) comes from the root ܒܘܣ; (c) means 'rejoicing'; and (d) was probably associated with the Resurrection.

In the preceding pages we have intermittently suggested that the meanings 'consolation' and 'resurrection' were obtained by בעותא only in earliest Christian Aramaic. We now turn to the *Odes of Solomon*, which was probably composed in an early form of Syriac (Aramaic) around 100 CE in or near Antioch,[16] in order to discover if either of these meanings is supported by it.

In *Ode* 17.13b we find the following difficult line:

ܘܒܥܘܬܝ ܒܚܘܒܐ ܕܝܠܝ

The translations of this line are equivocal and ambiguous. In his final edition of the *Odes*, J.R. Harris was forced to append the following note: 'The sense is very doubtful.'[17] The confusion is caused by ܒܥܘܬܐ. Applying the meaning found in most lexicons, we obtain the following translation of v. 13:

> And I offered my knowledge generously,
> And my petition through my love.

Obviously something is wrong. Harris's final attempt at a solution was to amend the text to read, 'And their request to me with my love.' This conjecture is unacceptable for three reasons. First, the manuscripts agree at this point so an emendation is purely subjective. Second, the conjecture destroys the synonymous parallelism since 'my knowledge' is not parallel with 'their request'. Finally, it is not easy to understand the meaning of 'I offered...their request.'

---

16. See J.H. Charlesworth, *The Odes of Solomon* (Oxford: Clarendon Press, 1973) (reprinted as *The Odes of Solomon: The Syriac Texts* [Missoula, MT: Scholars Press, 1978]). See Chapter 4 of this book for the original language of the *Odes*.

17. Harris and Mingana, *The Odes and Psalms of Solomon*, II, p. 291. In 1911 Harris had translated the verse as follows: 'and I imparted my knowledge without grudging: and my prayer was in my love' (*The Odes and Psalms of Solomon*, p. 114). In 1912 J.H. Bernard presented the same translation (*The Odes of Solomon*, p. 82). Both of these early translations were relegated by the later recognition that the *Odes* are composed in verse. Verse 12 is constructed according to *parallelismus membrorum*.

While the meaning 'petition' does not fit into the context of this verse, the meaning 'consolation' fulfills the requirements. It restores the parallelistic construction, and makes the verse coherent and lucid. The verse so translated would read as follows:

> And I offered my knowledge generously,
> And my consolation through my love,

What is the precise meaning of 'consolation' in this passage? Let us now turn to the Ode with this question in mind.

The evidence points toward the assumption that consolation in this verse means 'resurrection'. First, we should note that the particular context favors it. Since the Odist frequently emphasizes that eternal life is the result or reward of belief in Christ, it is only natural that he would have written that Christ offered his knowledge and his resurrection (the passage is written *ex ore Christi*). Note that the first person, singular suffix shows that the 'consolation' is not some abstract idea but a personal offering. No emendation is needed, and the synonymous parallelism is palpable.

Second, it is important to observe that the general context adds great weight to the deduction that ⲣⲇⲁⲟ in *Ode* 17.13 means 'resurrection'. Prior to v. 13 the Odist is probably developing the subtle meanings of the resurrection of Christ. In v. 11 he claims that Christ is 'the opening of everything' and in v. 12 he states the result of his resurrection. These verses are as follows:

> And nothing appeared closed to me,
> Because I was the opening of everything.
>
> And I went towards all my bondsmen in order to loose them;
> That I might not leave anyone bound or binding.

The two verses that follow v. 13 speak of 'my fruits' and 'my blessing', both of which are parallel to ⲟⲇⲁⲟⲟ. Since the former two gifts by Christ result in the 'bondsmen' being 'transformed' and 'saved', it is highly likely that ⲟⲇⲁⲟⲟ meant 'and my resurrection'. Moreover, if this passage concerns the *descensus ad inferos* (cf. *Ode* 42.10ff.), then the only consolation that would be effective is the resurrection from the dead.

In summation, we have found that ⲣⲇⲁⲟ in the *Odes of Solomon* has precisely the meaning that Torrey speculated it would have in an early Christian, Aramaic (Syriac) manuscript. Incidentally, we may have found supportive evidence that the provenience of the *Odes* is not in eastern Syria, as most scholars have argued,[18] but somewhere in western Syria or northern Palestine.[19]

In conclusion, ܪܕܐܬ probably denoted 'consolation' and sometimes connoted 'resurrection' among the earliest Aramaic-speaking Christians in Palestine. These meanings alone explain the passages in the Sinaitic Palimpsest, clarify the etymology of the Arabic word *bâ'ûth*, and remove the difficulty in *Odes* 17.

18. The scholars who have defended this thesis, accompanied with the date of their publication, are the following: J. de Zwaan (1937), R.M. Grant (1944), J. Daniélou (1957), A. Vööbus (1958) and G. Quispel (1965). Also included in this list are the scholars who contended that Bardaiṣan may be the author of the *Odes*: W.R. Newbold (1911), M. Sprengling (1911), and F.M. Braun (1957). A full bibliography for their publications is given in Charlesworth, *The Odes of Solomon*, pp. 149-67.

19.   Numerous scholars hold the opinion, expressed *viva voce* to me, that the word 'Syriac' must be used solely for documents written in Edessa. 'Aramaic', on the other hand, should be used to signify western writings. This distinction between early Syriac and Aramaic is no longer tenable. For example, one of the heretofore cherished distinctions between Aramaic and Syriac is that the former uses the preformative yud in the imperfect but the latter uses the preformative nun. This distinction no longer holds. Early Syriac inscriptions have been found containing the preformative yud. The two most important publications on this point are the following: K. Beyer, 'Der reichsaramäische Einschlag in der ältesten syrischen Literatur', *ZDMG* 116 (1966), pp. 242-43; and E. Jenni, 'Die altsyrischen Inschriften', *TZ* 21 (1965), p. 381.

Chapter 6

PARONOMASIA AND ASSONANCE IN THE SYRIAC TEXT
OF THE *ODES OF SOLOMON*

Of all the biblical books, canonical and extra-canonical, one of the most beautifully composed is the earliest Christian hymnbook, pseudony-mously called the *Odes of Solomon*. The Odist was a linguistic and poetic genius. Above all, he was fond of creating paronomasia and assonance. In the following essay, we shall clarify the Odist's mastery of early Syriac poetry and then draw some related conclusions.

At the outset and for clarification, let me express my own opinion regarding the higher critical problems involved.[1] Foremost among these, for the present study, are the following contentions: the original language of the *Odes* is a form of early Syriac (or Aramaic-Syriac). They were composed by one individual who was profoundly influenced on the one hand by Jewish ideas and on the other by specifically Christian traditions. The Odist probably had been a Jew before his conversion to Christianity; and probably composed the *Odes* around 100 CE in or near Antioch.

Since the discovery of a Syriac manuscript of the *Odes* (John Rylands Lib. Cod. Syr. 9) by J.R. Harris in 1909,[2] the *Odes* have evoked volumi-nous scholarly research. At the center of such study have always been linguistic and philological questions. However, the discussions have

---

1. These conclusions are developed in Charlesworth, *The Odes of Solomon*, and in other chapters of the present book. Relevant bibliographical information can be found in the edition just cited. All translations are by the author, unless otherwise mentioned. Versification is according to the translation and text of the edition just noted. No effort has been made in the following essay to illustrate the obvious fact that the *Odes* are structured according to *parallelismus membrorum*. These reflec-tions are dedicated to the memory of W.F. Stinespring, erudite philologue, unusu-ally effective pedagogue, and cherished friend.

2. J.R. Harris, 'An Early Christian Hymn-Book', *The Contemporary Review* 95 (April 1909), pp. 414-28.

almost always been limited to the question of the original language. The linguistic and poetic beauty of the extant Syriac manuscripts[3] has been almost totally ignored.

Paronomasia

The Odist loved to create paronomasia. His plays on words can be divided into three types: repetition, *double entendre*, and *double entente*.

Repetition

Because of the atomistic structure of Semitic languages, viz. the predominance of the triliteral root as an indivisible foundation, there is the ability to make paronomasia by repeating the same root. Though inordinate and redundant to a Western mind, such repetition was orderly and ideal to a Semitic poet. Moreover, two observations support the Semitic feeling for this norm. First, the degree of inflection separates the English translation from the Semitic: that is, in English one change of form alone, usually a minor suffix, distinguishes a noun (e.g. work) from its cognate verb (e.g. worked); but in Semitics the change is usually multiple, involving prefix, suffix, and infix (see the examples from Syriac mentioned below). Hence, repetition is usually blandly artless in English but subtly artful in Semitics. Second, in Semitics this paronomasia has the additional qualities of harmony, assonance, and euphony.

The *Odes* abound with repetition.[4] Sometimes this phenomenon is merely the result of grammatical laws. For example, as in Hebrew, so in

---

3.   In 1912 F.C. Burkitt discovered another Syriac MS of the *Odes*, which had been housed for seventy years in the British Museum (MS Add. 14538). Burkitt, 'A New MS of the Odes of Solomon'.

4.   The two best articles on repetition in biblical Hebrew that I have found are the ones by I. Eitan ('La Répétition de la Racine en Hébreu', *JPOS* 1 [1920–21], pp. 170-86) and J. Muilenburg ('A Study in Hebrew Rhetoric: Repetition and Style', in VTSup 1 [Leiden: E.J. Brill, 1953], pp. 97-111). Taking a grammatical approach, Eitan presents examples of repetition in the Old Testament to express interjection, apostrophes, superlatives, imperatives and contrarieties. He notes that repetition is often employed to add emphasis and continuity. Taking a more literary approach, Muilenburg lucidly demonstrates how repetition focuses the reader's attention upon the poet's controlling perspective, and how this literary device lends continuity to the flow of thought.

Syriac the superlative can be denoted by repeating in the plural the self-same word. Hence, in *Ode* 36.4 we read, 'Because I was the most glorified (*m⁽šabbaḥ*) among the glorious ones (*bamšabb⁽ḥê*), / And the greatest (*w⁽rabh*) among the great ones (*b⁽rawr⁽bhānê*).' Likewise, according to the rules of good Syriac and Hebrew, an action is intensified by placing an infinitive absolute before its cognate participle or finite verb. We find this rule applied in the following passages: 'He never falls but standing (*m⁽qām-ū*) he stands (*qā'em*)' (*Ode* 12.6 [ᴫᴅᴇ ᴀᴏ ᴢᴀᴅᴚ ᴋᴧᴋ']). 'Blessing (*m⁽bharrākhû*) he has blessed me (*bharr⁽kani*)' (*Ode* 28.4). We should observe that this philological rule is parallel to, but different from, the Odist's choice of phrase in *Ode* 33.2—'And he destroyed (*w⁽'awbedh*) the destruction (*la'bhdānâ*) from before him.'

Usually the repetition found in the *Odes* is the result of the Odist's skill in creating paronomasia. The Odist's use of repetition can be separated into five interrelated groups:

(a) Repetition is frequently applied in order to bring out the dynamic quality of a noun. The most important examples of this usage are the following:

'Sprinkle (*rûs*) upon us your sprinklings (*resîsaik*)' (*Ode* 4.10).

'And lived (*waḥyaw*) by the living (*ḥayyê*) waters of eternity' (*Ode* 6.18). // 'And who grow (*w⁽yā'ein*) in the growth (*b⁽maw'îthâ*) of your trees' (*Ode* 11.19).

'They who work (*de'ābhedhîn*) good works ('⁽bhādhê*)' (*Ode* 11.20).

'And like the flowing (*rādheyâ*) of waters, truth flows (*rādhê*) from my mouth' (*Ode* 12.2).

'And created things in their courses (*b⁽rahṭaihein*) run (*rahⁱṭan*), // And their works (*wa'bhādhaihein*) they work ('ābh⁽dhān*)' (*Ode* 16.13).

Transcription of Syriac words is as follows: Spirantization is denoted by the letter *h*. Long vowels written *plene* are represented by the circumflex accent. Shewa *mobile* is transcribed by the supralinear vowel. My effort in transliterating is to bring out phonetics and draw attention to the pleasing sounds in Syriac. Literalistic English translations are often selected because they represent the Syriac paronomasia better.

'I am a priest (*kāhnâ*) of the Lord, /And to him I serve as a priest (*mᵉkhahen-nâ*); / And to him I offer (*mᵉqarrebh-nâ*) the offering (*qûrbānâ*) of his thought' (*Ode* 20.1-2).[5]

'But the chasms were submerged (*waṭbha'u*) in the submersion of the Lord (*bᵉṭûbhā 'eh dᵉmāryâ*)' (*Ode* 24.7).

'For they travailed (*ḥabbelu*) from the beginning, /And the end of their travail (*dᵉḥûbhālᵉhôn*) was life' (*Ode* 24.8).

'And my heart gushed forth (*waghsâ*) like a gusher (*gᵉsîthâ*) of righteousness' (*Ode* 36.7).

(b) The Odist sometimes juxtaposes a noun with its cognate verb in order to accentuate the source or cause of an action. The two words are often connected by a preposition. Examples of the Odist's use of repetition in order *to emphasize* the source of an action are the following:

Then they spoke the truth,
From the breath (*nᵉphāḥâ*) *breathed* (*danphaḥ*) *into them by the Most High* (*Ode* 18.15).[6]

And I was covered (*wᵉ'ethkassîth*) with the covering (*bᵉthakhsîthâ*)
    of your spirit (*Ode* 25.8),

And caused me to stand on my feet in the Lords' high place,
Before his perfection and his glory (*wᵉtheshbûḥtheh*),
Where I continued glorifying (*mᵉshabbaḥ-nâ*) (him)
    by the composition of his odes (*Ode* 36.2).

Because I was the most glorified among the glorious ones
    (*kadh mᵉshabbaḥ-nâ bamshabbᵉhê*),
And the greatest (*wᵉrabh-nâ*) among the great ones (*bᵉrawrᵉbhānê*).

For according to the greatness (*rabbûtheh*) of the Most High,
    so she made me;
And according to his newness (*ḥûdhātheh*).
    he renewed me (*haddᵉtani*) (*Ode* 36.4-5).

May we also be saved (*nethpᵉreq*) with you,
Because you are our Savior (*pārôqan*) (*Ode* 42.18).

5.   Also note that the palatals, *k* and *g*, unify the verses and create a subtle alliteration.
6.   Note that many of these deliberate paronomasiae are also contiguous in Syriac (but rarely in English): ܒܚܝܢ ܕܦܚ (18.15).

Examples of the Odist's use of repetition in order *to stress the cause or means of an action*—usually love, grace, and trust—are the following 'I am loving[7] the Beloved (*larḥimâ*) and I myself love (*weˀrāḥmâ*) him' (*Ode* 3.5). 'On account of this he was gracious to me (*ḥanani*) in his abundant grace (*baḥnaneh*)' (*Ode* 7.10). 'I trusted (*haimeˀneth*), consequently I was at rest; / Because trustful (*damhaiman-û*) is he in whom I trusted (*deˀhaimeˀneth*)' (*Ode* 28.3). 'And let our faces shine (*weˀnenheˀrān*) by his shining (*beˀnûhreh*)' (*Ode* 41.6). 'Let us exult (*neˀdhûṣ*) with the exultation (*deˀyāṣeh*) of the Lord' (*Ode* 41.7). One should note that the Odist frequently places contiguously the two cognate words.

(c) The Odist liked to play with three different forms of the same root (compare *Ode* 28.3 cited above). For example, note the following: 'And the restraints (*kelyānê*) of men were not able to restrain it (*keˀlāˀûhi*), / Nor even the arts of them who habitually restrain (*deˀkhālein*) water' (*Ode* 6.9). 'The Seers (*ḥazzāyê*)...shall be seen (*weˀnethheˀzôn*)...and he sees (*weˀḥāze'*)' (*Ode* 7.18-19).

(d) The Odist occasionally uses a word in an active sense and then repeats it in a passive sense. Examples of this paronomasia are the following: 'Keep (*ṭaru*) my mystery, you who are kept (*deˀmethnaṭrîn*) by it; / Keep (*ṭaru*) my faith, you who are kept (*deˀmethnaṭrîn*) by it' (*Ode* 8.10). 'And I forsook the folly being cast (*šadhyâ*) upon the earth, / And I stripped it off and cast it (*wašdîthâh*) from me' (*Ode* 11.10). 'And they condemned me (*weˀḥayyeˀbhûni*) when I stood up, / me who had not been condemned (*meˀḥayyeˀbhâ*)' (*Ode* 31.8). This verse seems to be a subtle reference to Jesus' trial, stressing that Jesus 'stood' and was not brought down.

(e) The Odist sporadically applies a verb so that the action is brought to bear upon the noun with which it is cognate. In *Ode* 10.3 we read, 'And to capture (*walmešbâ*) a good captivity (*šeˀbhîthâ*) for freedom.' The best example of this type of repetition is found in *Ode* 31.2, 'Error (*ṭā 'yûthâ*) erred (*ṭeˀˀāth*) and perished on account of him.' Note that the paronomasia is contiguously arranged. Surely this attractive choice of words is the work of a skilled Semitic poet: ܛܥܝܘܬܐ ܛܥܬ (31.2).

One of the uses of repetition that is exasperating for the translator is found in *Ode* 36.3:

---

7. The verb form is from the root ܚܡ (Pa. which means 'to love passionately' or 'embrace' [not Aph. *'ḥb* 'to kindle' or 'to love']) and not ܪܚܡ (Pe. 'to love', 'to delight in').

> And because I was the Son of Man (ܒܪܢܫܐ),
> I was named the Light, the Son of God (ܒܪܗ ܕܐܠܗܐ).

The use of repetition in this verse is perplexing since one cannot be certain that the Odist intended the repetition of *bar* to accentuate synonymity or stress antithesis. Scholars who opt for the latter possibility would translate the first colon as, 'And although I was a man.'[8]

The most noteworthy example of repetition in the *Odes* is found in *Ode* 19.9:

ܘܠܐ ܣܢܝܩܐ ܚܝܬܐ
ܡܛܠ ܕܐܚܝܗ

> And she did not require a midwife (*hayyᵉthâ*),
> Because he caused her to give life (*dᵉ'aḥyāh*).

Two observations help clarify the ingenious aspect of this play on the root *ḥy'*. First, such paronomasia is possible only in Syriac (or Aramaic). In Hebrew, for example, 'midwife' would probably be the piel feminine participle of ילד, but 'he caused her to give life' would be the hiphal of the root חיה.[9] Second, the paronomasia is highlighted by the parallelistic construction.

The most striking example of repetition in the *Odes* is the fivefold paronomasia in *Ode* 38.9:

> And the corrupting (ܘܡܚܒܠܘܬܗ) of the Corrupter (ܕܚܒܠܐ)
> I saw when the Bride who was corrupting (ܕܡܚܒܠܐ) was adorned,
> And the bridegroom who corrupts (ܕܡܚܒܠ) and is corrupted (ܘܡܬܚܒܠ).

---

8   See A. Hamman, *Naissance des lettres chrétiennes* (Paris: Editions de Paris, 1957), p. 62; Bernard, *The Odes of Solomon*, p. 121. Harris–Mingana's translation is confusing: 'And although a Son of Man' (*The Odes and Psalms of Solomon*, II, p. 384). For a defense of the translation given above, see Charlesworth, *The Odes of Solomon*, note *ad loc.*

9.   This skillful paronomasia, I am convinced, originated in Syriac; hence it appears far more likely that the Odist composed this passage in Syriac than it is that a later translator invented it (see Chapter 4 of the present book). A. Mingana contended that this repetition clinched the argument for a Syriac *Urtext*: 'Cette coincidence est capitale et péremptoire, car la mot *sage-femme* ne signifie vivificatrice, et ne provient du verbe ܐܚܝ qu'en syriaque. Cette seule phrase donc? suffirait peut-être à trancher la question.' See his 'Quelques mots sur les Odes de Solomon. I', p. 239. Harris and Mingana also pointed out that the Syriac in 19.9 'is curiously well worded'; see their *The Odes and Psalms of Solomon*, II, p. 301. Note esp. their insight: '...the Syriac sentence would involve a mental conception and a play on words which could be accounted for exclusively through a Syriac channel' (II, p. 301). The word-play is also possible in Aramaic.

The Odist's use of repetition has five desirable features. First, it draws attention to and *accentuates* the central idea. Second, the repetition of sound and central concept usually *unifies* a verse or knits it tightly with the immediately preceding one.[10] Third, the repetition provides *continuity* in the development of the poem. Fourth, the reiteration of a basic sound produces *assonance and euphony*. Fifth, by juxtaposing variations of a root, *subtle differences* in meaning appear, and an idea is seen from more than one perspective. There is, therefore, a clear tendency to extend the reader's attention beyond what is actually said to something essentially unutterable, though pointed at through repetition of one basic thought.

Double entendre

The Odist often places two or more forms of a root in close proximity in order to make a play on similar-sounding words that have different meanings. This type of paronomasia is very appealing because of the etymological relationship. We have called this form of word-play *double entendre*.[11] There is such a play on the ܣܒܠ in *Ode* 8.11, 'And understand (*wᵉdha'u*) my knowledge (*yidha'ti*) you who know (*yādheʿin*) me in truth'.

In *Ode* 11 there are two good examples of the Odist's ability with *double entendre*. The first three verses play on two different meanings of the root ܓܙܪ. The verb means 'to prune' or 'cut back' a tree or flower; it also has the technical denotation 'to circumcise'. The paronomasia is as follows: 'My heart was pruned (*'ethgᵉzar*) and its flower appeared... / For the Most High circumcised me (*gazᵉrani*) by his Holy Spirit. /And his circumcising (*gᵉzûrᵉtheh*) became my salvation.' Thus the first colon of vv. 1, 2 and 3 of *Ode* 11 contain an alteration of the self-same root.

The second example of *double entendre* in *Ode* 11 is found in v. 5: 'And I was established (*wᵉ'eštarrᵉreth*) upon the rock of truth (*dašrārâ*).' The noun translated as 'truth' and the verb translated as

---

10. In addition to the examples given above, note the following: 'And turn (ܐܬܦܢܘ) from wickedness to your pleasantness. / For they turned away (ܐܬܦܢܝܘ) from themselves the bitterness of the trees' (*Ode* 11.20-21). Other examples of repetition are noted in the discussions on *double entendre*, *double entente*, and assonance (*vide infra*).

11. *Double entendre* in the *Odes* has been discussed by J.R. Harris and A. Mingana (*The Odes and Psalms of Solomon*, II, pp. 101-103) and J.A. Emerton ('Some Problems of Text and Language').

'was established' come from the root ܬܩ. The ethpaal form of this root basically means 'to be firmly set'; the substantive fundamentally means 'firmness' (note that in *Ode* 31.11 'solid rock' is *kîphâ šarirᵉthâ*). Moreover, one should note that in 11.5 the Odist has not employed the usual word for rock, ܟܐܦܐ, but has chosen another, ܫܘܥܐ. The reason for his choice seems to be the desire to create assonance on the sibilant shin: *wᵉ'eštarrᵉreth 'al šû 'â dašrārâ*.

In *Ode* 18.12 the Odist plays on two different meanings of the root ܣܪܩ. The noun denotes 'vain people' and the verb form means 'to be emptied out', 'left bare', 'to be impoverished'. The verse reads as follows:

> And vain people (*sᵉrîqê*) thought that it[12] was great,
> And they became like its type and were impoverished (*wᵉ'estarraqu*).

In three odes the Odist has made a pun on the Syriac word ܪܝܫ. The noun has numerous meanings, denoting 'head', 'summit', 'beginning', 'chief', 'superior', and 'source.' In *Ode* 23 the Odist employs a play on this noun to state that at the *beginning* of 'the letter' (v. 17) was seen the '*head*' (chief, superior one, prince):

> And there was seen at its head,
>   the head (ܒܪܝܫ ܪܝܫܐ) which was revealed,
> Even the Son of Truth from the Most High Father (*Ode* 23.18).

Notice that the paronomasia is also achieved by placing the words contiguously, thus accentating the alliteration and pun. Also, the Odist has carefully chosen a repetitive use of the sonorous shin.

ܒܪܝܫ ܪܝܫܐ...ܕܪܝܫܐ

Earlier the Odist confessed that the *head* of the members (viz. those who were saved, *Ode* 17.15; cf. Rom. 12.4-5) is 'our *head*' (cf. Col. 1.18):

> Because they became my members,
> And I was their head (*rîšᵉhôn*).

> Glory to you, our Head (*rîšan*), O Lord Messiah (*Ode* 17.16-17) .

As in other passages, so here the Odist was so corporately united with 'the Messiah' that he composed *ex ore Christi*. When the Odist stated

---

12. The pronoun refers back to the noun 'ignorance', which the Odist described as appearing 'like the foam of the sea'.

that 'the Lord' was his head, he was not speaking figuratively but descriptively (*vide infra* the concluding remarks).

Another pun on the word ‮ܪܝܫ‬ is found in *Ode* 24.1:

> The dove fluttered over the head (*rîšeh*) of our Lord Messiah,
> Because he was her head (*d^erîšâ*).

The first colon of this bicolon probably refers back to the tradition that the dove hovered over the head of Jesus at his baptism in the River Jordan. The second colon declares that he was her head (her Lord).

In *Ode* 25.8-9 we find repetition and *double entendre:*

> And I was covered (*w^e'ethkassîth*).
> with the covering (*b^ethakhsîthâ*) of your spirit,
> And I removed (*w^e'arîmeth*) from me my garments of skin.
>
> Because your right hand exalted me ('*arîmtani*),
> And caused sickness to pass from me.

After reading v. 8 one might wonder why the Odist had not employed the usual Syriac verb for 'to remove' (viz. ‮ܫܠܚ‬) as he had in *Ode* 21.3. The answer is precisely that he wanted to accentuate that the action was both one of removal and exaltation, as clarified by the *double entendre* with the aphel of ‮ܪܘܡ‬ in the next bicolon. Hence, we discover how important a proper appreciation of the Odist's use of *double entendre* is for an understanding of his otherwise enigmatic expressions.

In *Ode* 31.8-9 the Odist plays on the root *ḥwb*. First, as we have seen, there is an example of repetition ('condemned'…'had not been condemned'); then there is an instance of *double entendre* since 'was owed' derives from the self-same root. Thus the two verses are tightly knit together, and 'nothing was owed (*metht^ehîbh*) them' is an echo of 'Me who had not been condemned (*m^eḥayy^ebhâ*)'.

Two verses later in the same Ode there is a variant reading that has been ignored by critics and translators. In favor of the neglected reading is the fact that it is preserved by the older Syriac MS, and the observation that it alone preserves *double entendre*. The Syriac noun *kîphâ* means primarily 'rock', but it also denotes 'column'. *Ode* 31.11 is as follows:

> But I stood undisturbed like a solid rock (*kîphâ*),
> Which is continuously pounded by columns (*kîphê*)[13]
>> of waves and endures.

In *Ode* 36.1-2 we find a cleverly constructed *double entendre*:

> I rested on the Spirit of the Lord,
> And she lifted me up (*we'arîmtani*) to heaven (*l'rawmâ*);
> And caused me to stand on my feet in the Lord's
>> high place (*b'rawmeh*).

'To lift up', 'heaven' and 'high place' all derive from the root ܪܡ
Moreover, there is a rhyme between the end of the first colon in v. 1 and the end of the first colon in v. 2: *rûḥeh d'mâryâ...b'rawmeh d'mâryâ*.

Finally, one of the most beautiful examples of *double entendre* is found in the final ode. In 42.2 the Odist plays on two different meanings of ܦܫܝܛ:

> And my expansion (*waphšîṭûthi*) is the common (*ph'šîṭâ*) cross,
> That was lifted up on the way of the Righteous One.

Moreover, this verse is linked by means of repetition with the preceding one, 'I extended (*pešṭeth*) my hands and approached my Lord.'

Double Entente

Closely related to the Odist's fondness for *double entendre*, though not as predominant, is his ability with *double entente*. He often creates a pun by playing on two different meanings of a single word. We have called this type of paronomasia *double entente*. Although this feature of his style could easily lead to ambiguity, it often exhibits under his genius the inseparably double aspect of a theological subtlety. Consequently, his intention seems to be not that either interpretation should be chosen but that both are necessary in order to express the complexity of an idea. Of course, the concepts that he is wrestling with concern the revelation of the long-awaited Messiah.

His efforts to make his expressions bear a double load may reflect something more: his awareness that the language with which he had to work was a poor vehicle for expressing the various dimensions of his

---

13. The MS (British Museum Add. 14538) actually has ܟܐܦܐ. There is no problem in emending a final joined 'alaph to a final joined yud since scribes often had the tendency to sweep upward the tail of a final yud. These two letters, for example, are often indistinguishable in John Rylands Lib. Cod. Syr. 9.

thoughts, and conversely that his thoughts were limited because they themselves were somewhat dependent on language.

In the following discussion we have limited our comments to four examples of his use of *double entente.* First, Harris and Mingana (*The Odes and Psalms of Solomon,* II, p. 267) translated *Ode* 11.15 as follows:

> And my breath was refreshed
> By the pleasant odor of the Lord.

This translation, however, does little justice to the beautiful subtleties of the Syriac. There are two dimensions to the Odist's thought. The translation above conveys only one of these: the nose received a pleasant smell. The Syriac verse is presented below.

$$\text{ܐܬܒܣܡܬ ܢܫܡܬܝ,}$$
$$\text{ܒܪܝܗ ܒܣܝܡܐ ܕܡܪܝܐ}$$

> *wᵉʾethbassᵉmath nešmathi*
> *bᵉrîheh basîmâ dᵉmāryâ*

There is *double entendre* since the first word in the first colon and the second word in the second colon both derive from the root ܒܣܡ. Moreover, the euphony and assonance unite the bicolon. Most important, however, is the *double entente:* the Odist is not only stating that the 'nose' received a 'fragment smell' (ܪܝܚ means both 'fragrance' and 'smell'), but also clarifying that his life (ܢܫܡܐ means 'breath', 'spirit', 'living being' and later even meant 'soul') was refreshed by the Lord's fragrance. A better translation, perhaps, might be the following:

> And my spirit-breath was refreshed
> By the pleasant fragrance of the Lord.

Second, in *Ode* 19.10 the Odist describes the virginal conception, stating that she bore *bᵉthaḥ wîthâ.* The preposition can mean both 'with' and 'according to', and the noun *taḥwîthâ* means 'example' and 'manifestation'. One wonders if the Odist means both that 'she bore with manifestation' (i.e. exemplarily) and that 'she bore according to the manifestation' (by Gabriel; cf. Lk. 1.26ff.). Since the preposition can also mean 'because', the second meaning is likewise conveyed by the following translation: 'she bore because of the manifestation' (by Gabriel). While the second meaning is suggested by the base root *ḥwʾ*, 'to make manifest', the first is suggested by the first line of the tricolon:

'She brought forth like a strong man with desire.' It appears that the Odist may have been attempting to convey both meanings.

Third, the subject of *Ode* 33 is a dualism of two ways: the ways of 'the Corrupter' and the ways of 'the perfect Virgin'. The contrast between allegiance to 'the Corrupter' and obedience to 'the Virgin' may be subtly woven into the first colon of v. 8. The speaker of this verse is 'the perfect Virgin':

> And I will enter into you,
> And bring you forth from destruction,
> And make you wise in the ways of truth.

There may be *double entente* in the first colon since it could also have been translated as 'he enticed you to sin'. The 1st common singular Pe'al imperfect of *'l*, 'to enter', is identical in unpointed texts with the 3rd masculine singular 'Aphal perfect of *'wl*, 'to sin'. The second meaning may be subtly hidden behind the first.

Fourth, on a first reading, *Odes* 41.12 seems to mean:

> The man who was humbled,
> But was exalted because of his own righteousness.

The verb in the first colon, *'ethmakkakh*, may also be taken reflexively: 'The man who humbled himself'. This translation is in better harmony with the following verse, which is clearly about the incarnation ('The Son of the Most High appeared'). Although the usual verb employed to denote the lifting up on a cross is *z°qaph*, in the second colon the Odist employed the Ethpe'el of the root *rwm*; and this verb form means 'to be exalted' or 'to be lifted up'. Significantly, it is the Ethpe'el of *rwm* that the author of the Gospel of John in 12.32 in the Peshitta chose to denote 'I am lifted up', and the subsequent verse shows that the reference is to the lifting up on the cross. Moreover, the noun *zadîqûthâ* also means 'alms'. This verse, therefore, can also be translated as follows:

> The man who was humbled,
> And was lifted up upon his own alms.

Translated in this way, the verse refers to the crucifixion with multivalent meanings. The first translation brings out antithetical parallelism, the second synonymous parallelism.[14] The second colon can be translated to refer either to the lifting up upon the cross or the lifting up in exaltation. *The Odist probably meant both*: Jesus' exaltation was his crucifixion. In this belief the Odist was distinct from Luke's trifurcation of crucifixion, resurrection, and exaltation; but he was in harmony with the interpretation found in the Gospel of John.

Assonance

In the discussions above we have occasionally referred to the Odist's feel for assonance. We noted alliteration through the use of the palatals *k* and *g* in *Ode* 20.1-2. Repetition of the sibilant shin produces assonance in *Ode* 11.5. We have seen that the repetition of a root usually produces assonance, especially when it is repeated more than twice (viz. *Odes* 6.9; 7.18-19; 38.9). There are five additional instances of assonance in the *Odes* that should be mentioned.

In *Ode* 4.11 the odist has brought out both repetition and assonance. There is a word-play on the root *tw'*, 'to regret', but most interesting is the Odist's created assonance. Instead of the usual prepositions for 'with' (*be* or *'am*), he employs a preposition that frequently means 'towards', though it sometimes also means 'with'. The obvious reason for the Odist's choice is the desire to create assonance with the contiguous verb: *tᵉwāthâ lᵉwāthākh*. The verse reads as follows:

> For there is no regret (*tᵉwāthâ*) with you (*lᵉwāthākh*);
> That you should regret (*dᵉthethweʾ*) anything which you have promised.

The contiguity of the assonance and paronomasia is stunning; it most likely reflects original compostion and not ingenious translation.

Verses 13 and 14 of *Ode* 5 are linked together by means of rhythmic assonance. There is even a type of alliteration in the beginning of each colon. The result is a very pleasant, even-flowing composition. The beginning of each colon is as follows: *wᵉʾen…ʾenâ…wᵉʾen…ʾenâ*.

In *Ode* 34.1 the Odist has juxtaposed two nouns because of their resonant assonance. The first colon of this Ode is separated into two rhythmic portions, each of which is closed by a similar sounding word: ܿܪܠܝܣܘ ܪܠܝ ܪܣܝܪ ܪܕܝܣܘ ܪܘܛܐܪ ܕܝܠ. Phonetically this may be

---

14. As A. Berlin points out, 'Parallelism is the most prominent rhetorical figure in ancient Near Eastern poetry, and is also present, although less prominent, in biblical prose' (A. Berlin, 'Parallelism', *ABD*, V, pp. 155-62).

vocalized as follows: *laitᵉ ûrḥâ qᵉšîthâ 'aikâ dhᵉlebbâ pheŝîṭâ.*[15] The colon means 'There is no hard way where there is a simple heart'.

The best example of assonance, as the result of the play on one root, is found in *Ode* 26.11:

> Who can interpret (*dantargem*) the wonders of the Lord?
> Though he who interprets (*damtargem*) will be destroyed,
> Yet that which was interpreted (*dᵉmethtargam*) shall remain.

Moreover, the expression 'the wonders of the Lord' is very pleasing to the ear: *tedhmᵉrātheh dᵉmāryâ.* Note the juxtaposition and repetition of the dental dalath and the sonant sounds of mem with resh.

The cleverest and most pleasing assonance, as the result of the play on several roots, is found in *Ode* 35.4b-5. In one-and-a-half verses the Odist has created a beautiful play on four roots, each of which begins with the plosive dental teth: *ṭelāl* ('shade'), *ṭelê* ('child'), *ṭeʿen* ('to carry') and *ṭal* ('dew'). The poetic beauty of this passage is palpable:

> More than shade (*ṭelālâ*) was he to me, and more than foundation.
> And like a child (*ṭalyâ*) by its mother was I carried (*methṭeʿen*),
> And he gave me milk, the dew (*ṭaleh*) of the Lord.

In antiquity the pronunciation of the plosive teth would have been emphatic, and the resonant and echoing sound would have united three main thoughts: 'shade', 'child', and 'dew'.[16] Each of these deeply symbolic words, as is well known, had obtained polysemic theological meaning within biblical circles by the first century CE.

Conclusions

The preceding discussion reveals that the Odist was fond of paronomasia and assonance. He was a true poet, concerned with sound, form, and thought.

We observed how recognition of the Odist's love for paronomasia can help in deciding between variant readings (e.g. *Ode* 31.11). It can

15. This sentence is significant proof that the original language is Syriac-Aramaic.
16. I have been impressed by such precision in Semitics by Bedouin and colleagues in the Hebrew University, Jerusalem.

also help to restore a lacuna. A part of the first colon in *Ode* 6 has been worn away. There is room for about three or four letters, and the final alaph is joined to the preceding letter which is lost. Harris and Mingana (*The Odes and Psalms of Solomon*, I, *loc. cit.*; II, pp. 232-34) conjectured restoring ܐܝܕܐ ('hand'), but this restoration is improbable because the alaph would not be connected to the preceding consonant. Nevertheless, Mar Yosip, Bernard, Abbott, Bruston, Labourt, Flemming, Bauer, Holstijn, and others followed their restoration.[17]

It is probable that what has been partially lost is ܪܘܚܐ ('wind', 'spirit').[18] Three observations support this restoration: first, in the suggested restoration the alaph is connected to the heth. Second, in the manuscript the scribe penned an alaph with a preceding ligature; that is, a portion of the consonant connected to the alaph remains, and since the stroke goes back to the side of the missing consonant, that consonant must be heth, yudh, or shin. Third, the restoration presents a *double entendre* with ܪܘܚܐ in the next verse. *Ode* 6.1-2, with this restoration, reads as follows:

> As the wind (*rûḥâ*) glides through the harp
> And the strings speak,

> So speaks through my members the Spirit (*rûḥeh dᵉmāryâ*) of the Lord,
> And I speak through his love.

Here, therefore, we have a *double entendre* as in Jn 3.8 in which the same word (*pneuma*) means first 'wind' and then 'Spirit'.[19]

The Odist's ability with paronomasia, assonance, and early Syriac in general distinguishes him as a brilliant, erudite, and sensitive person. We frequently read that earliest Christianity appealed primarily to the lower echelons of society; it must not be forgotten, however, that its

---

17. For bibliographical details, see the comment in note 1.

18. The first scholar to suggest this emendation was W.E. Barnes in his article 'An Ancient Christian Hymn Book', *Exp* 10 (1910), p. 57. Harris and Mingana (*The Odes and Psalms of Solomon*, II, p. 234) recognized Barnes's suggestion, but apparently preferred their own restoration (see vol. 2, p. 232).

19   The similarity between the *Odes* and the Gospel of John has been recognized by almost every scholar who has studied the *Odes*. One wonders what literary or historical relationship best explains the shared paronomasia on the verb 'to lift up' (*Ode* 41.12 and Jn 12.32) and the noun 'wind – Spirit' (*Ode* 6.1-2 and Jn. 3.8)? See Chapters 9 and 10 of the present book for my discussion of the probable relation between the *Odes* and the Gospel of John.

message sometimes won the hearts of sophisticated individuals like the Odist, Paul, and the authors of John, Matthew, Luke, Hebrews, and Revelation.

One final question must receive our attention. Why was the Odist so fond of paronomasia? Interest in language as an end in itself will never suffice as an answer, because he was too involved with the proclamation of the thrilling 'good news' ('And like the flowing of waters, truth flows from my mouth, / And my lips declare his fruits' *Odes* 12.2). There seem to be two likely answers.

It is well known that the Odist was deeply influenced by the Old Testament; the Psalter was his model for composition. He could have been influenced by the paronomasiae scattered intermittently throughout the Old Testament.[20] For example, as a former Jew he probably would have known that Eve (חוה), the mother of all living (כל־חי [Gen. 3.20]), was called woman, because she was taken out of her man לזאת יקרא אשה כי מאיש לקחה־זאת [Gen. 2.23]).[21] Likewise, he may have remembered Amos's pun on 'summer fruit' (קיץ) and 'the end' (הקץ) (Amos 8.1-2); and the famous paronomasiae in Isa. 5.7 (ויקו למשפט והנה משפח לצדקה והנה צעקה). To be sure, the Odist was most likely influenced by the Old Testament's paronomasiae; but he was probably more influenced by paronomasiae among his fellow Semites.

Principal Matthew Black demonstrated 'that Jesus did employ the medium of alliteration, assonance, and word-play'.[22] The Odist could have been influenced by Jesus' paronomasiae which may be mirrored in the Peshiṭta; note especially the following examples:

> every one who does (*deʻābhedh*) sin is a slave (*ʻabhdāh*) of sin (Jn 8.34).[23]
> We piped to you, and you did not dance (*raqqedhtûn*),
> We mourned unto you, and you did not lament (*ʻarqedhtûn*)
> (Mt. 11.17).

---

20. See especially the lucid article by W.F. Stinespring, 'Humor', *IDB*, II, pp. 660-62. In addition to the bibliography given in Stinespring's; article, see G. Boström, *Paronomasi i den äldre Hebreiska Maschalliteraturen med särskild hänsyn till proverbia* (Lund: C.W.K. Gleerup, 1928); and A. Guillaume, 'Paronomasia in the Old Testament', *JSS* 9 (1964), pp. 282-90.

21. Following the variant reading of the Samaritan Pentateuch, Septuagint and Targum.

22. *An Aramaic Approach*, p. 185.

23. A.S. Lewis drew attention to this pun. See Black, *Aramaic Approach*, p. 171.

Which of you shall have a beast (*b^ereh 'aw tawreh*) fallen into a pit
(*b^ebîrâ*) (Lk. 14.5).[24]

While we cannot be certain that the Odist was influenced by Jesus'
paronomasiae, at least three considerations point toward that probability: first, it is logical to assume that his poetry would be influenced by
the poetic utterances traditionally linked with his Master. Second, the
Odist frequently asserts that it is not so much he who speaks as it is his
Messiah who speaks through him (viz. 'The Lord has directed my
mouth by his Word' [*Ode* 10.1]; 'I will open my mouth, / And his spirit
will speak through me' [*Ode* 16.5; cf. 6.1-2; 12.1]). The resulting
compositions would tend to be influenced by the poetic style that the
tradition attributed to Jesus. Finally, and perhaps most importantly, the
Odist's language, Syriac, is closely related to (indeed, sometimes identical with) Jesus' native language, Aramaic. We may reasonably assume,
therefore, that the Odist's poetic compositions were influenced by
Jesus' poetic expressions—at least as they were remembered in the
decades after 70 CE.

In conclusion, one of the weaknesses in the discussion above is the
flaw inherent in any analytical examination: it tends to dissect and
separate that which has been carefully brought together. One should be
encouraged to see the synthesis of the Odist's carefully constructed
compositions. For example in *Ode* 36 we have the following poetic
features. In vv. 1 and 2 there are *double entendre* (a) and repetition (b).
Repetition is again employed in v. 3. In v. 4 there is repetition to denote
the superlative (greatest) followed in the next verse by an echoing
repetition (greatness) plus an additional repetition (b) on another root
('to renew'). In v. 6 there are two poetic features that have not been
noted above. First, the verb form 'and he anointed me' (*w^emašhani*)
would have evoked in the reader the *terminus technicus* the Anointed
One, the Messiah—especially so since the passage was composed *ex ore
Christi*. Hence, we have a sort of *double entente*. Second, there is an
alliteration on the consonant mem: *w^emašhani men m^ešamleyûtheh*. In
v. 7, as we noted above, there is repetition (a). In the final verse 'my

24. Emendation and translation by Black, *Aramaic Approach*, pp. 168-69.
E. Russell concluded his dissertation with the well-documented observation that 'In
the gospels, as we should expect, by far the greater number of paronomasias are
found in the sayings of Jesus.' For further examples of paronomasiae in the New
Testament, see his *Paronomasia and Kindred Phenomena in the New Testament*
(Chicago: University of Chicago Libraries, 1920), the quotation is found on p. 42.

approach' (*qûrrābhi*) may be an example of *double entendre* with 'those who are near him' (*qarrîbhaw-hi*) in v. 6. The Ode concludes with pleasing vocalic assonance and rhyme: *wᵉ'eštarrᵉreth bᵉrûḥâ damdabhrānûthâ. / hallelûya'*. Consequently, the Odist's efforts to present his thoughts in a well-composed poetic form are evident in each verse of *Ode* 36.

Semitic poetry has two advantages over English and most modern languages. First, it was designed to be read out loud so that the resounding sounds and echoes could help tie thoughts together. The echoeing repititions served as *Stichworten* (words that unite units of thought) which re-unite separated sounds. Second, all Semitics (Hebrew, Aramaic, Syriac, and Arabic) feature sounds unheard in English and Western languages; these sounds are often gutturals, dentals, fricatives, and plosive consonants (such as heth and teth). Even to an ear untrained in Semitics such sounds as these are pleasing, *ṭelālâ... ṭalyâ...methṭᵉ'en...ṭaleh*. The sounds resonant and unite 'shade', 'child', 'carried', and 'dew' and thus illustrate the bonded unity between nature and the human:

> More than shade (*ṭelālâ*) was he to me, and more than foundation.
> And like a child (*ṭalyâ*) by its mother was I carried (*methṭᵉ'en*),
> And he gave me milk, the dew (*ṭaleh*) of the Lord.

Such repetitive assonance has been celebrated in English poetry. For example, T.S. Eliot concludes his masterful *The Waste Land* by borrowing from the *Brihadaranyaka Upanishad* the words for 'give', 'sympathize' and 'control': 'Datta. Dayadhvam. Damyata'.[25] These words are reminiscent of the Odist's brilliant constructions, as in the *dantargem...demtargem...dᵉmethtargam*:

> Who can interpret (*dantargem*) the wonders of the Lord?
> Though he who interprets (*damtargem*) will be destroyed,
> Yet that which was interpreted (*dᵉmethtargam*) shall remain (26.11).

Especially ingenious is the Odist's construction in 34.1, *laitᵉ ûrḥâ qᵉšîthâ 'aikâ dhᵉlebbâ phešîṭâ*.

The observations presented above should lay to rest F.C. Burkitt's erroneous opinion that the Syriac of the *Odes* was 'stiff', lacked any

25. T.S. Eliott, *The Waste Land and Other Poems* (New York: Harvest Books, 1934 [1958]), p. 46.

'really characteristic native idiom', and was 'exotic'.[26] We have seen evidence that the Odist was a linguistic genius and a consummate artist. His poems distinguish him as worthy to be called the poet laureate of earliest Christianity.

APPENDIX

For an important study of the poetic and linguistic skills of the Odist see M. Franzmann, *The Odes of Solomon: An Analysis of the Poetical Structure and Form* (NTOA, 20; Freiburg: Universitätsverlag; Göttingen: Vandenhoeck & Ruprecht, 1991). She judges the above chapter to be the 'most important and helpful contribution so far in the area of poetical analysis' of the *Odes* (p. 7). Generally on Semitic poetry see M. O'Connor, *Hebrew Verse Structure* (Winona Lake, IN: Eisenbrauns, 1978, 1980), W.G.E. Watson, *Classical Hebrew Poetry: A Guide to its Techniques* (JSOTSup, 26; Sheffield: JSOT Press, 2nd edn, 1986). Extremely helpful is A. Berlin, 'Parallelism', *ABD*, V, pp.155-62 (note esp. the extensive bibliography).

---

26. F.C. Burkitt, 'New MS of the Odes of Solomon', *JTS* 13 (1912), pp. 373-74.

Chapter 7

HAPLOGRAPHY AND PHILOLOGY: A STUDY OF *ODE OF SOLOMON* 16.8

Scholars continue to puzzle over the meaning of the Syriac in *Ode* 16.8, despite the extended discussions it has provoked during the last century. Recently a critic, unfamiliar with the scholarly debates, claimed incorrectly that the verb ܘܓܠܐ cannot be an active participle and should be vocalized to mean 'and that which is revealed'. It is timely, therefore, to discuss afresh the probable meaning of this verse.

The Syriac and translation, as presented in my edition of *The Odes of Solomon*,[1] is as follows:

ܡܠܬܗ ܓܝܪ ܕܡܪܝܐ ܒܨܐ ܟܣܝܐ ܡܕܡ ܕܠܐ ܡܬܚܙܐ
ܘܓܠܐ ܡܚܫܒܬܗ

> For the Word of the Lord investigates that which is invisible,
> And reveals His thought.

The first observation is obvious. The bicolon is uneven. Why would the Odist break his norm and compose lines so uneven?

The second observation is clear only to the translator. What is the derivation of the verb in the second colon? S.P. Brock thinks that the verb is from the root *gl'* and that as pointed in my edition, *wᵉdāghlâ*, it must be translated 'and deceives'. He claims that the translation 'and reveals' demands a different vocalization: *wad-gālê*. Such a translation 'is not possible' for Brock, because the antecedent subject is feminine. He argues that the verb should be repointed as *wᵉda-gᵉlê* in order to obtain the following translation: 'For the Word of the Lord investigates that which is invisible, and his thought that which is revealed.'[2]

Brock, who judges my edition 'quickly to become standard', notes correctly that the subject of the verb *wdgl'* is a feminine noun, *mlt'*.

1. Charlesworth, *The Odes of Solomon*, pp. 69-71.
2. S.P. Brock, review of J.H. Charlesworth, 'The Odes of Solomon', *JBL* 93 (1974), p. 624.

Although this noun is often masculine when used to represent the divine Logos, it is feminine in this verse, because the accompanying verb is a feminine participle, ܒܨܝܐ, *bāṣyâ*. Brock's translation is possible since *maḥšabhteh* ('his thought'), which presupposes this participle, is also feminine. In favor of his translation is the *parallelismus membrorum* and the attractive parallel between 'that which is invisible' and 'that which is revealed'.

One must ask, nevertheless, if the translation suggested makes good sense and is likely in the context. The first line is clear and has not been the point of controversy; it means that the Word of the Lord inquires or searches into the things that are invisible to the human. The second line has caused the debate. Brock's 'and his thought that which is revealed' would mean that the thought of the Lord inquires into the things visible to the human. Is this statement logical?[3] If things are visible to the human, what need is there for the thought of the Lord to search into them, presumably for human benefit? Syriac conceptually links sight with cognition; *ḥˀzîthâ*, the adjective related to *metʰˀzê* in *Ode* 16.8a, means not only 'visible' but also 'well known'; *gˀlê*, the passive participle which Brock surmises is found in 16.8b, means not only 'uncovered' but also 'evident'.

Also against the probability of this translation is the contrast drawn between the function of the Word of the Lord and the thought of the Lord, a distinction not found, indeed resisted by the Odist.

Note an idea that follows the problematic v. 8:

> And the worlds are by his Word
> And by the thought of his heart (16.19).

The context is also against pointing the verb in the passive voice; all the preceding verbs are in the active voice, and most are active participles. The following verbs are active, with a predominance of active participles, except for v. 14 which is required by the acknowledgment of the Lord as creator ('And the hosts are subject to his Word'). Against Brock's vocalizing *wdgl'* (v. 8b) as a passive participle is the immediate context. Verses 8a, 9a and 9b all contain verbs that are feminine active participles. One should first attempt to vocalize *wdgl'* also as a feminine active participle; this is the vocalization in the recent edition

---

3. We could object by asking why the Odist should make sense. The proper response, of course, is that to presume otherwise would be fruitless.

(*wᵉdāghlâ*), a pointing inherited from J.R. Harris and A. Mingana. As
we shall see below, the verbal root is probably not *gl'*.

Next we must ask whether we should follow Brock's advice and take
maḥšabhteh ('his thought') as the subject. The answer to this question
is probably negative. In 9b the word *lᵉmaḥšabhteh* is clearly the object
of the verb, as the *nota accusativi* emphasizes. Verses 6-19 have nouns
with pronominal suffixes and each is objective (his hands, his fingers,
his mercies, his Word, his works, his thought, his works, his Word, his
Word, his heart). In v. 9a, moreover, the noun is in the accusative and
without the *nota accusativi*. The presumption would then favor taking
maḥšabhteh in 8b as objective, as in my translation. J.A. Emerton
presents a similar translation:

> For the Word of the Lord searches out what is unseen,
> And perceives his thought; ...[4]

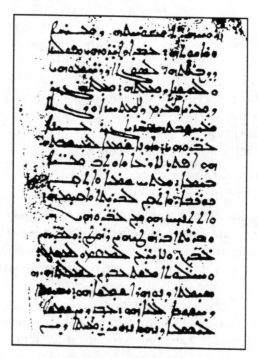

Fig. 1. Odes of Solomon 16.5-16. John Rylands Lib. Cod. Syr. 9, fol. 12 *b*. Reproduced
by permission of the trustees of the John Rylands University Library of Manchester.

4.   J.A. Emerton, 'The Odes of Solomon', in H.F.D. Sparks (ed.), *The Apocryphal Old Testament* (Oxford: Clarendon Press, 1984), p. 706.

Textual Restoration

Two likely translations of *Ode* 16.8b have evolved out of decades of scholarly debate. It is possible that a word has been omitted in this line. In 1911 J. Labourt suggested that 'le second ܟܬܒܐ n'a pas été copié'. He restored the text as follows: ܐܠ [ܟܬܒܐ]ܬܐ.[5]

Many scholars would resist emending the *Odes* since they are preserved in Coptic, Greek and in two Syriac manuscripts. In favor of a restoration, however, are two significant factors. First, *Ode* 16 is *preserved only in John Rylands Lib. Cod. Syr. 9* (MS H).

Second, *the scribe who copied MS H frequently omitted a word or phrase.* He accidentally omitted 'and you will know the grace of the Lord' in *Ode* 23.4; 'the head of our Lord' in *Ode* 24.1; most of the second line in *Ode* 40.3; 'who knew me [not], / Because I shall hide myself from those' in *Ode* 42.3; 'And I placed their faith in my heart' in *Ode* 42.19. The presumption that he is guilty of haplography in *Ode* 16.8 is heightened by the recognition that he committed parablepsis at least twice in copying this verse but corrected himself by writing above the line ܒܩ and then ܐܠ.[6] Labourt probably did not have access to a photograph of MS H, but he would most likely have been pleased to learn that the copyist was inclined towards parablepsis and that he omitted initially at least two words in the problematic v. 8. Labourt's intuition may have been correct but his restoration fails to explain why ܒܩ and ܐܠ were initially omitted and why ܘܐܠ was copied correctly with the connective waw. Conceivably the exemplar had the following:

$$\text{ܡܠܬܗ ܓܝܪ ܕܡܪܝܐ}$$
$$(ܒܩ)^{7}\ ܡܪܐ\ ܡܪܗ (ܐܠ)ܘܐܠܓ\ ܟܬܒܐ\ ܡܣܬܒܪ\ [ܕܡܪܝܐ}$$
$$[ܡܪܗ ܕܡܪܝܐ]$$

For the Word of the Lord investigates whatever is invisible,
And [what is visible] reveals the thought [of the Lord].

5.   J. Labourt and P. Batiffol, *Les Odes de Salomon*, p. 17.

6.   See J.H. Charlesworth (ed.), *Papyri and Leather Manuscripts of the Odes of Solomon* (Dickerson Series of Facsimiles, 1; Durham, NC: The Center, 1981), plate 51.

7.   Parentheses denote words initially omitted by the copyist; square brackets circumscribe the attempted restoration.

The copyist wrote the first ܟܬ݂ܒܐ and his eye wandered to the second putative ܟܬ݂ܒܐ, perhaps because of homoeoteleuton (as suggested above), inadvertently omitting the intervening words. The scribe of MS H then copied ܟܪܘܙ ܡܢܕ ܟܘܬ݂ܒܐ, and continued copying correctly until he came to ܡܬܒܪܗ when he noticed his mistakes. Subsequently, he restored both the ܟܝܢ and the ܐܠ, but since there was no room on the line he was forced to add them above the line he had completed transcribing. Incorrectly thinking that he had restored all the words he had missed, he continued copying after the words he had written previously, and copied the next verse, ܚܙܐ ܓܝܪ ܥܝܢܐ, 'for the eye sees'. He remembered that he had already copied ܟܬ݂ܒܐ ܡܢܕ ܟܪܘܙ, but he erred in thinking that they appeared only once in his exemplar.

This suggestion helps explain how some words were first omitted. If it seems too complicated, an examination of the haplography in *Ode* 42.19b shows that this phenomenon is often accompanied by other errors. In favor of the restoration is the meaning and the harmony of following 'And [what is visible] reveals the thought [of the Lord]' with 'For the eye sees his works, / And the ear hears his thought.'

Also in favor of some restoration is the length of the second colon in 16.8. In *Ode* 16 each of the bicolons and tricolons are of similar length as demanded by poetic scanning and *parallelismus membrorum*; that is, except for v. 8, which, as extant, seven words are paralleled by only two. According to my suggested restoration seven are paralleled by five.

Emendations and restorations are naturally speculative and are attractive primarily to those who suggest them. But, some restoration seems demanded because of the truncated second colon. A second observation regarding the translation of 16.8 may appeal to more critics.

Philological Recognition

Three questions are raised by a careful study of *Ode* 16.8. First, why is the second colon out of balance? Second, why did the copyist of the only extant manuscript miss some words and then place some of them above the line? Third, what is the philological explanation of the Syriac verb ܡܚܘܐ? We have reflected, and hopefully answered the first two questions; we now turn to the third.

The verb in *Ode* 16.8 is not from *gl'*, according to many scholars, but from *dgl*, which in the peal means 'to perceive'. According to Harris and Mingana the form means 'it fathomed', 'it scrutinized', and 'it saw clearly'.[8] According to C. Brockelmann *dgl* means 'it aimed (at)' and 'it considered'.[9] Some Syriac scholars are ignorant that *dgl* was used in the peal; perhaps the reason for this misapprehension is that R. Payne Smith represented it inadequately,[10] and F. Schulthess,[11] J. Payne Smith (Mrs Margoliouth),[12] R. Köbert,[13] and M.H. Goshen-Gottstein[14] failed to record the use and meaning of *dgl* in the peal. Each of these philologians worked primarily from R. Payne Smith's massive *Thesaurus Syriacus*, but he recorded the meaning of the Syriac words in the manuscripts then extant. The *Odes of Solomon* had not yet been discovered in Syriac.

The Syriac ܕܓܠ in the peal is an Akkadian (= Assyrian) loan-word. In Akkadian *dagālu* means 'to look', 'to take aim', 'to wait for, to attend to a matter or person', 'to receive', and 'to hand over'.[15] The root *dgl* in

---

8. *The Odes and Psalms of Solomon*, II, pp. 284-85.
9. *Lexicon Syriacum*, p. 141.
10. *Thesaurus Syriacus*, col. 820. He recorded that *dgl* in the peal means 'levit', 'illevit', 'decepit', 'mentitus fuit', but failed to note that it also means 'examinavit'. L. Costaz also recorded only that *dgl* in the peal denotes 'to direct (the dart), to aim at' (*Dictionnaire syriaque–français; Syriac–English Dictionary* [Beirut: Imprints catholique, 1963], p. 8).
    The additional meaning of *dgl* is not recorded in the supplements to the *Thesaurus*: J.P. Margoliouth, *Supplement to the Thesaurus Syriacus* (Oxford: Clarendon Press, 1927); J. Schleifer, 'Berichtigungen und Ergänzungen zum Supplement des Thesaurus Syriacus', *Orientalia* NS 8 (1939), pp. 25-58.
11. *Lexicon Syropalaestinum* (Berlin: Georg Reimer, 1903), p. 42.
12. *A Compendious Syriac Dictionary* (Oxford: Clarendon Press, 1903; repr. 1957), p. 83. Syriac *dgl* is listed as meaning only 'to falsify, outwit, scheme, be cunning' in E.S. Drower and P. Macuch, *A Mandaic Dictionary* (Oxford: Clarendon Press, 1963), p. 102.
13. *Vocabularium Syriacum*, p. 39; *idem*, 'Addenda ad Vocabularium Syriacum, Romae 1956', *Orientalia* NS 39 (1970), pp. 315-19.
14. *A Syriac–English Glossary* (Wiesbaden: Otto Harrassowitz, 1970), p. 15.
15. I.J. Gelb *et al.*, *The Assyrian Dictionary* (Chicago: Oriental Institute; Gluckstadt: Augustin, 1959), III, pp. 21-25. The brilliant Semitist G.R. Driver noted the importance of Akkadian (= Assyrian) for an understanding of the *Odes*; 'Notes on Two Passages in the Odes of Solomon', *JTS* NS 25 (1974), pp. 434-37.

Syriac also can mean 'to look'; note the following statement by Gregory of Cyprus (late fourth century).[16]

ܠܢܬܪ ܐܝܟܘܬܗܐ ܕܢܗܝܪܐ
ܘܚܕܐ ܕܠ ܕܐܝܬ ܪܐ ܐܝܬ ܒ...

> my eyes fly over the countries of the luminaries,
> *and see clearly* all that is found in...[17]

Additional evidence that ܓܠܐ in the peal denotes 'to see' or 'to perceive' is the meaning of the noun derived from it, *degîlûtâ*, which means 'sight'.

The first scholar to argue that *wdgl'* in *Ode* 16.8b is from ܓܠܐ, and not ܓܠܐ, was W. Frankenberg in his *Das Verständnis der Oden Salomos*.[18] He influenced many other translators, especially L. Tondelli,[19] who alone was credited for this insight by Harris and Mingana.[20] The peal singular feminine participle of this root is *dāglâ* and the meaning of *Ode* 16.8b would then be 'And it (the Word) perceives his thought'.[21]

Conclusion

The preceding discussion permits us to evaluate the various attempts to understand *Ode* 16.8. There are numerous suggestions. First, some published translations are too preliminary to warrant serious consideration; they have been obviated by debates among critical scholars. All of these translations date from the first years of research into the *Odes*

16. W. Wright, *A Short History of Syriac Literature* (London: A & C. Black, 1894; Amsterdam: Philo, 1966), pp. 42-43.

17. The translation is by Harris and Mingana. For more of the Syriac and translation see their *The Odes and Psalms of Solomon*, II, p. 285.

18. Pp. 39, 17.

19. *Le Odi di Salomone*, p. 187.

20. *The Odes and Psalms of Solomon*, II, p. 285.

21. In the edition published by Scholars Press, I corrected 'it reveals' to 'it perceives'. Even though *dagalu* in Akkadian (= Assyrian) can mean 'to hand over' (especially in legal and covenantal relationships), I erred in thinking *dgl* in the peal could be stretched to mean 'exposes' or 'reveals'. 'Perceives' is preferable to 'scrutinizes' (Harris and Mingana); the Word of the Lord would not need to examine the thought of the Lord. I am tempted to restore the text since the only extant manuscript bears ample signs of haplography. Perhaps it is wise to be conservative since a text should receive an emendation only when it is incomprehensible without it.

and all derived *wdgl'* incorrectly from *gl'*, but most contained notes signifying a problem with v. 8. Among this first group are the publications by J.R. Harris in 1909[22] and 1911,[23] J. Flemming in 1910,[24] H. Grimme in 1911,[25] and J.H. Bernard in 1912.[26]

Second, only one scholar, S.P. Brock in 1974,[27] attempted to obtain meaning by vocalizing *wdgl'* as a passive participle. This translation is laudable, if one ignores the root ܠܓܐ. Brock has admirably struggled with the grammatical force of the feminine subject ܡܠܬܐ; but Brock's suggestion is unpersuasive because all the contiguous verbs are active.

Third, two attempts have been made to restore the second colon. The first was by J. Labourt, who influenced A. Hamman,[28] and the second is the one offered in the preceding examination:

> Car le Verbe du Seigneur scrute ce qui est invisible,
> Et ce [qui est visible] manifeste son dessein.[29]

> For the Word of the Lord investigates whatever is invisible,
> And [what is visible] reveals the thought [of the Lord].

A restoration is attractive because of three main reasons: (a) the need to restore some words to recreate the necessary length of the bicolon; (b) the thought obtained; and (c) because the copyist of MS H is frequently guilty of haplography—especially in this section of MS H. I do not think the suggested restoration is based on too much speculation, and an emendation is sometimes necessary in MS H.

Fourth, most translators rightly assume that *wdgl'* derives from *dgl*. In this group are included the differing translations published by W. Frankenberg in 1911,[30] C. Bruston in 1912,[31] L. Tondelli in 1914,[32]

22. *The Odes and Psalms of Solomon* (1st edn, 1909), *ad loc.*
23. *The Odes and Psalms of Solomon* (2nd edn, 1911), p. 111.
24. Harnack and Flemming, *Ein jüdisch-christliches Psalmbuch*, pp. 45-45.
25. *Die Oden Salomos*, pp. 38-39.
26. *The Odes of Solomon*, p. 80.
27. S.P. Brock, review of J.H. Charlesworth, *Odes of Solomon*, *JBL* 93 (1974), p. 624.
28. *Naissance des lettres chrétiennes*, p. 40.
29. Labourt and Batiffol, *Les Odes de Salomon*, p. 17. I have placed their translation in parallel lines according to the rules of Semitic poetry. This form has become standard for the *Odes* ever since R.H. Charles's dictum that nothing less would suffice ('A Church Hymnal of the First Century', *Times Literary Supplement* 430 [7 April 1910], p. 124).
30. *Das Verständnis der Oden Salomos*, p. 17.

H. Gressmann in 1922,[33] W. Bauer in 1933,[34] M. Mar Yosip in 1948,[35] and J.H. Charlesworth in 1973 and 1985.[36] Hence, given the weight of the available data and scholarly debates, the most probable translation of *Ode* 16.8 is as follows:

> For the Word of the Lord investigates that which is invisible,
> And [what is visible] perceives his thought.

This verse, therefore, apparently means that the human should not worry because the Word of the Lord has investigated that which is invisible and thus potentially threatening to the human. That which is visible to the human reflects the Lord's gracious thought. The Word can then communicate[37] the thought of the Lord, since it (he) functions as the mediator of the invisible to the human as clarified in *Ode* 41.14, 'And light dawned from the Word / That was before time in him.'

This research shows the necessity of various dimensions of research on the *Odes of Solomon*. First, the manuscripts must be studied carefully both directly and through photographs, and—as with the Dead Sea Scrolls—sometimes with infra-red photography or digitizing and computer analysis. Second, it is necessary to emend the text of the *Odes*, especially when there is only one witness that is defective. Third, scholars must not rely on lexicons that do not represent the full range of meanings now available in Syriac, Coptic, or Greek.

The preceding study should help to reveal the beauty of the *Odes* and should also show more clearly the need to comprehend them from within themselves, not from comparisons with other documents. As Labourt wrote, 'Les *Odes de Salomon* se distinguent des écrits similaires par une fraîcheur d'inspiration et une ferveur religieuse tout exceptionnelles.'[38]

---

31. *Les plus anciens cantiques chrétiens*, p. 57.

32. *Le Odi di Salmone*, p. 187.

33. 'Die Oden Salomos', in Hennecke (ed.), *Neutestamentliche Apokryphen*, p. 452.

34. *Die Oden Salomos*, p. 33.

35. *The Oldest Christian Hymn-Book*, p. 59.

36. *The Odes of Solomon*, pp. 69, 71; *OTP*, II, p. 749.

37. Note that in Akkadian (= Assyrian) *dgl* can mean 'to hand over'. It is possible that *dgl* in the peal in Syriac also denotes 'to communicate' or 'to make clear'.

38. 'The Odes of Solomon are distinguished from similar writings by a freshness of inspiration and a completely exceptional religious fervor.' Labourt and Batiffol, *Les Odes de Salomon*, p. 1.

Part III

GNOSTICISM, THE *ODES OF SOLOMON*, THE DEAD SEA SCROLLS
AND THE GOSPEL OF JOHN

Chapter 8

THE *ODES OF SOLOMON*—NOT GNOSTIC[*]

One of the most exciting and important discoveries at the beginning of this century was the recovery of some long-lost hymns of the early Church referred to by the Early Fathers as the *Odes of Solomon*. Immediately after their publication by J.R. Harris in 1909 they were the topic of conversation among biblical scholars in Italy, Germany, France, Britain, the United States, and elsewhere. Public interest was so aroused that these conversations frequently extended beyond scholarly journals into such publications as *The Times Literary Supplement* and *The Evening Bulletin* (Philadelphia). An authority on Christian Origins, A. Harnack, remarked that the discovery of the *Odes* was 'geradezu epochemachend' for the understanding of the provenience of the Fourth Gospel;[1] and subsequently R. Bultmann used the *Odes* as a foundation for his monumental commentary on John. Yet all this enthusiasm about the *Odes* seems to have subsided as one scans the literary productions of the last few decades; neither C.K. Barrett nor R.E. Brown relies upon them in their commentaries on the Fourth Gospel and few of the introductions to the New Testament even mention them.

One wonders why the *Odes* have been so neglected. Perhaps it is because the beautiful spontaneity and freshness of these hymns has been buried beneath the weight of lengthy and laborious discussions. In fact the analysis of the *Odes* has resulted in such different assessments that the authorities have been placed these hymns in such mutually exclusive categories as the Old Testament Pseudepigrapha (O. Eissfeldt), the New Testament Apocrypha (E. Hennecke), and the Patristic

[*]   I acknowledge my gratitude to the United States–United Kingdom Educational Commission for the Fulbright Research Fellowship under which I pursued this research.
    1.   Harnack and Flemming, *Ein jüdisch-christliches Psalmbuch*, p. 119.

Literature (J. Quasten, C.K. Barrett, C.H. Dodd). One of the main reasons that biblical scholars have tended to neglect the *Odes* is the general belief that they are heretical and so have little to say to the mainstream of the biblical tradition. They have been shelved and branded as gnostic literature. Recent discoveries and studies indicate that a re-examination of this thesis is both timely and desirable.

The Gnostic Hypothesis

As early as 1910 H. Gunkel presented the thesis that the *Odes* are a gnostic hymnbook of the second century CE;[2] shortly thereafter numerous scholars[3] defended his hypothesis. In the last two decades such distinguished scholars as H.M. Schenke,[4] R.M. Grant,[5] S. Schulz,[6] F.M. Braun,[7] and H. Jonas[8] have argued for the similarity between the *Odes*

2.   Gunkel, 'Die Oden Salomos', pp. 291-328; *idem*, 'Die Oden Salomos', *DR* 154 (1913), pp. 25-47; *idem*, 'Die Oden Salomos', in *Reden und Aufsätze* (Göttingen: Vandenhoeck & Ruprecht, 1913), pp. 163-92; *idem*, 'Salomo Oden', pp. 87-90.

3.   C. Clemen, 'Die neuentdeckten Oden Salomos', *TRev* 14 (1911), pp. 1-19; H. Duensing, 'Zur vierundzwanzigsten der Oden Salomos', *ZNW* 12 (1911), pp. 86-87; W.R. Newbold, 'Bardaisan and the Odes of Solomon', *JBL* 30 (1911), pp. 161-204; *idem*, 'The Descent of Christ in the Odes of Solomon', *JBL* 31 (1912), pp. 168-209; M. Sprengling, 'Bardesanes and the Odes of Solomon', *AJT* 15 (1911), pp. 459-61; H. Gressmann, 'Die Oden Salomos', *DL* 32 (1911), pp. 1349-56; H. Gressmann, 'Les Odes de Salomon', *RTP* 1 (1913), pp. 195-217; *idem*, 'Die Oden Salomos', in Hennecke (ed.), *Neutestamentliche Apokryphen*, pp. 437ff.; E. Hora, 'Die Oden Salomos', *TGl* 5 (1913), pp. 128-40; W. Stölten, 'Gnostische Parallelen zu den Oden Salomos', *ZNW* 13 (1912), pp. 29-58; H. Schlier, 'Zur Mandäerfrage', *TRev* 5 (1933), pp. 1-34, 69-92; R. Abramowski, 'Der Christus der Salomooden', pp. 44-69; M. Dibelius, *A Fresh Approach to the New Testament and Early Christian Literature* (New York: Charles Scribner's Sons, 1936), p. 249; L.G. Rylands, *The Beginnings of Gnostic Christianity* (London: Watts, 1940), pp. 36-44.

4.   *Die Herkunft des sogenannten Evangelium Veritatis* (Göttingen: Vandenhoeck & Ruprecht, 1959), pp. 26-29. Schenke, however, cautions that the conclusion that these two texts come from the same gnostic circle is 'nur ein Schluss möglich'.

5.   Grant contends the *Odes* are Valentinian. 'Notes on Gnosis', *VC* 11 (1957), pp. 149-51; *idem*, *Gnosticism and Early Christianity* (New York: Columbia University Press, 1959), p. 169.

6.   'Salomo-Oden' (3rd edn), pp. 1339-42.

7.   'L'énigme des Odes de Salomon', pp. 597-625; *idem*, *Jean le Théologien*, pp. 232-51.

and gnostic literature, especially the *Gospel of Truth* and the *Hymn of the Pearl*. Recently K. Rudolph attempted to show why the *Odes* are gnostic.

A Re-examination of the Gnostic Hypothesis

Our present task is neither to discuss the character of Gnosticism nor to consider the sundry relationships between the *Odes* and Gnosticism; our purpose is limited to a refutation of the charge that the *Odes of Solomon* are gnostic. R. Bultmann's arguments for a gnostic interpretation of the *Odes* will not be considered precisely because he contends they are distinct from second-century Gnosticism and are an early form of oriental Gnosis.[9]

In the following pages we hope to show in three steps that the *Odes* are not gnostic: first by refuting Rudolph's arguments for a gnostic interpretation, then by observing that the mood of the *Odes* is not gnostic, and finally by presenting nine reasons why the *Odes* should not be considered gnostic. First, however, it is necessary to clarify the terminology that will be employed; indeed, it seems safe to say that there is a consensus among biblical scholars that no other branch of knowledge suffers as much from inexact definitions as does Gnosticism.[10]

The colloquium of authorities on Gnosticism that met at Messina from April 13–18, 1966, considered it advisable to distinguish between

8.   *Gnosis und spätantiker Geist* (Göttingen: Vandenhoeck & Ruprecht, 1954), I, pp. 327f.; *idem*, The *Gnostic Religion: The Message of the Alien God and the Beginnings of Christianity* (Boston: Beacon Press, 1958), pp. 119-21.

9.   'Ein jüdisch-christliches Psalmbuch', p. 28. Also see his *Das Evangelium des Johannes* (Göttingen: Vandenhoeck & Ruprecht, 13th edn, 1953), esp. pp. 13ff.

10.   It is interesting to note that the Messina Colloquium showed quite clearly that a short definition of Gnosticism is actually impossible at the present time. For example, after T.P. van Baaren finished his lecture, 'Towards a Definition of Gnosticism', he was asked by Dr Ugo Bianchi, 'Une définition du gnosticisme, brève et dont les éléments s'impliquent, est-elle possible?' Professor van Baaren replied, 'A short definition is not really possible, in my opinion; we will have to give a rather long description of what gnosticism, even 2nd cent. gnosticism, is.' It is significant that M. Mansoor begins his discussion of 'The Nature of Gnosticism in Qumran' with the 'firm belief' that a definition of Gnosticism at the present stage of our knowledge is 'tantamount to attempting the impossible'. (U. Bianchi [ed.], *Le Origini dello Gnosticismo: Colloquuio di Messina 13–18 Aprile 1966* [Leiden: E.J. Brill, 1967], pp. 180, 389).

Gnosticism and Gnosis. Gnosticism was to designate the specific group of systems that flourished in the second century CE; but Gnosis, a more general term, was to include phenomena that predated Gnosticism, and was regarded as 'knowledge of the divine mysteries reserved for an elite'.[11] M. Mansoor correctly remarked that 'when we say "gnosticism" we mean the term for the heretical movements that arose in the second century, originally known only from the references and polemics of the Church Fathers.'[12] 'Gnostic' is the adjective used to refer to the ideas and concepts peculiar to this movement. It seems wise to accept the definitions proposed by the authorities in this field.

It appears that Professor Rudolph had assumed a similar definition of Gnosticism for two main reasons. He advocated a strong connection between the *Odes* and the Valentinian *Gospel of Truth*. He concluded a comparison between the *Odes* on one side and the *Thanksgiving Hymns* and Mandean literature on the other with the contention that the former could not have been written in the first century CE.[13] Applying the definition of Gnosticism proposed by the Messina Colloquium, and apparently assumed by K. Rudolph, let us now examine the latest arguments for the hypothesis that the *Odes* are gnostic.

Professor Rudolph claims that the 'gnostic character of the *Odes of Solomon* is a well-established fact (eine feststehende Tatsache)'.[14] Their gnostic character is readily apparent, he contends, once one realizes that the root *yd'* (to know) and its two derivatives, *yidha'tâ* (knowledge) and *madha'* (understanding), are abundantly used and that the predominant use of these words characterizes the gnostic perception.[15] It is unfortunate that he does not elaborate why the Odist's use of the verb 'to know' and its derivatives should obtain gnostic connotations. The Gnostics had no monopoly on this word. It is abundant in such pre-gnostic works (i.e. prior to and not characteristic of Gnosticism) as the *Thanksgiving Hymns* (56 times in 18 columns) and the Fourth Gospel (*gnosis* does not appear but *ginoskein* is found 60 times). W.D.

11. Bianchi (ed.), *Le Origini dello Gnosticismo*, p. xxvi.
12. 'The Nature of Gnosticism in Qumran', in Bianchi (ed.), *Le Origini dello Gnosticismo*, p. 389.
13. 'War der Verfasser der Oden Salomos ein "Qumran-Christ"?', pp. 526, 553.
14. 'War der Verfasser der Oden Salomos ein "Qumran-Christ"?', p. 525.
15. 'War der Verfasser der Oden Salomos ein "Qumran-Christ"?', p. 525.

Davies,[16] M. Burrows,[17] Bo Reicke,[18] and others[19] have convincingly shown that the Dead Sea Scrolls are not gnostic. Likewise, Quispel,[20] Barrett,[21] Braun,[22] Dodd,[23] and Brown[24] have demonstrated quite conclusively that John is not gnostic.

Perhaps one of the reasons Professor Rudolph and some of the other scholars with international reputations and impressive credentials have labeled the *Odes* gnostic is because they came to these hymns *via* gnostic documents. When the *Odes* are approached from this direction, it is easy to see them as reflecting gnostic ideas. In the endeavor to ascertain whether or not these *Odes* are gnostic, let us begin with the text itself.

First, one should note that in the *Odes* knowledge is *not* the gnostic idea of salvation through a comprehension of the nature of the soul's heavenly origin, subsequent imprisonment in the world of matter, and possible ascension to its native abode. In the *Odes* knowledge is always

16. *Christian Origins and Judaism* (Philadelphia: Westminster Press, 1962), pp. 124-44. G.G. Scholem also contended that the scrolls are not gnostic (*Jewish Gnosticism, Merkabah Mysticism, and Talmudic Tradition* [New York: Jewish Theological Seminary of America, 1960], p. 3).

17. *The Dead Sea Scrolls* (New York: Viking, 1955), pp. 252-60.

18. 'Traces of Gnosticism in the Dead Sea Scrolls?' *NTS* 1 (1954–55), pp. 137-41.

19. R.McL. Wilson, 'Gnostic Origins Again', *VC* 11 (1957), pp. 104-10. M. Mansoor has also argued that the Qumran sect should not be considered gnostic and H. Ringgren suggested that 'the Qumran sect could represent an early Jewish variation of the general tendency that manifested itself as Gnosticism even if all details do not fit the pattern exactly' (Bianchi [ed.], *Le Origini dello Gnosticismo*, esp. p. 383). Contrast K. Schubert's remark that 'Im Sektenkanon En Feshcha III, 13-IV,26 liegt der älteste derzeit bekannte gnostische Text vor.' See his 'Der gegenwärtige Stand der Erforschung der in Palästina neu gefundenen hebräischen Handschriften', *TLZ* 78 (1953), pp. 495-506. Also see his discussion 'Die gnostische Lehre des Sektenkanons von 'En Fesha', in K. Schubert (ed.), *Die Religion des nachbiblischen Judentums* (Vienna: Verlag Herder Freiburg, 1955), pp. 85-87.

20. G. Quispel, 'Het Johannesevangelie en de Gnosis', *NThT* 11 (1956–57), pp. 173-203.

21. C.K. Barrett, 'The Theological Vocabulary of the Fourth Gospel and of the Gospel of Truth', in W. Klassen and G.F. Snyder (eds.), *Current Issues in New Testament Interpretation* (London: SCM Press, 1962), pp. 210-23; *idem*, *The Gospel According to St. John*, pp. 31-33.

22. *Jean le Théologien*, pp. 113-33.

23. C.H. Dodd, *The Interpretation of the Fourth Gospel* (Cambridge: Cambridge University Press, 1953, 1960), pp. 97-114.

24. *The Gospel According to John*, pp. lii-lvi.

of Christ, the Most High, and the Lord, in that order of frequency; in Gnosticism, as Grant rightly remarks,[25] it is essentially self-knowledge. Let us now closely examine the use of the root *yd'* and its derivatives in the *Odes*, following the sequence listed by Rudolph.

Ode 7.13   For toward knowledge He has set his way,
            He has widened it and lengthened it and brought it to
            complete perfection.[26]

The subject of this sentence is 'He who created me' (v. 9) and 'the Father of the worlds' (v. 11). He is clearly also the one who is to be praised (v. 19); hence this passage is not gnostic because the creator is condemned in Gnosticism.

Ode 7.21   For ignorance was destroyed upon it,
            Because the knowledge of the Lord arrived upon it.

This verse cannot be gnostic because the creator is praised; also the object of knowledge is 'the Lord'.

Ode 8.8   Hear the word of truth,
            And receive the knowledge of the Most High.

Again knowledge is not of the soul's predicament but of 'the Most High'.

Ode 8.12   And understand my knowledge,
            You who know me in truth.

The reader is told to understand 'my knowledge', an expression that is parallel to 'my faith' in the preceding line; in Gnosticism, however, knowledge and faith are somewhat antithetical. Also Christ seems to be the speaker in vv. 8-21 so that the object of knowledge is Christ.

Ode 11.4   From the beginning until the end
            I received his knowledge.

We read of 'his knowledge', but 'his' refers to 'Most High' in v. 2.

Ode 12.3   And he has caused his knowledge to abound in me,
            Because the mouth of the Lord is the true Word,
            And the entrance of his light.

Again knowledge is not of oneself but of the Lord, the true Word. One should also clearly note the emphasis on proclamation and the open or

25. *Gnosticism and Early Christianity*, p. 10.
26. All translations of the *Odes of Solomon* are by the author.

missionary quality of the 'truth' in the preceding two verses ('He has filled me with words of truth, / That I may proclaim Him'). This is the opposite of the esoteric emphasis in Gnosticism.

> *Ode 7.7a*   And He who knew and exalted me,
>   Is the Most High in all his perfection.

The subject of 'He who knew and exalted me' is obviously 'the Most High' and the object appears to be Christ, who is the speaker in vv. 6-15. The verses that follow 7.7 do not speak about the ascent of a gnostic through various cosmic spheres; they sing of Christ's descent into Hell and the gift of his resurrection to those who are bound there.

> *Ode 17.12*   And I offered my knowledge generously
>   And my resurrection through my love.

Since Christ is the speaker in this verse, 'my knowledge' refers to both to Christ's knowledge and to knowledge offered by Christ. The contiguous verses of this passage reflect the Odist's belief in the *Descensus ad inferos*; the 'doors that were closed' in v. 8 refer to the 'gates of Hell'.

> *Ode 23.4*   Walk in the knowledge of the Lord
>   And you will know the grace of the Lord generously;
>   Both for his exultation and for the perfection of his
>   knowledge.

That 'the knowledge of the Lord' in this verse is not gnostic appears obvious from the parallelism with 'the grace of the Lord'. The passage is very biblical.

As for *Ode* 35.5, neither *yidha'tâ* nor *madha'* nor any form of the root *yd'* appears either in this verse or in this Ode, yet Rudolph includes the verse in his list.

> *Ode 18.13*   But the wise understood and contemplated,
>   And were not polluted by their thoughts,
>   Because they were in the mind of the Most High.

'The wise understood' is an axiomatic statement. Also the reason for this understanding is not because of some esoteric *gnosis* but because 'they were in the mind of the Lord'. Significantly enough, the last Syriac noun that was translated as 'mind' also means 'doctrine' or 'belief'. K. Rudolph claims that the gnostic distinction between 'belief' and 'knowledge' is found in the *Odes*;[27] this contention, however, is an

---

27. 'War der Verfasser der Oden Salomos ein "Qumran-Christ"?', p. 525.

example of what can be read into the *Odes* but is not there to be read out of them.

Ode 18.11 And ignorance appeared like dust,
        And like the foam of the sea.

This passage is characteristically Jewish and free of gnostic overtones as is seen by the biblical names for the deity in the contiguous verses: 'my God' (v. 8), 'the Lord' (v. 13), 'the Most High' (v. 15).

It is fruitful to compare these passages in the *Odes* with the following gnostic statement on knowledge and salvation:

What liberates is the knowledge of who we were, what we became;
where we were, whereinto we have been thrown; whereto we speed,
wherefrom we are redeemed; what birth is, and what rebirth
                        (*Exc. Theod.* 78.2).[28]

Knowledge in the *Odes* is not used in this sense; it is not an understanding of our origin before birth or of our destiny. As stated at the beginning of this examination, knowledge in the *Odes* is recognition of the Lord, the Messiah, or of the Most High. At times the use of the term 'knowledge' probably has the Old Testament meaning of acknowledgment (esp. *Ode* 23.4).

The conclusion to this systematic analysis of the use of *yd'* and its derivatives by the Odist shows that the emphasis on knowledge in the *Odes* is *not* evidence of Gnosticism. As the preponderance of Church members in the United States does not baptize the nation Christian, so the predominance of the word 'knowledge' in a manuscript does not christen the text gnostic.

Second, Professor Rudolph believes the *Daseinsverständnis* is thoroughly gnostic and is expressed in line with the *Erlösermythos*. As proof of his contention, he cites references to descent (*Odes* 22; 1.11) and ascent (*Odes* 21.2, 38, 1ff.; 29.1-9; 18.6f.). When one examines these passages, however, one notices that only *Ode* 22.1 reflects a cosmic dimension, and a gnostic rendering would have demanded a descent and ascent between the numerous worlds. Moreover, the ascent 'up out of the depths of Sheol' in *Ode* 29.4 is not a progression from one of the gnostic's many spheres; it is a movement upward from the Hebraic underworld, namely, Sheol.

28. As cited by Jonas, *The Gnostic Religion*, p. 45.

Third, Rudolph suggests that the references to the strangeness of Christ's appearance (*Odes* 17.6; 28.10; 41.8), only apparent death (*Odes* 28.7f.; 42), divine help (*Odes* 22.5ff; 41.9), conquest of Hell (*Ode* 42.11ff.), awakening of belief (*Ode* 42), and deliverance (*Odes* 10; 15.9; 17.8ff.; 22.1ff.; 29.2ff.; 31; 39) show that the Redeemer in the *Odes* is portrayed in terms of the gnostic *Erlösermythos*.[29] But are not these attributes either profoundly Christian or typically docetic? Docetism, the mythological view that Jesus only seemed to be a man but was really an angelic redeemer of celestial substance, must not be confused or equated with Gnosticism. Recent debates on Gnosticism have centered around the problem of whether it was preceded by proto-Gnosticism or only pre-Gnosticism; moreover, the precise meaning of these terms themselves is a subject of considerable debate. Regardless of the outcome of this discussion, however, docetism clearly predates Gnosticism.[30] For example, clear condemnation of docetism appears in Ignatius ('Jesus Christ...truly born...truly persecuted...truly crucified and died...' *Trallians* 9f.), in 1 Jn 4.1ff., and in 2 John 7. Polycarp[31] also condemned docetism.[32] To contend, therefore, that the Christology of the *Odes* is sometimes docetic does not suggest that it is gnostic.[33] The Christology of the *Odes* is influenced by docetic tendencies,[34] but this

29. 'War der Verfasser der Oden Salomos ein "Qumran-Christ"?', p. 526.

30. Thus Cullmann can conclude his critical examination of *The Christology of the New Testament* with the claim that 'Docetism...is branded already in the New Testament as the fundamental Christological heresy.' O. Cullmann, *The Christology of the New Testament* (trans. S.C. Guthrie and C.A.M. Hall; Philadelphia: Westminster Press, 1959), p. 324.

31. E.g. *Phil.* 7.12. C.H. Dodd suggests that this passage from Polycarp should be dated shortly after 115 CE (*The Johannine Epistles* [London: Hodder & Stoughton, 1946], p. xii).

32. So also W. Kramer, *Christ, Lord, Son of God* (trans. B. Hardy; SBT, 50; London: SCM Press, 1966), pp. 16f. C.H. Dodd correctly remarks that the only fact we are presented with is that the dissenters denied the reality of the Incarnation and so were Docetists. He claims, furthermore, that the errors with which 1 John is concerned were 'on the track which led to later Gnostic heresies' (*The Johannine Epistles*, pp. xix, 149).

33. Frequently there has been a tendency to equate docetism and Gnosticism (e.g. J.F. Bethune-Baker, *An Introduction to the Early History of Christian Doctrine* [London: Methuen, 1903], pp. 79-81).

34. E.g. *Odes* 28.16-17; 19.8; 42.10; cf. 7.4-6. A. Mingana correctly remarked, 'Strictly speaking, Gnosticism has no strong support in the Odes...on the other hand, there are sentences which seem to betray slight tendencies towards

factor does not relegate their composition to the second-century gnostic circles.

We now leave a refutation of the specific reasons why Rudolph believes the *Odes* are gnostic. Before we present nine observations why the *Odes* should not be considered gnostic, it is imperative to perceive the complex milieu in which early Christianity developed and then observe the general mood of the *Odes*.

Previous discussions about Gnosticism have often evolved under the tacit presupposition that what was not 'orthodox' must be in some way gnostic. Research has sometimes proceeded under the unexamined assumption that early Christianity was bifurcated into two somewhat distinct groups: the gnostics and the non-gnostics.[35] Only in the last few decades has there been an awareness that 'orthodox' and 'heretical' are labels that must not be applied to ideas and documents in this early period (a thought fathered by W. Bauer),[36] that the Church in the first two centuries was evolving contiguously with a multifarious array of somewhat analogous phenomena such as Jewish mysticism (a movement exposed by G.G. Scholem),[37] sectarian Judaism (proved by the discovery of the Dead Sea Scrolls), Encratism (which is found both in the New Testament and in the *Gospel of Thomas*)[38] and Hellenistic philosophy. While full-blown Gnosticism is found only in the second century, the question of its antecedents is hotly debated, and its variegated nature is now recognized (so that we hear about Valentinian Gnosticism, Babylonian Gnosticism, Egyptian Gnosticism, Manichean Gnosticism, and Jewish Gnosticism).

Docetism.' 'Odes of Solomon', in J. Hastings (ed.), *Dictionary of the Apostolic Church* (Edinburgh: T. & T. Clark, 1992), II, p. 106. P. Batiffol claimed the Christology of the *Odes* was docetic (Labourt and Batiffol, *Les Odes de Salomon*, pp. 94ff.). In contrast, Harris claimed that *Odes* 41.15 ('The Messiah in truth is one') was written against Docetism (*The Odes and Psalms of Solomon*, II, pp. 77, 83).

35. In 1942 R.E. Messenger thought that there were only two alternatives: the origin of the *Odes* was either gnostic or Christian (*Christian Hymns of the First Three Centuries* [New York: Hymn Society of America, 1942], p. 21).

36. *Rechtglaubigkeit und Ketzerei im ältesten Christentum* (Tübingen: J.C.B. Mohr [Paul Siebeck], 2nd edn, 1964).

37. See especially his *Major Trends in Jewish Mysticism* (New York: Schocken Books, 2nd edn, 1946) and *Jewish Gnosticism*.

38. See G. Quispel's comments in J.P. Hyatt (ed.), *The Bible in Modern Scholarship* (New York: Abingdon Press, 1965), esp. p. 257.

In light of these phenomena during the early Christian centuries, it is important to recognize that it is not the presence of such terms as light, darkness, truth, sleep, knowledge, etc., that characterizes Gnosticism; rather it is the interpretation of these terms and the metaphysical framework in which they are given expression that is uniquely gnostic! As H. Jonas remarked, 'the mood or tone of gnostic statement; the style of gnostic mythologizing…is not an extraneous consideration but an element in the intrinsic meaning of the gnostic position itself.'[39] As examples of the gnostic mood, he singles out the rebellious temper, the sophisticated nature of the myth which is 'often contrivedly allegorical rather than authentically "symbolical"' and the polemical use of Jewish sources.[40] It is highly significant that none of these factors is found in the *Odes*: the *Odes* are not rebellious but joyous, not speculatively allegorical but naïvely symbolical, not polemically Jewish but Jewish-Christian. Great weight must be given to the general observation that the mood of the *Odes* is not gnostic. Another nine particular considerations follow.

1.   The Creator in the *Odes* is called the Lord (*Ode* 4.15), the Word (*Odes* 21.10; 16.8-19), the Father (*Ode* 7.7-12), and Christ, in passages where it is probable that they are *ex ore Christi* (*Ode* 8.18-20). Clearly the Creator is the object of 'glory and honor' (*Ode* 16.20). How strikingly different this conception is from Gnosticism where the world is the result of evil desires or of an unfortunate accident. In the *Odes* there is no hint of a creator of lower rank or demiurge as in Gnosticism. The vast difference between the *Odes* and Gnosticism on this point is graphically illustrated by a juxtaposition of an ode with a gnostic speculation[41] on the creation of the world (see below).

2.   As in the Fourth Gospel so in the *Odes* there is no attempt to describe or conceptualize the procession of the Logos from the Father.

Ode 16.8-20	*Gospel of Truth* 17.15-35
8. For the Word of the Lord searches out anything which is invisible, And reveals his thought.	Error elaborated its own Matter in the Void, without knowing Truth. It applied itself to the fashioning of a for-

---

39.   See his article, 'Le problème des origines du gnosticisme', in Bianchi (ed.), *Le Origini dello Gnosticismo*, pp. 1-27.

40.   Bianchi (ed.), *Le Origini dello Gnosticismo*, pp. 100-104.

41.   The translation is by Jonas, *The Gnostic Religion*, p. 190.

Ode 16.8-20	*Gospel of Truth* 17.15-35
9. For the eye sees his works And the ear hears his thoughts.	mation, trying to provide in beauty a substitute of Truth… Not having any root, it remained in a fog with regard to the Father while it was engaged in preparing Works and Oblivions and Terrors in order to attract with their help, those of the Center and to imprison them.
10. It is he who made the earth broad, And placed the waters in the sea.	
11. He expanded the heaven, And fixed the stars.	
12. And he fixed the creation and set it up, Then he rested from his works.	
13. And created things run according to their courses, And they work their works, For they can neither cease nor fail.	
14. And the hosts are subject to his Word.	
15. The reservoir of light is the sun, And the reservoir of darkness is the night.	
16. For he made the sun for the day so that it will be light; But night brings darkness over the face of the earth.	
17. And by their portion one from another They complete the beauty of God.	
18. And there is nothing outside of the Lord, Because he was before anything came to be.	
19. And the worlds are by his Word, And by the thought of his heart.	
20. Glory and honor to his name Hallelujah.	

This shared nonchalance towards cosmology is quite distant from Gnosticism.

3. H. Jonas has remarked that dualism 'is omnipresent in all Gnosticism as, first and foremost, a radical mood that dominates the gnostic attitude and unites its widely diversified expressions. The dualism is between man and world, and again between the world and God.'[42] This characteristic gnostic dualism, however, is not found in the

---

42. Bianchi (ed.), *Le Origini dello Gnosticismo*, p. 94.

Odes as K. Rudolph himself remarks 'dass wir in den *Oden Salomos* keinen ausgeprägten Dualismus vor uns haben'.[43]

4.   There is no hint of man having a spark of eternal light within him as in almost all gnostic systems nor of men being separated into mutually exclusive groups according to the amount of *gnosis* they possess as in Gnosticism.[44]

5.   The typically gnostic language with such terms as sleep, intoxication, awakening, call, etc. is absent.

6.   The Old Testament is not rejected as it is in most forms of Gnosticism,[45] but it is the pattern and norm for composition and expression as previous studies have shown.[46]

7.   In contrast to the emphasis in Gnosticism on revelation as essentially secret, the *Odes* openly proclaim God's revelation, for example *Ode* 12.1: 'He has filled me with words of truth, / That I may proclaim Him.' In *Ode* 30 there is a description of the 'water from the living fountain of the Lord' which came *boundless* and was for *all* the thirsty. Indeed, the Odist's thoughts are strikingly dissimilar to the following gnostic idea: 'He who has received that light will not be seen... And again when he goes out of this world he has already received the truth in the images...it is revealed to him alone...hidden in a perfect day and a holy light' (*Gos. Phil.* 127).[47]

---

43.   'War der Verfasser der Oden Salomos ein "Qumran-Christ"?', p. 526. After the above-mentioned reasons for categorizing the *Odes* as gnostic, Professor Rudolph presents a list of terms shared by the *Odes* with the Mandean literature. However, it is significant that the majority of these terms are not unique to Mandeanism or Gnosticism, that such *termini technici* as Enosh, Mana, and Manda d'Hayye are not found in the list, and that he finds it necessary to note at the end that 'die *Oden Salomos* die mythologische Redeweise stark reduziert haben' (Bianchi [ed.], *Le Origini dello Gnosticismo* p. 535).

44.   See the enlightening comments by H. Jonas and T.P. van Baaren in Bianchi (ed.), *Le Origini dello Gnosticismo*, pp. 94ff. and 179. F.M. Braun correctly remarked, 'Si, au moment où il écrivait ses poèmes, le pseudo-Salomon avait été un gnostique, on relèverait dans les *Odes* certaines allusions à la répartition des hommes en groupes étanches' (L'énigme des Odes de Salomon), p. 605.

45.   See the interesting hypothesis presented by H. Jonas in Bianchi (ed.), *Le Origini dello Gnosticismo*, pp. 101ff.; and note T.P. van Baaren's comments on pp. 178-79 in the same book.

46.   See Harris and Mingana, *The Odes and Psalms of Solomon*, and Charlesworth, *The Odes of Solomon*.

47.   Translated by R.McL. Wilson, *The Gospel of Philip* (London: Mowbray, 1962), p. 62.

8.   There is no suggestion in the *Odes* of a divine Redeemer who has descended from above to release men's souls and lead them back to the realm of light.

9.   The imagery in the *Odes* evolved out of imagination which borrowed heavily from the Old Testament, and not out of abstract intelligence or bizarre speculation as was characteristic of the gnostics. The truth of this statement is manifest when one holds up any passage in the *Odes* against the following excerpt from the detailed description of the creation of the prototype of Man:

> He made [the], navel of his belly after the likeness of the Monad (*monas*) which is hidden in the Sêtheus (*sêtheus*). He made the great intestine after the likeness of the Sêtheus (*sêtheus*) who is Lord over the Pleroma (*plêrôma*), and the small intestine he made after the likeness of the Ennead (*hennas*) «hidden in» the Setheus (*sêtheus*).
>
> (*Codex Brucianus* 3.12-19)[48]

Conclusion

Finally, two other facts militate against a gnostic interpretation of the *Odes*. First, if the *Odes* are gnostic, as so many excellent scholars from Gunkel to Rudolph have suggested, then why did the author of the *Pistis Sophia* deem it necessary to append a gnostic Targum to each?[49] Second, it is significant that an authority on Gnosticism in the first half of this century, a man most sympathetic to Gnosticism, remarked that the *Odes* were not gnostic. After mentioning that the gnostics were prolific writers of hymns, psalms and odes, and that these contained 'the most beautiful forms and ideas', G.R.S. Mead remarked, 'Our *Odes* are certainly not of this order, but they as certainly use a mystic symbolism.'[50] Gnosticism was primarily a soteriological and metaphysical

---

48.   Translated by C.A. Baynes, A *Coptic Gnostic Treatise Contained in the Codex Brucianus* (Cambridge: Cambridge University Press, 1933), p. 17.

49.   As F.C. Burkitt accurately remarked, the *Odes* show 'no more affinity to the doctrines found in *Pistis Sophia* than the Psalms of David do' (*Church and Gnosis* [Cambridge: Cambridge University Press, 1932], p. 71). W.H. Worrell wrote, 'That it is the intention of the *Pistis Sophia* to quote a non-Gnostic or orthodox Ode and not a Gnostic version of the same is evident from the fact that the Davidic Psalms are treated in the same way, and quoted without any attempt to gnosticize them' ('The Odes of Solomon and the *Pistis Sophia*', *JTS* 13 [1912], p. 31).

50.   G.R.S. Mead, review of *The Odes and Psalms of Solomon*, by Harris, in *The Quest* 1 (1909/10), p. 565.

system, knowledge of which was the secret of the gnostic group. If it will be accepted that mysticism is primarily an experienced relationship with the transcendent which is grasped intuitively by the individual, then the *Odes* are not gnostic but they are mystic.

In retrospect it is safe to say that *the Odes of Solomon are not gnostic.* In prospect it appears probable that the *Odes* are a tributary to Gnosticism which flows from Jewish apocalyptic mysticism (viz. *4 Ezra,* the *Books of Enoch,* the *Thanksgiving Hymns* [1QH], the *Book of Mysteries* [1QH 27]) through such works as the *Hymn of the Pearl* and the *Gospel of Thomas* to the full-blown Gnosticism of the second century. The *Odes* are not 'heretical'—such a word is anachronistic at this time in the development of Christian thought—but rather a Jewish-Christian hymnbook of the late first or early second century CE. Such discussion, however, goes beyond the confines of the present essay.

APPENDIX

This essay remains essentially unchanged since it has served as a watershed which introduced the period in which the *Odes of Solomon* are no longer labeled 'gnostic' by informed critics without further qualification. The specialists in the field of Gnosticism have considered the *Odes of Solomon* a form of 'early Gnosticism' which is very different from Gnosticism, in my opinion. I hesitate to label Paul and the author of the Gospel of John 'gnostics'. They, and the author of the *Rule of the Community,* were certainly influenced by forms of Gnosis that appreciably antedates Gnosticism. The chaos in the field of Christian origins sometimes results from imprecise definitions; and that is never more acute than in the use of the terms 'gnostic' and 'Gnosticism'.

Henry Chadwick was the first to comment on 'The Odes of Solomon—Not Gnostic'. He noted that his article 'was already printed when there came into my hands the article of Dr J.H. Charlesworth, "The Odes of Solomon—not gnostic"... the acute learning and conclusions of which I wish to salute', 'Some Reflections', p. 270). The second scholar to accept my arguments and one who repeated them at length is B.D. Fanourgakis in his Αι Ωδαι Σολομωντος, pp. 126-27. E. Yamauchi apparently accepts the argument that the *Odes of Solomon* are not to be branded heretical and gnostic. Yamauchi, *Pre-Christian Gnosticism* (Grand Rapids: Eerdmans, 1973), p. 94.

Emerton argues against the gnostic interpretation of the *Odes of Solomon*: 'there is no evidence in the *Odes* either of the characteristic Gnostic doctrine of emanations from a distant God, or of a radical dualism between matter and spirit: on the contrary, *Ode* xvi witnesses to a doctrine of Creation which would have been impossible for any thoroughgoing Gnostic. ...the *Odes*...show no trace of any developed, or logically formulated, Gnostic system' (Emerton, 'The Odes of Solomon', p. 684). A. Peral and X. Alegre offer an assessment similar to my own: 'el autor se encuentra dentro de las corrientes teológicas que culminaron en el gnosticismo, aspecto este que viene confirmado cuando se analiza más a fondo la teología de las odas' ('Odas de Salomon', p. 64).

M. Lattke recognizes the problems of labeling the *Odes of Solomon* 'gnostic', and prefers to refer to the Odist as 'ein früher, vielleicht gnostisch-synkretistischer Christ' (*Oden Salomos*, p. 34). E. Azar also notes the problems of calling the *Odes of Solomon* 'gnostic', and concludes that nothing excludes 'la possibilité d'une certaine influence de la mythologie et de la philosophie grecque' (*Les Odes de Salomon*, p. 41).

Chapter 9

QUMRAN, JOHN AND THE *ODES OF SOLOMON*

Scholars now generally agree that John is influenced by Essene thought. There has been no question that John and the *Odes* are conceptually related; the question concerns the direction of influence. Recent research discloses that the *Odes* are indebted in many ways to the Essenes.[1] It is therefore appropriate to search for the relationship between Qumran, John, and the *Odes*. Since dualistic thought[2] is found in each of these, and since the relationship between John and Qumran and also between the *Odes* and Qumran is most impressively evident when comparison is followed along the lines of dualism, it is wise to limit our present concern to an examination and comparison of the dualism found in these ancient manuscripts.

The development of the chapter is as follows. First, Qumran's dualism, John's 'dualism', and the *Odes'* 'dualism' will be analyzed separately. Second, the relationship between the *Odes'* and John's 'dualism', the correlation between the *Odes'* 'dualism' and Qumran's dualism, the comparison between John's 'dualism' and Qumran's dualism, and the relationships among the 'dualisms' in the *Odes*, in John, and in the Qumran Scrolls will be discussed consecutively. Third, the broader consequences obtained from this research will be organized as conclusions in retrospect) and prospect.

---

1. Carmignac, 'Les affinités qumrâniennes', pp. 71-102; *idem*, 'Un qumrânien converti au christianisme', pp. 75-108; Braun, 'L'énigme des Odes de Salomon', pp. 597-625; pp. 224-59; Charlesworth, 'Les Odes de Salomon et les manuscrits de la Mer Morte', pp. 522-49.

2. Definitions for the types of dualism mentioned herein may be found in the first footnote in J.H. Charlesworth, 'A Critical Comparison of the Dualism in 1QS 3.13–4.26 and the "Dualism" Contained in the Gospel of John', in *idem* (ed.), *John and the Dead Sea Scrolls* (Christian Origins Library; New York: Crossroad, 1991), p. 76.

The breadth of the subject and the brevity of this chapter demand that the remarks be merely programmatic. Our eyes will be focused on the texts, hence consideration of recent publications will be kept to a minimum.

Analyses

The following analyses and comparisons are built on conclusions obtained elsewhere. Most important of these are the following:

1.   The Dead Sea Scrolls antedate both John and the *Odes* and are Essene.[3]

3.   This conclusion is held by most scholars. See, for example, M. Black, *The Essene Problem* (London: Dr William's Trust, 1961). The two major dissenting voices have been G.R. Driver and S. Zeitlin. Rejecting the usual inferences from the archaeological (see esp. p. 398) and palaeographical (see esp. p. 416) data, Driver claims that the authors of the Scrolls should be identified with the Zealots (*The Judaean Scrolls* [Oxford: Blackwell, 1965], pp. 75, 106-21, 237-51). Further, he dates the major scrolls between 46 and 132 CE (p. 373). Although Driver is exceedingly erudite, his hypotheses are highly improbable. See R. de Vaux, 'Esséniens ou Zélotes? A propos d'un livre récent', *RB* 73 (1966), pp. 212-35. For an English version of part of this article and one by M. Black on Driver's book, see review of G.R. Driver, *The Judean Scrolls*, *NTS* 13 (1966–67), pp. 81-104.

Zeitlin's position is even more extreme and untenable. He claims that the Scrolls are written by a fringe group of the Karaites in the Middle Ages. S. Zeitlin, *The Dead Sea Scrolls and Modern Scholarship* (Philadelphia: Dropsie College for Hebrew and Cognate Learning, 1956). His articles are found in *The Jewish Quarterly Review*; see esp. 'The Dead Sea Scrolls: Journalists and Dilettanti', *JQR* 60 (July, 1969), pp. 75-79. Also see his 'The Slavonic Josephus and the Dead Sea Scrolls: An Exposé of Recent Fairy Tales', *JQR* 58 (1968), pp. 173-203. It is significant that an authority on Karaism, N. Wieder, argues that on purely theological grounds alone (dualistic world-view, predestination) it is extremely unlikely that the Qumran documents emanate from Karaite circles. N. Wieder, *The Judean Scrolls and Karaism* (London: East and West Library, 1962), p. 253.

Under the influence of Driver's hypothesis, Principal Black has qualified his position that the sect should be identified with the Essenes. He now holds that 'the Essene group who held the fort at Qumran at the outbreak of the first Revolt' had 'thrown in their lot with Zealot and Pharisaic groups' (*The Dead Sea Scrolls and Christian Doctrine* [London: Athlone Press, 1966], p. 4). The men who had composed the Scrolls would still have been Essenes; hence, I prefer to agree with F.M. Cross, Jr, who has reaffirmed his earlier opinion that the men of Qumran were Essenes. See his 'The Early History of the Qumran Community', *McCormick Quarterly* 21 (1968), p. 254.

2. The extant Gospel attributed to John, herein abbreviated as John, was originally composed in Greek from numerous sources, some of which were Aramaic.[4]

3. The *Odes of Solomon* were originally composed in Syriac and are contemporaneous with John; both were composed around 100 CE.[5]

Qumran's Dualism

It is well known that the Dead Sea Scrolls are characterized by dualism. In the treatise concerning the two Spirits in the *Rule of the Community* (1QS 3.13–4.26) a brilliant Jew, probably the Righteous Teacher, under the influence of Zurvanism, a Zorastrian sect, developed this dualistic paradigm based on the opposition of light to darkness.[6]

4. This position is held by most scholars. See especially the following: Black, *An Aramaic Approach*, esp. pp. 75ff., 149-51; *idem*, 'Aramaic Studies and the Language of Jesus', in M. Black and G. Fohrer (eds.), *In Memoriam Paul Kahle* (Berlin: Alfred Töpelmann, 1968), pp. 17-28; M. Black, 'The "Son of Man" Passion Sayings in the Gospel Tradition', *ZNW* 60 (1969), pp. 1-8. S. Brown, 'From Burney to Black: The Fourth Gospel and the Aramaic Question', *CBQ* 26 (1964), pp. 323-39; H. Ott, 'Um die Muttersprache Jesu: Forschungen seit Gustaf Dalman', *NT* 9 (1967), pp. 1-25; M. Wilcox, 'The Composition of John 13.21-30', in E.E. Ellis and M. Wilcox (eds.), *Neotestamentica et Semitica: Studies in Honour of Matthew Black* (Edinburgh: T. & T. Clark, 1969), pp. 143-56; Brown, *The Gospel According to John*, pp. xxiv-xi, cxxix-cxxxvii.

There is currently keen interest in recovering the sources behind the Fourth Gospel. Two attempts are to be noted: R. Fortna, *The Gospel of Signs: A Reconstruction of the Narrative Source Underlying the Fourth Gospel* (SNTSMS, II; Cambridge: Cambridge University Press, 1970); see also his article, 'Source and Redaction in the Fourth Gospel's Portrayal of Jesus' Signs', *JBL* 89 (June 1970), pp. 151-66. Another significant attempt at diagnosing the strata in the Fourth Gospel was presented by E. Haenchen in his commentary on John: *John: A Commentary on the Gospel of John* (trans. R.W. Funk and U. Busse; 2 vols.; Hermeneia; Philadelphia: Fortress Press, 1984). Some of his ideas regarding the Evangelist's sources are conveniently collected in his *Gott und Mensch: Gesammelte Aufsätze* (Tübingen: J.C.B. Mohr [Paul Siebeck], 1965) and *Die Bibel und Wir* (Tübingen: J.C.B. Mohr [Paul Siebeck], 1968).

5. The date given to John is the one accepted by most scholars. That is the date of the extant Fourth Gospel. For the date attributed to the *Odes* see Charlesworth, *The Odes of Solomon*.

6. For text, translation, and introduction, see Charlesworth, 'The Rule of the Community', in *idem, Rule of the Community and Related Documents* (PTSDSSP, 1; Tübingen: J.C.B. Mohr [Paul Siebeck]; Louisville, KY: Westminster/John Knox

Monotheism
God of Israel (3.24)
From the God of knowledge comes all (3.15)
He establishes all (3.15)

Cosmic and Divided Angelology

Spirit of Truth (3.18-19; 4.21, 23)	Spirit of Deceit (3.19, 4.9, 20, 23)
Angel of Truth (3.24)	
spring of light (3.19)	well of darkness (3.19)
source of truth	source of deceit
Prince of Lights (3.20)	Angel of Darkness (3.20f.)
spirits of light (3.25)	spirits of darkness (3.25)
God loves (3.26)	God loathes (4.1)
illuminates human hearts (4.2)	causes hardness of heart (4.11)
	causes blindness of eye
cause the human to fear God's	deafness of ear (4.11)
judgments (4.2)	
Holy Spirit (4.21)	
nature of truth (3.19)	nature of deceit (3.19)

Bifurcated Humanity

Sons of Light (3.13, 24f.)	[Sons of Darkness][7]
Sons of Righteousness (3.20, 22)	Sons of Deceit (3.21)
Sons of Truth (4.5,6)	
upright ones (4.22)	
the perfect in the Way (4.22)	
a mans' share in truth (4.24)	his inheritance in the lot of deceit (4.24)

Human Conduct

in the ways of light they walk (3.20)	ways of darkness (3.21, 4.11)
ways of true righteousness (4.2)	ways of ungodliness (4.19)
ways of truth (4.17)	doings of deceit (4.17)
in the light of life (3.7)	
walk in wisdom (3.24)	walk in vileness (4.24)
	walk in the ways of darkness (3.21; 4.11)
walking with reservation (4.5)	pride and haughtiness (4.9)
righteous (4.24)	deceit (4.24)

Press, 1994), pp. 1-51. Space allows listing only the first few times a *terminus tech-nicus* appears.

7.   It is surprising how seldom the *terminus technicus* 'Sons of Darkness' appears in the Dead Sea Scrolls; it is found in 1QS only in 1.10; for occurrences see J.H. Charlesworth *et al.*, *Graphic Concordance to the Dead Sea Scrolls* (Tübingen: J.C.B. Mohr [Paul Siebeck]; Louisville, KY: Westminster/John Knox Press, 1991), *ad loc. cit.*

concealing the truth of the mysteries of knowledge (4.5)	wickedness and falsehood (4.9)
a glorious purity (4.5)	filthy ways in unclean worship (4.10)

The Appointed Time of Judgment (4.20)

great peace in long life (4.7)	eternal perdition (4.12)
endless joy (4.7)	everlasting terror (4.12)
a crown of glory (4.7)	endless shame (4.13)
all the glory of Adam (4.23)	
resplendent attire in eternal light (4.7)	bitter misery in dark abysses (4.13)
everlasting life (4.7)	to be destroyed (4.14)

In the following examination we will attempt to see to what extent the features of this dualism are contained or modified in the major sectarian scrolls.

Putting aside for the moment the question of the development of dualism in Qumran theology,[8] it is necessary to emphasize that dualism appears in each of the major sectarian Scrolls. Observe the following representative excerpts.[9]

> And to love all the Sons of Light,
>   each according to his lot in the plan of God;
> And to hate all the Sons of Darkness,
>   each according to his guilt in the vengeance of God (1QS 1.9-11).

> And he (the God of Knowledge) appointed
>   for him (man) two Spirits
>   in order that he should walk in them until
>   the time of his visitation;
>   they are the Spirits of Truth and Falsehood (1QS 3.18-19).

> And then at the time of Judgment the sword of God will act
>   quickly,
> And all the sons of his tr[u]th shall be roused

8.   Obviously this is not the place to discuss the date of composition for the instruction concerning two Spirits (1QS 3.13–4.26) or for portions thereof (especially 1QS 3.13–4.14). P. von der Osten-Sacken (*Gott und Belial: Traditions-geschichtliche Untersuchungen zum Dualismus in den Texten aus Qumran* [SUNT, 6; Göttingen: Vandenhoeck & Ruprecht, 1969]) and Murphy-O'Connor, ('La genèse littéraire') conclude their minute examinations by the contention that 1QS 3.13–4.26 is a later addition to the Rule. However, see also the position of A.-M. Denis, 'Evolution de structures dans la secte de Qumrân', in *Aux origines de l'église* (RechBib, 7; Louvain: Desclée de Brouwer, 1965), pp. 23-49.

9.   Unless otherwise noted, all translations are by the author.

to [destroy the sons of] wickedness;
And all the sons of iniquity shall be no more (1QH 6.29-30).

For in proportion to the Spirits
   [You have divi]ded them (men)
   between good and evil (1QH 14.11-12).

For formerly Moses and Aaron arose
   by the hand of the Prince of Lights;
   but Belial raised Jannes and his brother... (CD 5.17-19).

And no one who has entered the Covenant of God shall
   take from or give to the sons of the Pit
   except[10] through trade (CD 13.14-15).

...the war, the beginning is when the
   Sons of Light stretch forth their hand in order
   to begin against the lot of the Sons of Darkness... (1QM 1.1).

And You have assigned us to the lot of light
   for your truth. And from of old you
   appointed the Prince of Light
   to help us...
And you made Belial, the
   Angel of Hatred, to corrupt, his dominion is
   in darkness (1QM 13.9-11).

The above excerpts from the Scrolls display Qumran's dualism. It was not an absolute dualism, however, because it was subsequent to, inferior to, and dependent on an overriding and fervent monotheism. As we look back at the above excerpts, we note that according to 1QS 3.18-19 the 'two Spirits' are under God's appointment and are to perform their functions only as long as he wills it ('until the time of his visitation'). Monotheism dominates the dualism found not only in the *Rule of the Community* but also in the other major sectarian Scrolls (see 1QH 1.1-20; CD 2.2-13; 1QM 1.8-14). The first characteristic feature of Qumran dualism is that it is limited in power, extent and time.

In these Scrolls we find the belief in two warring cosmic Spirits. In the *Rule of the Community* they are called by various names, the 'Prince

---

10. The Hebrew literally means 'except hand for hand'. The idiom clearly means that the member of the covenant of God must receive payment for what he gives and pay for what he receives.

of Light' and the 'Spirit of Truth' vis-à-vis the 'Angel of Darkness' and the 'Spirit of Perversity'. In the *Thanksgiving Hymns* several passages refer to the idea that there are two ruling Spirits, one evil, the other good (1QH 1.9, 17ff.; 4.31; 7.6-7; 11.12-13; 14.11-12; 16.9ff.; 17.23ff.). In the *Damascus Document* and the *War Scroll* the war rages between the 'Prince of Lights' [or Light] (CD 5.18; 1QM 13.10)[11] and Belial (CD 4.13, 15 *et passim*; 1QM 1.1, 5, 13 *et passim*) and the 'Angels of Destruction (Corruption)' (CD 2.6; 1QM 13.12). Behind the diversity of terminology lies the belief that the world is ripped into two realms by two warring, cosmic Spirits. This is the second characteristic of Qumran dualism.

Under the sheer brilliance of the dualism promulgated in 1QS 3.13–4.26, we often have the impression that Essene dualism is a system in which there are two warring Spirits, distinguished and separated by their identification either with light or with darkness. In fact J. Daniélou remarks that 'the conflict between light and darkness…is nothing else but the *leitmotif* of Qumran.'[12] The remark is somewhat misleading because the *Rule*'s dualism has been read into other documents. The Hodayot do not contain the expression בני אור, 'sons of light', or the term בני חושך, 'sons of darkness', nor do they have the phrase Prince, Angel or Spirit of Light. The Qumranic *Damascus Document* does not contain the word חושך, 'darkness'. The light–darkness paradigm,[13] therefore, is not always the typical feature of Qumran dualism.

The omission of the terminology in the *Thanksgiving Hymns* probably results from the focus of the speaker. The words are directed not to

11. H. Ringgren argues that in 1QM 13.2-4, 'it is not a question of two spirits under God's supremacy but of God and Belial'. H. Ringgren, *The Faith of Qumran: Theology of the Dead Sea Scrolls* (New York: Crossroad, 1995), p. 75 (an English translation of *Tro och liv enligt Döda-havsrullarna* [Stockholm: Diakonistyrelsens Bokförlag, 1961]). It would not be wise to build too much on the observation that the Levites (*et al.*) bless God but curse Belial. The 'Prince of Light' is not mentioned in lines 2-4; however, it is appropriate to praise not the messenger from God but God himself.

12. S. Daniélou, *The Dead Sea Scrolls and Primitive Christianity* (New York: New American Library; London: New English Library, 1958), p. 107.

13. The light–darkness paradigm means more than that there is a dualism sometimes expressed in terms of light and darkness. It signifies that there are two opposites primarily described as light (which symbolically represents life, truth, knowledge, and eternal life) or darkness (which tends to represent death, falsehood, ignorance, and extinction).

a person's situation but to God's. The speaker apparently assumes the light–darkness paradigm: 'and my light shines in Thy glory. For Thou hast caused the light to shine out of darkness' (1QH 9.26-27). The first two lines of the final column of the *Thanksgiving Hymns* begin with the expression 'Thy light'. The author then confesses, 'For with Thee is light' (1QH 18.3).

The observation that חושׁך is not found in the *Damascus Document* should be combined with the recognition that in this same scroll we read that 'the Prince of Lights' (CD 5.18) is opposed by 'Belial' (CD 5.18). Since the noun Belial abounds in this Scroll (6 times) and since the composition is clearly later than the earliest portions of the *Rule*, it is possible that Belial was a frequent substitute by the *later* sectarians for the 'Angel of Darkness'. The possibility is strengthened by the observation that Belial is a favourite expression in the *War Scroll* (12 times), which is the latest of the major sectarian Scrolls. Further corroborative evidence is that the term Belial is found only in the preface (1QS 1.18, 24; 2.5, 19) and concluding hymn (1QS 10.21) of the *Rule*;[14] and these sections are dated by J. Murphy-O'Connor to approximately the same date: 'The setting in life of the final hymn in 1QS is the same as that of 1QS 1.16–2.25a.'[15] The time when these additions were made to the *Rule of the Community* corresponds approximately to the date of composition for the *Damascus Document*.

What are we to say about the use of Belial in the *Thanksgiving Hymns*, where it is also frequent (12 times)? Since the substitution of Belial for the 'Angel of Darkness' would necessitate the cosmic conception of the former, we must ask another question: is Belial conceived of as a hypostatic individual in the *Thanksgiving Hymns*? Only in four passages does this term probably have a cosmic dimension (1QH 2.22; 3.28; 3.29; 3.32); in the other eight occurrences it has a non-cosmic or psychological meaning (1QH 2.16; 4.10; 4.13 [*bis*]; 5.26; 5.39; 6.21; 7.3). It is impressive to discover that each one of the latter group of passages is taken from sections that G. Jeremias has attributed to the Righteous Teacher.[16] The passages containing a cosmic meaning probably come

14. 'Belial' in 1QS 10.21 does not denote the cosmic evil Spirit. This observation alone, however, is not sufficient to place the hymn in the time of the Righteous Teacher.

15. J. Murphy-O'Connor, 'La genèse littéraire', p. 545.

16. *Der Lehrer der Gerechtigkeit*. Jeremias argues that in the *Thanksgiving Hymns* 'Belial' means 'Bosheit, Ränke, nicht der Eigenname des göttlichen Gegenspielers'

from later stages in the life of the community. Moreover, in his *Kon-kordanz* Kuhn reports that the word Belial as *nomen proprium* does not appear in the *Thanksgiving Hymns* (*q.v. ad loc.*). The evidence seems to converge towards the supposition that Belial as a synonym for the 'Angel of Darkness' is peculiar to the later texts. By the time the *Damascus Document* was composed, 'Belial' had become a surrogate for the 'Angel of Darkness'. The absence of the word 'darkness' in this Scroll is not as stunning as formerly supposed.

We may now conclude our discussion of the light–darkness paradigm in the Scrolls. While the paradigm is not emphasized in each of the major sectarian documents, it is nevertheless characteristic of the Scrolls as a collection. This schema is so sophisticated in the Scrolls as to distinguish them from most literature with which they were con-temporaneous.[17] The lone exception is the *Testaments of the Twelve Patriarchs*.[18] This document, however, may originate in Essene circles.

(*Der Lehrer der Gerechtigkeit*, p. 194). M. Delcor also remarks, 'Ce terme y sert à désigner des personnes ou des êtres mauvais ou qui veulent du mal, mais non le Démon lui-même' (*Les Hymnes de Qumran*, p. 44; see also pp. 37 and 185f.).

17. This is certainly not the place to discuss the concepts of light and darkness in the early Jewish and extra-canonical literature. Suffice it to state that in this literature 'darkness' is not always portrayed as something intrinsically bad: for example, in the *Song of the Three Children* (v. 48) light and darkness are exhorted to bless and praise the Lord. The authors of the Scrolls, *Odes*, and John would never have conceived such an exhortation for darkness. The light–darkness paradigm is also not found in the rabbinic literature. It may, however, be behind some portions of the Ethiopic *Book of Enoch* (e.g. 58.3ff.; 92.4ff.). The uniqueness of the light–darkness paradigm to Qumran (in contrast to other sects of pre-Christian Judaism) has recently been intimated by H. Kosmala: 'Previous to the discovery of the Dead Sea Scrolls such expressions as "the children of light", "light" and "darkness", "enlightened", and many, many others were thought to be exclusively terms of the theological language of the New Testament and early Christian literature' ('The Parable of the Unjust Steward in the Light of Qumran', in *idem* (ed.), *Annual of the Swedish Theological Institute* [Leiden: E.J. Brill, 1964], III, pp. 114-21; the quotation is from p. 115). F. Nötscher discusses some of the peculiarities of Qumran's dualism in his *Zur theologischen Terminologie der Qumran-Texte* (BBB, 10; Bonn: Hanstein, 1956) pp. 103-48.

18. E.g. *T. Levi* 19.1-2, 'choose...either the light or the darkness, either the law of the Lord or the works of Beliar' (cf. *T. Naph.* 2.7-10); *T. Jos.* 20.2, 'the Lord shall be with you in light, and Beliar shall be in darkness with the Egyptians'. Even in the *Testaments of the Twelve Patriarchs*, as F. Nötscher and O. Böcher observed, the paradigm is not combined with the idea that there are two ways, which appears only once (*T. Ash.* 1.3-5); see Nötscher, *Zur theologischen Terminologie*, p. 114;

Therefore, the third characteristic of Qumran dualism is the light–darkness paradigm.

Pervading the Scrolls, as is well known, is the Essenes' belief that they were living in the last days and that the future had irrupted into the present.[19] At times the Scrolls suggest that the postbiblical Jewish division of time between 'this age' and 'the age to come' had clearly dissolved. Often the Essene projects himself into the future and speaks as if the end has already come (1QH 3.23-36). At other times the Scrolls uphold a division within time. According to P. von der Osten-Sacken, the oldest form of Qumran dualism, found in the *War Scroll* and the first section of the *Rule* (1QS 3.13–4.14), emphasizes the imminent eschatological combat (*Endkampfdualismus*).[20] The decisive eschatological act still lay in the future. At the end of the impending conflict, the 'sons of light' will receive 'every continuing blessing and eternal joy in eternal life, and a crown of glory with a garment of majesty in eternal light' (1QS 4.7-8; cf. 1QH 9.25). The 'sons of darkness', however, will be annihilated 'until they are exterminated without remnant or escape' (1QS 4.14; cf. 1QM 1.4-7). The fourth characteristic of Qumran dualism, therefore, is the eschatological dimension.

Each of the major sectarian Scrolls—that is, those that most likely were composed at Qumran or reflect Essene thought—contains the idea that humankind is bifurcated into two mutually exclusive camps. Although the terminology changes, the dualism is clear; and persons are categorized either as 'Sons of Light' (1QS and 1QM), 'Sons of Truth' (1QS, 1QH and 1QM), 'sons of Zadok' (1QS and CD) or as 'Sons of Darkness' (1QS and 1QM), 'Sons of Perversity' (1QS and 1QH) and 'sons of the Pit' (CD). Since men are divided according to their virtues and vices, we have running through the Scrolls an ethical dualism. This

O. Böcher, *Der johanneische Dualismus in Zusammenhang des nachbiblischen Judentums* (Gütersloh: Gütersloher Verlagshaus, 1965), p. 97, see also pp. 96-101, 15. A succinct comparison of the dualism contained in the *Testaments of the Twelve Patriarchs* with that in the Scrolls is found in von der Osten-Sacken, *Gott und Belial,* pp. 197-205. Although *Jubilees* contains dualistic thought (e.g. 'sons of perdition' [10.3]—'sons of the righteous' [10.6]), it does not contain the light–darkness paradigm.

19. The point is developed with erudition in a recent monograph: Kuhn, *Enderwartung und gegenwärtiges Heil.* J. Carmignac questioned the appropriateness of the term 'eschatology'. See his 'La notion d'eschatologie dans la Bible et à Qumrân', *RevQ* 7 (1969), pp. 17-31.

20. Von der Osten-Sacken, *Gott und Belial.*

is the fifth characteristic of Qumran dualism.

The ethical dualism is usually expressed in terms of preordination. Note the predestinarian strain in the following excerpts:

> From the God of Knowledge (מאל הדעות) comes all that is occurring and shall occur (כול הויה ונהייה). Before they came into being he established all their designs; and when they come into existence in their fixed times (לתעודותם) they carry through their task according to his glorious design (1QS 3.15f.).[21]

> But during all those (years), (God) raised raised up for himself those called by name (שם קריאי) so as to leave a remnant for the land (פליטה לארץ)... But those whom he hated he caused to stray (CD 2.11-13).[22]

> And you have cast upon man an eternal lot (1QH 3.22; 15.13-21).

> You have cast us in the lot of light (ובגורל אור) according to your truth... You have made Belial to corrupt (עשיתה בליעל לשחת), a hostile angel.[23] (1QM 13.9-11).

Other passages suggest the possibility of conversion from sin ('to pardon them that return from sin' [CD 2.5; cf. 1QS 10.20; 1QH 2.9; 6.6; 14.24]), others attribute an individual's fate not to God's foreordination but to his foreknowledge ('For God did not choose them from the beginning, and before they were established He knew their works' [CD 2.7-8]),[24] but these ideas are exceptions. There is wide agreement today

---

21. For the Hebrew and English translation, see J.H. Charlesworth (ed.), *The Dead Sea Scrolls: Hebrew, Aramaic, and Greek Texts with English Translations*. I. *Rule of the Community and Related Documents* (Tübingen: J.C.B. Mohr [Paul Siebeck], 1995]), pp. 1-51. H. Ringgren argues that תעודה means predestination. See Ringgren, *The Faith of Qumran*, pp. 53f.

22 . For Hebrew and English translation, see J.M. Baumgarten and D. Schwartz, 'The Damascus Document', in J.H. Charlesworth (ed.), *The Dead Sea Scrolls: Hebrew, Aramaic, and Greek Texts with English Translations*. II. *Damascus Document, War Scroll and Related Documents* (Tübingen: J.C.B. Mohr [Paul Siebeck], 1995]), pp. 5-57.

23. This idea frees Belial of responsibility for his sins. The thought is thus inferior to the brilliant balance obtained in 1QS 3.13–4.26. For the Hebrew and translation, see J. Duhaime, 'War Scroll', in Charlesworth (ed.), *The Dead Sea Scrolls*, II, pp. 80-198.

24. E. Cothenet entitles the section CD 2.2-13 'Prédestination des Justes et des Impies', in *Les Textes de Qumran* (Paris: Letouzey & Ané, 1963), II, p. 152. Accord-

that the authors of the Scrolls held a dualism that contained predestinarian features.[25] This is the sixth characteristic of Qumran dualism.

The most conspicuous feature of Qumran dualism is the ethical dimension. The cosmic struggle centres in the heart of human beings. Synonyms for the 'Sons of Light' and 'Sons of Darkness' are respectively the 'Sons of Righeousness' and 'Sons of Perversity'. The pervasive eschatological tone of the Scrolls clarifies the results of ethical dualism: eternal life for the 'sons of piety' (1QH 7.20), extinction for the 'sons of transgression' (1QH 5.7; 6.30; 7.11). The lot of a human being is predetermined. In summation, humankind is divided not according to metaphysical but ethical categories.

John's 'Dualism'
In the following paragraphs it should become evident that the most systematic dualism in the New Testament is found in John.

A cosmic dualism is assumed by the author of John, not in the sense of two opposing celestial spirits, but in the sense of two distinct and present divisions in the universe. The universe is bifurcated into the 'world above', which is the source of all things, especially power (1.3, 10; 19.11), and the 'world below', which hates the 'world above' (7.7) and is similar in meaning to κόσμος, which is frequently presented as an inferior force in rebellion against God. The cosmic dualism is modified since the two worlds are not two equal and eternal concepts. The 'world below' is limited in quality and quantity:

> And he (Jesus) said to them (the Ioudaioi [Jews or Judeans]), 'You are from below, I am from above. You are from this world, I am not from this world. Therefore, I declared to you that you will die in your sins' (8.23f.; cf. 6.48-51, 58; 4.13-14; 3.3ff., 31; 11.41; 19.11).

ing to our interpretation the heading is misleading because *some* verses in the section intimate foreknowledge not foreordination.

The omission of the word הושע and the presence of passages that are not 'predestinarian' have led me to entertain the idea that CD was not directed to those in the Community. This idea is now developed by J. Murphy-O'Connor, 'An Essene Missionary Document? CD II, 14–VI, 1', *RB* 77 (1970), pp. 201-29.

25. Contrast A. Marx who argues that when talking about the Scrolls we ought to avoid 'le terme de "prédestination" et de parler tout simplement de grâce!' ('Y a-t-il une prédestination à Qumrân?' *RevQ* 6 [1967], pp. 163-81; the quotation is from p. 181).

The first characteristic of John's 'dualism', therefore, is a modified cosmic dualism between the 'world above' and the 'world below'.

Each world exhibits a force. From above the force is Christ, from below it is the κόσμος. The main actors in the drama are Jesus and the Ioudaioi. Hence, while there is no metaphysical dualism (i.e. God is not opposed by an evil angel), there is a cosmic struggle between Jesus Christ and the κόσμος (= the Ioudaioi). Since Jesus represents[26] God (5.36ff.; 12.50) and since the Ioudaioi symbolize the Devil ('You are of your father the devil [τοῦ διαβόλου]' [8.44]) we are justified in calling this aspect of John's 'dualism' an extremely modified metaphysical dualism.[27] This is the second characteristic of John's 'dualism'.

Pervading John's 'dualism' is the light–darkness paradigm; his penchant for 'light' and 'darkness' distinguishes him from the other evangelists.[28] He uses the word 'light' more than three times as much as either Matthew or Luke, and 23 times more than Mark (φῶς, 'light': Mt. [7], Mk [1], Lk. [7], Jn [23]).[29] His application of the word 'darkness' is slightly more frequent than that of the other evangelists, but his use of σκοτία to designate 'darkness' is unique (Mt. [2], Mk [0], Lk. [1], Jn [8]). The 'world above' and the 'world below' are respectively categorized by 'light' and 'darkness'. All persons are in darkness; however, the appearance of light brought judgment: 'But this is the judgment: although light came into the world men loved *darkness* rather than *light*, because their deeds were evil' (3.19 [italics mine]). Ironically, judgment resulted from God's attempt to save humanity, since the appearance of Christ, 'the light of the world' (8.12; 9.5) was for humanity's benefit: 'I have come as *light* into the world, that whoever believes

---

26. Jesus is sent from God: it is not Jesus alone who speaks, but God speaking through him; it is not Jesus himself who heals the sick, but God's power manifest in and through him. The concept of Jesus as one sent and its relationship to the Old Testament and gnostic literature is presented by J. Kuhl, *Die Sendung Jesu und der Kirche nach dem Johannes-Evangelium* (SIMSVD, 11; Siegburg: Steyler Verlag, 1967).

27. Some verses reflect the idea that Jesus has already fought and defeated the devil (e.g. 12.31; 16.33).

28. So also P.H. Bakotin, *De notione lucis et tenebrarum in Evangelio S. Joannis* (Croatia, Dubrovnik, 1943), and Nötscher, *Zur theologischen Terminologie*, p. 123.

29. For these statistics I am indebted to R. Morgenthaler, *Statistik des neutestamentlichen Wortschatzes, loc. cit.* See also Brown, *The Gospel According to John,* I, pp. 515-16.

in me may not remain in *darkness*' (12.46 [italics mine]). Humankind, therefore, is bifurcated into two categories: on one side there is light, which is associated with belief (12.35f.), truth (3.21; 8.31f.), life (1.4; 8.12), and knowledge (1.9f.); on the other is darkness, which is linked primarily with evil (3.19f.) and ignorance (1.5; 12.35). One who does not believe 'walks in the darkness' (12.35); one who follows Jesus 'will not walk in *darkness*, but will have the *light* of life' (8.12 [italics mine]). John's cosmological and soteriological dualism, discussed below, are couched in terms of the light–darkness paradigm. This is the third characteristic of John's 'dualism'.

An important feature of John's 'dualism' is the division of eschatology into the future that has broken into the present and the future that is about to break into the present. Like a cascading waterfall, time has rushed on, leaving behind those who cling to a past revelation, the law (1.17), and sweeping with it those who grasp the present revelation, Jesus (1.17; 8.12). John's realizing eschatology is the logical result of his Christology, the hour has come (12.23), the Devil is defeated (12.31; 16.11), Christ has overcome the world (16.33). In John, therefore, the distinct eschatological dualism between the present time and a future awaited day (the distinction between 'this age' and 'the age to come') has become modified.[30] Those who belong to the light have eternal life (3.16);[31] those who are of the darkness shall be destroyed (3.16, 18). This modified eschatological dualism is the fourth characteristic.

Although humankind is not initially divided into two mutually exclusive categories, one's individual response to Jesus' call for faith categorizes one as either 'from God' (8.47; cf. 'children of God' in 1.12) or 'not from God' (8.47). After the invitation to believe, one is categorized by one's response; a person is either 'one who believes' (3.16; 12.36) or 'one who does not believe' (3.18). The fifth characteristic of John's 'dualism', therefore, is a soteriological dualism.

Consistent with his soteriology is John's insistence on the human ability to choose.[32] While some passages tend to suggest preordination

30. There are exceptions posed by Jn 5.28-29; 6.39, 40, 44, 51c-58; and 12.48.

31. S. Vitalini correctly notes that for John the reception of light signifies participation in 'la vita divina' and the presence of eternal life (*La nozione d'accoglienza nel Nuovo Testamento* [Studia Friburgensia, NS 35; Fribourg: Edizioni Universitarie, 1963], pp. 68-69).

32. Contrast E. Käsemann's recent claim that for John faith is restricted to the elect: 'To decide in favour of Jesus is a divine gift and possible only for the elect.'

(1.12ff.; 6.37-45), the main thrust in John is that the invitation to believe is sent to *all* people: 'For God so loved the world that he gave his only son, so that *everyone who believes in him* may not perish but have life eternal' (3.16 [italics mine]). Christ's death on the cross was not for an elect group alone, but for all: 'when I am lifted up from the earth, I will draw all men to myself' (12.32). The human ability to choose is the sixth characteristic of John's 'dualism'.

The most important characteristic of Johannine 'dualism' is the soteriological.[33] Pervading the Gospel is the emphasis on the result of acceptance or rejection of Jesus Christ. John conceived of everything either being for or against Christ, in light or darkness, truth or error, righteousness or sin, life or death. Though cosmic dualism did not originate from his soteriological dualism, it was reminted and colored by it. Everything is transposed into a higher key because of the arrival of the promised σωτήρ, 'Saviour'; hence the essential 'dualism' is soteriological.

'Dualism' in the Odes

Unlike the Scrolls and John, the *Odes of Solomon* have not been examined for their dualism. A cursory reading of the *Odes* would probably give the impression that there is relatively little, if any, dualism in them. In the following pages we shall see that the *Odes* contain a dualism, even if it is subdued.

Like the Scrolls and John the *Odes* are monotheistic. There is one Creator upon whom all creatures and created things are dependent. In *Ode* 4.15 we read, 'And you, O Lord, have made all.' In *Ode* 6.3-5 the odist wrote the following:

This interpretation became possible because Jn 3.16 was judged to have come not from the Evangelist himself but from a 'traditional primitive Christian formula', which was employed solely 'to stress the glory of Jesus' mission, that is to say the miracle of the incarnation' (*The Testament of Jesus: A Study of the Gospel of John in the Light of Chapter 17* [Philadelphia: Fortress Press, 1968], pp. 64, 60). It is quite likely, however, that Jn 3.16 is from the Evangelist; 3.1-21 is a well-organized discourse. So also Brown, *The Gospel According to John*, I, pp. 136-37, 147.

33. Perhaps this is what Käsemann meant when he declared that 'The Johannine dualism marks the effect of the Word in that world in which the light has always shone into the darkness... The decisions for or against the Word constantly take place on an earth which has already been separated into two hostile spheres through the event of the Word' (*The Testament of Jesus*, p. 63). Cf. A. Wikenhauser, *Das Evangelium nach Johannes* (RNT, 4; Regensburg: Pustet, 3rd edn, 1961), p. 176.

For he (the Spirit of the Lord) destroys whatever is alien,
And everything is of the Lord.

For thus it was from the beginning,
And it will be until the end.

So that nothing shall be contrary,
And nothing shall rise up against him.

As we saw above when considering the Dead Sea Scrolls and John, the dualism is decisively modified by the monotheistic belief.

In several verses the Creator is called the 'Word' (12.10; cf. 7.7f.; 16.8-12, 19). In *Ode* 7.7, however, the Creator is specified as the 'Father of knowledge (ܐܒܐ ܕܝܕܥܬܐ)'. The striking parallels between the former (the 'Word') and John and the latter ('Father of knowledge') and the Scrolls will be discussed in the following pages.

The Odist, like John, inherited the Old Testament idea that the universe is separated into two worlds.[34] Occasionally the Odist mentions the descent of the 'Word' (12.5f.) and the Lord: 'And his (the Lord's) will descended from on high' (23.5). Elsewhere the ascent of the believer is mentioned: 'And I was lifted up in the light' (21.6), 'I rested on the Spirit of the Lord, / And she lifted me up to heaven' (36.1). Like John, the cosmic dualism of two worlds is modified because the 'world above' is so vastly superior:

The likeness of that which is *below*
Is that which is *above*.
For everything is from *above*,
And from *below* there is nothing;
But it is believed to be by those in whom there is no understanding
(*Ode* 34.4-5 [italics mine]).

---

34. O. Böcher correctly argues that according to the Old Testament the universe is divided into the world above, heaven, and the world below, earth (Gen. 1.1ff.; 14.19, 22). Sheol, the so-called 'underworld' and abode of the dead (cf. especially Isa. 14.9), is not a world separate and beneath the earth, 'but apparently on the Earth itself' (*Der johanneische Dualismus*, p. 23). Seen in this light *Ode* 22.1-2 does not reflect belief in a trifurcated universe. It is also possible that these verses reflect the Odist's belief that Christ descended from heaven, lived on the earth, died, descended into hell, and then ascended into heaven again (*Ode* 42.11-20 is clearly about the *descensus ad inferos*). According to *Ode* 29.4, Sheol is the abode of the dead on the earth.

The first characteristic of the Odist's 'dualism', therefore, is a modified cosmic dualism of two worlds.

As one reads through the *Odes*, one is confronted by a belief in two Spirits, one good ('the Spirit of the Lord, which is not false' [3.10]; 'his [the Lord's] Spirit' [16.5; cf. 14.8; 7.3; 8.6; 21.2; 25.2]), the other evil ('the Evil One' [14.5]). The dualism, however, does not depict a cosmic struggle between two Spirits; here the good Spirit (or the Lord) saves or has saved the believer from the evil Spirit (14.4f.). Near the end of the collection, we find a clearer expression of this dualism; in *Ode* 33 the two 'Spirits' do not fight each other but vie for man's allegiance. *Ode* 33.3-7 reads as follows:

> And he (the Corruptor) stood on the peak of a summit and cried aloud
> From one end of the earth to the other.
>
> The he drew to him all those who obeyed him,
> For he did not appear as the Evil One.
>
> However the perfect Virgin stood,
> Who was preaching and summoning and saying:
>
> O you sons of men, return,
> And you their daughters, come.
>
> And leave the ways of the Corruptor,
> And approach me.

The dualism contained in this Ode, including the remaining verses, may be expressed in diagram form as follows:

'the perfect Virgin' (33.5)	'the Corruptor' (33.1, 7)
	='the Evil One' (33.4)
'the ways of truth' (33.8)	'the ways of that Corruptor' (33.7)
'my (the Virgin's) ways' (33.13)	
'obey me (the Virgin)' (33.10)	'all those who obeyed him' (33.4)
'be saved and blessed' (33.11)	'destruction' (33.8f.)
'possess incorruption in the new world' (33.12)	'perish' (33.9)

In *Ode* 38 we find a dualism between Truth and Error, both of which are personified, and later a dualism between two sets of brides and bridegrooms. Truth is not depicted as fighting against Error, but as the protector of the Odist from Error, over whom he is definitely superior ('For Error fled from him' [38.6]). Likewise in the second section of this Ode the 'Bride who was corrupting' and the 'Bridegroom who corrupts and is corrupted' do not confront but imitate 'The Beloved and his Bride'. The dualism contained in this Ode may be outlined as follows:

The Lord (38.20)

Truth (38.1)	Error (38.6)
'light of Truth' (38.1)	('The way of error' 15.6)
'the upright way' (38.7)	('walking in error' 18.14)
'I walked with him (Truth)' (38.5)	
'immortal life' (38.3)	death (38.8)
Truth (38.10)	the Corruptor (38.9)
'the Beloved and his Bride' (38.11)	'the Bridegroom who corrupts and is corrupted' (38.9)
	'the Bride who was corrupting' (38.9)
	='the Deceiver and the Error' (38.10)
	'cause the world to err and corrupt it' (38.11)
(drink 'from the Most High' 6.12; *Ode* 30 complete)	'the wine of their intoxication' (38.12)
wisdom and knowledge (38.13)	nonsense (38.13)
	no understanding (38.15)
the Truth (38.16)	the Deceivers (38.16)

In this Ode, therefore, we find emphasis placed on two ways, each of which is headed by a hypostatic figure.

In the *Odes* we have discovered a 'dualism' of two opposing creatures. Since the two figures do not confront each other as they do in the *War Scroll* (viz. 1QM 7.6; 12.8; 16.11; 18.1), this aspect of the odist's 'dualism' can be called a modified metaphysical dualism. This is the second characteristic.

As with the Scrolls and John, the *Odes* express the dualistic ideas in terms of the light–darkness paradigm (cf. 5.4-6; 6.17; 7.14; 12.3; 25.7; 29.7; 31.1; 32.1; 38.1; 41.6, 14).[35] Note the following symbolic uses of 'light' and 'darkness':

'And to walk with watchfulness in his light' (8.2).
'the Lord…possessed me by his light' (11.11).
Blessed are they who 'have passed from darkness to light' (11.18f.).

---

35. Verses cited as examples in parentheses are usually meant to be representative not exhaustive.

'He is the light and dawning of thought' (12.7).
the Lord 'he is my Sun, /...
And his light has dismissed all darkness from my face' (15.2).

The Odist makes full use of this light–darkness paradigm in 21.3 ('And I put off darkness, / And put on light') and 18.6:

Let not light be conquered by darkness,
Nor let truth flee from falsehood.

The synonymous parallelism shows that light is associated with truth (cf. 15.5) and darkness with falsehood. The third characteristic of the Odist's 'dualism' is the emphasis put upon the light–darkness paradigm.

Like John, the *Odes* portray a realizing eschatology. The Odist believed that the Messiah had come (41.3f., 11-15), taking human form:

He became like me that I might receive him.
In form he was considered like me
    that I might put him on.

And I trembled not when I saw him,
Because he was gracious to me.
Like my nature he became
    that I might understand him.
And like my form
    that I might not turn away from him. (7.4-6)

The struggle between good and evil still continues (8.7; 9.6; 28.6; 29.9) but the decisive battle has been fought so that 'the persecutors' are now 'blotted out' (23.20; 42.5), because the Messiah has already captured the world ('I took courage and became strong and captured the world, / And it became mine for the glory of the Most High, and of God my Father' [10.4 (*ex ore Christi*); cf. 29.10; 31.1f.]) and 'possessed everything' (23.19), even conquering Sheol and death ('Sheol saw me and was shattered, / And death ejected me and many with me' [42.11 (*ex ore Christi*); the remainder of this ode concerns the *descensus ad inferos*]). As with John, so in the *Odes* 'eternal life' is not merely a future reward but primarily a present actuality for the believer ('And he [the Lord] has caused to dwell in me His immortal life' [10.2; see 15.10]). Some verses in the *Odes*, however, such as Jn 5.28f., reflect a futuristic eschatology (e.g. 'And they who have put me [the perfect Virgin] on shall not be falsely accused, / But they shall possess incorruption in the new world' [33.12]). Nevertheless, throughout the *Odes* the concept of time is not that of the present versus the distant or even imminent future, but of *the breaking in of the future into the present.* The similarities with John are striking. Hence we may refer to this fourth characteristic of the *Odes*' 'dualism' as a modified eschatological dualism.

Pervasive in *sotto voce* throughout the *Odes* is a soteriological dualism. The Syriac word for 'to save', ܦܪܩ, and its derivatives such as 'Saviour', ܦܪܘܩܐ, are employed no less than 34 times. This frequency is remarkable, since it is roughly equal to the number of times 'to praise' and its derivatives are used (35 times); and the *Odes* are primarily 'thanksgiving hymns'. Although the noun 'Saviour' is found in only two verses (41.11; 42.18), the Odist continually praises the Lord for his salvation. His petition is for salvation from the Evil One ('let me be saved from the Evil One' [14.5; cf. 18.7]). Often he declares that he is saved ('And I walked with him and was saved' [17.4; cf. 17.2, 15; 25.2, 4; 28.10; 35.2, 7; 38.2f., 17]). It is important to note that the Odist is saved from the Evil One (14.5), the 'way of error' (15.6), and that it is because of salvation that the Lord ('the Son' [7.15]) possesses everything (7.16).

Occasionally 'the Lord' signifies 'God' (29.6a), but usually it represents 'the Messiah' (29.6b; 24.1). The Messiah is the one who rejects all who do not belong to the truth (24.10-12), the one who dispels darkness (15.1-2), and the Salvation-Bringer ('And because the Lord is my salvation, / I will not fear' [5.11; cf. 31.12f.]). He is portrayed in dualistic terms:

> The way of error I have forsaken,
> And I went toward him and received salvation from him abundantly.
> (15.6; cf. 21.2)

Like John, the *Odes* reflect the idea that the coming of the Saviour has split humankind into two groups; but unlike John, the *Odes* do not describe the division as 'those who do not believe' and 'those who believe'. Only implicit in John but prominent in the *Odes* is the description of the two sections of humankind according to the paradigm error–ignorance vis-à-vis truth–knowledge. On the one hand are those who do not belong to the truth (24.10-12), the 'vain people' (18.12); on the other are those who wear 'the crown of truth' (1.2; 9.8ff.) and 'the wise' (18.13). The division of persons is frequently expressed in terms of two ways:

'the way of error' (15.6)	'the way of truth' (11.3)
'walking in error' (18.14)	'walk in the knowledge of the Lord' (23.4)

The bifurcation of humankind is also expressed in terms of an ethical dualism, although it is less prominent than the error-versus-truth schema. In two of the passages just cited knowledge is associated with 'love' (11.2; 23.3; cf. *Ode* 3.1-7). *Ode* 17.2-5 implies that the Odist has been freed from the realm of 'vanities' and condemnation to that of 'salvation' and 'truth'. In *Ode* 7.20f. 'knowledge' is not only contrasted with 'ignorance' but 'hatred' and 'jealousy' as well. The ethical aspect is clearest in *Ode* 20.3-6 in which 'the world' and 'the flesh' are contrasted with 'righteousness', 'purity of heart and lips', 'compassion' and other ethical norms. We may describe this fifth aspect of the 'dualism' in the *Odes* as a soteriological dualism expressed frequently in terms of error versus truth and occasionally in terms of an ethical dualism.

Since the question of predestination in both the Scrolls and John has been examined, it is appropriate to say a few words about this subject in the *Odes*. As one would expect in a hymnbook, there is no discussion on this question; however, a few passages reflect that the Odist would have opted for the idea that the human being has a choice. The Odist apparently advocated universalism; he states that the stream (the spread of the good news; see 6.12ff.) 'spread over the surface of *all* the earth, / And it filled *everything*. / / Then *all* the thirsty upon the earth drank' (6.10f. [italics mine]). In *Ode* 33, as we saw above, 'the Corruptor' and 'the perfect Virgin' are not playing chess with human beings as pawns; they are vying for human allegiance. Note that 'the perfect Virgin' is not described as teasing men, but as 'preaching, summoning and saying: /...return, /...come' (33.5f.). The Odist's use of the term 'the elect ones', therefore, does not mean those foreordained to election, but those who accept the invitation (see also 8.13-18; 23.2f.).[36] In 33.13 'My elect ones' is paralleled by 'them who seek me'. The sixth characteristic of the *Odes*' 'dualism' is that human beings can choose.

Of these six aspects of the 'dualism' in the *Odes*, the fifth, soteriological dualism, is clearly the most important to the Odist. He composed these *Odes* to praise God for his recent action in history. Everything tended to be viewed from a soteriological perspective because he was joined to his Saviour:

> I have been united because the lover has found the Beloved,
> Because I love him that is the Son, I shall become a son (3.7).

---

36. *Ode* 8.13-18 refers not to foreordination but to foreknowledge; recognition (v. 13) precedes election (v. 18).

Not only in the entire third Ode but throughout the *Odes*, we find evidence that the Odist is united with his Lord. Frequently it is difficult to discern whether the Odist or 'Christ' is the speaker.

In conclusion it is necessary to state that unlike the author of 1QS 3.13ff. the Odist did not promulgate a theory concerning dualism. Unlike John the Odist did not write a Gospel or develop a theological position. He was a poet who wrote hymns. From this perspective and from the insight that the authors of the *Thanksgiving Hymns* softened their own developed dualism, a new light is thrown on the observation that the *Odes* contain a dualism. The above data are sufficient to show that the Odist held a rather sophisticated dualism. If he did not develop it, he probably inherited it from his predecessors or contemporaries. With this thought we enter the second section of the chapter in which the comparisons between the dualisms discussed above will be examined.

Comparisons

Critics who demand an exact quotation as the only proof that one document is dependent on another need not proceed further. A mind is needed with perceptions more keen and categories more subtle. An early Christian who borrowed from the Dead Sea Scrolls was dependent on them regardless of whether he altered these traditions little or greatly. A priori we should assume that an early Christian would have reminted an inherited Jewish tradition in line with his shift in eschatology and messianism: the end of time has come, the long-awaited Messiah is Jesus of Nazareth. Hence, as a prism refracts light, so the belief in the new dispensation would have altered old traditions. During the present comparisons the problem of deciphering whether there is dependency on the Qumran Scrolls will be extreme precisely because both John and the *Odes* are characterized by the extent to which they rework their sources.[37]

---

37. This feature of John is well known and discussed in most of the commentaries. For the *Odes*, see my comments in 'Les Odes de Salomon et les manuscrits de la Mer Morte'. Early Christians sometimes deliberately altered a passage borrowed (e.g. cf. *1 En.* 1.9, ἔρχεται, 'he is coming', with Jude 14, ἦλθεν, 'he came').

The 'Dualisms' of the Odes and John

Both the *Odes* and John inherit a modified cosmic dualism of two worlds. This similarity, at first glance, is unimpressive because most Christian texts written around 100 CE inherited from the Old Testament a dualistic cosmology. On closer examination, however, the similarity with which the *Odes* and John express this aspect of their 'dualisms' and the conjoined thoughts raises the possibility that there is some dependence between them. It is significant that the *Odes* hold the Johannine belief that the universe was created by 'the Word'. This striking similarity is evident below [italics mine]:

In the beginning was the *Word*, and *the Word* was with God, and *the Word* was God. He was in the beginning with God; *all things were made through him*, and without him was not anything made that was made.[38] In him was life, and the life was the light of men. The light shines in the darkness, and the darkness has not overcome it (Jn 1.1-5 RSV).

For *the Word* of the Lord searches out
   anything that is invisible,
And reveals his thought.

For the eye sees his works,
And the ear hears his thought.

It is he who made the earth broad,
And placed the waters in the sea.

He expanded the heaven,
And fixed the stars.

And he fixed the creation and set it up.
Then he rested from his works (*Ode* 16. 8-12).

And they[39] all were stimulated by *the Word*,
And knew him who had made them,
Because they were in harmony (*Ode* 12. 10).

38. Compare also 1QS 11.11, 'And through his [God's] knowledge all is brought into being, and through his thought all life is established, and without him nothing is made.' S. Schulz also sees a strong relationship between Jn 1.3 and 1QS 11.11. See his 'Die Komposition des Johannesprologs land die Zusammensetzung des 4. Evangeliums', in K. Aland, F.L. Cross, *et al.* (eds.), *Studia Evangelica* (TU, 73; Berlin: Akademie Verlag, 1959), p. 356. Also compare Jn 1.3 and 1QS 11.11 with *Ode* 16.18 ('And there is nothing outside of the Lord, / Because he was before anything came to be') and *Ode* 6.3 ('And everything is of the Lord').

39. 'They' are 'the generations' mentioned in v. 7.

It is clear that in both the *Odes* and John the Creator is called the 'Word' (see also *Ode* 7.7). The similarity between the *Odes* and John is increased by the observation that neither in the Old Testament[40] nor in the extra-canonical literature[41] is there an emphasis on the personification of the 'Word'. Unlike the other early Christian literature, the *Odes* and John stand out by their thoroughgoing depiction of the Messiah (*Odes* 9.3; 41.14) as the 'Word'. Moreover, both of them conceive of the 'Word' as pre-existent (*Odes* 32.2; 41.14; Jn 1.1f.), the Creator (*Odes* 7.7; 12.10; 16.8-14; Jn 1.3), incarnate (*Odes* 7.1-6; 39.9; 41.11f.; Jn 1.14), equated with light (*Odes* 10.1; 12.3; 16.14; 32.2; 41.14; Jn 1.4; 8.12), and the essence of love (*Odes* 12.12; Jn 13.34), truth (*Odes* 8.8; 12.3, 12; 32.2; Jn 14.6), and life (*Odes* 41.11; Jn 14.6), especially immortal life (*Odes* 10.1; 15.9; Jn 3.16 *et passim*). These similarities are too numerous, pervasive and substantial to be mere coincidence. Numerous passages, many of which are cited below, are so close as to support the probability that there is some level of dependence between the *Odes* and John.

Numerous scholars, most recently R. Schnackenburg,[42] have argued that the *Odes* are dependent on John. This conclusion is unlikely first because the evidence is equivocal: in one passage the *Odes* seem dependent on John, in another the reverse seems to be the case. It is improbable secondly and chiefly because of the following consideration. The Syriac texts of John use only ܡܠܬܐ to represent the divine 'Word'. This is true not only of the Peshitta and the Curetonian recensions (the first 24 verses of John are missing in the Sinaitic Palimpsest),

---

40. Compare the *Odes* and John with Gen. 1.1ff. and Ps. 33.6 ('By the word of the Lord the heavens were made').

41. *Pr. Man.* 3 ('Who hast bound the sea by the word of thy command') is closer to Gen. 1.1ff. than to Jn 1.1ff. *Jub.* 12.4 ('the God of heaven… has created everything by His word'), however, is closer to John and the *Odes*. The idea of creation by the Word is also reflected in Ps. 148.5, 2 Pet. 3.5 and *2 Bar.* 21.4 (if the text is amended from ܡܪܚܡܘ to ܡܠܬܐ). Compare *Acts of John* 101. The translations from the Apocrypha and Pseudepigrapha are those found in R.H. Charles (ed.), *The Apocrypha and Pseudepigrapha of the Old Testament* (2 vols.; repr.; Oxford: Clarendon Press, 1963–68 [1913]). See now *OTP* and Sparks's *The Apocryphal Old Testament*.

42. *The Gospel According to St John*, I, p. 145. See also F.M. Braun, 'L'énigme des Odes de Sal.', *RevThom* 57 (1957), pp. 615-19.

but also of the Syriac commentaries on John.[43] In the *Odes*, however, ܡܠܬܐ (10 times) as well as ܡܠܬܐ (11 times) signifies the divine 'Word'. This observation has not received the attention it deserves; it reduces the possibility that the *Odes* are dependent on John. If the *Odes* borrow from John's use of the 'Word', then it is practically impossible to explain why in *Ode* 12, the only Ode in which both ܡܠܬܐ and ܡܠܬܐ are found, ܡܠܬܐ means 'speech' but in four separate verses (3, 5, 10 and 12) ܡܠܬܐ denotes the divine Logos, to use the familiar Greek term.

The conclusion to this first comparison is that while both the *Odes* and John have borrowed some of their modified cosmic dualism from the Old Testament, other parts of it are so unique in the history of ideas and so similar to each other as to raise the question of some level of dependence. It is improbable that the Odist systematically borrowed from John. The most probable solution, at this stage in our research, is that both the author of John and the Odist contemporaneously shared not only the same milieu but perhaps also the same community.

In the discussion above we called the second aspect of John's dualism 'an extremely modified metaphysical dualism' and the *Odes'* 'dualism' a 'modified metaphysical dualism'. To reiterate, the struggle in John is between Jesus, who represents God, and the Ioudaioi, who are frequently equated with the *kosmos* or Satan. In the *Odes* this aspect of the 'dualism' is more pronounced and may be outlined as follows:

the Spirit of the Lord	the Evil One
the perfect Virgin	the Corruptor
Truth	Error
the Beloved and	the Bridegroom who corrupts and is corrupted
his Bride	the Bride who was corrupting
	the Deceiver

Since the Odist himself equates the Corruptor with the Evil One (33.4) and the evil Bride and Bridegroom with the Deceiver and the Error (38.10), it appears that he assumed the existence of one pair of evil creatures. Likewise, he thought that the good forces were also a pair: the Spirit of the Lord (the Beloved) and the perfect Virgin (his Bride).

43. L.A. Herrick, who has worked on Moses bar Kepha's commentary on John (MS Add. 1971 [Cambridge]), informs me that the *terminus technicus* for the divine Word in this MS is ܡܠܬܐ; ܡܠܬܐ is used exclusively in the sense of 'text' or 'phrase'.

Here the differences between the 'dualisms' in the *Odes* and John are most extreme. First, in the *Odes* the imagery is more fully developed. As with the Scrolls, numerous names are given to the hypostatic creatures, and Truth and Error are clearly personified and juxtaposed. Second, in the *Odes* the evil creatures never confront the good figures, with the possible exception of *Ode* 33.1; they meet only obliquely as they vie for human allegiance. In contrast, John portrays the Ioudaioi (sometimes 'Jews' but in some passages 'Judeans') in confrontation with Jesus. Third, the names given to the opposing figures are strikingly different. The Odist's imagery of the Bride and Bridegroom is closer to letters attributed to Paul (2 Cor. 11.2; Eph. 5.25f.) than to John. Fourth, in the *Odes* the metaphysical dualism is less modified, hence closer to that of the Scrolls.

Some of the above differences could be the result of the poetic aspect of the *Odes*, which is in contrast to the narrative and kerygmatic character of John. Others can be due to the frequently anti-Gentile characteristic in the *Odes*,[44] which is distinct from the occasional anti-Jewish bias in John (especially 8.12–9.41). However, we must not fail to observe that a considerable amount of independence must be accounted for when comparing the *Odes* and John.

In summary, the *Odes* are clearly closer than John to the Scrolls' concept of two warring cosmic Spirits. Observations made below raise the probability that some of the differences mentioned above between the *Odes* and John are caused by more direct Essene influence on the Odist.

One of the most impressive similarities between the 'dualisms' in the *Odes* and John is that both have woven into the fabric of their thought the light–darkness paradigm. Since neither of them develops the schema but presents it at a sophisticated level, it is clear that each has inherited the paradigm from an earlier tradition. Of all the dualisms by which the *Odes* and John could have been influenced, it is that developed in the Scrolls that comes closest to being the source. Only in the Scrolls, the *Odes*, and John is light associated with truth, knowledge, and everlasting (eternal) life, while antithetically darkness is linked with falsehood, ignorance, and extinction. Both the *Odes* and John probably inherited this paradigm from the Essenes.

---

44. *Odes* 10.5, 'And the Gentiles..., / I was not defiled by my love (for them)'. R.H. Charles correctly remarked that 'Christ apologizes after a fashion for His reception of the Gentiles into the Church' ('A Church Hymnal', p. 124).

Some elaborations of this paradigm, however, come from the fact that both the *Odes* and John are Christian (hence the schema is seen soteriologically), but the conception that the Messiah (Christ) is 'Light' suggests either some level of dependence between the *Odes* and John or that they both come from the same or contiguous communities. Compare *Ode* 41.14 ('And light dawned from the Word / That was before time in him') with the prologue to John, and *Ode* 10.1 ('The Lord directed my mouth by his Word, / And opened my heart by his light') or *Ode* 15.2 ('Because he (the Lord) is my Sun, /...; / And his light has dismissed all darkness from my face')[45] with Jn 8.12 ('I am the light of the world'). In conclusion, therefore, the data reveal that both the *Odes* and John have been independently influenced by the light–darkness paradigm promulgated in the Scrolls, but that in developing it for the new dispensation they have been related dependently in some way, or independently influenced by a shared community.

It is not impressive that both the *Odes* and John present a modified eschatological dualism since both, as Christian documents, affirm that the Messiah has come and that the future has irrupted into the present.[46] It is significant, however, that both depict the coming of the Messiah in such similar terms. *Ode* 12.12 ('For the dwelling place of the Word is man, / And his truth is love') is parallel to Jn 1.14 ('And the Word became flesh and dwelt among us').[47]

Two observations raise the possibility that on this point there is some relationship between the two documents. First, both clearly accentuate the reward of eternal life as the will of the Lord for all people (*Odes* 9.4; 10.2; 11.16f., *et passim*; Jn 3.15-16; 3.36; 4.14 *et passim*). Second, both describe 'eternal life' not as a distant dream but as a present reality for those who belong to the light (*Odes* 3.9; 11.12; 15.8-10; Jn 3.36; 4.14 *et passim*). The first point certainly does not suggest dependence on the Scrolls, because of their exclusiveness (viz. 1QS 1.9f.). The second, however, might reflect the Essenes' contention that the 'Sons of Light'

45. Of all the variegated aspects of sectarian Judaism that we know today, only the Essenes venerated the sun and accentuated the symbolic importance of light.

46. O. Betz correctly states that the *Odes* stress the present aspect of salvation even more so than John. O. Betz, *Der Paraklet: Fürsprecher im häretischen Spät-judentum, im Johannes-Evangelium und in neu gefundenen gnostischen Schriften* (AGSU, 2; Leiden: E.J. Brill, 1963), p. 215.

47. Also see *Ode* 39.9-13 and especially *Ode* 41.11-15.

would receive 'eternal life' (1QS 4.7) and the belief that their Community was an antechamber of heaven.

We saw that the most important feature of the 'dualism' in the *Odes* and John is the fifth aspect, soteriological dualism. It would be difficult to show dependence between them here precisely because they share this characteristic with other Christian literature. A few observations, however, help clarify the possibility of dependence.

In contrast to Qumranic dualism, neither the *Odes* nor John portrays the bifurcation of humankind as a primordial fact but as the result of each person's response to the Saviour's call to repent. We mentioned above that both the *Odes* and John referred to the Creator as the 'Word'; likewise both conceive of the Saviour as the 'Word'. It is clear that the author of John held this identification although he never says so explicitly, and the parallelism in *Ode* 41.11 shows that the Odist made the equation:

> And his Word is with us in all our way,
> The Saviour who gives life and does not reject us.

Two observations suggest that there is some level of dependence between the *Odes* and John in terms of the development of the soteriological dualism. First, both put an extraordinary amount of emphasis on the salvific aspects of 'to know' (ܝܕܥ as a verb is employed 44 times in the *Odes*, γινώσκειν occurs 56 times in John). In both, 'to know' is frequently synonymous with 'to follow' or 'to belong' to the Saviour, Jesus Christ. In *Ode* 42.3, 'those who knew me [not]' is paralleled by 'those who possessed me not', an idea that is similar to the dualistic dialogue in Jn 8.32-58 (cf. 14.20; 17.25). Correlatively, in both 'Truth' is not only personified as the Saviour (viz. 'The Truth led me' [*Ode* 38.1] 'I am...the truth' [Jn 14.6]) but is also portrayed as the spiritual abode of the believer (viz. 'And [Truth] became for me a haven of salvation' [*Ode* 38.3] 'Every one who is of [ἐκ] the truth hears my voice' [Jn 18.37; cf. 8.44]).[48]

Second, for both the distinguishing mark of one who belongs to the Saviour is 'love'. 'For I should not have known how to love the Lord, / If he had not continuously loved me' (*Ode* 3.3) is strikingly similar to 'We love him, because he first loved us' (1 Jn 4.19 [clearly 1 John and

---

48. Frequently the Odist's use of 'truth' has a 'Johannine' ring to it. In one verse (12.12) he conceptually combines 'Word', 'truth' and 'love'. In *Ode* 32.2 he writes, 'And the Word of truth who is self-originate'.

the Gospel of John are closely linked, some way).[49] Permeating the *Odes* is the emphasis put on love (ܐܚܒ, 25 times; ܚܘܒ, 24 times). The possibility of dependence, in some direction, is increased by the observation that only John records Jesus' commandment 'to love' ('A new commandment I give to you, that you love one another; even as I have loved you' [Jn 13.34]).

As we attempt to discover the level and direction of possible influence between the *Odes* and John, we should make the following observation. In both, the Lord (= the Saviour) lifts up his voice (*Ode* 31.4; in Jn 17.1 Jesus 'lifted up his eyes...and said') towards the Most High (*Ode* 31.4; in Jn 17.1 'to heaven') and offers to him (*Ode* 31.4; Jn 17 *passim*, especially vv. 9f.) those whom 'his Holy Father' (*Ode* 31.5; 'Holy Father' in Jn 17.11) 'had given to him' (*Ode* 31.5; Jn 17.2, 6, 9 *et passim*), those who now possess 'eternal life' (*Ode* 31.7; Jn 17.2f.). The similarities between *Ode* 31.4-5 and John 17 are sufficient to raise the question of some dependence. The initial reaction would be to assume that the Odist was influenced by John 17. This hypothesis, however, fails to convince on closer examination; there are too many expressions in these two verses of *Ode* 31 that are neither attributable to John 17 nor to the peculiar vocabulary of the Odist. Is it improbable that the connection could be traced to the same community from which the *Odes* and John might have come? Further research is needed before we can be certain.

The sixth characteristic of the 'dualisms' in the *Odes* and John is that every human being has the ability to choose his or her own way. Perhaps it is here that both are farthest from Qumran and its exclusivism. Any relationship between the *Odes* and John at this point would be due not to dependence of one on the other but to the universalism of burgeoning Christianity with its missionary zeal.

In concluding this comparison between the 'dualism' in the *Odes* and John, we may say that there are numerous and striking similarities. There is clearly some relationship between these two early Christian documents. The problems arise when one tries to analyse in which direction the dependence should be traced: are the *Odes* dependent on John, is John developing ideas found in the *Odes*, are the similarities the result of a shared community? The last possibility looms large not only in the light of the data amassed above, especially because only the *Odes*

49. See D.M. Smith, 'Did the Same Author Write the Gospel and Letters?', in *First, Second, and Third John* (Louisville, KY: John Knox Press, 1991), pp. 11-15.

employ ܦܬܓܡܐ as a *terminus technicus* for the 'Word', but also because it now seems highly probable that John is not the effort of a genius working alone but of a school of scholars.[50] There is certainly much yet to be done before we can make sweeping generalizations about the relationship between the *Odes* and John. Certainly we must become more aware of our presuppositions and perceptions; because John is more familiar to us, because we read it first, and because it is in the canon are not sufficient reasons to proceed as if it must be the source for the *Odes*.

'Dualism' in the Odes and Dualism at Qumran

Both the 'dualism' in the *Odes* and the dualism in the Scrolls are modified by an overriding monotheism. This idea and the belief that the universe is bifurcated into heaven and earth display the Odist's and Essenes' Old Testament heritage. A possible relationship between them might be the shared conception of the community as an antechamber of heaven, the dwelling of 'the holy ones'. In *Ode* 22.12 we read the following:

> And the foundation of everything is your rock.
> And upon it you have hast built your kingdom,
> And it became the dwelling-place of the holy ones.

This imagery is similar to that of the Scrolls in which the 'heavenly Community'—'the dwelling of perfect holiness' (1QS 8.8; cf. 1QM 12.2; 1QH 12.2; 1QSb 4.25)—is also conceived of as 'founded upon rock' (1QH 6.25).[51]

Here the possibility of dependence by the Odist upon ideas found in the Scrolls is displayed by the observation that both specify the Creator as ܐܒܐ ܕܝܕܥܬܐ, 'the Father of knowledge' (*Ode* 7.7) or מֵאֵל הַדֵּעוֹת, 'from the God of Knowledge' (1QS 3.15; 1QH 1.26; 12.10; fragment 4.15), peculiar concepts rarely found in the Old Testament (the closest parallels are 1 Sam. 2.3: אֵל דֵּעוֹת, 'God of knowledge'; and Isa. 11.2: רוּחַ דַּעַת, 'the spirit of knowledge'), the New Testament, the Old Testament Apocrypha (contrast the closest parallel in

---

50. In my judgment the core of John ultimately goes back to a disciple, but the present form is the result of a Johannine school. R.E. Brown presents this solution as an '*ad hoc* theory' in *The Gospel According to John*, I, pp. xcviii-cii.

51. See Charlesworth, 'Les Odes de Salomon et les Manuscrits de la Mer Morte', pp. 529-32. (See also J.H. Charlesworth, *The Beloved Disciple: Whose Witness Validates the Gospel of John?* [Valley Forge, PA: Trinity Press International, 1995].)

Wis. 9.2), or the Old Testament Pseudepigrapha (contrast *1 En.* 63.2). The absence of parallels outside of the *Odes* and the Scrolls raises the probability that the Odist inherited the concept and expression from the Scrolls, where it is found not only in the *Rule of the Community* but also in the *Thanksgiving Hymns.*

The two warring cosmic Spirits, which play such a prominent role in Qumran's dualism, may be disguised in the *Odes'* 'dualism', even though the terminology is quite different. Also the cosmic figures in the *Odes* are not described as warring with each other as they are, for example, in the *War Scroll* and the *Rule of the Community.* The Odist may have borrowed the broad lines of the Qumran dualistic imagery, but in so doing he completely reminted the idea so that it is 'the perfect Virgin' who vies with 'the Corruptor'. Behind this Christian garb may lie a disguised Qumran dualism of two warring Spirits, a possibility that should be taken seriously since both in the *Odes* (especially 33.3-7) and the Scrolls (viz. 1QS 3.18; 4.23) the struggle is for human allegiance. Moreover, on two accounts the similarity is striking: the Odist's 'the Spirit of the Lord, which is not false' (3.10) may be a reminted 'Spirit of Truth' (1QS 3.19 *et passim*); 'the Corruptor' (*Odes* 33 and 38) corresponds to the Essenes' 'angels of destruction (corruption)' (1QS 4.12; 1QM 13.12; CD 2.6). It is logical to assume that here the Odist is influenced by Essene imagery.

The most striking similarity between the *Odes'* 'dualism' and the Scrolls' dualism is the pervasiveness of the light–darkness paradigm in each. In both, 'light', which represents 'truth', is contrasted with 'darkness', which signifies 'falsehood'. Compare, for example, *Ode* 18.6,

> Let not light be conquered by darkness,
> Nor let truth flee from falsehood.

with the *Rule of the Community* (1QS 3.19),

> In a dwelling of light is the origin of Truth,
> And in a fountain of darkness is the origin of Perversity.

We mentioned above that the development of the light–darkness paradigm is unique to Essene or Essene-influenced documents; it is found neither in the Old Testament nor in other 'intertestamental literature'. We are left with two logical possibilities: either the Essenes and the Odist developed this paradigm independently, or the Odist has been influenced by Essene promulgations. The first possibility is unlikely because the Odist did not develop but inherited the paradigm. The second possibility looms probable and should be viewed in light of other striking similarities.[52] Moreover, it is significant that the *Odes* and the Scrolls are distinguished from documents with which they were contemporary by the inordinate degree to which they accentuate the importance of the sun (compare *Ode* 15.2 with 1QH 12.3-9; 11QPs[a] 26.4; 4Q *Morgen- und Abendgebete*).

The fourth characteristic of the dualistic thought found in the *Odes* and Scrolls is respectively the modified and unmodified eschatological dimension. It would be easy to report only how different the two eschatologies are: while the Odist repeatedly praises the marvelous advent of *the* Messiah, the Essenes yearn for the future coming of *a* messiah(s); while the Odist proclaims that the decisive battle has been fought and that the Messiah has captured the world, the Essenes look to a future decisive battle. Behind these differences, however, there may be some impressive similarities, and we must not overlook the logic that an early Christian who borrows an idea or symbol from the Essenes is dependent on them regardless of whether he remints or alters it in line with the eschatological ramifications of the new dispensation.

Under this fourth characteristic there is the striking similarity of future rewards and punishments. Both stress that those who belong to the light shall receive a 'crown' (*Odes* 1.1-3; 9.8f.; 1QS 4.7-8; 1QH 9.25) and possess 'eternal life' (viz. *Odes* 10.2; 15.10; 1QS 4.7-8); but that those who belong to the darkness shall receive not eternal punishment (cf. Dan. 12.2; *1 En.* 10.4-13; 67.4-13) but extinction (e.g. *Ode* 33.8-9; 1QS 4.14). It is conceivable that these similarities are mere coincidences; but it is more likely that the Odist and the author of John shared the same milieu, and perhaps community, and did not simply independently receive these ideas and images from a shared Jewish background.[53]

The fifth and most important characteristic of the 'dualism' in the *Odes* is that it is soteriological, while that in the Scrolls is ethical. Earlier we noted that, unlike John, the *Odes* emphasized the bifurcation of humanity according to the paradigm truth–knowledge vis-à-vis error–ignorance. Note for example that the Odist and Essenes talk about the way or ways of truth (*Odes* 11.3; 33.8; 1QS 4.17) and the way of error or

---

52. See Charlesworth, 'Les Odes de Salomon et les Manuscrits de la Mer Morte'.
53. See the next chapter.

unrighteousness (*Ode* 15.6; 1QH 14.26).[54] Occasionally the Odist describes the soteriological dualism in terms of an ethical dualism (compare *Ode* 20.3-6 with the long ethical lists found in 1QS 4.2-11). Here the *Odes* are closer than John to Qumranic dualism.

There are tremendous differences between the *Odes* and Qumran's sixth characteristic feature. It is a difference that results from early Christianity's universalism and missionary zeal, which was antithetical to Qumran's exclusiveness (1QS 1.9ff.).

The similarities mentioned above are striking and pervasive. Certain of these may be mere coincidences (e.g. the Odist's description of the soteriological dualism); others might be the result of the general Jewish background of the *Odes* to which Qumran thought belongs (e.g. monotheism, angelology, the concept of future rewards or punishments). Others, however, are caused by ideas and images peculiar to the Scrolls (e.g. the concept of the Community as an antechamber of heaven, terminology such as the description of the Creator as the 'Father of knowledge', the development of the idea that there are two opposed cosmic figures, the centrality of the light–darkness paradigm). The logical conclusion, therefore, is that the *Odes* are probably influenced by the Scrolls; indeed in some passages they may be directly dependent on them.

John and Qumran

The preceding analyses permit us to make this section of the discussion brief. John and the Dead Sea Scrolls contain a modified dualism; in John it is at first inconspicuous but in the Scrolls frequently obvious. John borrows his dualism, but the author(s) of columns three and four in the *Rule* promulgates a dualism, employing ideas borrowed from elsewhere (viz. Zurvanism). John inherits the concept of two worlds from the Old Testament, but animates the worlds and sets them up as two opposing forces. The Essenes, on the other hand, merely assume the existence of two worlds (viz. 1QH 16.3). John probably borrowed the light–darkness paradigm from the Essenes, who had developed it.[55]

---

54. We should expect the Syriac ܐܠܚܘܬ (*Ode* 15.6) to correspond to the Hebrew תועה, both of which mean 'error'; but the Syriac noun is very close to the Hebrew עולה (1QH 14.26), which means 'unrighteousness' or 'wrong'.

55. Contrast Bakotin, who argued that John inherited the paradigm from the Old Testament; however, he wrote before the Scrolls were discovered. He correctly saw that John's 'dualism' should not be traced to Gnosticism (*De notione lucis et*

John's modified eschatological dualism, soteriological dualism, and concept of the freedom of the will are clearly distinct from the corresponding concepts in the Scrolls. These differences, however, are demanded by the affirmation that the long-awaited Messiah has come, and wills to save all persons from destruction (viz. Jn 1.14; 3.16; 12.32). The similarities show that John probably has been influenced by Essene thought; this is especially evident by the terminology he employed to present his 'dualism'.

Odes, John, and Qumran

In the following pages we shall attempt to organize the main observations regarding the relationships among the dualisms found in the *Odes*, John, and the Qumran Scrolls. The conclusions to the above analyses are conveniently arranged in the following chart (an asterisk marks the most conspicuous emphasis, italics signify the closest parallels):

Odes	*John*	*Qumran*
1. modified cosmic dualism of two worlds	1. modified cosmic dualism of two worlds	1. modified dualism of two worlds
2. *modified metaphysical dualism*	2. an extremely modified metaphysical dualism	2. *2 warring cosmic Spirits*
3. *light–darkness paradigm*	3. *light–darkness paradigm*	3. *light–darkness paradigm*
4. modified eschatological dualism	4. modified eschatological dualism	4. eschatological dualism
*5. soteriological dualism (plus ethical dualism)	*5. soteriological dualism	*5. ethical dualism
6. choice	6. choice	6. predestination

First, the *Odes*, John, and Qumran have inherited their basic cosmology from the Old Testament: there are two worlds, the one above, heaven, and the one below, earth. These two worlds are implicit in the Scrolls, explicit in the *Odes*, and emphasized with new dualistic connotations in John. We have seen that the similarities between the *Odes* and John on this first point are so impressive, especially in the shared terminology (viz. 'Word') as to warrant the probability that both come

tenebrarum, pp. 84-87). See also G. Baumbach, *Qumran und das Johannes-Evangelium* (Wissenschaft vom Alten Testament, 6; Berlin: Evangelische Verlagsanstalt, 1958), p. 51; and R.E. Murphy, *The Dead Sea Scrolls and the Bible* (Westminster, MD: Newman, 1956), pp. 71-79.

from an identical milieu, perhaps even the same community. While John, however, shows no dependence here on the Scrolls, the *Odes* are apparently influenced by their thoughts and expressions. The conception of the community as an antechamber of heaven and the description of the Creator as the 'Father of knowledge' suggest that the Odist has borrowed from the Scrolls.

From this first comparison we see that the Odist may have belonged to the same community as John, but apparently was more influenced by the Essenes than he. These possibilities could be accounted for by the assumption that Essenes lived in the community, by the hypothesis that the Odist had been an Essene before his conversion to Christianity, or both, since the two are not mutually exclusive.

Second, we have seen that the *Odes*, John, and the Scrolls portray a cosmic struggle headed by two hypostatic figures, a concept only in the background of John's thought (e.g. Christ, the representative of God, against the Ioudaioi, the representatives of the Devil), but in the foreground of the Odist's and Essenes' metaphysics. We should not be mesmerized by differences; the *Odes* and Scrolls share images and expressions that are sufficiently similar as to warrant the hypothesis that the Odist has been influenced by the Essenes.

Third, and most significantly, the *Odes*, John and the Scrolls are distinguished by the inordinate degree to which they employ the light–darkness paradigm. No other documents dating from this time portray a dualism that is so permeated by light and truth versus darkness and falsehood. There can be little question that, as Christian writings essentially indebted to Judaism, the *Odes* and John probably inherited the paradigm from the dualistic ideas of pre-Christian Judaism. Therefore the probable source for this paradigm was the Essenes, who—as far as we can detect—developed and promulgated the light–darkness paradigm. It is highly improbable that the *Odes* have borrowed the schema from John or vice versa; it seems that both independently inherited the imagery from the Essenes.

Fourth, the chart presented earlier shows, on the one hand, that the eschatology in the *Odes* and John is similar, and on the other, that their eschatology is clearly distinct from that of the Essenes. Here particularly, however, we must allow for the prism effect of the Christian contention that the Messiah has come. Also, the similarities between the *Odes* and John should not be dismissed as merely one of the characteristics of early Christianity. The *Odes* and John are peculiar in two ways:

the coming of the Messiah is described as the incarnation of the 'Word', and victory is assured since the Messiah has overcome the world (compare *Ode* 10.4 with Jn 16.33).

Both the *Odes*[56] and John are distinguished by their emphasis on the reward of eternal life for those of the light and the punishment of extinction for those of the darkness; moreover, both portray eternal life as a present possession. Certainly these striking similarities should be seen in conjunction with the observation that the Essenes taught the same rewards and punishments, and implied that they, the Sons of Light, already had eternal life since their Community was an antechamber of heaven in which angels were present.[57] Likewise, the *Odes*, John, and the Scrolls accentuate that one who belongs to the light possesses 'living water', a symbolism that frequently connotes the possession of eternal life. In pre-Christian literature the expression 'living water' is not peculiar to the Scrolls, but it is clearly emphasized only in them.[58] Consequently, the presence of this concept in the *Odes* and John certainly strengthens the probability that they are influenced by the thought of the Scrolls.[59]

Fifth, the most conspicuous emphasis in the *Odes* and John is a soteriological dualism, that in the Scrolls an ethical dualism. In the *Odes* and John the bifurcation of humankind is caused by the appearance of

56. E. Schweizer correctly remarks that in the *Odes* the Redeemer is frequently identified with the redeemed (p. 76). He also notes the terminological relationship between John and the *Odes* (p. 56). See his *Ego Eimi* (Göttingen: Vandenhoeck & Ruprecht, 2nd edn, 1965). One of the difficulties confronted in translating the *Odes* is to decide when the Odist begins to compose *ex ore Christi*.

57. Contrast the surprising conclusion obtained by A. Feuillet in his 'La participation actuelle à la vie divine d'après le quatrième évangile: les origines et le sens de cette conception', *SE* 1, pp. 295-308, see esp. p. 307: 'More than all the other writings in the New Testament, it [John] seems turned toward the Greek world.' Clearly such a statement is anachronic. Also, contrast our position with that of J. Carmignac, 'Une qumrânien converti au christianisme', p. 89 and n. 42.

58. See Charlesworth, 'Les Odes de Salomon et les Manuscrits de la Mer Morte', pp. 534-37.

59. O.D. Szojda has compared the symbolism of water in the Scrolls with the self-same imagery in John, and concludes that John probably knew the Essene symbolic and ritualistic use of water. He cautions, however, that John has completely reworked the symbolism of water so one must not claim that John is 'directly dependent' on the Scrolls. O.D. Szojda, 'Symbolika Wody w Pismach Sw. Jana Evangelisty i w Qumran', *RocTK* 13 (1966), pp. 105-21.

the Saviour; in the Scrolls the division dates from the time the two Spirits were created. There seems to be some dependence between the *Odes* and John because both conceive of the Saviour as the 'Word', accentuate the soteriological aspects of the verbs 'to know' and 'to love', and either explicitly (*Odes*) or implicitly (John) depict the division in terms of the schema error–ignorance vis-à-vis truth–knowledge. Here again we see that the *Odes* are a little closer to the Scrolls than John because they occasionally present the soteriological dualism in terms of an ethical dualism.

Another observation needs reporting at this time. All three denigrate the importance of sacrificing in the Jerusalem Temple (*Odes* 6; 12.4; 20.1-4; Jn 4.21-24; 1QS 9.3-5)[60] and accentuate the importance of bearing fruit, which in the *Odes* and Scrolls is frequently synonymous with 'praise' (*Odes* 8.1f.; 11.1; 14.7f.; 16.2; Jn 15; 1QS 10.6-8).[61] These similarities are by no means mere coincidences. When they are taken with the numerous other parallels mentioned throughout this chapter, it seems likely that the *Odes* and John are influenced by the Scrolls.

Sixth, the tremendous difference between the *Odes*' and John's belief that an individual can choose and the Essenes' idea that one is predestined should be viewed in the light of the missionary aspects of burgeoning Christianity, which has clearly left its mark on these two documents (*Ode* 6, 10;[62] Jn 20.31). No dependence can be traced here in any direction among the *Odes*, John, and the Scrolls.

60. O. Cullmann contends that the type of Christianity represented by John is as old as that of the Synoptics primarily because there is such strong similarity between the nonconformist Jewish sects (Qumran), the Johannine group, and the Stephen-led branch of early Christianity. All three denigrate the present Temple cultus. See Cullmann's chapter in *Neutestamentliche Studien für Rudolf Bultmann* (BZNW, 21; Berlin: Alfred Töpelmann, 1954), pp. 35-41; and his article in *ExpT* 71 (1959–60), pp. 8-12, 39-43 [= *NTS* 5 (1958-59), pp. 157-73]. See also Carmignac, 'Les affinités qumrâniennes', pp. 100f.

61. These parallels are discussed by R. Borig, *Der wahre Weinstock: Untersuchungen zu Jo 15, 1-10* (SANT, 16; Munich: Kösel, 1967). Borig correctly reports that there is no literary borrowing between the *Odes* and John; the relationship is probably through a shared milieu (p. 127).

62. A.A.T. Ehrhardt compares *Ode* 10 with 1QH 7.26-33 and claims that in particular what is new in the ode is 'a strong missionary spirit' (*SE* 1, pp. 586f.).

Conclusion

Retrospect

The numerous and pervasive parallels between the *Odes* and John cannot be explained by literary dependence of the Odist on John or vice versa (also see next chapter). The most likely explanation for the similarities analyzed above is that the Odist and John shared the same milieu, and it is not improbable that they lived in the same community.

The *Odes* and John clearly share numerous parallels with the Dead Sea Scrolls; these similarities are seldom in terms of fundamental concepts, occasionally in images, and frequently in terminology.[63] Both the Odist and John could have been influenced independently by the Essenes or Essene literature, or could have received these influences at approximately the same time from Essenes living within or contiguous with their community. In the case of the Odist, we should take seriously the possibility that he is a converted Essene.[64] Subsequent research will reveal how possible or probable these tentative conclusions are.

Prospect

The discussion shows that we are no longer justified in speaking about the *Odes* and John as if they were late and gnostic.[65] Moreover, if both the *Odes* and John share the same milieu, as is extremely probable, and

---

63. E. Best holds that 'The Qumran material has led to a re-opening of the question of the background from which John was issued; for a dualism similar to John's appears in Qumran as well as in Hellenistic Judaism and in Gnosticism' ('New Testament Scholarship Today', *Biblical Theology* 20 [1970], p. 22). I must disagree; the dualism in the Dead Sea Scrolls is dissimilar to that in Gnosticism, but it is similiar to that in John.

64. See also Carmignac, 'Un qumrânien converti au christianisme', pp. 75-108.

65. See Professor H. Chadwick's lucid and brilliant 'Some Reflections'. See the excellent article recently presented by B. Reicke, 'Da'at and Gnosis in Intertestamental Literature', in Ellis and Wilcox (eds.), *Neotestamentica et Semitica*, pp. 245-55. Permit me to raise a question: is it insignificant that the Righteous Teacher is anonymous in the Scrolls, the Beloved Disciple is unnamed in John, and anonymity characterizes the *Odes*? See an interesting attempt at answering part of this question by J. Roloff, 'Der johanneische "Lieblingsjünger" und der Lehrer der Gerechtigkeit', *NTS* 15 (1968), pp. 129-51. Roloff concludes, 'dass das Johannes-Evangelium seine Wurzeln in dem gleichen sektiererisch-täuferischen Milieu am Rande des palästinischen Judentums hatte, in dem auch die Qumran-Sekte beheimatet war' (p. 150). (See my further reflections in Charlesworth, *The Beloved Disciple*.)

if the *Odes* were originally composed in Syriac, as some scholars have argued,[66] then it would be well for us to look to northern Palestine and Syria for the provenience of the *Odes* and of at least one recension of John.[67] Antioch, of course, should be considered as a prime candidate, and in this connection we must recall the numerous parallels between the *Odes*, John, and the letters of Ignatius of Antioch, and the recent illustration of how these letters frequently resemble the imagery of the Dead Sea Scrolls.[68]

These observations raise questions that extend far beyond the scope of this chapter. Before we can adequately answer such questions and learn how and where John[69] and the *Odes* received their Essene influence, we need to know how geographically widespread the Essenes were, and when the Essenes ceased to be a strong influence upon Christianity.

The new perspectives obtained above show how far biblical research has advanced since 1947, when Cave 1 near Qumran was discovered. In many ways we are dealing with issues undreamed of by scholars who

66. See Emerton, 'Some Problems of Text and Language'; see also Chapter 4 of this book.

67. Although T.E. Pollard's treatment of this issue is too brief, he tends toward the same conclusion (*Johannine Christology and the Early Church* [SNTSMS, 13; Cambridge: Cambridge University Press, 1970], p. 34). Contrast J.N. Sanders's contention that the numerous parallels between the Scrolls and John strengthen the indications that John Mark, 'a member of the priestly aristocracy in Jerusalem', wrote the Fourth Gospel; but that he composed it at the end of his life in Ephesus; see B.A. Mastin (ed.), *A Commentary on the Gospel According to St John* (London: A. & C. Black, 1968), esp. pp. 50-51. Also contrast our position with Irenaeus' comment (*Adv. Haer.* 3.11.1), recently developed by F. Neugebauer, that connects the origin of John with the imminent division in Christianity caused by Cerinthus' 'heretical' cosmology and Christology (*Die Entstehung des Johannesevangeliums* [Arbeiten zur Theologie, 1.36; Stuttgart: Calwer Verlag, 1968]). F.L. Cribbs is certainly correct in urging us 'to make a reassessment of this gospel in the direction of an earlier dating and a possible origin for John against the general background of Palestinian Christianity' ('A Reassessment of the Date of Origin and the Destination of the Gospel of John', *JBL* 89 [1970], pp. 38-55 [39]).

68. V. Corwin argues that Ignatius knew some of the *Odes* and displays some of the frequent parallels between Ignatius, the *Odes* and John, in *St Ignatius and Christianity in Antioch* (Yale Publications in Religion, 1; New Haven: Yale University Press, 1960), esp. pp. 71-80.

69. See W.H. Brownlee, 'Whence the Gospel of John?', in *John and the Dead Sea Scrolls*, pp. 166-94.

worked during the first half of the twentieth century. These exciting new insights into the origins of Christianity appear not primarily because of modern methods, but because of the recovery of such compositions as the long-lost *Odes of Solomon*, and manuscripts, like the Dead Sea Scrolls, actually copied or composed during the life of Jesus of Nazareth.

APPENDIX

J. Ashton concludes that the author of John 'had dualism in his bones... The evangelist may well have started life as one of those Essenes', whose thought is found in the Dead Sea Scrolls; they were found in large numbers in every town (Josephus, *War* 2.124). See J. Ashton, *Understanding the Fourth Gospel* (Oxford: Clarendon Press, 1991), p. 237. E. Ruckstuhl offers his opinion that the Beloved Disciple may well have been a member of the Qumran settlement in Jerusalem. See E. Ruckstuhl, *Jesus im Horizont der Evangelien* (Stuttgarter Biblische Aufsatzbände, 3; Stuttgart: Katholisches Bibelwerk, 1988), esp. pp. 393-95. H. Koester thinks that the *Odes of Solomon* 'may have been written at about the same time as the prologue of the Gospel of John...' (*Introduction to the New Testament*. II. *History and Literature of Early Christianity* [Philadelphia: Trinity Press International, 1982], p. 217).

J. Guirau and A.G. Hamman rightly contend that 'L'auteur des *Odes* semble connaître les hymnes esséniens et s'en inspirer.' See their *Les Odes de Salomon* (Paris: Desclée de Brouwer, 1981), p. 9. In *Les Odes de Salomon* Azar agrees that the *Odes* and John come from the same milieu: 'Il nous semble toutefois qu'il [les *Odes*] aurait une origine commune avec la tradition johannique' (p. 42). In his *Oden Salomos* Lattke offers his insight that the 'Ursprungszeit der Oden Salomos' is close to that of the *Corpus Johanneum* (pp. 33-34). In his Αι Ὠδαι Σολομωντος Fanourgakes points out numerous parallels between the *Odes* and John (p. 128).

Chapter 10

THE *ODES OF SOLOMON* AND THE GOSPEL OF JOHN

The *Odes of Solomon* are a neglected key for unlocking the historical and theological enigmas of John.[1] Despite his misleading hypothesis of

1. This chapter was written by Charlesworth and Culpepper; it was edited by Charlesworth. Herein John denotes neither the Apostle nor the Evangelist but the extant Gospel. The following works are cited alphabetically, by author: B.W. Bacon, in *The Gospel of the Hellenists* (ed. C.H. Kraeling; New York: Holt, 1933); Barrett, *The Gospel According to St John*; Bernard, *The Odes of Solomon*; G. Bert, *Das Evangelium des Johannes* (Gütersloh: Bertelsmann, 1922); Betz, *Der Paraklet*; Borig, *Der wahre Weinstock*; Braun, *Jean le théologien*; Brown, *The Gospel According to John*; Bruston, *Les plus anciens cantiques chrétiens*; C.F. Burney, *The Aramaic Origin of the Fourth Gospel* (Oxford: Clarendon Press, 1922); H. van den Bussche, *Jean* (Paris: Desclée, 1967); Corwin, *St. Ignatius*; Dodd, *The Interpretation of the Fourth Gospel*; Grimme, *Die Oden Salomos*; Hamman, *Naissance des lettres chrétiennes*; Harnack and Flemming, *Ein jüdisch-christliches Psalmbuch*; Harris and Mingana, *The Odes and Psalms of Solomon*; Kuhl, *Die Sendung Jesu*; M.-J. Lagrange, *Evangile selon Saint Jean* (Paris: Librairie Lecoffre, 1936); W. von Loewenich, *Das Johannes-Verständnis im zweiten Jahrhundert* (Giessen: Alfred Töpelmann, 1932); J. Marsh, *Saint John* (Harmondsworth: Penguin, 1968); E. Massaux, *Influence de l'évangile de saint Matthieu sur la littérature chrétienne avant saint Irénée* (Universitas Catholica Lovaniensis, 2.42; Louvain: Publications Universitaires de Louvain, 1950); P.-H. Menoud, *L'évangile de Jean* (Neuchâtel: Delachaux & Niestlé, 1947); L. Morris, *The Gospel According to John* (Grand Rapids: Eerdmans, 1971); H. Odeberg, *The Fourth Gospel* (Uppsala: Almquist & Wiksells, 1929); E. Percy, *Untersuchungen über den Ursprung der johanneischen Theologie* (Lund: Hakan Ohlssons, 1939); Rylands, *The Beginnings of Gnostic Christianity*; J.N. Sanders, *The Fourth Gospel in the Early Church: Its Origin and Influence on Christian Theology up to Irenaeus* (Cambridge: Cambridge University Press, 1943); J.N. Sanders and B.A. Mastin, *The Gospel According to St John* (London: A. & C. Black, 1968); D.A. Schlatter, *Der Evangelist Johannes* (Stuttgart: Calwer Verlag, 1930); Schnackenburg, *The Gospel According to St John*; Schweizer, *Ego Eimi*; H. Strathmann, *Das Evangelium nach Johannes* (Göttingen: Vandenhoeck & Ruprecht, 1951): Tondelli, *Le Odi di Salomone*; Wikenbauser, *Das Evangelium nach Johannes*; M.F. Wiles, *The Spiritual Gospel: The*

a Jewish *Grundschrift*, Harnack in 1910 correctly sensed that the recovery of the *Odes* was 'nothing short of epoch-making' ('geradezu epochemachend') for an understanding of John.[2] For the following 30 years the *Odes* were used extensively in works on John by Bert, Bauer, Odeberg, and Bultmann. They are now, however, essentially ignored by such Johannine scholars as Menoud, Strathmann, Morris, Wilkens, Wiles, Wikenhuaser, van den Bussche, Marsh, Sanders, Dodd,[3] Barrett, and Brown.

This practice apparently evolves from a judicious rejection of Harnack's redaction hypothesis and from the supposition that the *Odes* are gnostic and late. Recent research, however, suggests that the *Odes* are neither gnostic nor late.[4] It is appropriate, therefore, to re-evaluate the relation between the *Odes* and John.

The main issue is not the possibility of a relationship, but the cause of the numerous parallels. The purpose, therefore, of this chapter is primarily to encourage and facilitate further study of the relation between the *Odes* and John by clarifying the issues involved, and by presenting a bibliographical summary of scholarly conclusions.

Examination of the Evidence

As the reader examines the parallels below, he or she should consider that the *Odes* were probably composed in Syriac,[5] but John in Greek, that the style of the *Odes* is poetic, but that of John usually prosaic, and that the *Odes* and John habitually remint inherited traditions. Direct quotations are, therefore, obviated at the outset.

Interpretation of the Fourth Gospel in the Early Church (Cambridge: Cambridge University Press, 1960); W. Wilkens, *Die Entstehungsgeschichte des vierten Evangeliums* (Zollikon: Evangelische Verlag, 1958).

2.   Harnack and Flemming, *Ein judisch-christliches Psalmbuch*, p. 119.

3.   Bultmann correctly criticized Dodd for not considering the *Odes*, especially in his discussion of the Logos concept and of the symbolic use of 'light' and water. See his review of Dodd's commentary in *NTS* 1 (1954–55), pp. 77-91 (ET 'Rudolf Bultmann's Review of C.H. Dodd's *The Interpretation of the Fourth Gospel*', *Harvard Divinity Bulletin* 27 [1963], pp. 9-22).

4.   Charlesworth, 'Les Odes de Salomon et les manuscrits de la Mer Morte', pp. 522-29; see also Chapters 8 and 9 of the present volume. Carmignac, 'Les affinités qumrâniennes; *idem*, 'Un qumrânien converti au christianisme'; Chadwick, 'Some Reflections', pp. 266-270.

5.   See Emerton, 'Some Problems of Text and Language'; see also Chapter 4 of the present volume.

Evidence of a Verbal Relationship

The *Odes* and John share numerous, striking, and often unique expressions. The following parallels are listed according to their appearance in the *Odes*.[6]

The Odes 1.	John
...and he *loves me* / / For *I* should not have known how to *love ther Lord,* / *If he had not* continuously *loved me.* / / (3.2f.; cf. 3.5-7) [See parallel 9.]	...and *he* that *loveth me* shall be *loved* of my Father, and *I* will *love him*...(14.21) *We love, because he* first *loved us.* (1 Jn 4.19; cf. 1 Jn 4.10; Jn 15.16)

This parallel reveals the emphasis on 'love' in the *Odes*, John, and 1 John; at least the latter two come from the same school.

Harris and Mingana noted the 'strongly Johannine cast of the Ode', claimed that the Ode's theme was taken from 1 Jn 4.19, and concluded 'Whether we are to recognize actual quotations or distinct references depends on the general decision as to the priority of the Odes to the Fourth Gospel and the Pauline Epistles, or the contrary.'[7] Massaux[8] also considered *Ode* 3 to be a hymn written on the 'Johannine' concept of 'love', but F. Spitta disagreed. He denied a special relation between the *Odes* and the Johannine writings, and rejected the parallels between *Ode* 3 and 1 Jn 4.19 or Jn 14.21, because in the *Odes* 'ist die Liebe als Forderung und nicht als Tatsache, als Pflicht der Dankbarkeit und nicht als Naturnotwendigkeit hingestellt'.[9] Contrary to Spitta's opinion, 'love' in the *Odes*, as in John and 1 John, is a present reality for the believer: 'I am putting on the love of the Lord' (*Ode* 3.1). The significance of the first parallel should be seen in terms of the cumulative force of the others that follow.

---

6.   This arrangement has been chosen because frequently several themes appear in the same verse, making a topical arrangement difficult. Charlesworth's translation is followed for the *Odes*. The American Revised Version of 1901 is used for John because of its mechanical, literal translation of the Greek. See Addendum I for a list of the parallels according to their order in John.

7.   Harris and Mingana, *The Odes and Psalms of Solomon*, II, p. 218

8.   Massaux, *Influence de l'évangile*, p. 210

9.   F. Spitta, 'Die Oden Salomos und das Neue Testament', *MPTh* 7 (1910), p. 95.

2.

... And *where his rest is, there also am I. / /* (3.5)	...for I go to prepare *a place* for you. And if I go and prepare *a place* for you. I come again, and will receive you unto myself; *that where I am, there ye may be also.* (14.2f.) Father, I desire that they also whom thou hast given me be *with me where I am...* (17.24)

'His rest' is parallel to 'place' or *monai*, possibly night-stops or resting places,[10] in John.

3.

Indeed he who is joined to h*im who is immortal, /Truly shall be immortal. / /* (3.8)	...*because I live, ye shall live also.* (14.19; cf. 10.10; 3.16; etc.)

The language is different, but the thought is similar. In both the *Odes* and John the Lord is the source of life even *eternal life*, which is a *present reality* resulting from the indwelling of the believer in the Lord and also the Lord in the believer, symbolically represented by the drinking of life-giving water (see parallels 4, 6, 13, 15, 22 and the discussion on 'living water' below), and by the garland (*Ode* 1) and vine with branches (John 15).

4.

And he who delights in *the Life /Will become living. / /* (3.9; cf. 9.4; 10.2; 28.7f.) [See parallel 11.]	... I am the resurrection, and *the Life*: he that believeth on me, though he die, *yet shall he live.* (11.25; cf. 1.4; 5.26, 40; 10.10, 28; 14.6)

In both the *Odes* and John 'Life'[11] is a surrogate for Jesus. The expression 'delight in' and 'believeth on' may be considered synonymous in the parallel above. In both writings the concept of the present is

10. See Brown, *The Gospel According to John*, pp. 618f. For a brief discussion of the connection between knowledge and rest in the *Odes*, see O. Hofius, *Katapausis: Die Vorstellung vom endseitlichen Ruheort im Hebräerbrief* (WUNT, 11; Tübingen: J.C.B. Mohr, 1970), pp. 83f.

11. For a discussion of the concept 'life' in the *Odes* and John, see the following: J. Lindblom, 'Om lifvets idé hos Paulus och Johannes samt i de s.k. Salomos oden', *Uppsala Universitets Årsskrift 1910* (Teologi, 1; Uppsala: Akademiska boktryckeriet, E. Borling, 1911), pp. 1-187; Percy, *Untersuchungen*, pp. 333f.

permeated by the influx of the future promise of life and eternal life, because of the unity between the believer and the 'Life' (see parallels 1 and 3, and compare *Ode* 1 with Jn 15).[12]

5.

This is *the Spirit of the Lord, which is not false,* / *Which teaches* the sons of men to know his ways. / / (3.10)	...*the Spirit of truth:* (14.17, 15.26) ...*he shall teach* you all things, and bring to your remembrance all that I said unto you. (14.26)

This verse in the *Odes* contains three ideas that parallel the Johannine concept of the Paraclete: 'the Spirit' is true, it teaches human beings, and the subject taught is 'his ways' or Jesus' words. A spirit 'which is not false' is probably a spirit that is true, and that is close to John's 'Spirit of truth'. The parallel to the Dead Sea Scrolls is significant.[13]

6.

For *there went forth a stream,* and it became *a river* great and broad; / Indeed it carried away everything, and it shattered and brought (it) to the Temple. / /... Then all *the thirsty* upon the earth *drank,* / And the *thirst was relieved and quenched;* / / for *from the Most High the drink was given.* / / Blessed, therefore, are *the ministers of that drink,* / Who have been entrusted with *His water.* / /... And *lived* by the *living water of eternity.* / / (6.8, 11-13, 18) [See parallels 13, 15, 22.]	...*if any man thirst,* let him come unto me and *drink.* He that believeth on me, as the scripture hath said, from within him shall flow rivers of *living water.* (7.37f.) ...*and he would have given thee living water.* (4.10) but *whosoever drinketh* of the *water* that I shall give him *shall never thirst;* but the *water that I shall give* him shall become in him a well of *water* springing up unto *eternal life.* (4.14) And when the ruler of the feast tasted the *water* now become wine, and knew not whence it was (but *the servants* that had drawn the water knew)... and when men have *drunk* freely... (2.9f.)

Both authors emphasize the gift of 'eternal life' and describe its presence as 'living water' (see below). R.H. Strachan suggested that the

---

12. Borig, *Der wahre Weinstock*, p. 127, correctly notes the imagery shared by the *Odes* and John and remarks, 'In keinem dieser Fälle ist jedoch eine direkte literarische Beziehung zwischen der joh. Weinstockrede und dem Text der Oden zu sichern.'

13. See Charlesworth (ed.), *John and Qumran*, pp. 130, 132f.; see also Chapter 9 of the present volume.

'ministers' in this Ode are to be related to the pericope of the marriage at Cana, and that the strange reference to becoming intoxicated in *Ode* 11 (see parallel 13 below) is related to the word *methusthosin* ('they have drunk freely') in Jn 2.10.[14]

7.

He became like me that I might *receive Him.* / In form he was considered like me, ... the *Word* of Knowledge. /... *He was gracious to me* in his *abundant grace,* /... He has allowed him *to appear to them that are His own;* / In order that they might recognize *him that made them,* / And not suppose that they came of themselves. / / (7.4, 7, 10, 12) [See parallels 16, 18, 24, 26.]	He was in the world, and the world was *made through him,* and the world *knew him not.* He came unto his own, and *they that were his own received him* not. But as many as *received him...* And the *Word became flesh,* and dwelt among us... *For of his fullness we all received, and grace for grace.* (1.10-12, 14, 16)

See the discussion on 'Word' below. The strength of this parallel lies in the number of parallel *termini technici* and concepts: Word, the creative function of the Word, appearance to 'His own', receiving Him, and the gift of 'abundant grace'. After summarizing this parallel in John, E.A. Abbott correctly concluded: 'All this agrees with the thought in the Ode, but in the obscure and condensed language of the latter there is no trace at all of borrowing from the Gospel. The two writers assume the same fundamental axioms.'[15]

8.

For *I turn not my face from my own,* / Because I *know them.* / / (8.12) [See parallel 22 below.]	... *I know my own...* (10.14) All that which the Father giveth me shall come unto me; and him that cometh to me *I will in no wise cast out.* (6.37; cf. 1.11; 17.6-10)

The similarity between *Ode* 8.12 and Jn 10.14 does not lead to the hypothesis that one is a quotation of the other. The different context, which is significantly echoed elsewhere, might suggest that the two writings emanate from the same community.

14. R.H. Strachan, 'The Newly Discovered Odes of Solomon, and their Bearing on the Problem of the Fourth Gospel', *ExpTim* 22 (1910), p. 11.

15. Abbott, *Light on the Gospel*, p. 203

9.

And my righteousness goes before them, / and they shall not be deprived of my *name*; / for it is *with them*. // [Composition *ex ore Christi* ceases and the odist himself speaks] Pray and increase, And *abide in the love of the Lord*; / And you who are loved in the Beloved, / and *you who are kept in him* who lives, / (8.19-21) [See parallel 1.]	Holy Father, *keep them in thy name* which thou hast given me... While I was *with them, I kept them* in thy *name*... (17.11f.) ...*abide ye in my love*. If ye keep my commandments, ye shall *abide in my love*; even as I have kept my Father's commandments and *abide in his love*. (15.9f.)

The strength of these parallels lies in the presence of several so-called Johannine concepts in the Ode: abiding in 'the love of the Lord', being kept, and the association of these ideas with His 'name'. The parallels are palpable but direct literary dependence, in either direction, is dubious.

10.

And also *that those who know him may not perish, /*... (9.7)	... *that whosoever believeth on him should not perish*... (3.16)

Both the language and thought are similar; this may have been a common saying in the 'Johannine' *Urgemeinde*. In both documents 'to know' and 'to believe' appear often to be synonymous.

11.

And he caused to *dwell in me* his immortal life, / And permitted me to proclaim the *fruit of his peace*. // (10.2) [See parallels 4, 6, 9, 11 and discussions.]	... He that *abideth in me, and I in him*, the same beareth much *fruit*... (15.5)... *Peace* I leave with you: *my peace* I give unto you... (14.27)

12.

And the Gentiles *who had been dispersed* were *gathered together*, /... (10.5)	...but that he might also *gather together* into one the children of God *that are scattered abroad*. (11.52)

C.F. Burney cited Rev. 11.15; 21.3, 24 as well as Jn 11.52 and stated:

Ode 10.5-6 is a passage which illustrates very remarkably the Poet's use of the Johannine writings. His theme is the gathering of the Gentile nations into the Church; and he seems deliberately to have selected the outstanding passages on this subject from Jn. and Apoc., and worked them up in a manner which utilizes their most striking phrases.[16]

The obvious difference, however, is between 'the Gentiles' and 'the children of God'; the latter might denote the Diaspora. The language is noticeably different, and the parallel may be due to the prevalence of this thought in the Jewish apocryphal literature.

13.
And *speaking waters* touched my lips / From the *fountain* of the Lord generously. / / And so *I drank* and became *intoxicated,* / From the *living water that does not die.* / / And my *intoxication* did not cause ignorance; / But I abandoned vanity. / / (11.6-8)
[See parallels 6, 15, 22.]

[See parallel 6 above.]

See the discussion on 'living water' below.

14.
Indeed, there is much room in your paradise. / (11.23)

In my Father's house are many mansions... (14.2)

The thought behind these verses is similar even though the imagery is dissimilar. In support of this parallel P. Smith stated: 'The "abundant room in Paradise" (*Ode* XI, 20) is but another name for the "many mansions" of John 14.2.'[17]

15.
And like *the flowing of waters,* truth flows *from my mouth,* / (12.2; cf. 40.2)

[See parallels 6, 13, and 22 above.]

See the discussion on 'living water' in the following pages.

16.
For the *dwelling* place of *the Word is the human,* /... (12.12)

[See parallels 7, 18, 24, and 26 above.]

Harris and Mingana contended:

16. Burney, *The Aramaic Origin*, p. 169.
17. P. Smith, 'The Disciples of John and the Odes of Solomon', *The Monist* 25 (1915), p. 173. A parallel between Jn 14.2 and *2 En.* 61.2 should be mentioned.

This Ode is a Hymn concerning the Divine Logos, or the Divine Wisdom which becomes the Logos. It is not an easy Ode to translate nor to understand. It comes very close in one sentence to the Gospel of John, 'the dwelling-place of the Word is Man'. This is very near to the statement that the 'Logos dwelt among us.' but does not involve the personal incarnation nor the assumption of flesh.[18]

Spitta, however, accentuated the difference: 'Der Satz 12.11 (12.12): "Der Wohnsitz des Wortes ist der Mensch", hat mit Joh. 1.14 nichts zu tun, da es sich nicht um das persönliche Wort und um dessen Wohnen in der Mitte der Menschen handelt.'[19]

The numerous parallels between the *Odes* and the Prologue of John, of course, were popularized and emphasized by Bultmann in his commentary. They are now carefully re-examined in a positive light by J.T. Sanders.[20] See the discussion on 'Word' in the following pages.

17.
And let your gentleness, O Lord, [See parallels 9 and 11 above.]
abide with me, / And the *fruits of your love.* / / (14.6)

Evidence for a parallel lies in the appearance of three symbolic words in the same context in both *Odes* 14 and John 15: abiding, fruit, and love.

18.
And *there is nothing outside of the Lord,* / Because he *was before anything came to be.* / / And *the worlds are by his Word,* / And by the thought of his heart. / / (16.18f.)

In the beginning was the Word, and the *Word* was with God, and the *Word* was God. The same was *in the beginning* with God. *All things were made through him;* and; *without him was not anything made that hath been made.* (1.1-3)

[See parallels 7, 16, 24, 26.]

For a discussion of 'Word', see below. Harris and Mingana commented that

Evidently in this Ode we see the Logos-theology in its making. Some persons will perhaps object and say that we see it already made. But that

18. Harris and Mingana, *The Odes and Psalms of Solomon,* II, p. 275.
19. Spitta, 'Die Oden Salomos', p. 95.
20. Sanders, *The New Testament Christological Hymns,* pp. 38f. Also see Brown, *The Gospel According to John,* pp. xxxii, 21.

raises the question as to what it was made of, and takes us back to Prov. 8.22ff.[21]

Harris and Mingana[22] and Massaux[23] observed that the parallel in Col. 1.17 may be closer than the one in John. The odist and John, however, mention creation by the Word, and weave pre-existence out of a Word Christology. In Colossians 1 the *terminus technicus* is not Word but *prototokos*.

19.

And nothing appeared closed to me, / Because *I* was *the opening of every-thing.* / / (17.11; cf. 42.15-17)	I am *the door...* (10.9; cf. 14.6)

Scholars have differed on the evaluation of this parallel. Bauer[24] and Bultmann[25] cited it, Massaux claims it is 'fort frappant',[26] and F.M. Braun observes 'Comme en Jo. x, 7, Jésus est la Porte, à la fois parce qu'il a le pouvoir de pénétrer où il veut (x, 2), et qu'il faut passer par lui pour être sauvé (x, 9).[27] Odeberg,[28] however, rejected the parallel, claiming that in the *Odes* the door is before 'the house of bondage' but in John it is 'the entrance to the innermost abode of the Godhead'.

Odeberg perceived the dissimilarity, but failed to observe that the ode and John portray Jesus as the door or gate through which the believer comes into salvation.[29] The parallel remains even though *Ode* 42 is probably about the *Descensus ad inferos*.

20.

Let not *light be conquered by darkness,* / Nor let truth flee from falsehood. / / (18.6; cf. 11.11, 19; 15.1f.)	And the *light* shined in the *darkness:* and the *darkness apprehended it not.* [= has not *overcome* it.] (1.5, *et passim*)

21. Harris and Mingana, *The Odes and Psalms of Solomon*, p. 286.

22. Harris and Mingana, *The Odes and Psalms of Solomon*, p. 286.

23. Massaux, *Influence de l'évangile*, p. 212

24. W. Bauer, *Das Johannesevangelium* (Tübingen: J.C.B. Mohr, 1925), p. 139.

25. R. Bultmann, 'Die Bedeutung der neuerschlossenen mandäischen und manichäischen Quellen für das Verständnis des Johannesevangeliums', *ZNW* 24 (1925), p. 135. See also Schweizer, *Ego Eimi*, p. 34.

26. Massaux, *Influence de l'évangile*, p. 210.

27. Braun, *Jean le théologien*, I, p. 243.

28. Odeberg, *The Fourth Gospel*, pp. 320-21.

29. See also Brown, *The Gospel According to John*, pp. 385, 393-95.

Harris and Mingana called this a 'quasi-parallel';[30] Braun remarks that the idea in the Ode 'répond bien' to the idea in John,[31] and Massaux contends that the opposition of light and darkness in *Odes* 18.6 has 'une teinte johannique'.[32] This parallel, however, should be viewed in light of the conclusion that both the *Odes* and John are probably independently influenced by the earlier Qumranic light–darkness paradigm.[33]

21.

And I did not perish, because I was not their brother, / *Nor was my birth like theirs.* / / And *they sought my death but were unsuccessful,* / Because *I was older than their memory;* / And in vain did they *cast lots against me.* / / And those who were *after me* / sought *in vain* to destroy the memorial of *him who was before them.* / / (28.17-19)	The Jews therefore said unto him, Thou art not yet fifty years old, and hast thou seen Abraham? Jesus said unto them, verily, verily, I *say* unto you, *before* Abraham was born, *I am*. They took up stones therefore *to cast at him: but Jesus hid himself...* (8.57-59; cf. 1.1, 15, 27, 30)

These verses in *Ode* 28 contain several words and ideas found in the passage cited from John: the pre-existence of the Lord, an unsuccessful attempt to kill him, the importance of the verb 'to cast', and the play on 'before...after'. The parallel between the 'I' of this *ex ore Christi* passage in the *Odes* and the 'I am' of John is significant. A further, extensive examination of such parallels should inform our search for *ipsissima verba Jesu*.[34]

22.

Fill for yourselves water from the living *fountain* of the Lord, / Because it has been opened for you.	[See parallels 6, 13, and 15, and Rev. 22.17.]

30. Harris and Mingana, *The Odes and Psalms of Solomon*, II, p. 297.

31. Braun, *Jean le théologien*, I, p. 243.

32. Massaux, *Influence de l'évangile*, p. 210.

33. See Charlesworth's discussion of this issue in 'Les Odes de Salomon et les manuscrits de la Mer Morte', pp. 524-29, and in *John and Qumran*, pp. 76-106 and 107-36. On the basis of such parallels as 'das Gegensatzpaar Wahrheit und Lüge, das Parallelenpaar Licht und Leben', M. Dibelius argued that the *Odes* and John come from the same 'Gedankenwelt' ('Johannesevangelium', p. 359).

34. Unfortunately they are usually ignored when the *religionsgeschichtliche* background to the 'I am' of John is discussed, e.g. P.B. Harner, *The 'I am' of the Fourth Gospel: A Study in Johannine Usage and Thought* (Philadelphia: Fortress Press, 1970).

/ / And *come all you thirsty ones and take a drink,* / And rest beside the *fountain* of the Lord / /... Because *it flowed from the lips of the Lord,* / and it named from the heart of the Lord. / / And it came boundless and invisible, / And until *it was set in the middle they knew it not.* / / (30.1f., 5f.)	... I baptize in *water: in the midst of you standeth one whom ye know not.* (1.26)

See parallels 6, 8, 13 and 15 above; and the discussion on 'living water' below. Both in the *Odes* (44 times) and John (20/12/28/56/16/50)[35] there is an unusual emphasis placed on the paradigm 'to know' vis-à-vis 'to be ignorant'.

23.

And he *lifted his voice* toward the Most High, / And offered to him those that had become sons through him. / / And his face was justified, / Because thus his Holy *Father had given* to him. / / (31.4f.)	...and *lifting up his eyes* to heaven, he said, *Father* ...unto the men whom thou *gavest* me... I pray for them: I pray not for the world, but for *those* whom thou hast *given* me... (17.1, 6, 9; cf. 1.12)

The parallel is clear and striking; the direction of influence is open to question. Is the Ode recalling the prayer in John 17? Was the elaborate prayer in John composed on the basis of a tradition like that preserved in the Ode? Or, did the two arise independently of each other but dependent on a common tradition? These questions can be answered only within the context of all the parallels, and in light of related literature.[36] Massaux's suggestion that *Ode* 31.4 is an echo of Jn 17.9 is unlikely,[37] as is literary dependence in either direction. This parallel indicates, it seems to me, that both compositions probably come from the same community or school.

24.

And *the Word* of truth who is self-originate, / / (32.2) [See parallels 7, 16, 18, 26.]	In the beginning was *the Word*... (1.1; cf. 1.3)

35. These and the following statistics from the New Testament are taken from Morgenthaler, *Statistik des neutestamentlichen Wortschatzes*.
36. See the discussion in the previous chapter of the present volume.
37. Massaux, *Influence de l'évangile*, p. 212.

See the discussion on 'Word' in the following pages.

25.

And he stood on the peak of a summit and cried aloud / From one end of *the earth* to the other. / / Then *he drew to him all* those who obeyed him, / For he did not appear as the Evil One. / / (33.3f.; cf. 42.2)	And I, if I be *lifted up* from *the earth, will draw all* men unto myself. (12.32)

The problem in this parallel is whether the odist is referring to the Lord or 'the Evil One'. Strachan cited this parallel, claiming: 'the subject is apparently the Messiah... The idea in both passages is the world-wide reign of the Messiah.'[38] Harris and Mingana[39] cited Prov. 8.1-4 as a parallel, and claimed that the odist identified Christ with Wisdom. These comments are misleading if the subject is 'the Evil One', as I think it is. Regardless, the parallel to John does have the strength of a similar progression of ideas: being on a high point on the earth and drawing all (cf. *Ode* 33.3f. with Jn 1.7, 12; 3.16ff., *et passim*).

26.

And his *Word* is with us in all our way, / The Savior who *gives life* and *does not reject ourselves*. / / The man who humbled himself, / but was exalted because of his own righteousness. / / The Son of the Most High appeared / In the perfection of his Father. / / And *light dawned from the* Word / *That was before time in him.* / / The Messiah in truth is one. / And he was known *before the foundations of the world*, / That he might *give life* to persons for ever by the truth of his name. / / (41.11-15; cf. 10.1f.) [See parallels 7, 16, 18, 24 and the discussion on 'Word'.]	For the bread of God is that which cometh down out of heaven, and *giveth life* unto the world. ...and him that cometh to me I *will in no wise cast out.* (6.33, 37) ...the glory which I had with thee *before the world was*... for thou lovedst me *before the foundation of the world.* (17.5, 24; cf. 1.1-5, 9, 14)

Massaux claims: 'On nierait difficilement un rapprochement litté-raire' between *Odes* 51.14 and Jn 1.1.[40] The importance of this parallel is

38. Strachan, 'The Newly Discovered Odes', p. 12.
39. Harris and Mingana, *The Odes and Psalms of Solomon*, II, pp. 376f.
40. Massaux, *Influence de l'évangile*, p. 210.

heightened by the superabundance of 'Johannine' terms and concepts present in the ode: Word, way, 'The Savior who gives life' and does not reject those who come to him, exaltation in and through humility, Son, Father, light, pre-existence and truth.

The preceding 26 parallels are not exhaustive but they do reveal a relationship between the *Odes* and John. In fact, the *Odes* contain more striking parallels to John than any other non-canonical writing prior to Justin Martyr. The mandate, of course, is to explain the cause of these parallels; but in attempting an explanation it becomes evident how little is known about some aspects of Christian origins.

Evidence of a Conceptual Relationship

Do the concepts and images in the above parallels suggest that the *Odes* and John developed in the same community? In an attempt to answer this question, attention will be focused on two of the most important shared themes: 'Word' and 'living water'.

Word

The concept of the Word is certainly prominent in both writings; note parallels 7, 16, 18, 24, and 26. In the following pages an attempt will be made to summarize the nature and function of the Word in the *Odes* and John, and to report the observations made by earlier studies.

The 'Logos' doctrine is very similar in each. The Word was in the beginning with God, all things were made through him, and without him was not anything made that was made. In him was life and light. Nowhere, however, does the odist explicitly state that the Word became flesh. R.M. Grant, consequently, contended that

> the Odist will not take the final step of admitting that the Word became flesh, incarnate. Even the statement in the twelfth Ode, 'For the dwelling-place of the Word is man,' is concerned with the Light that lighteth every man, the Logos as reason, rather than with the mode of the incarnation.[41]

The Odist is not as concerned as the Fourth Evangelist with the mode of the incarnation, but Grant incorrectly asserts that Word in the *Odes* means only 'the Light that lighteth every man'. The Word in the *Odes*

---

41. R.M. Grant, 'The Odes of Solomon and the Church of Antioch', *JBL* 63 (1944), p. 366.

does sometimes mean reason, as Dodd[42] and others have stated, but it is also hypostatic, as J.T. Sanders[43] emphasized. The Odist, I believe, did not wish to distinguish between the 'Word' and the incarnate Lord: 'For there is a helper for me, the Lord. /.../ / He became like me.../ / And I trembled not when I saw him, /.../ / Like my nature he became,.../ And like my form' (*Ode* 7.3-6). Few will miss the incarnational dimension of *Ode* 37.3: 'His Word came toward me.' Dodd, therefore, correctly wrote about *Ode* 12, 'This is the Word which was incarnate in Christ, as in Od. Sol. xli. 13-14, etc.'[44] One should neither exaggerate the similarities here between the *Odes* and John,[45] nor ignore them or explain them away.

What is the most likely explanation of this relationship? An answer can come only after a careful and detailed analysis of the meaning of the two nouns used by the Odist to express 'Word': ‏ܡܠܬܐ‎ and ‏ܦܬܓܡܐ‎.[46] Harris and Mingana[47] argued accurately that since only the odist uses ‏ܦܬܓܡܐ‎ to express the divine Word and that the noun is inappropriate in the history of ecclesiastical terms, the *Odes* must not be appreciably later than John. Scholars who have studied these *termini technici* for 'Word' in the *Odes* correctly conclude that the *Odes* must be either contemporary with (Bert)[48] or earlier than John (Bultmann,[49] Sanders[50]). Either possibility proves the importance of the *Odes* for an understanding of Johannine theology.[51]

42. Dodd, *The Interpretation of the Fourth Gospel*, pp. 272f.

43. Sanders, *The New Testament Christological Hymns*, pp. 115-20.

44. Dodd, *The Interpretation of the Fourth Gospel*, p. 272. Also see parallel 7.

45. Rylands, *The Beginnings of Gnostic Christianity*, p. 226, wrote, 'The Johannine Word is precisely the Word of the Odes; a spiritual being capable of becoming immanent in men.'

46. Bert, *Das Evangelium des Johannes*, p. 97, after juxtaposing excerpts of the two terms in the *Odes*, concluded: 'Es kann darnach nicht zweifelhaft sein, dass wir in den "Oden Salomos" die Logoslehre selbst unter diesem ihrem Namen in derselben Weise wie im Johannes-Evangelium vor uns haben.'

47. Harris and Mingana, *The Odes and Psalms of Solomon*, I, pp. 92-93. See also Mingana, 'Odes of Solomon', *Dictionary of the Apostolic Church*, II, p. 106; and Metzger, 'Odes of Solomon', , p. 812.

48. Bert, *Das Evangelium des Johannes*, p. 98.

49. Bultmann, 'Ein jüdisch-christliches Psalmbuch', pp. 23-29; *idem, The Gospel of John*, pp. 30f.

50. Sanders, *The New Testament Christological Hymns*, pp. 115-20.

51. The importance of the Word in the dualism shared by the *Odes* and John leads to the conclusion that 'It is improbable that the Odist systematically borrowed

Living Water

Not only is 'living water'[52] an important concept in the *Odes* (6.18; 11.7) and John (4.10, 11; 7.38), but 'water' itself is peculiarly empha- sized and developed in the *Odes* (11 times) and John (7/5/6/21/7/1—18 times in Revelation). 'Living water', however, also occurs in the Old Testament, Qumran Scrolls, Mishnah, Mandean literature, and Corpus Hermeticum. The problem, therefore, of identifying a credible concep- tual relationship between our two documents is considerable. Spitta questioned the significance of 'living water' in the *Odes* and John and called for more specific evidence.[53]

A study of this relationship should begin by examining the shared symbolic meaning of 'living water'. Brown argues that in John it represents both the revelation and the Spirit that Jesus gives to believers.[54] He cites or refers to numerous and significant parallels to John in the Old Testament, the apocryphal literature, the Qumran Scrolls, the New Testament, and the rabbinic literature; Bultmann, however, relates a similar exegesis of John to the *Odes*:

> However the idea of 'living water,' combined with the water of baptism as a divine power, can be used figuratively, or better *symbolically, to refer to the divine revelation, or alternatively to the gift bestowed by the revelation.* This usage is to be found principally in the Odes of Solomon. 'Draw your water from the life-source of the Lord!' cries the singer, and confesses: ... [11.6-8].
>
> It is this usage which must give us the clue to Jn 4.10-15.[55]

from John. The most probable solution, at this stage of our research, is that both the author of John and the Odist contemporaneously shared not only the same milieu but perhaps also the same community' (Charlesworth, *John and Qumran*, p. 125).

52. See parallels 6, 13, 15 and 22 above. 'Living water' is found in the following odes: 6.18; 11.7; 12.2; cf. 6.9, 13; 11.6; 16.10; 28.15; 30.1, 4; 40.1-2.

53. Spitta, 'Die Oden Salomos', p. 95.

54. Brown, *The Gospel According to John*, I, pp. 178-79 and 328; also see the selected bibliography on p. 331.

55. Bultmann, *The Gospel According to John*, pp. 184f. (italics in the original). Also see the discussion of 'living water' by Fabbri, 'El tema del Cristo vivificante', pp. 487-95. C. Goodwin recognizes the parallel between the concept of water in the *Odes* and John, but concludes that John may or may not have had passages of the *Odes* in mind. One cannot know because the Fourth Evangelist 'was capable of changing his sources beyond recognition' (E.E. Fabbri, 'How Did John Treat his Sources?', *JBL* 73 [1954], p. 72).

A decision whether to follow Spitta's skepticism or Bultmann's confidence may be facilitated by the following outline of the symbolic use of water in the *Odes* and John:

1. Water (= living water) is a gift from God (*Ode* 6.12; 30.1 and Jn 4.10).
2. Water (= living water) quenches thirst (*Ode* 6.11 and Jn 4.14).
3. Living water gives life (*Ode* 6.18 and Jn 4.14).
4. Living water is associated with eternity and eternal life (*Odes* 6.18; 11.7, 22f. and Jn 4.14).
5. An invitation is extended to all who are thirsty (*Ode* 30.2 and Jn 7.37).
6. Water (= living water) flows from within the Lord (*Ode* 30.5 and Jn 7.38).[56]
7. The flow becomes a river (*Odes* 6.8 and Jn 7.38).
8. Both in the *Odes*[57] and John[58] 'living water' has obtained baptismal motifs.
9. The salvific connection between 'water' and 'rest' is explicit in the *Odes* (viz. 30.1-6) and implicit in John. See parallels 2 and 22 above.
10. Both claim that 'the living fountain of the Lord' (*Ode* 30.1 = Jn 4.14, 'a well of water springing up unto eternal life') has been opened for (*Odes*) or placed in (John) the believer.
11. The *Odes* and John use water, or living water, to symbolize both the revelation and Spirit which the Lord (= Jesus) gives to the believer, and the latter is more emphasized in both (*Ode* 6.7f.; cf. 30.1-7; Jn 7.39).

Is the shared symbolism not impressive?[59] Is it not significant, both for an evaluation of the relationship between the *Odes* and John and for

56. On the difficulty of interpreting Jn 7.38 see Brown, *The Gospel of John*, pp. 319-31. In *Ode* 30.5 'his heart' means the Lord's heart. In Jn 7.38 the pronoun 'his' may refer to the Lord, certainly the Lord is the source.

57. Bernard, *The Odes of Solomon*, p. 42, introduced the thesis that the *Odes* are 'baptismal hymns intended for use in public worship, either for catechumens or for those who have recently been baptized'. Although Bernard clearly overstated his case, there is a consensus today that the *Odes* do contain baptismal motifs. Contrast P. Batiffol, who claimed that the odist 'n'a pas le baptême en vue. L'eau est un symbole de la foi, de la grâce, de la connaissance, symbolisme analogue aux images johannines.' P. Batiffol, 'Les Odes de Salomon', *RB* 8 (1911), p. 44.

58. See, for example, Brown, *The Gospel of John*, p. 180.

insight into the so-called Johannine school, that 'living water' or 'water of life' is found in the New Testament only in John and in Revelation (7.17; 21.6; 22.1, 17)? The data reveal a significant relationship between the *Odes* and John, and these 11 shared ideas obviate Braun's conclusion: 'Sans doute, le rapport est-il dans les images plutôt que dans les idées.'[60]

The concept of water and living water is not necessarily more developed in the *Odes*, even though they speak of 'ministers of that drink' (6.13), the size and power of the river (6.8-10), and the effect of drinking it ('intoxication did not cause ignorance' [11.8]). Images can be more developed in mystical hymns than in a gospel. Is it not probable, furthermore, that the careful, subtle use of the water motif in John reflects a sophisticated development?

It has been suggested that both the *Odes* and John probably inherited the concept of living water from the *Thanksgiving Hymns* of Qumran.[61] This suggestion does not necessarily weaken a relationship between the *Odes* and John. Both authors could have borrowed the basic imagery from the same source; they certainly developed it along the same lines.[62]

The discussion of the impressive parallels between the concepts of Word and living water in the *Odes* and in John shows that these two writings are significantly related. The importance of these parallels should be viewed in light of the numerous other shared concepts such as the following: the doctrine of the Trinity and the heightened relationship of Father and Son; the manifest tendency toward mysticism;

59. See Bacon, *The Gospel of the Hellenists*, p. 179.

60. Braun, *Jean le théologien*, I, p. 242.

61. Charlesworth, 'Les Odes de Salomon et les manuscrits de la Mer Morte', pp. 534-38.

62. After comparing the symbolism of living water in the *Odes*, John, and the Dead Sea Scrolls, J. Daniélou arrived at a similar conclusion: 'It is difficult to think that the Odes of Solomon depend on John, but on the other hand their connection with the Qumran writings is certain. They represent a parallel development whose context is Judaeo-Christian'; J. Daniélou, *Primitive Christian Symbols* (trans. D. Attwater; Baltimore: Helicon Press, 1964), p. 48. See also Gibson, 'From Qumran to Edessa', p. 16; and O. Cullmann, 'The Significance of the Qumran Texts for Research into the Beginnings of Christianity', *JBL* 74 (1955), pp. 222-24. Both Gibson and Cullmann argue for a relation between Qumran, the *Odes*, and John.

the connection between abiding and the image of the vine;[63] a developed dualism that contains unique characteristics;[64] the emphasis on 'love', 'truth', the verb 'to know', the identification of the Lord's crucifixion and exaltation and paronomasia on the verb 'to lift up';[65] the delineation of the paradigm 'to have eternal life' or 'to perish'; and the emphasis on the present experience of the former by those who are united with the Lord.[66]

Essene influence on the *Odes* and John, which was apparently obtained independently,[67] suggests that both reflect a community influenced by Essene traditions. This conclusion does not demand that the community be identical, but it does limit the time for such variegated and fluid influence to an early and approximately contemporaneous time. Certainly it is now clear that both writings were composed before 125 CE, and probably earlier than that date. In attempting in the future to diagnose more precisely the lines of convergence, one should consider the evidence that the letters of Ignatius of Antioch contain parallels to the Dead Sea Scrolls, the *Odes*, and John.[68]

63. See Brown, *The Gospel of John*, p. 511. See parallels 4, 9, 11, 17. *Ode* 1 and Jn 15, for example, share a similar image. In *Ode* 1 a plaited wreath is described as not only upon the head of the believer but also entwines him so that he exclaims that the wreath has 'caused your branches to blossom in me'.

64. Charlesworth, 'Les Odes de Salomon et les manuscrits de la Mer Morte', pp. 524-29. See also Haenchen, *Die Bibel und Wir*, p. 212; and Kuhl, *Die Sendung Jesu*, p. 36.

65. Compare, for example, *Ode* 41.12 ('The man who humbled Himself, / But was exalted because of His own righteousness') with Jn 12.32.

66. Betz, *Der Paraklet*, p. 215, judiciously remarks that the *Odes* stress the present aspect of salvation even more so than John. Earlier Harris (J.R. Harris, *The Doctrine of Immortality in the Odes of Solomon* [London: Hodder, n.d. (?1912)], pp. 45f.), had argued that 'It appears, therefore, that the Odist viewed his immortality experimentally and qualitatively, rather than in the remote future, or in the language of mere duration.' He also noted the parallels between *Odes* 3 and in Jn 11.25 and 14.19 (p. 22), but never made a clear statement regarding the relation between the *Odes* and John. In his book, however, Betz tended to reject the hypothesis that the *Odes* depend upon John (*Der Paraklet*, p. 71).

67. See the discussion in Charlesworth, *John and Qumran*, pp. 107-36.

68. See R.M. Grant, 'The Odes of Solomon and the Church of Antioch', pp. 370ff.; Burney, *The Aramaic Origin*, pp. 159-66, 170f., Harris and Mingana, *The Odes and Psalms of Solomon*, II, p. 53; Corwin, *St Ignatius*, pp. 71-80. C.H. Kraeling reached the following noteworthy conclusion: 'In the writings of a number of earlier authors...particularly Ignatius there has come to light a number of such

Summary of Scholarly Conclusions

We have seen that the relation between the *Odes* and John is impressive. Further research is demanded on each parallel. In order to facilitate future research, the remainder of the present article will contain a summary of the major works on the subject.

The Odes Depend on John

Many scholars have concluded that the *Odes* depend on John; yet none of them has published a critical investigation of the relationship. The issue is dismissed in a cavalier fashion, characterized by statements such as that by A.C. Headlam, who after citing verses from *Odes* 3, 6, 7, 12, 38 and 41 advised,

> Now we readily admit that no single passage above can be called a quotation, but we also believe that not one of them could 'have been written unless the Fourth Gospel had been written and had been known to the writer.'[69]

H. Leclercq,[70] J. Wellhausen,[71] C. Bruston,[72] M.-J. Lagrange,[73] C.F. Burney,[74] F.M. Braun,[75] R. Schnackenburg,[76] and J.H. Bernard[77] suggested that the *Odes* depend on John. Most of these scholars merely cite parallels; yet, unfortunately, this hypothesis is the one frequent in

---

striking analogies to the thought and expression of the Odes as to make it almost certain that the analogies are the result of free quotation from our text. The lines of patristic evidence converge upon Antioch and require that our Hymns have been in existence prior to the date of the Ignatian letters, that is about the year 100 CE.' C.H. Kraeling, 'The Odes of Solomon and their Significance for the New Testament', *Lutheran Church Review* 46 (1927), p. 228.

69. A.C. Headlam, 'The Odes of Solomon', *CQR* 71 (1911), p. 291.

70. H. Leclercq. 'Odes de Salomon', in F. Cabrol and H. Leclerq (eds.) *Dictionnaire d'archéologie chrétienne et de liturgie* (Paris: Letouzey et Ané, 1936), XII.2, p. 1910.

71. Wellhausen, review of *The Odes and Psalms of Solomon*, by Harris.

72. Bruston, *Les plus anciens cantiques chrétiennes*, pp. 12, 18, 20.

73. Lagrange, *Evangile selon Saint Jean*, p. xxviii.

74. Burney, *The Aramaic Origin*, pp. 132 and 169.

75. Braun, *Jean le théologien*, I, p. 245.

76. Schnackenburg, *The Gospel According to St John*, I, p. 145.

77. Bernard, *The Odes of Solomon*, p. 31.

summaries.[78] R.E. Brown apparently places himself in this company by claiming that some passages in the *Odes* 'are possibly dependent on John'.[79] W.H. Raney claimed the hypothesis was 'suggestive'.[80] L. Tondelli argued that the *Odes* not only borrowed from John but also partook of that living tradition and the same spiritual atmosphere.[81] Although H. Gressmann[82] and W. Bauer[83] did not speak directly concerning the relationship, they popularized this hypothesis in German-speaking circles by means of the claim that the *Odes* are a second-century gnostic hymnbook. Since no conclusive evidence is cited by any of the scholars mentioned, it appears that they reached their conclusions on the basis of a priori judgments, rather than from an analysis of the verbal and conceptual parallels.[84]

John Depends upon the Tradition Represented in the Odes
The position taken by Harnack is complex. He claimed that the author of John may have once been a Jew from the same circle as the Odist,[85] and that the Christian interpolator of the *Odes* probably knew John. Consequently, the importance of the *Odes* for an understanding of John was twofold:

78. E.g. Hamman, *Naissance des lettres chrétiennes*, p. 20; B. Altaner, *Patrology* (trans. H.C. Graef; Freiburg: Herder, 1958), p. 63; Quasten, *Patrology*, I, p. 162. A. Robert and A. Feuillet, *Introduction to the New Testament* (trans. P.W. Skehan *et al.*; Paris: Desclée, 1965), p. 633. This position was originally advocated by T.E. Pollard ('The Fourth Gospel: Its Background and Early Interpretation', *AusBR* 7 [1959], p. 50), but he appears to have abandoned it (*Johannine Christology*, p. 34).

79. Brown, *The Gospel of John*, p. 21.

80. W.H. Raney, *The Relation of the Fourth Gospel to the Christian Cultus* (Giessen: Alfred Töpelmann, 1933), p. 58.

81. Tondelli, *Le Odi di Salmone*, p. 123: 'Le Odi non dipendono però soltanto dagli *scritti* giovannei: esse sembrano aver vita e calore direttamente da quella tradizione viva spirituale che in quegli scritti trovò la sua più alta e diretta manifestazione: questi documenti vivono nella stessa atmosfera di idee e di sentimenti.'

82. Gressmann, 'Die Oden Salomos', in Hennecke (ed.), *Neutestamentliche Apokryphen*, p. 437.

83. W. Bauer, 'Die Oden Salomos', in Hennecke and Schneemelcher (eds.), *Neutestamentliche Apokryphen*, p. 577.

84. It is surprising to find this hypothesis stated as fact in the introduction to John in *La Sainte Bible* (Paris: Cerf, 1956), p. 1396.

85. Harnack and Flemming, *Ein jüdisch-christliches Psalmbuch*, p. 106.

Für 'Johannes' hat also sowohl der ursprüngliche jüdische Verfasser als auch der christliche Interpolator die grösste Bedeutung. Das ist geschichtlich die wichtigste Frucht, welche uns diese Oden bringen, dass sie in doppelter Weise das vierte Evangelium, d.h. seine Religion und seine Theologie, beleuchten. Was sie hier lehren, ist ebenso neu wie aufklärend zugleich und wird die Kirchenhistoriker noch lange beschäftigen. Man hat hier den Steinbruch vor sich, aus dem die johanneischen Quadern gehauen sind![86]

H. Grimme claimed that his research, which had centered on an examination of the original language of the *Odes*, strengthened Harnack's hypothesis.[87] In 1910 Bultmann, closely following Harnack's position, contended that

Ein doppeltes Licht fällt also von unsern Oden auf das Johannesevangelium: wir lernen erstens einen jüdischen Kreise kennen, der als die Vorstufe der johanneischen Frommigkeit und Theologie anzusehen ist;

86. 'For "John", therefore, not only the original Jewish author, but also the Christian interpolator had the greatest importance. This is historically the most important fruit that the Odes bear: in a two-fold manner they illuminate the religion and theology of the Fourth Evangelist. What they teach here is new as well as at the same time enlightening and will occupy the Church historian for a yet long time.' Harnack and Flemming, *Ein jüdisch-christliches Psalmbuch*, pp. 110f. We think that Harnack later changed his mind about the relation of the *Odes* to John. Two years later he wrote again about the *Odes* but neither developed nor reiterated his theory about them. (See his review of 'A New MS of the Odes of Solomon', by Burkitt, in *TLZ* 37 [1912], p. 530.) It is surprising to find that he never again mentioned the relation of the *Odes* to John, despite such publications as the following: *New Testament Studies. VI. The Origin of the New Testament* (trans. J.R. Wilkinson; London: Williams, 1925); 'Zum Johannesevangelium', in *Erforschtes und Erlebtes* (Giessen: Alfred Töpelmann, 1923), pp. 36-43; 'Das "Wir" in den johanneischen Schriften', *Sitzungsberichte der Preussischen Akademie der Wissenschaften* 17 (1923), pp. 96-113; 'Johannes', in *Die Entstehung der christlichen Theologie und des kirchlichen Dogmas* (Darmstadt: Wissenschaftliche Buchgesellschaft, 1927, 1967), pp. 58f.; 'Zur Textkritik und Christologie der Schriften des Johannes', in *Studien zur Geschichte des Neuen Testaments und der alten Kirche* (Arbeiten zur Kirchengeschichte, 19; Berlin: W. de Gruyter, 1931), pp. 105-52.
It is significant that in the 1921 Festschrift, K.L. Schmidt, on p. 41, and M. Dibelius, on p. 110, discuss the *Odes* but make no mention of Harnack's earlier work on them (*Harnack-Ehrung* [Leipzig: J.C. Hinrichs, 1921]). The biographies of Harnack, moreover, fail to mention his hypothesis about the *Odes* and their importance for John.
87. Grimme, *Die Oden Salomos*, pp. 136f.

und wir lernen ferner einen Christen kennen,—nämlich eben den Bearbeiter—der dem Johannes verwandte Züge aufweist.[88]

Fifteen years later Bultmann argued that the *Odes* reflect the kind of 'gnostic' and hymnic sources used by the Fourth Evangelist. He claimed that John knew and used sources which contained an *Erlösungsmythos* and that evidence of such a myth permeates the *Odes*. At one time he almost contended that John used the *Odes*: 'Ich will aber hier schon bemerken, dass mir für einzelne Partien des Joh-Ev. die Benutzung schriftlicher Quellen, Offenbarungsreden etwa in der Art einiger Oden Salomos, wahrscheinlich ist.'[89]

Bultmann's general position, however, is that found in his commentary. The *Odes* are earlier[90] than John and best represent the religious background of John.[91]

J.T. Sanders commented on the relation between the *Odes* and John. Concluding that it is highly unlikely that the *Odes* are influenced by John, he suggests that they are earlier than John:

> hypostatization in the *Odes of Solomon*, particularly the hypostatization of the Word, has proceeded independently of the prologue of John and is in some respects logically prior in its development to the hypostasis of the Logos in the prologue of John.[92]

Except for Sanders, scholars have usually assumed that the *Odes* are influenced by John. Harnack, Grimme, and Bultmann's position on the relation between the *Odes* and John has been lost in the judicious

---

88. 'A double light falls, therefore, from our Odes upon the Johannine gospel. We learn first to understand a Jewish circle, which can be seen as the background material of Johannine piety and theology; and, moreover, we come to understand a Christian, namely the reviser, who exhibits characteristics similar to John.' Bultmann, 'Ein jüdisch-christliches Psalmbuch', p. 28.

89. Bultmann, 'Die Bedeutung', p. 141.

90. Bultmann often gives the impression that the *Odes* could be roughly contemporaneous with John. For research that claims to confirm Bultmann's position, see H. Becker, *Die Reden des Johannesevangeliums und der Stil der gnostischen Offenbarungsrede* (FRLANT, NS 50; Göttingen: Vandenhoeck & Ruprecht, 1956), esp. pp. 16-18.

91. 'The result of this enquiry is that the Prologue's source belongs to the sphere of a relatively early oriental Gnosticism, which has been developed under the influence of the O.T. faith in the Creator—God... The Odes of Solomon prove to be the most closely related' (*The Gospel of John*, pp. 30f.). Bultmann's emphasis upon 'development' and his qualification of 'Gnosticism' have generally been ignored.

92. Sanders, *The New Testament Christological Hymns*, p. 119.

rejection of Harnack's interpolation hypothesis, Grimme's Hebrew hypothesis, and Bultmann's concept of Gnosticism. Rylands incorrectly suggested that John knew the *Odes*,[93] but his position is certainly closer to the truth than Spitta's contention that there is no special relationship between the *Odes* and John.[94] None of the above explanations, however, allows for the subtleties contained in the parallels previously discussed. The following hypothesis, therefore, is the only one that is probable.

John and the Odes Come from the Same Religious Environment
Harnack, as just noted, claimed that the Christian interpolator of the *Odes* and the author of John probably were later members of the same circle as the Odist. Almost all scholars who have published a detailed comparison of the *Odes* and John have concluded that it is highly improbable that the *Odes* depend on John.[95] Harris,[96] Grant,[97] Massaux,[98] Dodd,[99] Borig,[100] and Bert[101] correctly concluded that the *Odes* and

93. Rylands, *The Beginnings of Gnostic Christianity*, p. 225.

94. Spitta, 'Die Oden Salomos', p. 95. In a similar vein Barrett (*The Gospel According to St John*, p. 55) contended, 'Both draw upon the inheritance of Oriental-Hellenistic religion. The major resemblances (such as they are) between the two works are due to this common drawing upon a non-Christian source of religious terminology.'

95. Note, for example, the comments by the following authorities: Harris, *The Odes and Psalms of Solomon*, 2nd edn, pp. 74f.; Harris and Mingana, *The Odes and Psalms of Solomon*, II, p. 120; Mingana, 'Odes of Solomon', p. 106; Kraeling, 'The Odes of Solomon and their Significance', pp. 235f.; Daniélou, *Primitive Christian Symbols*, p. 48; Sanders, *The New Testament Christological Hymns*, p. 118. See also P. Feine, J. Behm and W.G. Kümmel, *Introduction to the New Testament* (trans. A.J. Mattill Jr; New York: Abingdon Press, rev. edn, 1966), p. 159: 'A dependence of the "Odes of Solomon" upon John (Schmid, *op. cit.*) is extremely improbable.' H. Jordan argued that the odist's belief 'ist geflossen aus einer Frömmigkeit, wie sie in den johanneischen Kreisen lebendig war und Ausdruck gefunden hatte im Johannesevangelium.' Jordan, *Geschichte der altchristlichen Literatur* (Leipzig: Quelle, 1911), p. 458.

96. See note 66. 'It is when we come to the Gospel and Epistles of John that we find the community of ideas to be the most pronounced' (Harris, *The Odes and Psalms of Solomon*, p. 74). See also R. Harris, *The Origin of the Prologue to St John's Gospel* (Cambridge: Cambridge University Press, 1917), pp. 29f.

97. Grant, 'The Odes of Solomon and the Church of Antioch', p. 368; *idem*, 'The Origin of the Fourth Gospel', *JBL* 69 (1950), p. 321.

98. Massaux, *Influence de l'évangile*, p. 214.

99. Dodd, *The Interpretation of the Fourth Gospel*, p. 272.

100. Borig, *Der wahre Weinstock*, p. 127.

John come from the same spiritual environment. Bert, who presented the most complete analysis of this relationship, concluded, 'Wir können uns diese Verwandtschaft nur dadurch erklären, dass beide örtlich, zeitlich und geistig demselben Mutterboden entstammen.'[102]

Carmignac, who has published several articles on the *Odes*,[103] is impressed by their relationship both to the Dead Sea Scrolls and to John. He concludes that the parallels to each are pervasive and profound; the Odist did more than merely study the Dead Sea Scrolls and John. 'Pour être si profondément marqué, il a dû vivre assez longtemps dans des communautés qumrâniennes et johanniques, avec le désir sincère d'en assimiler les richesses spirituelles.'[104]

Conclusions

The first hypothesis, that the *Odes* depend on John, is the least likely of the three main positions presented by critical scholars. The 26 parallels summarized above do not suggest that the Odist was working from John. It is significant, moreover, that no scholar who has systematically examined the parallels between the *Odes* and John, has concluded that the Odist knew John. It is precisely this hypothesis, nevertheless, that is accepted by the majority of contemporary scholars; and they sometimes even go so far as to present it as a fact.[105]

101. Bert, *Das Evangelium des Johannes*, p. 98. E.C. Selwyn argued that the *Odes* and John are contemporaneous, and that the source of their theology, especially baptismal imagery, is Isa. 60–62 [LXX!], which alludes to the Feast of Tabernacles and the ceremony of bearing water (living water) from Siloam to the Temple. E.C. Selwyn, 'The Feast of Tabernacles, Epiphany, and Baptism', *JTS* 13 (1912), pp. 225-40.

102. 'Only by the fact that both [John and the Odes] stem geographically, temporally and religiously from the very same nurturing ground can we illumine their relationships.' Harnack and Flemming, *Ein jüdisch-christliches Psalmbuch*, p. 114, concluded that either the Odist knew John or both came from the same circle. Cf. W.F. Howard, *The Fourth Gospel in Recent Criticism and Interpretation* (rev. C.K. Barrett; London: Epworth, 1955), p. 77.

103. See note 4 above.

104. 'To be so profoundly marked he must have lived for a long time in the Qumran and Johannine communities with a sincere desire to assimilate from them their spiritual riches.' 'Les affinités qumrâniennes', p. 68.

105. 'Déjà, dans la première moitié du IIe siècle, nous voyons que le quatrième évangile est connu et utilisé par nombre d'auteurs: saint Ignace d'Antioche, l'auteur des Odes de Salomon, Papias…' (*La Sainte Bible traduite en français sous la direction de l'Ecole Biblique de Jérusalem* [Paris: Cerf, 1961], p. 1396).

The second hypothesis, that John depends on the tradition represented in the *Odes*, suffers primarily because it places the *Odes* appreciably earlier than John.

The third hypothesis, that the *Odes* and John come from the same religious environment, is the best explanation of the data summarized above. Moreover, it is the conclusion obtained by most scholars who have seriously studied the relation between the *Odes* and John.

It is clear that the *Odes* and John contain numerous and impressive parallels, and that these neither suggest that the *Odes* depend on John nor the reverse.[106] Both reflect the same milieu, probably somewhere in western Syria, and both were probably composed in the same community.[107] Continued research may eventually indicate that the Odist probably had been an Essene, though perhaps a non-Qumran Essene,[108] who composed the *Odes* in the 'Johannine' community or school. If this reconstruction is correct, the *Odes* have begun to unlock the historical enigmas of John and promise to be a most important key to the theological mysteries.

106. E.A. Abbott, who published a voluminous work on the *Odes*, claimed that the thought of the *Odes* is 'not in orthodox or at least not in familiarly orthodox form. But it is not Gnostic. It is poetic. It seems to recognise, as the Fourth Gospel does, a personal *Logos* or Word who is also incarnate Light and Life, but it recognizes also—an aspect about which the Fourth Gospel is silent—one who is Babe as well as Son, a Messiah born of the Virgin Daughter of Zion to be at once the Lord of Israel and the embodiment or body of Israel. In this body, or in these 'members'—to use the word employed almost at the outset of the Odes—every true Israelite finds himself to be incorporate. This doctrine—or poetic meditation—seems to go back to a time before orthodoxy had crystallized, when Christian thinkers and seers and poets were still in the atmosphere of that stupendous Life, which was also their life, and which they could not analyse or systematically and dogmatically define while they were still breathing it' (Abbott, *Light on the Gospel*, pp. xxxviif.).

107. Since John is heterogeneous, containing sections that may be separated by as much as 50 years, and since there is no need to assume that the 42 *Odes* were composed within the same year or decade, the actual relationship between our two documents may be exceedingly complex. By these statements, however, we do not mean to imply direct literary dependence.

108. Charlesworth, 'Les Odes de Salomon et les manuscrits de la Mer Morte'; *idem, John and Qumran*, pp. 107-36.

ADDENDUM I

In order that references in John may be checked more easily, the twenty-six parallels cited above are here given in the order in which they appear in John. Only those
passages which are quoted above are included.

John	Odes	John	Odes
1.1-3	16.18f; 32.2; 41.11-15	11.52	10.5
1.5	18.6; 15.lf.	12.32	33.3f.
1.10-12	7.4, 12	14.2f.	3.5; 11.23
1.14	7.4, 7, 12; 12.2	14.17	3.10
1.16	7.10	14.19	3.8
1.26	30.5-6	14.21	3.2f.
2.9f.	6.11-13; 11.6-8	14.26	3.10
3.16	9.7	14.27	10.2
4.10	6.11-13, 18; 11.6-8	15.5	10.2; 14.6
4.14	6.11-13, 18; 11.6-8; 30.1-2	15.9f.	8.19-21; 14.6
6.33	41.11-15	15.26	3.10
6.37	8.12; 41.11-15	17.1	31.4f.
7.37f.	6.8, 11-13, 18; 11.6-8; 12.2; 30.1f., 5f.	17.5	10.1f.; 41.11-15
8.57-59	28.17-19	17.6	31.4f.
10.9	17.11	17.9	31.4f.
10.14	8.12	17.11f.	8.19-21
11.25	3.9; 9.4; 10.2; 28.7f.	17.24	3.5; 41.11-15
		1 Jn 4.19	3.2f.

ADDENDUM II

The above important parallels are not meant to be exhaustive. The possible parallels
are the following.

John	Odes	John	Odes
1.2	15.5	4.8	6.27
3.2f.	14.21; 15.16; 1 Jn 4.19	4.9b+c	15.16
3.2c-7	1: 12; 15.16	4.10b	4.14
3.5b	14.2f; 17.24	4.15a	1.3
3.8	14.19	5.3	1.16
3.9	1.4; 5.40; 10.10, 28; 11.25; 14.6	5.4	15.20; 16.2
		6.1	3.8
3.10	14.16f., 26; 15.26; 1 Jn 4.1-6	6.8	4.10; 7.37f.
		6.11f.	4.10; 7.37f.
4.6	6.37	6.13	2.9f.

John	Odes	John	Odes
6.18	4.14	17.11	10.9
7.2	14.6	18.6	1.5
7.4	1.10-12, 14	19.10	1.13
7.7	1.1	20.3	14.27
7.10b	14.13	21.6	3.14; 12.32
7.10f.	1.16	22.1	3.31
7.12a+b	1.10-12	22.12	14.3
7.14	8.12	24.1	1.32f.
7.21b	14.7	24.5	16.21
8.5	12.32	24.8	16.21
8.7	14.3, 27; 15.20	24.10b	8.44
8.8	14.7	24.12	8.44
8.11	14.7; 17.8	26.1	10.14; 17.6-9
8.12	1.11; 6.37; 10.14;	26.13	4.14
	17.6-10	28.9	15.20
8.14	6.27	28.17-19	1.1, 15, 27, 30;
8.19	14.12, 17.11f.		8.57-59
8.20	15.4-7, 9f.	29.7	8.12
8.21	14.19; 15.9; 17.11f.	30.1f.	4.10, 14; 7.37f.;
9.7	3.16; 14.7		Rev. 22.17
10.2	14.23, 27; 15.5	30.5f.	1.26
10.4a	16.33	31.4f.	1.12; 17.1, 6, 9
10.5	11.52; Rev. 11.15;	31.10	14.27
	21.3, 24	32.1	8.12
11.1	15.1-6	32.2	1.1, 3
11.3	14.6, 27	33.3f.	1.7, 12; 3.16; 12.32
11.6f.	4.10, 14	33.4f.	3.31
11.7f.	2.9f.	36.3	1.6, 9; 5.35
11.22	17.15	38.9	3.29
11.23	14.2	38.17-22	15.1-6
12.2	7.37f.	40.2	4.14; 7.37f.
12.3b	17.17	41.8	8.58
12.7	1.9	41.11	1.1-3; 6.33, 37
12.10	1.10	41.13-15	1.1-5, 9, 14; 17.5,
12.11	1.18		24
12.12	1.14	42.2	12.32
14.6	15.1-6	42.8	3.29
15.2	12.32	42.15-17	10.9
16.12b-13	5.17f.	42.20	17.6-10
16.18f.	1.1-3		

APPENDIX

No major publication comparing the *Odes of Solomon* and the Gospel of John has appeared since the previous chapter appeared in print. There have been comments by scholars; in particular those mentioned at the end of the previous chapter. E. Haenchen made one reference to the *Odes of Solomon* in his commentary: 'the Gospel of John was not influenced by Odes of Solomon 6.11-18' (Haenchen, *John: A Commentary*, I, p. 220). Ashton sees a profound similarity between the *Odes* and John in the concept of deathless life: 'Lying behind the eternal life of the Fourth Gospel, therefore, and the immortal life of the Odes of Solomon is not just a profound faith in God as the author of life but the very different belief that God would ultimately "swallow up death for ever"' (J. Ashton, *Understanding the Fourth Gospel* [Oxford: Clarendon Press, 1991], p. 218). D.M. Smith judges that the Gospel of John has closer affinities with the *Odes of Solomon* than with the *Gospel of Truth*, and he is impressed that the Odes of Solomon 'sometimes reflect the language or conceptuality of the Gospel of John, at just those points at which there is also an affinity with the sectarian documents of Qumran' (D.M. Smith, *The Theology of the Gospel of John* [New Testament Theology; Cambridge: Cambridge University Press, 1995]).

B. Lindars was convinced that the *Odes of Solomon* were 'certainly Gnostic' (what did he mean?), contain 'many Johannine expressions', and the most likely explanation is that the Gospel of John has influenced them. B. Lindars, *The Gospel of John* (London: Marshall, Morgan & Scott; Grand Rapids: Eerdmans, 1972, 1995), pp. 41, 80. Schnackenburg drew a contrast between the concept of love and joy in the Gospel of John and in the *Odes of Solomon*, in *The Gospel According to St John*, ET, III, p. 420.

Unfortunately, despite the obvious importance of the *Odes of Solomon* for understanding not only the origin but also the theology and Christology of the Gospel of John, most commentators ignore the *Odes of Solomon*. This situation particularly pertains to the commentaries by G. Sloyan (1988), G.R. Beasley-Murray (1989), D.A. Carson (1991), T.L. Brodie (1993), and L. Morris (1995). The *Odes of Solomon* are also not mentioned in such monographs as G.J. Riley's *Resurrection Reconsidered: Thomas and John in Controversy* (Minneapolis: Fortress Press, 1995); this omission is surprising because of the numerous links between the *Odes of Solomon* and the *Gospel of Thomas*.

SELECTED AND ANNOTATED BIBLIOGRAPHY
WITH STATUS QUAESTIONIS

This bibliography is a selection of the most important publications on the *Odes of Solomon*; for a fuller bibliography see Charlesworth's 'Bibliography on the Odes of Solomon', in *The Odes of Solomon*, pp. 149-67, and his *The Pseudepigrapha and Modern Research with a Supplement* (Septuagint and Cognate Studies, 7S; Chico, CA: Scholars Press, 1981), pp. 189-94, 301-303. Another helpful, and more up-to-date, guide bibliographically is Lattke's 'Chronologische Bibliographie 1910–1984', *Die Oden Salomos*, III, pp. 57-367 and his 'Literatur', *Oden Salomos*, pp. 239-54. I have seldom cited book reviews, and have focused on full-length books. In light of the preceding research, annotations will be focused seriatim on (a) original language, (b) provenience, (c) date, (d) character, (e) connection with the Dead Sea Scrolls, (f) relation to the Gospel of John, (g) possible 'gnostic' thought. Only when a specialist on the *Odes* devotes research to one of these comments is it included; obviously, category (e)—connection with the Dead Sea Scrolls—will not be possible for publications that antedate 1947, and seldom is a contribution characterized by comments on each of these issues. If a scholar has completed more than two major publications the annotation will come at the end of them. All entries under a name are listed chronologically, as is the separation of the bibliography into periods; it is necessary to observe the impact of improved methodologies and archaeological discoveries (which should not undermine my contention that some of the best work was published in the first decade by the world's leading experts in the study of Christian Origins). Usually focus will be directed to only the most important contributions or works by luminaries, such as R. Bultmann, R.H. Charles, H. Gunkel, A. Harnack, A. Loisy, G.R.S. Mead, E. Schürer, P. Smith, and J. Wellhausen.

Abbreviations
1.15, 80 = first publication of the scholar just listed, pages 15 and 80

Period of Discovery and Excitement (1909–20)
This period covers the time from the *editio princeps* to the publication of the second volume of Harris and Mingana. The period is one of unprecedented research on the *Odes*. The consensus was that the *Odes* were extremely early and important for understanding the origins of the Gospel of John, but it was impossible to agree whether they were originally Jewish or Christian (references to the complex composition history of the *Testaments of the Twelve Patriarchs* abound).

Abbott, E.A., *Light on the Gospel from an Ancient Poet* (Diatessarica, 9; Cambridge: Cambridge University Press, 1912).
(a) The original language of the *Odes of Solomon* is Hebrew; (c) 'a very early date

indeed, possibly even before 100 A.D.' (p. viii); (d) the *Odes* were pseudonymously attributed to Solomon, 'Jedidiah, "the beloved"',...'a first-century Christian Jewish poet, tinged by nationality, steeped in a new religion, but still a poet for the world' (p. xi); the *Odes* are 'a half-way house...between Judaism and Christianity' (p. xxix); (f) 'Throughout the Odes there appear to me something like the Johannine reiteration...combined with something like the Johannine variation' (p. xvi). Abbott's book is full of precious insights, dated, but contains many important insights into the symbolisms and theology of the *Odes* (a subject that is notably discussed deficiently in the field).

Bacon, B.W., 'The Odes of the Lord's Rest: I. The Problem of their Origin', *Exp* 8.1 (1911), pp. 193-209.

—'Songs of the Lord's "Beloved"' , *Exp* 8.1 (1911), pp. 319-37.

—'The Odes of Solomon: Christian Elements', *Exp* 8.2 (1911), pp. 243-56.

—'Further Light on the Odes of Solomon', *Exp* 8.4 (1912), pp. 459-62.

(d) The main purpose of Bacon's research is to stress that the *Odes* are basically Jewish (2.319), perhaps a Hellenized form of Judaism (3.254), maybe similar to 'an Egyptian writing of circ. 30' (3.255); the composition is shaped by an allegorizing interpolator (3.243); the one theme is redemption (1.206-07), the Odist favors images of mountains (1.205). *Odes* 8 and 19 and *2 Bar.* 21 and 51 are dependent someway (4.459).

[Contrast his views with the comments he published in 1933 annotated in the second phase of research.]

Bernard, J.H., *The Odes of Solomon* (Texts and Studies, 8.3. Cambridge: Cambridge University Press, 1912).

(a) Bernard argued that Aramaic or Syriac is the original language of the I (p. 10); (c) 'I incline, then, to a date between 150 and 200 for their origin' (p. 42); (d) 'Whoever the author may have been, he had something of the poetical *afflatus*; nor would it be easy to find Christian poems of any age which strike a higher spiritual note. "Solomon" is the first Christian poet in order of time, and not the least in order of inspiration' (p. v). The *Odes* are 'Hymns of the Catechumens, or Hymns of the newly baptized taught to Catechumens as part of their instruction' (p. vi). The 'Hallelujah' which concludes 'all' the *Odes* 'shews clearly that they...were intended for liturgical use' (p. 17). (f) '...the doctrine of Christ as the Logos...is not dependent on a few phrases in the Prologue to the Fourth Gospel; it is deep-rooted in his thought' (p. 31). (g) The *Odes* are not gnostic (pp. 28-30).

Bruston, C., *Les plus anciens cantiques chrétiens* (Paris: Librairie Fischbacher, 1912).

(a) Bruston was the first to argue that the original language of the *Odes of Solomon* is Syriac (pp. 30-37); (b) the *Odes* were composed in Antioch (pp. 36-37); (c) they date from the first half of the second century CE (p. 36); (d) the *Odes* are not docetic (*pace* Batiffol, p. 25): (f) the Odist knew 'les principaux livres du Nouveau Testament' (p. 12).

Bultmann, R., 'Ein jüdisch-christliches Psalmbuch aus dem ersten Jahrhundert', *MPTh* 7 (October 1910–September), pp. 23-29.

(a) The original language of the *Odes of Solomon* is Greek (1.24); (b) the *Odes* were probably composed in Palestine (1.24); (c) the *Odes* are originally Jewish and antedate the Gospel of John (1.29); and (f) they provide the mythology and background to this gospel (1.28).

Charles, R.H., 'A Church Hymnal of the First Century', *Times Literary Supplement* 430 (7 April 1910), p. 124.

The father of the modern study of the Pseudepigrapha thought the *Odes* were a first-century composition. He claimed rightly that the *Odes* must be translated with *parallelismus membrorum* in mind.

D'Alès, A., 'Les Odes de Salomon', *Etudes* [Paris] 129 (1911), pp. 753-70.

(g) The *Odes* are 'gnostic' like the works of Scripture are gnostic—hence, they are not gnostic.

Dhorme, P., review articles in *RB* NS 9 (1912), pp. 464-69.

(g) '...the resemblances are indeed fugitive: these *Odes* are less gnostic than this least gnostic of all Gnostics was himself' (p. 468).

Dietrich, G., 'Eine jüdisch-christliche Liedersammlung aus dem apostolischen Zeitalter', *Reformation* 9 (1910), pp. 306-10, 370-76, 513-18, 533-36.

(d) The first level is Essene (pp. 306, 370) and the subsequent one is Christian (related to Eastern heretics, i.e. Messalianismus).

Frankenburg, W., *Das Verständnis der Oden Salomos* (BZAW, 21; Giessen: Alfred Töpelmann, 1911).

(a) Convinced that the original language of the *Odes of Solomon* is Greek, Frankenburg was the first scholar to translate them into Greek; (d) the *Odes* are originally Jewish or at least Jewish-Christian (p. 1); (f) there is no relation to the Gospel of John but are close to Alexandrian exegesis.

Gressmann, H., 'Die Oden Salomos', *IW* 5.29 (July 1911), pp. 897-908, 949-58.

(g) The *Odes* are to be characterized as gnostic.

Grimme, H., *Die Oden Salomos: Syrisch–Hebräisch–Deutsch* (Heidelberg: Carl Winter, 1911).

(a) Grimme translated the *Odes of Solomon* into Hebrew because Harnack had influenced him into thinking that the original language is Hebrew (pp. iii, 107). He announces that a partial acrostic pattern emerges when the *Odes* are translated back into Hebrew, mistakes by the Syriac translator are corrected, and 'daß wir mit einem hebräischen Originale rechnen müssen' (p. 115).

Gunkel, H., 'Die Oden Salomos', *ZNW* 11 (1910), pp. 291-328.

(a) The original language of the *Odes of Solomon* is Greek (p. 292); (d) the theme of redemption characterizes the *Odes* (p. 324); (g) most importantly Gunkel claimed that the *Odes* are gnostic (p. 326).

Harnack, A., and J. Flemming, *Ein jüdisch-christlichen Psalmbuch aus dem ersten Jahrhundert* (TU, 35.4; Leipzig: J.C. Hinrichs, 1910).

—Review of the edition by Harris and Mingana in *TLZ* 46 (1921), pp. 6-7.

(a) 'dass die Oden hebräisch (aramäisch?) abgefasst werden...'; (b) from the Christian community in Palestine (1.iii); (c) 'ein Psalmbuch aus dem Zeitalter Jesu', perhaps as early as 50 BCE (1.10, 104), but reworked by a Christian around 100 CE (iii); (f) the *Odes of Solomon* antedate and help explain the origins of the Gospel of John (1.v, 106, 110-11). In his review Harnack accepted Harris's position: 'ich nunmehr gern kapituliere' (2.7). The *Odes* are a Christian work, a unity, and they were probably composed in the first century in Antioch (2.7). In fact, Harnack changed his mind on the *Odes* more than once. In 1891 he thought they were gnostic (Harnack, *Über das gnostische Buch Pistis-Sophia*, TU, 7.2 [Leipzig: J.C. Hinrichs, 1891], pp. 45-46).

Harris, J.R., *The Odes and Psalms of Solomon: Now First Published from the Syriac Version* (Cambridge: Cambridge University Press, 1909).

—*An Early Christian Psalter* (London: James Nisbet, 1909).

—*The Odes and Psalms of Solomon: Published from the Syriac Edition* (Cambridge: Cambridge University Press, 2nd edn, 1911).

—*The Doctrine of Immortality in the Odes of Solomon* (London: Hodder & Stoughton, 1912).

—and A. Mingana, *The Odes and Psalms of Solomon* (2 vols.; Manchester: University Press; London: Longmans, Green, 1916–20).

—'The Odes of Solomon and the Apocalypse of Peter', *ExpTim* 42 (1930), pp. 21-23.

(a) First Harris thought the *Odes* were composed in Greek (1 and 3.48), but then he changed his mind: they were composed in 'Syro-Aramaic' (5.165); (b) they were composed in Antioch (5.67)—'...the Odes of Solomon belong to Palestine as their origin, and to a date which cannot differ much from the close of the first century after Christ' (2.viii); (c) they are a first-century hymnbook (5.67) composed probably soon after 70 CE (3.58) —it is 'more probable that they belong to the second century of the Christian era than to the first' (4.10); (d) the *Odes* are a unity and clearly Christian (4.14)—the character of the *Odes* is Jewish-Christian (all)—perhaps the *Odes* contain Essene doctrines (4.11); (f) the *Odes* are 'filled with Johannine phraseology and ideas' (3.13) but it is not clear the *Odes* depend on the Gospel of John (3.75, 4.82); the *Odes* are not gnostic (3.13, 5.205).

Kittel, G., *Die Oden Salomos: Überarbeitet oder Einheitlich?* (Beiträge zur WAT, 16; Leipzig: J.C. Hinrichs, 1914).

(a) The original language is Greek; (d) Kittel argued against Harnack; he sifted the debate over the unity of the Odes to recognize their homogeneity.

Labourt, J., and P. Batiffol, *Les Odes de Salomon: Une oeuvre chrétienne des environs de l'an 100–120* (Paris: Librairie Lecoffre, 1911).

(a) The original language of the *Odes of Solomon* is Greek (p. 116); (b) the provenience is Syria (p. 121); (c) they were composed between 100 and 120 CE (p. 121); (d) the Christology is docetic.(pp. 94-98); (f) the *Odes* are not dependent on the Gospel of John, have a Logos Christology different than in it, and breathe a type of Christianity known from the Johannine writings and Ignatius (pp. 118-19); (g) there is absolutely nothing gnostic about the *Odes* (p. 121). [The ideas are those of Batiffol.]

Lindblom, J., *Om Lifvets Idé hos Paulus och Johannes Samt I de S. K. Salomos Oden* (Uppsala: Akademiska Boktryckeriet, 1911).

(d) The *Odes* are Jewish: 'Officiell judendom finna vi ej i Salomos oden; vi finna en judisk mystik med gnostisk färg (p. 34)', they were composed between 50 BCE and 67 CE and were revised by a Christian around 100 CE (pp. 40-41)—he is obviously influenced by Harnack. (e) While the *Odes* come from Jewish gnostic and mystical circles ('judiska gnostiskt-mystika kretsar', p. 187) and talk about a timeless gnostic mysticism ('mystisk-gnostisk tidlös spekulation'), the Gospel of John concerns a historical reality, the historical person Jesus (om ett historiskt faktum...Jesus historiska person', pp. 185-86). The study of Paul and the Gospel of John is improved by an appreciation of the *Odes*, which reflect Jewish mysticism that has been influenced by other cultures.

Loisy, A., 'La mention du temple dans les Odes de Salomon', *ZNW* 12 (1911), pp. 126-30.

(a) The original language of the *Odes of Solomon* is Greek; (d) the Temple mentioned in *Odes* 4 is not the Jerusalem Temple, the odist's temple is 'le lieu mystique où entrent ceux qui ont été abreuvés par le déluge d'Esprit, c'est-à-dire la société des prédestinés' (p. 129).

Mead, G.R.S., Review of *The Odes and Psalms of Solomon*, by Harris, in *The Quest* 1 (1909–10), pp. 561-70.

(a) the original language is Greek (p. 561); (c) the *Odes* are early, *Ode* 4 could have been composed by an Essene and it seems to antedate 70 and the destruction of the Temple (p. 566); (d) the *Odes* were composed by 'Jews by birth' and should be labeled 'Judaeo-Christian' (p. 566).

Menzies, A., 'The Odes of Solomon', *Interpreter* [London] 7 (1910), pp. 7-22.

(d) Menzies tried to prove that Harnack was correct: the *Odes* are a Jewish composition. He concluded that the *Odes* are the 'Psalms of the Proselytes' (p. 17).

Nestle, E., review of *Ein jüdisch-christliches Psalmbuch*, by Harnack and Flemming, and *Die Ode Salomos* (Neue Studien zur Geschichte der Theologie und der Kirche, 9; Berlin: Trowitzsch, 1911), by G. Diettrich, in *TLZ* 36 (1911), pp. 586-88.

Nestle viewed the *Odes* as epoch-making for understanding the Gospel of John (p. 587).

Newbold, W.R., 'Bardaiṣan and the Odes of Solomon', *JBL* 30 (1911), pp. 161-204.

(d) Bardaiṣan composed all, or at least some, of the *Odes* [contrast de Zwaan and Drijvers]; (g) the *Odes* are not gnostic but a man filled with gnostic ideas.

Schürer, E., review of *The Odes and Psalms of Solomon*, by Harris, in *TLZ* 1.35 (1910), pp. 6-7.

(a) Greek is the original language [he is primarily quoting Harris]; (g) the *Odes* are not gnostic.

Smith, P., 'The Disciples of John and the Odes of Solomon', *The Monist* 25 (1915), pp. 161-99.

(d) The Odist was perhaps a disciple of John the Baptist.

Spitta, F., 'Zum Verständnis der Oden Salomos', *ZNW* 11 (1910), pp. 193-203, 259-90.

(d) The Odist was a Jew and the work is Jewish.

Sprengling, M., 'Bardesanes and the Odes of Solomon', *AJT* 15 (1911), pp. 459-61.

(d) Bardaiṣan knew the *Odes*; (g) there is gnosis in the *Odes*.

Stölten, W., 'Gnostische Parallelen zu den Oden Salomos', *ZNW* 13 (1912), pp. 29-58.

(g) The *Odes* are gnostic.

Tondelli, L., *Le Odi di Salomone: Cantici Christiani degli inizi del II Secolo* (Rome: Francesco Ferrari, 1914).

(a) The original language of the *Odes of Solomon* is Greek (pp. 46-50); (c) the *Odes* were composed sometime between 90 and 150, and most likely near 120 CE (p. 134); (f) the 'Odi dipendono dal IV Vangelo' (p. 133).

Wellhausen, J., review of *The Odes and Psalms of Solomon*, by Harris, in *GGA* 172 (1910), pp. 629-41.

(a) The original language is Greek (p. 631); (d) all the *Odes* originate 'aus derselben Sphäre' if not the same author and they are not Jewish but Christian (p. 639); they are extremely close to the Gospel of John which they may know (p. 641); (g) but they are not gnostic although 'gnosis' is in the foreground (p. 641).

Zahn, T., 'Die Oden Salomos', *NKZ* 21 (1910), pp. 667-701, 747-77.

(a) Greek is the original language (p. 764); (b) the *Odes* do not betray evidence of a provenience (p. 774); (c) the *Odes* date from circa 120–50 CE (p. 774); (d) 'ein von Anfang bis zu Ende christliches Produkt sind diese Lieder insgesamt' (p. 760); (f) the

Odist probably had read Matthew, the Gospel of John and the *Apocalypse of John* (pp. 764-65).

Zwaan, J. de, 'Een Dichter uit den tijd der Apostolische Vaders', *Onze Eeuw* [Haarlem] 11 (1911), pp. 223-46.

—'Ignatius and the Odist', *AJT* 15 (1911), pp. 617-25.

(a) The original language of the *Odes of Solomon* is Syriac perhaps (3.287); (b) they may have been composed in Antioch (1.245); the *Odes* and Ignatius share the same spiritual setting but there is no clear literary dependence (2.625).

Period of Denigration (1921–58)
The period is from the publication of Harris and Mingana, vol. 2, to the publication of Bodmer Papyrus XI. This period provides no significant advance in understanding the *Odes*. It is often assumed, without insight or new research, that the *Odes* are gnostic; but the caution of Gunkel and others that the *Odes* are a form of extremely early gnosis is not perceived. Those who wrote on the *Odes* in this period usually only continued their studies that antedate 1921.

Abramowski, R., 'Der Christus der Salomooden', *ZNW* 35 (1936), pp. 44-69.

(c) The *Odes* were composed around 100 CE (pp. 45-47); (g) the *Odes* are to be categorized as gnostic, but notice the qualification: 'wobei Gnosis als allgemeine Religion der mittel-orientalischen (arabischen) Kultur zu verstehen ist' (p. 47).

Bacon, B.W., *The Gospel of the Hellenists* (ed. C.H. Kraeling; New York: Henry Holt, 1933).

The *Odes* are 'a second-century hymn-book of the Syrian church, in which Oriental religious mysticism is blended with the themes of Deutero-Isaiah and with the beliefs of apocalyptists and Wisdom writers' (p. 145, cf. p. 179). [This conclusion clashes with his work annotated in the first phase of research.]

Bernard, J.H., *Gospel According to St. John* (2 vols.; ICC; Edinburgh: T. & T. Clark, 1928).

(c) The *Odes* are 'Christian hymns composed about 160 or 170 A.D.' (p. cxlvi); (f) the *Odes* 'show how deeply rooted in Christian devotion was the Johannine doctrine of the Word, within seventy years of the publication of the Fourth Gospel' (p. cxlvii).

[See Bernard's book on the *Odes* annotated in the previous period of research.]

Bousset, W., *Kyrios Christos: Geschichte des Christusglaubens von den Anfängen des Christentums bis Irenaeus* (Göttingen: Vandenhoeck & Ruprecht, 2nd edn, 1921).

Under the influence of Gunkel and Gressmann, Bousset assumed the *Odes* were gnostic, but a very early form (p. 28). He used the *Odes* extensively throughout his influential tome. It is enlightening to note that this attribution hindered Bousset from using the *Odes* 'als Zeugnis für das genuine Christentum' (p. 29). (d) The 'Hauptthema' of the *Odes* is 'die Höllenfahrt des Messias' (p. 29).

Bultmann, R., 'Die Bedeutung der neuerschlossenen mandäischen und manichäischen Quellen für das Verständnis des Johannesevangeliums', *ZNW* 24 (1925), pp. 100-46.

—*The Gospel of John: A Commentary* (ed. R.W.N. Hoare and J.K. Riches; trans. G.R. Beasley-Murray; Oxford: Blackwell, 1971 [translated from the 1964 edition, but the work essentially antedates 1959]).

(f) The *Odes* provide the mythology and background to this gospel (1.100, 141).
(g) The *Odes* are an example of 'early oriental Gnosticism' (1.104; 2.8, 29). [Notice how he started with supporting Harnack and concluded by seeing the *Odes* as an early form of Gnosticism.]

Burt, G., 'Verwandtschaft des Evangeliums des Johannes und der Oden Salomos', in *Das Evangelium des Johannes: Versuch einer Lösung seines Grundproblems* (Gütersloh: Bertelsmann, 1922), pp. 75-100.

This major study of the *Odes* and John is apparently unknown to the major commentators on the Gospel of John. (f) The *Odes* and the Gospel of John share the same 'geistig und zeitlich, vielleicht auch örtlich' (p. 75)—his conclusion is persuasive: 'Wir können uns diese Verwandtschaft nur dadurch erklären, daß beide örtlich, zeitlich und geistig demselben Mutterboden enstammen' (p. 98).

Dibelius, M., 'Johannesevangelium', *RGG* (2nd edn, 1929), pp. 349-63.

(g) The *Odes* belong to 'Gnosis' understood 'im weiteren Sinne' (p. 358).

Gaster, M., *The Jewish Guardian* (September 1920), p. 6.

(d) The *Odes* are 'unquestionably of Jewish origin…an important contribution to ancient Jewish Hymnology'.

Goodspeed, E.J., 'The Odes of Solomon', in *A History of Early Christian Literature* (Chicago: University of Chicago Press, 1942), pp. 170-74.

(a) The *Odes* 'were almost certainly written in Greek' (p. 173); (b) perhaps in Antioch (p. 173); (c) in the middle of the second century CE (p. 173); (d) they are obviously Christian (p. 172); (f) and 'recall characteristic touches in the Gospel and Letters of John' (p. 172); (g) the gnostic phrases and terms do not make the *Odes* gnostic (p. 173).

Grant, R.M., 'The Odes of Solomon and the Church of Antioch', *JBL* 63 (1944), pp. 363-77.

(a) the *Odes* were composed in Syriac; (b) in Edessa and were shortly thereafter known to Ignatius either there or in Antioch (p. 377).

Gressmann, H., 'Die Oden Salomos', in E. Hennecke (ed.), *Neutestamentliche Apokryphen* (Tübingen: J.C.B. Mohr, 2nd edn, 1924), pp. 437-72.

(a) The original language of the *Odes of Solomon* is Greek; he inaccurately claimed that most scholars conclude that the *Odes* are a gnostic work of the second century CE. [This influential review misled and misleads many German experts.]

Kroll, J. *Die christliche Hymnodik bis zu Klemens von Alexandreia* (Collected lectures to the Academy at Braunsberg in Summer 1921; Königsberg: Hartungsche Buchdrückerei, 1921), esp. pp. 35-36 (repr. Darmstadt: Wissenschaftliche Buchgesellschaft, 1968), esp. pp. 69-74.

—*Gott und Hölle: Der Mythos vom Descensuskampfe* (Studien der Bibliothek Warburg, 20; Leipzig, 1932) (repr. Darmstadt: Wissenschaftliche Buchgesellschaft, 1963).

(a) The *Odes* were composed in Syriac (1.69); (b) in Syria (1.69); (c) probably towards the end of the second century CE (1.69); (f) they are Christian (1.69); (g) and 'gnostic' when one 'den Terminus nicht zu streng faßt' (1.69)—under the influence of Gressmann (1924) Kroll later assumed the *Odes* are a 'gnostischen Liederbuchs' (2.308-309).

Leclercq, H., 'Odes de Salomon', in F. Cabrol and H. Leclercq (eds.), *Dictionnaire d'archéologie chrétienne et de liturgie* (Paris: Letouzey & Ané, 1936), XII.2, cols. 1903–21.

The *Odes* are clearly Christian, and are more a significant discovery than the recovery of the *Didache*. The higher critical issues are not addressed, but the discussion of the style and theology of the *Odes* is significant.

Mingana, A., 'A Summary of Recent Criticism of "The Odes of Solomon"', *BJRL* 6 (1921–22), pp. 176-85.

—'Odes of Solomon', in J. Hastings (ed.), *Dictionary of the Apostolic Church* (Edinburgh:

T. & T. Clark, 1922), II, pp. 100-106.

(a) The original language is Aramáic or Syriac (2.103-105); (c) the *Odes* date from around 100 CE [The first article is mainly a refutation of Bernard's criticism of the 1916–20 edition of the *Odes*]—the limits of the original date are 80 to 210 (2.105); (d) the odist is a 'semi-Gnostic Christian writer, whose orthodoxy is very doubtful' (2.106); (f) all the *Odes* are 'closely joined together in a series whose keynote is the Johannine theology and experience' (2.102); (g) 'Gnosticism has no strong support in the Odes' (2.106).

Tondelli, L., 'I Salmi e le Odi Salomone', *EncIT* 30 (1936), pp. 550-51.

(c) The *Odes* date from around 120 CE (p. 551).

Unnik, W.C. van, 'A Note on Ode of Solomon XXXIV,4', *JTS* 37 (1936), pp. 172-75.

The above and below pattern in the *Odes* derives from a lost apocryphon.

Zwaan, J., 'The Edessene Origin of the Odes of Solomon', in R.P. Casey, S. Lake and A.K. Lake (eds.), *Quantulacumque* (London: Waverly Press, 1937), pp. 285-302.

(a) The original language of the *Odes* is Syriac perhaps (p. 287); (b) they were composed in Edessa (pp. 292-301 [contrast his earlier position which placed them in Antioch]); (d) the *Odes* could not have been composed by Bardaiṣan because he had an aristocratic character while the *Odes* are 'vulgärchristlich' (pp. 292-94); (g) it is misleading to label the *Odes* 'gnostic' (pp. 286-89).

Period of Renewed Interest and Careful Study (1959–97)

With the publication of Bodmer Papyrus XI in 1959 and the growing importance of not only the Dead Sea Scrolls but also the Nag Hammadi Codices for understanding early Judaism and Christian origins, a new flurry of research on the *Odes* begins. The tendency is now to see the original language as Syriac and not Greek; a consensus seems to be that the *Odes* should not be branded as 'gnostic'.

Abramowski, L., 'Sprache und Abfassungszeit der Oden Salomos', *OrChr* 68 (1984), pp. 80-90.

(a) The *Odes of Solomon* were composed in Syriac (p. 90); (c) they date from the latter half of the second century (p. 90). Abramowski was often focused on Drijvers's dating which she eventually had to judge as unsuccessful (p. 90).

Adam, A., 'Die ursprüngliche Sprache der Salomo-Oden', *ZNW* 52 (1961), pp. 141-56.

(a) The *Odes* were composed in a type of Aramaic close to that of Edessene Syriac.

Alegre, Xavier, *El concepto de salvación en las Odas de Salomón: Contribución al estudio de una soteriología gnostizante y sus posibles relaciones con el cuarto evangelio* (Dissertation, Münster, 1977).

(c) The *Odes* can be dated 'entre finales del siglo I y mediados del II d. C.' (p. 473).

[See also A. Peral and X. Alegre.]

Ashton, J., *Understanding the Fourth Gospel* (Oxford: Clarendon Press, 1991, 1993).

(e) The *Odes* and the Gospel of John are often strikingly similar (pp. 185, 217-18, 403, 550).

Aune, D.E., 'The Present Realization of Eschatological Salvation in the Odes of Solomon', in *The Cultic Setting of Realized Eschatology in Early Christianity* (NovTSup, 28; Leiden: E.J. Brill, 1972), pp. 166-94.

—'The Odes of Solomon and Early Christian Prophecy', *NTS* 28 (1982), pp. 435-60.

—'The Odes of Solomon', in *Prophecy in Early Christianity and the Ancient Mediterranean World* (Grand Rapids: Eerdmans, 1983), pp. 296-99.

(a) Aune concludes 'tentatively' that Greek is the original language, but 'in a milieu in which Asianic rhetoric and Semitic poetics had a strong influence on Greek style' (pp. 168-69), he then changed his mind—they were composed in Syriac (3.296); (b) Syria, and Antioch, is the provenience (1.170, 173), but he then changed his mind: Edessa is more likely than Antioch (3.296); (c) the *Odes* were composed between 90 and 150, perhaps near to 120 CE (1.174) or 'the first quarter of the second century A.D.' (3.296); (g) the *Odes* and the *Gospel of Truth* should not be labeled as 'gnostic' (1.171-72). Aune rightly criticizes R.E. Brown, D.M. Smith and J.L. Martyn for failing 'to utilize the Odes in discussion of the history and character of the "Johannine community"...' (2.456).

Azar, E., *Les Odes de Salomon* (Paris: Cerf, 1996).
(a) The *Odes* were probably composed in Syriac (p. 50): (b) they come from Syria and perhaps Edessa (p. 70); (c) they were composed sometime between 100 and 125 (p. 70) ; (d) they are Jewish Christian (p. 71); (e) the *Odes* are influenced by the Dead Sea Scrolls (pp. 21, 41-42, 46)—one wonders if some of the *Odes* may be pre-Christian and Jewish (p. 46); (f) they have 'une origine comme avec la tradition johannique' (pp. 42, 45, 47, 71).

Baarda, T., '"Het Uitbreiden van mijn Handen is zijn Teken": Enkele notities bij de gebedshouding in de Oden van Salomo', in *Loven en Geloven* (Festschrift H.N. Ridderbos; Amsterdam: Bolland, 1975), pp. 245-59.
(d) The *Odes* are Christian and should be studied within early Christian literature; (e) the Dead Sea Scrolls, esp. the *Hodayot*, are an important background for these odes.

Barrett, C.K., 'Jews and Judaizers in the Epistles of Ignatius', in R. Hamerton-Kelly and R. Scroggs (eds.), *Jews, Greeks and Christians* (Festschrift William David Davies; Leiden: E.J. Brill, 1976), pp. 220-44.

—*The Gospel According to St John* (London: SPCK, 2nd edn, 1978).
(c) Barrett is convinced that the *Odes* may 'well have been written somewhat later than Ignatius or the Gospel of John (1.240-41). (f) Both the *Odes* and the Gospel of John contain 'the terminology of Oriental-Hellenistic religion' (2.65), and while the evidence does not suggest any direct dependence (2.112), it is conceivable that the Odist knew the Gospel of John; in any case, the *Odes* are important for Johannine studies (2.113); (g) the *Odes* are gnostic (2.41).

Bauer, W., 'Die Oden Salomos', in E. Hennecke and W. Schneemelcher (eds.), *Neutestamentliche Apokryphen* (Tübingen: J.C.B. Mohr [Paul Siebeck], 3rd edn, 1964), II, pp. 576-625.
(a) Bauer thought that the 'Grundsprache der S.-O. ist das Griechische'; (g) he qualifies his claim that the *Odes* are gnostic: '*Gnostisch* ist dabei in einem weiten Sinne zu fassen' (p. 577). To strech the technical term 'gnostic' so much is to render it virtually meaningless for any insight into Christian origins.

Beskow, P., and S. Hidal, *Salomos Oden: Den äldsta kristna sångboken översatt och kommenterad* (Stockholm: Proprius, 1980).
(a) Much of the evidence suggests that the *Odes* were composed in Syriac (pp. 76-77); (d) they are Jewish Christian and heavily indebted to 'judisk poetisk tradition' (p. 73); (c) they probably date from the beginning of the second century: 'Det finns goda möjligheter att de är samtida i varje fall med de sist tillkomna skrifterna i Nya testamentet' (p. 7); (e) there are strong similarities between the *Odes* and the *Hodayot* along with other Qumran texts (pp. 79, 83); (f) the *Odes* share with the

Gospel of John the same theological vocabulary (p. 83); (g) they are not gnostic (pp. 78-79).

Blaszczak, G.R., *A Formcritical Study of Selected Odes of Solomon* (HSM, 36; Atlanta: Scholars Press, 1985).

This study is prolegomenous; it shows the importance of studying the *Odes* in light of form criticism. See Charlesworth's' review in *JBL* 107 (1988), pp. 134-35.

Brown, R.E., *The Community of the Beloved Disciple* (New York: Paulist Press, 1979).

(f) The *Odes* have affinities with the Gospel of John (p. 147).

Braun, F.M., 'L'énigme des Odes de Salomon', *RevThom* 57 (1957), pp. 597-625 (repr. in *Jean le théologien et son évangile dans l'église ancienne* [Paris: Librairie Lecoffre, 1959], I, pp. 224-51).

(g) The Odist was cognizant of gnostic terminology such as we find in the *Gospel of Truth* which represents Valentinian Gnosticism (p. 237); they were most likely composed by Bardaiṣan (pp. 238-42).

Brownson, J., 'The Odes of Solomon and the Gospel of John', *JSP* 2 (1988), pp. 46-69.

(a) The *Odes* were written in Syriac, (b) perhaps in Antioch or Edessa; (c) 'some of the material in the Odes could both precede and follow the Gospel from a developmental point of view' (p. 61); (d) 'it does seem clear that the Odes represent a particular variety of Johannine Christianity' (p. 61); (e) 'there are points of contact between some Odes and Qumran which are not mediated elsewhere in Christian tradition' (p. 61); (f) the *Odes* may represent the large group of schismatics that left the Johannine community—'the writer of the Odes of Solomon looks very much like one of the "sessionists" of 1 John' (p. 60).

Bruce, F.F., *The Gospel of John* (Grand Rapids: Eerdmans, 1983, 1992).

(c) the *Odes* date from about the same period as 'Ignatius, bishop of Antioch (c. AD 100)' (p. 7); (g) the *Odes* have 'a gnostic flavor' (pp. 7, 267).

[N.B. 'When J. Rendel Harris discovered the *Odes of Solomon* in 1909 and suggested that they might even be of first-century date, the German scholar Adolf Jülicher is reported to have said, 'Then all our criticism of the Fourth Gospel is *kaput*' (T.R. Blover, *Cambridge Retrospect* [Cambridge, 1943], p. 73)' (p. 23).]

Buck, P.F., 'Are the "Ascension of Isaiah" and the "Odes of Solomon" Witnesses to an Early Cult of Mary?', in *De Primordiis Cultus Mariani* (Rome: Pontificia Academia Mariana Internationalis, 1970), IV, pp. 371-99.

(a) The issue of the original language is not yet solved (p. 385); (b) the author is from Syria (p. 386); (c) the *Odes* were composed 'about the year 100' CE (p. 388) —and 'at least a decade before St. Ignatius wrote his Letters' (p. 396); (d) he is a Christian (p. 386); (e) there are obvious similarities between the *Odes* and the *Hodayot* but it is not clear that there is any dependence (p. 384). His comments are frequently derived from a study of secondary sources and not from original research, but he is well read. More experts need to study and compare the Christianity in the *Odes* with the Christianity preserved in the documents preserved in the Old Testament Pseudepigrapha.

Cameron, P., 'The "Sanctuary" in the Fourth Ode of Solomon', in W. Horbury (ed.), *Templum Amicitiae: Essay on the Second Temple Presented to Ernst Bammel* (JSNTSup, 48; Sheffield: JSOT Press, 1991), pp. 450-63.

Cameron laments the lack of consensus regarding the *Odes* and the wooden translations. He then offers a new translation of *Ode* 4 and draws attention to the need to explore the relation of this ode with John 4.

Carmignac, J., 'Les affinités qumrâniennes de la onzième Ode de Salomon', *RevQ* 3 (1961), pp. 71-102.

—'Un qumrânien converti au christianisme: L'auteur des Odes de Salomon', in H. Bardtke (ed.), *Qumran-Probleme* (Deutsche Akademie der Wissenschaften zu Berlin, 42; Berlin: Akademie Verlag, 1963), pp. 75-108.

—'Recherches sur la langue originelle des Odes de Salomon', *RevQ* 4 (1963), pp. 429-32.

    (a) The original language of the *Odes of Solomon* is Hebrew (similar to that at Qumran); (c) the odist was a Christian who had been a Qumran Essene.

Chadwick, H., 'Some Reflections on the Character and Theology of the Odes of Solomon', in P. Granfield and J.A. Jungmann (eds.) *Kyriakon* (Festschrift Johannes Quasten; 2 vols.; Münster: Aschendorff, 1977), I, pp. 266-70.

    (a) '…the weight of opinion now leaning strongly towards a Syriac original' (p. 266); (d) the author of the *Odes* is a Christian (p. 266); (e) 'who can deny that he may have been an Essene Jew who transferred his allegiance to Jesus the Messiah?' (p. 266); (g) the *Odes* are not gnostic.

Charlesworth, J., 'The Odes of Solomon—Not Gnostic', *CBQ* 31 (1969), pp. 357-69.

—'Les Odes de Salomon et les manuscrits de la mer morte', *RB* 77 (1970), pp. 522-49.

—'Paronomasia and Assonance in the Syriac Text of the Odes of Solomon', *Semitics* [Pretoria] 1 (1970), p. 12-26.

—'בעותא in Earliest Christianity', in J.M. Ewrd (ed.), *The Use of the Old Testament in the New and Other Essays: Studies in Honor of William Franklin Stinespring* (Durham, NC: Duke University Press, 1972), pp. 271-79.

—'Qumran, John and the Odes of Solomon', in *idem* (ed.), *John and Qumran* (London: Geoffrey Chapman, 1972; New York: Crossroad, 1991), pp. 107-36.

—'Tatian's Dependence on Apocryphal Traditions', *HeyJ* 15 (1974), pp. 5-17.

—*Odes of Solomon*, *IDBSup* (1976), pp. 637-38.

—*The Odes of Solomon* (Oxford: Clarendon Press, 1973; repr.; Chico, CA: Scholars Press, 1977).

—'Haplography and Philology: A Study of Ode of Solomon 16.8', *NTS* 25 (1978–79), pp. 221-27.

Charlesworth, J. (ed.), *Papyri and Leather Manuscripts of the Odes of Solomon* (Durham, NC: Duke University Center for the Study of Ancient Near Eastern Civilizations and Christian Origins, 1981).

—'Hymns, Odes and Prayers', in *The Old Testament Pseudepigrapha and the New Testament: Prolegomena for the Study of Christian Origins* (Cambridge: Cambridge University Press, 1985), pp. 119-23.

—'The Odes of Solomon', in *idem* (ed.), *The Old Testament Pseudepigrapha* (Garden City, NY: Doubleday, 1985), II, pp. 725-71.

—'Solomon, Odes of', *ABD* 6 (1992), pp. 114-15.

—'Ode of Solomon 5: Praise While Contemplating Persecutors', in M. Kiley *et al.* (eds.), *Prayer from Alexander to Constantine: A Critical Anthology* (London: Routledge, 1997), pp. 273-79.

Charlesworth, J., with R.A. Culpepper, 'The Odes of Solomon and the Gospel of John', *CBQ* 35 (1981), pp. 298-322.

    (a) The *Odes* were composed in Syriac; (b) somewhere in western Syria, northern Palestine or even Jerusalem; (c) they date from c. 100 CE; (d) they are clearly Christian; (e) the conceptual, linguistic and symbolic links between the Dead Sea Scrolls and the *Odes* lead to the supposition that the Odist had been an Essene before he became a Christian; (f) the *Odes* and the Gospel of John come from the same community; (g) they are not gnostic.

Corwin, V., *Ignatius and Christianity in Antioch* (New Haven: Yale University Press, 1950).

(c) Ignatius probably knew the *Odes* (p. 69); (d) the Christology of the *Odes* is 'naively docetic' (p. 102); (e) the Dead Sea Scrolls deepen our knowledge of the background of the Gospel of John, the *Odes*, and Ignatius (p. 13).

Cullmann, O., *Der johanneische Kreis* (Tübingen: J.C.B. Mohr [Paul Siebeck], 1975).

The *Odes* were composed (b) in Syria; (f) the *Odes* and the Gospel of John are connected in that they both represent a 'nichtkonformistischen Judentums' (p. 38).

Daniélou, J., 'Odes de Salomon', *DBSup* (1960), cols. 677-84.

—'Histoire des origines chrétiennes', *RSR* 49 (1961), pp. 576-79.

—*Primitive Christian Symbols* (trans. D. Attwater; Baltimore: Helicon Press, 1964).

—'Liturgical Texts', in *The Theology of Jewish Christianity* (trans. J.A. Baker; London: Darton, Longman & Todd, 1964), pp. 28-33.

(a) Bodmer Papyrus XI of the *Odes* is in 'grec, c'est-à-dire dans la texte original' (2.576)—'the original was certainly in Greek' (4.31); (b) the *Odes* originate in Syria (1.678; 4.31-32); (c) the *Odes* date from the end of the first century CE (2.576); (d) it is unacceptable to label the *Odes* 'purement juive', there is a unity of style that reflects Jewish Christianity (1.678; 2.576-77)—'everything in them speaks of Jewish Christianity' (4.30); (e) Carmignac has shown clear contacts with the Hodayoth—'Certain details recall the Qumran manuscripts...the *Odes* belong to the same literary genre as the *Psalms of Thanksgiving* of Qumran' (4.32)—'...the liturgical and ascetic structure of primitive Christianity was inspired by Essene Judaism' (4.36); (f) the links are close to the Gospel of John (2.577)—'It is difficult to think that the *Odes of Solomon* depend on John, but on the other hand their connection with the Qumran writings is certain' (3.48); (g) they are not gnostic (1.678). '...to conclude the *Odes* are the work of Jewish Christians in the tradition of the Great Church, who came from Eastern Syria, the home of Bar-Daisan, and among whom ascetic tendencies of an Essene type remained especially strong' (4.33).

Diez Macho, A., 'Odas de Salomon', in *Introducción general a los apocrifos del Antiguo Testamento* (Apocrifos del Antiguo Testamento, 1; Madrid: Ediciones Cristiandad, 1984), pp. 208-209.

(a) The original language is 'probablemente en siríaco'; (b) they may have been composed in Antioch; (c) they date from the turn of the first to the second centuries; they are 'judeocristianismo'; (d) the central theme is salvation and a 'unión místico-extática con Dios'; (g) gnostic influence is evident.

Driver, G.R., 'Notes on Two Passages in the Odes of Solomon', *JTS* NS 25 (1974), pp. 434-37.

A helpful improvement to the text and translation of the *Odes* by Charlesworth, assuming a rare *l* meaning 'indeed', 'surely', and an emendation in *Odes* 31.11 to obtain 'Which is continuously pounded by rolling rocks...'.

Drijvers, H.J.W., *Bardaiṣan of Edessa* (Assen: Van Gorcum, 1966).

—'Edessa und das jüdische Christentum', *VC* 24 (1970), pp. 4-33.

—'Die Oden Salomos und die Polemik mit den Markioniten im syrischen Christentum', in R. Lavenaut (ed.), *Symposium Syriacum 1976* (OCA, 205; Rome: Pontificium Institutum Orientalium Studiorum, 1978), pp. 39-55.

—'Kerygma und Logos in den Oden Salomos dargestellt am Beispiel der 23. Ode', in A.M.

Ritter (ed.), *Kerygma und Logos* (Festschrift C. Andresen; Göttingen: Vandenhoeck & Ruprecht, 1979), pp. 153-72.

—'The 19th Ode of Solomon: Its Interpretation and Place in Syrian Christianity', *JTS* NS 31 (1980), pp. 337-55.

—'Odes of Solomon and Psalms of Mani: Christians and Manichaeans in Third-Century Syria', in R. Van den Broek and M.J. Vermaseren (eds.), *Studies in Gnosticism and Hellenistic Religions* (Festschrift Gilles Guispel; Leiden: E.J. Brill, 1981), pp. 117-30.

—'Facts and Problems in Early Syriac-Speaking Christianity', *The Second Century: A Journal of Early Christian Studies* 2 (1982), pp. 157-75.

—'Solomon as Teacher: Early Syriac Didactic Poetry', in *idem et al.* (eds.), *IV Symposium Syriacum 1984: Literary Genres in Syriac Literature* (OCA, 229; Rome: Pontificium Institutum Studiorum Orientalium, 1987), pp. 23-34.

Since Drijvers's opinions change and he has published in separate years, it is possible to cite his position according to years. (a) Drijvers early stated that it is impossible to determine the original language of the *Odes* (1), but then eventually concludes that the *Odes* were composed in Syriac (2; 6); (b) the *Odes* were composed in 'perhaps Antioch or Edessa' (1), Edessa may be the provenience (2; 6); (c) Drijvers's work is characterized by the attempt to date the *Odes of Solomon* as late as conceivable: the *Odes* date from circa 125 CE (1), the *Odes* and the *Gospel of Thomas* are the oldest writings of Syriac theology (2.20), c. 200 CE and later (3), in the first half of the third century (4; 5), around 275 CE (6; 7); (d) the *Odes* 'belong to the 'vulgar' Christianity of the second century in Syria' (1.211), they are close to Judaism and reflect the Jewish apocalyptic cosmology of works such as *2 Baruch* (2)—the *Odes* are a unity which is originally ascribed to Solomon (8.124); (e) 'there are links between the *Odes of Solomon* and the Hôdayôt of the Qumrân community' and so Bardaiṣan cannot be the author (1.210 [see also 2.14]); (g) if the *Odes* are seen in light of 'gnostic' works, that term needs to be carefully defined (2). Though Drijvers is erudite, I find his attempts to see antimarcioniate tendencies in the *Odes*, antimanichean polemic in them, and the influence of the Diatessaron misleading (the reader needs to know that we do not have what Tatian wrote, usually we must reconstruct the 'Diatessaron' [a misnomer] from disparate versions). I can agree with him that third-century Syria is virtually an uncharted territory (6.119), and that the polemic in the *Odes* is 'concealed' (6.129).

Ehlers, B., 'Kann das Thomasevaneglium aus Edessa Stammen?', *NovT* 12 (1970), pp. 284-317.

(b) Ehlers concludes that the *Odes* are eliminated as a source for early Edessan Christianity (p. 301).

Emerton, J.A., 'Some Problems of Text and Language in the Odes of Solomon', *JTS* NS 18 (1967), pp. 372-406.

—'Notes on Some Passages in the Odes of Solomon', *JTS* NS 28 (1977), pp. 507-19.

—'A Problem in the Odes of Solomon XXIII.20', *JTS* NS 32 (1981), pp. 443-47.

—'The Odes of Solomon', in H.F.D. Sparks (ed.), *The Apocryphal Old Testament* (Oxford: Clarendon Press, 1984), pp. 683-731.

(a) The *Odes* were composed in Syriac (1; 3; 4); (b) in Syria (4); (c) and c. 100–120 CE (4); (d) they are obviously Christian but the composition was probably not originally attributed to Solomon [contrast Drijvers] (4); (e) the Odist may have been an Essene, as Charlesworth concludes, 'or at least subjected to very strong Essene influences' (4); (g) they are not gnostic (4).

Erbetta, M., 'Le Odi di Salomone', in M. Erbetta (ed.), *Gli Apocrifi del Nuovo Testamento* (Turin: Marietti, 1975), I.1., pp. 608-58.

(a) It is difficult to be certain, but the *Odes* seem to have been composed in Greek; (c) they seem to date from the second century CE, and (g) are most likely 'gnostico'.

Evans, C.A., 'Odes of Solomon', in M. Erbetta (ed.), *Gli Apocrifi del Nuovo Testamento* (Turin: Marietti, 1975), I.2, pp. 39-40.

(a) the *Odes* were composed in Aramaic or Syriac; (c) in the late first or early second century CE; (d) they are Christian and 'the theme of the *Odes* is one of thanksgiving for the advent of the promised Messiah'; (f) it is 'highly unlikely that the *Odes* themselves or the traditions they presuppose were drawn upon by the Fourth Evangelist'; (g) the *Odes* 'are no longer viewed as gnostic or as Jewish'.

Fanourgakis, V.D., ΑΙ ΩΔΑΙ ΣΟΛΟΜΩΝΤΟΣ (Analecta Vlatadon, 29; Thessalonika: Patriarchal Institute for Patristic Studies, 1979).

(a) The *Odes* were composed in Greek by a bilingual linguist who also rendered them in Syriac (pp. 89-90, 137); (b) perhaps in Edessa maybe by Bardaiṣan or his son, Harmonius, or other Bardaisanites (pp. 119, 138) [this hypothesis is unpersuasive since Bardaiṣan was not bilingual and he seems to have been virtually ignorant of Greek]; (c) the *Odes* date from the end of the second and beginning of the third century CE (p. 110); (d) they are clearly Christian (pp. 129-36); (e) Carmignac exaggerates the links with the Dead Sea Scrolls (p. 120); (f) the *Odes* are similar to the Gospel of John (p. 128); (g) gnostic elements do not categorize the *Odes* as gnostic and (influenced by Charlesworth) Fanourgakis concludes that the *Odes* are not the product of gnostic circles (p. 125).

Ferguson, E., 'Odes of Solomon', in E. Ferguson *et al.* (eds.), *Encyclopedia of Early Christianity* (New York: Garland, 2nd edn, 1997), p. 824.

(a) 'the majority of scholars hold to a Syriac original' (p. 824); (b) the *Odes* were composed in Syria or Palestine; (c) though the *Odes* have been dated from the first to the third centuries, 'most place the work at the earlier end of the time span' (p. 824); (d) they are not Jewish nor gnostic but Christian.

Fiorenza, E. Schüssler, 'Wisdom Mythology and the Christological Hymns of the New Testament', in R.L. Wilken (ed.), *Aspects of Wisdom in Judaism and Early Christianity* (University of Notre Dame Center for the Study of Judaism and Christianity in Antiquity; Notre Dame: University of Notre Dame Press, 1975), pp. 17-41.

Influenced by J.T. Sanders she suggests that the 'formal matrix from which some of the Odes and the New Testament hymns originated is the Jewish wisdom schools. From these schools come not only the thanksgiving psalms but also the New Testament hymns' (p. 25).

Franzmann, M., 'Portrait of a Poet: Reflections on "The Poet" in the Odes of Solomon', in E.W. Conrad and E.G. Newing (eds.), *Perspectives on Language and Text: Essays and Poems in Honor of Francis I. Andersen's Sixtieth Birthday, July 28, 1985* (Winona Lake, IN: Eisenbrauns, 1987), pp. 315-25.

—*The Odes of Solomon: An Analysis of the Poetical Structure and Form* (NTOA, 20; Freiburg: Universitätsverlag; Göttingen: Vandenhoeck & Ruprecht, 1991).

(a) '...the Odes remain a testimony to enthusiastic spiritual experience in the earliest centuries of the Christian church' (1.326); (c) the *Odes* show numerous signs of representing 'a worshipping community' (1.316); she rightly sees the probability that the Odist deliberately attributed his compositions to Solomon (1.325); although prolegomenous, the published dissertation is a major contribution to the poetic structure of the *Odes*.

Gero, S., 'The Spirit as a Dove at the Baptism of Jesus', *NovT* 18 (1976), pp. 17-35.

Ode 24, which depicts the baptism of Jesus which results in 'a cosmic catastrophe', preserves a pre-Marcan tradition that clarifies that a dove descending signifies a revelatory election motif. 'Ode 24, Christian in its present form, may well attest the first Christian linkage of the fairly common dove election motif with the baptismal setting, in a form as yet unallocated with the parallel but independent motif of the descent of the Spirit' (p. 19).

Guirau, J., and A.G. Hamman, *Les Odes de Salomon* (Paris: Desclée de Brouwer, 1981).

Hamman, who was co-translator, contributed the introduction; he claims that the *Odes* were probably composed (a) in Syriac, (b) in Syria, (c) around 100 CE, (d) by a Jewish Christian, (e) who seems to have known the Qumran hymnbook and was inspired by it (but there are apparent polemics against Qumran theology); (f) the *Odes* and the Gospel of John come from the same cultural milieu, and (g) are not gnostic. This position is impressive and I am convinced is generally correct.

Gruenwald, I., 'Knowledge and Vision: Towards a Clarification of Two "Gnostic" Concepts in the Light of their Alleged Origins', *Israel Oriental Studies* 3 (1973), pp. 63-107.

(e) The *Odes* contain passages that 'could have been written' by a Qumranite, and often one 'encounters a striking terminological affinity with the 'gnostic' terminology of the Dead Sea Scrolls'—the *Odes* 'carry on the terminological tradition of the (Qumran) sect, if not even more than that' (p. 106); (d) their 'Jewish origin lies on the surface' (pp. 1-6); they are a unique witness to the 'intermediate stage in the process of transmitting apocalyptic tradition towards gnosticism' (p. 105). These are brilliant and insightful conclusions.

Hengel, M., *Die johanneische Frage: Ein Lösungsversuch* (Tübingen: J.C.B. Mohr [Paul Siebeck], 1993).

The *Odes* were composed 'gegen Ende des 2. Jahrhunderts von der Kenntnis unseres Evangeliums' (p. 29).

Kee, H.C., 'The Odes of Solomon', in *The New Testament in Context: Sources and Documents* (Englewood Cliffs, NJ: Prentice-Hall, 1984), pp. 209-14.

(a) The *Odes* were written in Greek (p. 209); (b) in Syria (p. 209); (c) about the year 100 CE (p. 209); (d) they 'may have been composed by a Jew and subsequently slightly christianized by an interpolator, or perhaps they were written by a Greek-speaking Jewish-Christian' (p. 209); (e) they may have been composed by a former Essene (p. 210); (f) 'whatever the circumstances of their origin, they are akin to the lengthy and prolix discourses of the Gospel of John...' (p. 210).

Klijn, A.F.J., *The Acts of Thomas: Introduction, Text, Commentary* (NovTSup, 5; Leiden: E.J. Brill, 1962).

—'Die Oden Salomos', in *Edessa: Die Stadt des Apostles Thomas, Das älteste Christentum in Syrien* (Giessen: Neukirchener Verlag, 1965), pp. 45-64.

—'Christianity in Edessa and the Gospel of Thomas', *NovT* 14 (1972), pp. 70-77.

(a) The *Odes of Solomon* 'in griechischer Sprache verfasst wurden' (1.46-47; 2.169); (b) the *Odes* may have been composed in Antioch but were soon after known in Edessa (2.46)—the *Odes*, *Gospel of Thomas*, and *Acts of Thomas* may well have originated in Edessa (a critique of Ehlers, 3.77); (c) they were composed 'etwa gegen 125 n. Chr.' (2.46); (d) the *Odes* are to be understood in terms of early Jewish thought (the background of the *Odes*, 2.50-51), the foreground is 'die Sphäre des

Judenchristentums' (2.62), and the *Odes* are the 'ältesten Schrift aus der Kirche Syriens' (2.65); (f) the *Odes* represent 'der Gedankenwelt des Johannes' (= Gospel of John, 2.50); the *Odes* are not gnostic (2.63).

Köbert, R., 'Ode Salomons 20,6 und Sir 33,31', *Bib* 58 (1977), pp. 529-30.

On the basis of the 'sorgfältig und gut dokumentierte' edition of Charlesworth, it is possible to conclude that *Ode* 20.6 is linked with the Hebrew text of Sir. 33.31. This insight, I am convinced, tends to strengthen the Semitic and Syriac original for the *Odes*, since a Greek scholar would most likely have used the Greek version of Sirach.

Koester, H., *Introduction to the New Testament* (2 vols.; Philadelphia: Fortress Press; Berlin: W. de Gruyter, 1982).

(a) The original language is Greek (II, p. 216); (b) the *Odes* come from Syria; (c) the *Odes* may well have been composed at the same time as the Logos hymn that is now at the beginning of the Gospel of John, but a date in the early second century is 'likely' (II, p. 217); (g) it is not clear that the *Odes* are gnostic (II, p. 218).

Lattke, M., *Die Oden Salomos in ihrer Bedeutung für Neues Testament und Gnosis* (4 vols. [1, 1a, 2, 3]; Göttingen: Vandenhoeck & Ruprecht, 1979–86).

—'Zur Bildersprache der Oden Salomos', *Symbolon* NS 6 (1982), pp. 95-110.

—'The Apocryphal Odes of Solomon and New Testament Writings', *ZNW* 73 (1982), pp. 294-301.

—'Dating the Odes of Solomon', *Antichthon* 27 (1993), pp. 45-59.

—*Oden Salomos* (Fontes Christiani, 19; Freiburg: Herder, 1995).

Lattke is making the study of the *Odes* his life work. Sometimes his opinions of other scholars is insensitive and idiosyncratic, but he should be praised for the contributions he is making. He is preparing the first full commentary on the *Odes*. He has tended to reserve judgment on the key issues, but some of his ideas can be discerned. (a) The original language of the *Odes* is either Greek or Syriac (5.16-18); (c) the *Odes* date from the turn of the first to the second century CE (4; 5.33-34); (d) the grounds have disappeared for supporting Harnack's interpolation hypothesis, they are all by one author (*Symbolon*, 1982); (f) earlier he claimed (I think rightly) that the odist and the Gospel of John shared the same environment ('a heterodox Jewish, syncretistic early Gnosticism', 3.298), but now he seems to think that the odist probably had read the Gospel of John (1.80-81); (g) if the *Odes* are gnostic they represent an early form of Gnosticism (3.297-98; 5). There can be no doubt that Lattke is correct to claim that the *Odes* are important for the study of not only the New Testament but also the gnostic literature.

Licht, J., 'Solomon, Odes of', *EncJud* 15 (1971), pp. 114-15.

(c) The *Odes* date from 'the first century CE' (p. 114); (d) the 'early Christian poems' are similar to the *Hodayot* (*Thanksgiving Hymns*, pp. 114-15); 'the possibility that the *Odes* represent some group of Christians which was influenced by the Dead Sea sect (or some similar Jewish sect) cannot be denied' (p. 115); (g) 'there are some affinities to gnosticism' (p. 115).

Lindars, B., *The Gospel of John* (Grand Rapids: Eerdmans, 1972; London: Marshall, Morgan & Scott, 1981).

(g) The *Odes* are 'certainly Gnostic and contain many Johannine expressions (but this is probably due to Johannine influence)' (p. 41). In light of Charlesworth's work, Lindars notes that 'the relationship of the *Odes* to John would be not a matter of dependence on either side but of sharing a common background of speculative Jewish thought' (p. 41).

McCullough, W.S., 'The Odes of Solomon', in *A Short History of Syriac Christianity to the Rise of Islam* (Scholars Press General Series, 4; Chico, CA: Scholars Press, 1982), pp. 33-35.

(a) The *Odes* were composed in Syriac; (b) north-east Syria; (c) the latter half of the second century; (d) early Christian; (e) no comment regarding the relation to the Dead Sea Scrolls; (f) the *Odes* show 'a special interest in Johannine terminology' (p. 33).

McNeal, B., 'The Provenance of the Odes of Solomon: A Study in Jewish and Christian Symbolism' (PhD dissertation, University of Cambridge, 1977).

—'The Odes of Solomon and the Sufferings of Christ', in R. Lavenaut (ed.), *Symposium Syriacum 1976* (OCA, 205; Rome: Pontificium Institutum Orientalium Studiorum, 1978), pp. 31-38.

—'Le Christ en vérité est Un', *Irénikon* 2 (1978), pp. 198-202.

—'A Liturgical Source in Acts of Peter 38', *VC* 33 (1979), pp. 342-46.

—'Suffering and Martyrdom in the Odes of Solomon', in W. Horbury and B. McNeil (eds.), *Suffering and Martyrdom in the New Testament* (Cambridge: Cambridge University Press, 1981, 1993), pp. 136-42.

—'The Odes of Solomon and the Scriptures', *OrChr* 67 (1983), pp. 104-22.

(b) Provenience is unknown (6); (c) the *Odes* are contemporaneous with Hermas, Polycarp, Valentinus, the *Acts of John* and the author of *4 Ezra* (1; 2; 5) and date from the first half of the second century CE (3; 6); (f) though 'we find no passages which could establish that one author is dependent on the other', we conclude that, since the *Odes* post-date the Gospel of John, the *Odes*, in a qualified sense, 'are dependent on John' (1983).

Miranda, J.P., 'Die Oden Salomos', in *Der Vater, der mich gesandt hat* (Europäische Hochschulschriften, 23; Frankfurt: Peter Lang, 1972), pp. 195-202.

(f) The *Odes* and the Gospel of John both contain similar 'Sendungsaussage' (p. 195); (g) in the *Odes*, 'Die Erlösung wird rein gnostisch verstanden...' (p. 200).

Morrison, A.T., 'A Literary and Theological Comparison between the Odes of Solomon and the Johannine Literature' (PhD dissertation; University of Durham, 1980, N.V.).

Murray, R., 'On Early Christianity and Judaism: Some Recent Studies', *HeyJ* 13 (1972), pp. 441-51.

—*Symbols of Church and Kingdom: A Study in Early Syriac Tradition* (Cambridge: Cambridge University Press, 1975).

(a) Syriac is the original language (2.25); (b) Antioch is probably more likely than Edessa as the provenience (2.25); (c) the *Odes* are 'probably the earliest extant work in Syriac' (2.24); (d) they are Judaeo-Christian (2.25, 295); (e) show affinities with the Dead Sea Scrolls (2.255); (f) are 'not far in date and milieu from the Fourth Gospel and Ignatius' (2.25); and (g) are not to be branded as gnostic. While the fact that Aphrahat (*Dem.* 524.3-7) may know the *Odes* through oral tradition is more probable (2.326-27), it is clear that Ephrem (*Hymns on Paradise*) 'seems to know' *Ode* 11 and obtains his reference to 'Nothing in it is idle' from the description of paradise in that ode (2.255). 'I am not yet sure why I resist arguments about major Qumran influence on the Fourth Gospel but am ready to consider speculative hypotheses about the Odes of Solomon, but it is so. Consequently I find Charlesworth's own contributions here among the most impressive; students of the earliest Jewish Christianity are already in his debt...' (1.447).

Nibley, H.W., 'From the Odes of Solomon', in *The Message of the Joseph Smith Papyri* (Salt Lake City: Deseret, 1975), pp. 263-66.

Nibley, saluted as a genius by many non-Mormon scholars, claims that the *Odes* show 'undoubted affinities with the Dead Sea Scrolls' (p. 263). He is persuaded by Licht's comment that a relation between the *Odes* and the Dead Sea Scrolls cannot be denied, and he contends that a 'key to dating the Odes is the 4th Ode' which is to be dated either shortly after 70 CE or less likely shortly after 135 CE (p. 263). The theme of the *Odes* is 'the rites of the temple' (p. 263).

Philonenko, M., 'Conjecture sur un verset de la onzième Ode de Salomon', *ZNW* 53 (1962), p. 264.

(a) The *Odes* were composed in Greek.

Peral, A., and X. Alegre, 'Odas de Salomon', in A. Diez Macho *et al.* (ed.), *Apocrifos del Antiguo Testamento* (Madrid: Ediciones Cristiandad, 1982), III, pp. 61-100.

(a) The most likely solution is that Syriac is the original language of the *Odes* (p. 62); (b) influenced by Charlesworth they conclude that the *Odes* were composed in Syria or in the north of Palestine (p. 62); (c) the *Odes* date from the end of the first to the middle of the second century CE (p. 62); (d) they are a unity and Jewish-Christian community hymns (pp. 62-63)—and salvation is the central theme in the *Odes* (p. 64); (f) the links between the *Odes* and the Gospel of John are not only words (such as light, truth, life, knowledge, love, living water, spirit, Word, fruits) but also numerous motifs (such as pre-existence, the above as superior to the below) which suggest the two documents share a common spiritual milieu and perhaps community (here they are persuaded by Charlesworth and Culpepper, *Exploring the Gospel of John*, pp. 63-64); (g) the Odist evidences some ideas that eventually culminate in Gnosticism, thus they are 'de gnosis incipiente' (pp. 66, 64).

Pierce, M., 'Themes in the "Odes of Solomon" and Other Early Christian Writings and their Baptismal Character', *Ephemerides Liturgicae* 98 (1984), pp. 35-59.

The *Odes* were probably composed (b) in Syria, (c) in the late second or third century.

Pierre, M.-J., *Les Odes de Salomon* (Apocryphes: Collection de Poche de l'Aelac, 4; Belgium: Brepols, 1994).

(b) The Odist represents the 'milieu judéo-chrétien jérusalémite, proche du Temple... peut-être même lié à la famille de Jésus' (p. 54); (c) the *Odes* were composed in the 'premières années' of the second century CE (p. 50); (d) the *Odes* are Christian (p. 33) the links with the Dead Sea Scrolls are not clear because both the Qumranites and the Odist depended on biblical symbolism and language (p. 40); (f) the *Odes* are very close to the Gospel of John (pp. 13, 40); (g) the *Odes* are not gnostic but a 'texte pré-gnostique' (p. 50).

Pokorný, P., 'Das sogenannte Evangelium Veritatis und die Anfänge des christlichen Dogmas', *Listy Filologické* 87 (1964), pp. 51-59.

—*Tomášovo evangelium* (Prague: Edice Kalich, 1981).

—*Píseň o perle: Tajné knihy starověkých gnostiků* (Prague: Vyšehrad, 1986).

(b) The *Odes* come from Syria, perhaps Antioch or Edessa (2.23); (f) the *Odes* are close to the Gospel of John and the *Gospel of Thomas* (2.23); (g) the *Gospel of Truth* and the *Odes* come from 'demselben gnostischen Kreise' (1.54) and the *Odes* belong among the 'gnostickou literaturu' (3.38). It is essential to note that Porkoný defines Gnosis very broadly (and uses the adjective 'gnostic' in a similar fashion): 'Die Gnosis ist eine der bedeutendsten geistigen Bewegungen der Antike' ('Der Ursprung der

Gnosis', *Kairos* 9 [1967]), pp. 94-105; the quotation is on p. 94. See the warnings about defining such terms as 'gnostic' and Gnosticism by M. Smith, 'The History of the Term Gnostikos', in B. Layton (ed.), *The Rediscovery of Gnosticism* (Leiden: E.J. Brill, 1981), II, pp. 796-807.

Potterie, I. de la, *La vérité dans Saint Jean* (AnBib, 73; 2 vols.; Rome: Biblical Institute Press, 1977).

(d) In 'leur vocabulaire' the *Odes* 's'apparente surtout à la tradition sapientielle et apocalyptique du judaïsme' (p. 73); (f) the *Odes* are essential for understanding the Gospel of John (pp. 48, 74); in them 'living water' signifies revelation or truth (p. 689) and this helps us understand the same technical term in the Gospel of John and in Ignatius (*Rom.* 7.2); (g) the *Odes* have 'une coloration plus ou moins gnosticisante' (p. 73).

Quasten, J., 'The Odes of Solomon', in *Patrology* (Utrecht: Spectrum; Westminster, MD: Newman, 1962), I, pp. 160-68.

(a) The original language is Greek (p. 161); (b) they 'express the beliefs and hopes of Eastern Christianity' (p. 161); (c) composed in the first half of the second century CE (p. 161); (d) unity of style, the work of one person; (f) the 'exalted mysticism' of the *Odes* 'seems to be influenced by the Gospel of St. John' (p. 162); (g) the *Odes* 'cannot with complete assurance be dubbed a "Hymn Book of Gnostic Churches"' (pp. 160-61).

Quispel, G., 'Qumran, John, and Jewish Christianity', in Charlesworth (ed.), *John and Qumran*, pp. 137-55.

—'The Study of Encratism: A Historical Survey', in *La tradizione dell' enkrateia: Motivazioni ontologiche e protologiche* (Milan: Edizioni dell' Ateneo, 1983), pp. 35-81.

Quispel, one of the most creative and productive scholars in the field of Gnosticism, seldom cites the *Odes*. (a) The *Odes* were composed in Greek or Syriac (1.153); (b) provenience is unknown (1.153); (c) the date of the *Odes* is 'unknown' but they probably were 'written in the second century' because they 'are familiar with the *Gospel of the Egyptians* and the *Gospel of Thomas*' (2.55); (f, g) 'Certainly they are not gnostic, and they reflect a religiosity very much akin to that of the author of the Fourth Gospel' (1.153).

Rudolph, K., *Die Mandäer* (FRLANT NS, 56-57; 2 vols.; Göttingen: Vandenhoeck & Ruprecht, 1960, 1961).

—'War der Verfasser der Oden Salomos ein "Qumran-Christ"? Ein Beitrag zur Diskussion um die Anfänge der Gnosis', *RevQ* 16 (1964), pp. 523-55.

—'Gnosis und Gnostizismus, ein Forschungsbericht', *TRev* NS 34 (1969), pp. 221-25 [with regard to the *Odes*].

—*Gnosis: The Nature and History of Gnosticism* (trans. R. McL. Wilson; Edinburgh: T. & T. Clark, 1984; San Francisco: Harper & Row, 1987).

This sophisticated and brilliant gnostic expert thinks that (a) the original language of the *Odes* is either Greek or Aramaic (4.29) but most likely Syriac (3); (b) they are 'the song-book or prayer book of a Syrian gnostic-christian community' (4.221); (c) they were composed in the second century CE (4.306); (d) 'These hymns are of value particularly because of their figurative language, which links them with other gnostic documents of the East' (4.29)—they have been wrongly attributed to Bardaiṣan (4.328)—but they may have been composed by Satornil (1.226); (e) the *Odes* are dissimilar to the *Hodayot*; (f) the *Odes* are 'closely related to' the Gospel of John, but they post-date it (4.306, 346); (g) the *Odes*, like the *Hymn of the Pearl*, is an Iranian type of gnostic work 'formally very close to the Iranian-Zoroastrian dualism' (4.65, cf. 372)—'Der gnostische Charakter der *Oden Salomos* ist eine feststehende Tatsache...' (2.525; cf. 3.222).

I must add that the gnostic character of the *Odes* was accepted as a consensus only in the second period of research and by German experts.

Sanders, J.T., 'The Odes of Solomon', in *idem*, *The New Testament Christological Hymns: Their Historical Religious Background* (SNTSMS, 15; Cambridge: Cambridge University Press, 1971), pp. 101-10.

—'Nag Hammadi, Odes of Solomon, and NT Christological Hymns', in J.E. Goehring *et al.* (eds.), *Gnosticism and the Early Christian World* (Festschrift James M. Robinson; Sonoma, CA: Polebridge Press, 1990), pp. 51-66.

Sanders has focused much of his research on the *Odes*; he thinks that (a) the *Odes* date from 'the early part of the second century CE and therefore contemporary with or just a little later than the Fourth Gospel itself...' (2.61); (d) the *Odes* may reflect a pre-Christian complex that has been Christianized (2.56); (f) '...we...agree with Charlesworth that the *Odes of Solomon*, while Christian in their present form and containing many and striking parallels with the Johannine prologue, give evidence of parallel development and are not dependent on the Gospel of John' (2.56); (g) 'the provenance of all three documents'—the *Odes*, the Logos Hymn in the Gospel of John, and the *Trimorphic Protennoia*—'has to be explained together' (2.59).

Schenke, H.-M., *Der Herkunft des sogennanten Evangelium Veritatis* (Göttingen: Vandenhoeck & Ruprecht, 1959).

(g) Schenke rightly points out that the *Odes* and the *Gospel of Truth* derive from the same gnostic circles and that they share some unique symbolisms, like the Holy Spirit as the Father's breasts (*Gos. Truth* 1, 3.24, 9-11 and *Ode* 19 and the symbolic representation of truth as the Father's mouth (*Gos. Truth* 1, 3.26, 34-35) (pp. 26-29).

Schnackenburg, R., 'Christian-Gnostic Literature', in *idem*, *The Gospel According to St John* (trans. K. Smyth; New York: Crossroad, 1987), I, pp. 143-49.

(b) The *Odes* derive from Syria; (e) the *Odes*, esp. *Ode* 11, shows 'particularly strong affinities with the' Qumran *Hodayoth* (p. 143); (f) the 'closeness of the *Odes of Solomon* to John is shown' by the vocabulary and 'the elevated language for a joyous and intimate fellowship with God' (p. 144)—there is no proof that the odist knew the Gospel of John but somehow he seems dependent on it (p. 145); (g) the *Odes* are gnostic and 'the Valentinian connection has now become clear from the striking parallels in the *Gospel of Truth* (pp. 144-45).

Schulz, S., 'Salomo-Oden', *RGG* (3rd edn, 1961), cols. 1339-42.

(a) The original language probably is Greek (col. 1339); (c) they were composed in the first half of the second century CE (col. 1339); (d) the literary *Gattungen* are 'Lehrdichtung', 'Gemeindelieder', 'Individualoden' (cols. 1339-40); (e) there are impressive links with Qumran, esp. in the use of 'I', both a *filius proprius* and a *filius adoptivus* (col. 1341); (f) there is a special relation with the Gospel of John (col. 1340); they are gnostic (cols. 1340-41). [The strength of this publication is the attention to theology and *Gattungen*; the assessment of the gnostic hypothesis is definitely influenced by Gressmann and Bultmann (whom he cites) and thus reflects the second period (in which it was probably written).]

Segelberg, E., '*Evangelium Veritatis*: A Confirmation Homily and its Relation to the Odes of Solomon', *Orientalia Suecana* 8 (1959), pp. 3-42.

He concludes that the differences between the *Odes* and the *Gospel of Truth* are greater than the similarities (p. 42).

Smith, D.M., *Johannine Christianity: Essays on its Setting, Sources, and Theology* (Columbia, SC: University of South Carolina Press, 1984).

—*The Theology of the Gospel of John* (Cambridge: Cambridge University Press, 1995).

(e) 'The many affinities with the Odes of Solomon, which partly overlap those of Qumran, are not easily explained as the result of the odist's use of the Johannine literature' (1.27); the *Odes*' 'Christian character is often quite evident, and they sometimes reflect the language or conceptuality of the Gospel of John, at just those points at which there is also an affinity with the sectarian documents of Qumran' (2.70); (g) the *Odes* 'differ sharply from gnosticism' (2.71).

Terzoli, R., 'Le Odi di Salomone', in *Il Tema della Beatitudine nei Padri Siri* (Publicazioni del Pontificio Seminario Lombardo in Roma, 11; Rome: Morcelliana, 1972), pp. 17-28.

The *Odes* seem (a) to have been composed in Syriac (p. 17).

Testuz, M., *Papyrus Bodmer X–XII* (Cologne: Bibliothèque Bodmer, 1959).

(a) The Odist composed his poems in Greek; (c) the Odist was an Essene who lived sometime 'au courant du premier sièclce de notre ère.' (p. 58); (d) Testuz argued that *Ode* 11 'est l'oeuvre d'un Essénien' (p. 58).

Tosato, A., 'Il battesimo di Gesù e le Odi di Salomone', *Bibbia e Oriente* 18 (1976), pp. 261-69.

—'Gesù e gli zeloti alla luce delle *Odi di Salomone*', *Bibbia e Oriente* 19 (1977), pp. 145-54.

(c) '...l'opera di un giudeo-cristiano della fine del primo secolo' (1.262); d) 'Le *Odi di Salomone* sembrano dunque attribuire al mancato zelotismo di Gesù, e per converso allo zelotizmo dei Giudei, la causa del suo tragico ripudio' (2.153).

Tsakonas, V.G., ΑΙ ΩΔΑΙ ΣΟΛΟΜΩΝΤΟΣ (Athens, 1974).

This study is very careful, insightful and important. (a) The original language is Greek (pp. 9-11); (c) the *Odes* were probably composed in the late first century (pp. 6, 12-13); (d) the *Odes* are clearly Christian and the central theme, εἶναι ἡ ἀλήθεια (p. 27); (e) the *Odes* are close to the Gospel of John and were written about the same time and may have been influenced indirectly by it (pp. 13, 20-23); (g) they are not simply heretical and gnostic (pp. 8, 18-19).

Turner, J.D., 'Sethian Gnosticism: A Literary History', in C.W. Hedrick and R. Hodgson, Jr (eds.), *Nag Hammadi, Gnosticism, and Early Christianity* (Peabody, MA: Hendrickson, 1986), pp. 55-86.

Turner sees the *Odes* in light of spiritualizing protests 'against a failing or extinct sacrificial temple cultus'; they are close to the *Trimorphic Protennoia* and contain baptismal motifs (pp. 68-69).

Untergaßmair, F.G., *Im Namen Jesu: Der Namensbegriff im Johannesevangelium* (FzBr, 13. Stuttgart: Katholisches Bibelwerk, 1974).

The *Odes*, most likely, were composed (a) in Syriac; (b) in Syria; (c) in the 'erste Hälfte des W. Jhdt.' (p. 307); (f) the *Odes* shine significant light on the meaning of the concept 'name' in the Gospel of John (pp. 314-64); (g) there are ways in which the *Odes* may be considered gnostic (p. 311).

Vielhauer, P. 'Die Oden Salomos', in *Geschichte der urchristlichen Literatur* (Berlin: W. de Gruyter, 1975), pp. 750-56.

(a) The original language must be kept open, as either Syriac or Greek (p. 751);

(c) they were composed around the middle of the second century CE (p. 751);
(d) they are clearly Christian (p. 754) and 'das Grundthema ist die dem Einzelnen
bereits geschenkte Erlösung' (p. 752); (e) the 'enthusiastischen Erlösungsfrömmig-
keit' of the *Odes* distances them from the *Hodayot* (p. 753); (f) they are close to the
Gospel of John (p. 754); (g) they should be labeled as gnostic since they come to us
from 'christlich-gnostischen Kreises' (p. 750). [These conclusions represent the
rough consensus of the second period of research on the *Odes*, and the fact that this
volume derives from an earlier one (p. vii) clarifies why research on the *Odes* is
dated.]

Vööbus, A., 'The Odes of Solomon', in *History of Asceticism in the Syrian Orient* (CSCO,
14; Louvain: Secrétariat du Corpus SCO, 1958), pp. 62-64.

—'Neues Licht zur Frage der Originalsprache der Oden Salomos', *Mus* 75 (1962), pp. 275-
90.

(a) The *Odes of Solomon* were composed in Syriac; (b) they are one of the earliest
Syriac compositions.

Winterhalter, R., *The Odes of Solomon: Original Christianity Revealed* (St Paul, MN:
Llewellyn Publications, 1985).

(a) 'Most of the odes are the product of an inspired soul of the First Century A.D.'
(p. xiii); (d) they are Christian and reflect 'the original teaching and spirit of Jesus of
Nazareth more closely than any other work, with the possible exception of the Gospel
of John' (p. xiii).

Yamauchi, E.M., 'The Odes of Solomon', in *Pre-Christian Gnosticism: A Survey of the
Proposed Evidences* (Grand Rapids: Eerdmans, 1973), pp. 91-94.

(a) The original language may be Greek but Syriac seems more likely (p. 92); (c) if
Corwin is correct the *Odes* antedate 117 CE (p. 92); (g) the *Odes* do not seem to be
gnostic (p. 94). [His comments are essentially a report of others' research, as the
subtitle confirms.]

Status Quaestionis

Knowing that we scholars are trained to disagree, and that once we struggle with the assessment of a consensus on a work such as the *Odes* (that is, the conclusions obtained independently by a majority of leading scholars) and judiciously publish what is the consensus
two reactions immediately follow: there is the tendency to disagree with the obvious
consensus, and to change the consensus not because of the search for truth or assessment
of primary data but because of the need to disagree. That can be misleading and hinder
progress; hence I shall eschew articulating (at least at the outset) what may be a consensus
regarding the *Odes*; thus I begin by merely reporting my own opinion on trends in
research.

Separating research on the *Odes* into three periods helps to avoid the confusion that
there has been no development in this area of research. Those experts who claim that there
is no consensus among leading experts on the *Odes* confuse the first and second periods
with the present one. This error misleads other scholars and would not be tolerated in
other fields; for example, scholars do not mar the study of the Gospel of John by mixing
opinions from 1910 with those from the 1990s.

G.S. Sloyan states that the 'Fourth Gospel continues to baffle, to enrich, to infuriate, and to console as it has done for centuries'.[1] This may be true and the same may be reported about the *Odes*—but that does not mean there is no consensus in Johannine studies. The following assessment of *Odes* research indicates a definite and promising trend in discerning the original language, the provenience, the date of composition, the character, the relation to the Dead Sea Scrolls, the explanation of the striking parallels with the Gospel of John, and the proper assessment of the *Odes* relation with gnostic documents.

(a) *Original language*. In contrast to the second period of research on the *Odes*, there is a decided shift to affirm Aramaic-Syriac as the original language of the *Odes* (or at least to affirm that they were composed in a Semitic language). Earlier, leading scholars such as Bruston, Bernard, Abbott, Mingana, de Zwaan, and Harris with Mingana concluded that 'Syriac' is the original language. Now, numerous Syriac experts affirm that Aramaic-Syriac is probably the original language; among such scholars are Adam, Charlesworth, Emerton, Peral and Alegre, and Vööbus—and it is these scholars trained in Semitics who have prosecuted detailed research into the original language of the *Odes*. It must be stressed—a point missing in published research—that the extant Syriac manuscripts of the tenth and fifteenth centuries are but mirror reflections of the original, which would be a mixture of Aramaic and Syriac (such as found in the Old Syriac Inscriptions).

(b) *Provenience*. While most experts conclude that the *Odes* come from Syria, it is not clear exactly where. Edessa, Antioch, northern Palestine, and Jerusalem are each possible.

(c) *Date*. The date of the *Odes* has been the central area for disagreement. I sense that there is a burgeoning agreement that the *Odes* must antedate 135, the year in which Bar Kokhba's rebellion was defeated. Too much attention has been spent searching for a *terminus ad quem* and more work needs to be focused on the likely *terminus a quo*. Recognizing that the *Odes* may date from the latter half of the first century CE raises the question of just how earlier some of them may be. Obviously, all the hymns in a hymnbook were not written in the same year or decade. It would be good to see a discussion of the earliest date for some of the poems in the *Odes*. Is there any evidence that *Ode* 4 may antedate the 80s as Harnack, Harris, and so many specialists claimed at the beginning of this century?

(d) *Character*. While most scholars perceive that the *Odes* are Christian or Jewish-Christian, it is also obvious that they are far more Jewish than Christian; that is to say, the Jewishness of these Odes is exceedingly high and fundamental. We must note that some of them have no Christian elements at all, and may well have been written by a Jewish poet before he became a Christian. Recall that Harnack, Spitta, Diettrich, and Bacon saw the first layer of the *Odes* as Jewish, and that some scholars from Menzies and Grimme to Testuz and Gruendwald judge the *Odes* to be fundamentally or essentially Jewish.

(e) *Possible relation to the Dead Sea Scrolls*. It is surprising to report that, although the *Odes* are poetry and thus difficult to assess, most scholars trained in Dead Sea Scrolls research conclude that there is some significant link between the Dead Sea Scrolls and the *Odes* (Carmignac, Charlesworth, Emerton, Gruendwald).

(f) *Probable link with the Gospel of John*. There is wide agreement that there is some significant and fundamental relationship between the *Odes* and the Gospel of John. Many experts who have devoted years of study to each of these documents conclude that they may well share the same milieu. Much research needs to be prosecuted on this relationship, and the commentaries on the Gospel of John far too often relegate the *Odes* to an introduction or a note.

1.   G.S. Sloyan, *John* (*Int*; Atlanta: John Knox Press, 1988), p. 1.

(g) *Relation to Gnosis or Gnosticism.* The most surprising development is the perception that the *Odes* must not be simply branded as 'gnostic' and ignored. Many experts on the *Odes* and Gnosticism see correctly that the *Odes*, like the Gospel of John, the *Hymn of the Pearl*, the *Gospel of Thomas*, and the *Gospel of Truth* reflect in numerous ways early forms of Gnosis and are a tributary on the way to the full-blown Gnosticism of the second century CE. Thus the claims of Gunkel, Gressmann, Stölten, Kroll, and Abramowski need to be relegated to past opinions, or—better—recognized as conclusions that are modified by a broad definition of 'gnostic' or the clarification that the *Odes* are an early form of Gnosticism.[2]

It seems rather popular to celebrate or lament the lack of any consensus in the study of the *Odes*. For example, Cameron claims that 'there is such a difference of opinion on every aspect of the *Odes of Solomon* as a whole: date, place, authorship, original language are all legitimately disputed'.[3] On the one hand, readers might throw both hands into the air and give up; on the other hand, on further reflection there would be reason to say 'thank God!' It is good that all questions are debated and even 'disputed'. Is it not the same with the Gospel of John? But, with that document there is a clear consensus; and it is acknowledged (though, obviously debated). If the impression given is that *Odes* research is in chaos, then the false information has been obtained.[4]

I wish to turn the tide with this annotated bibliography and, deliberately going beyond the previous disclaimer, contend there is a remarkable consensus on the higher critical questions regarding the *Odes*. Take for example the entries on the *Odes* in the *Old Testament Pseudepigrapha* and the *Apocryphal Old Testament*: both Charlesworth and Emerton conclude that the *Odes* were (a) composed in Syriac; (b) in Syria or nearby; (c) sometime not far from 100 CE; (d) that they are clearly Christian; (e) somehow significantly influenced by the Dead Sea Scrolls (conceivably that the Odist had been an Essene); and (g) clearly not gnostic. I take such agreement to be remarkable, and it dominates intermittently in other publications dating from 1959 to the present. Hopefully, this review will serve as a

---

2.   G. MacRae warned that the *Odes* are not 'certainly Gnostic...' G. MacRae, 'Sleep and Awakening in Gnostic Texts', in U. Bianchi (ed.), *Le Origini dello Gnosticismo: Colloquio di Messina 13–18 Aprile 1966* (Studies in the History of Religions [Supplements to *Numen* 12]; Leiden: E.J. Brill, 1970), pp. 496-507 (504).

3.   P. Cameron, 'The "Sanctuary" in the Fourth Ode of Solomon', in W. Horbury (ed.), *Essays on the Second Temple Presented to Ernst Bammel* (JSNTSup, 48; Sheffield: JSOT Press, 1991), pp. 450-63 (450).

4.   It is distressing to note how often the *Odes* are never cited in major books on early Christian hymns, in collections of texts important for understanding Christian origins, in surveys on apocryphal works, and in monographs that concern the major ideas contained in the *Odes*. Geo Widengren, for example, states, 'Il existe enfin une autre collection de poèmes, les *Odes de Salomon*, qui mériterait une analyse, mais [*sic*] les éléments juifs, chrétiens, chrétiens et gnostiques, y sont tellement mêlés que cette recherche nous entraînerait trop loin' (p. 20). Thus, the *Odes* are not included in the important discussions found in *Apocalyptique Iranienne et Dualisme Qoumrânien* (Paris: Adrien Maisonneuve, 1995). The elements Widengren cites signify the uniqeness of the *Odes*, their extreme importance, and probably their early date. All these elements are why the *Odes* should be discussed and taken seriously in studying Qumran and its influences, the background and fore-ground of the Gospel of John, the origins of Christianity, and the development of Western culture. Because the provenience of the *Odes* is unclear, W. Cramer will not include them in *Der Geist Gottes und des Menschen in frühsyrischer Theologie* (Münsterische Beiträge zur Theologie, 46; Münster: Aschendorff, 1979), p. 25.

stimulus for young scholars to take the *Odes* seriously in the attempt to understand the New Testament and the origins of Christianity. They are indeed 'the Oldest Christian Hymnbook'.

JHC
Princeton
August 1997

INDEXES

INDEX OF REFERENCES

OLD TESTAMENT

12.5	207, 216	16.6-19	168
12.6	149	16.7	214
12.7	210	16.8-20	186
12.10	207, 214-16	16.8-14	215
12.11	240	16.8-12	207, 214
12.12	215, 216, 218, 239, 240	16.8	167-74
		16.9-20	187
		16.9	167, 168
		16.10	247
12.32	259	16.12	23
14	114, 126, 240	16.13	149
		16.14	167, 215
14.2	258, 259	16.18-19	186
14.3	259	16.18	214, 240, 258
14.5	208, 211		
14.6	240, 258, 259	16.19	167, 207
		16.20	186
14.7	228, 259	16.21	259
14.8	208	17	126, 134, 146
14.12	259		
14.13	259	17.1	259
14.16	258	17.2-5	212
14.19	258, 259	17.2	211
14.21	258	17.4-9	134
14.23	259	17.4	211
14.26	258	17.5	259
14.27	259	17.6-10	259
15.1-6	259	17.6-9	259
15.1-2	211	17.6	184, 259
15.1	241, 258	17.7–42.20	21
15.2	210, 218, 223	17.8	182, 184, 259
15.4-7	259	17.9	259
15.5	210, 258, 259	17.11	145, 241, 258, 259
15.6	209, 211, 224	17.12	90, 144, 145, 182
15.8-10	218	17.13	133, 144, 145
15.9	184, 215, 259	17.14	90
15.10	210, 223	17.15	154, 211, 259
15.16	258	17.16-17	154
15.20	258, 259	17.17	259
15.26	258	17.24	259
16	50, 169, 170	18	114, 126
16.2	228, 258	18.6	15, 183, 210, 222, 241, 242, 258
16.5	163, 208		

18.7	211
18.8	183
18.11	183
18.12	154, 211
18.13	182, 211
18.14	15, 209, 211
18.15	150, 183
19	24, 262
19.2	25
19.3	134
19.4	126
19.8	184
19.9	130, 152
19.10	157
20.1-4	228
20.1-2	129, 150, 159
20.3-6	212, 224
20.6	103
20.9	127
21	114
21.1	183
21.2	183, 208, 211
21.3	155, 210, 259
21.6	207
21.10	186
21.24	259
21.38	183
22	21, 126, 183
22.1-2	207
22.1	183, 184
22.2	119
22.5	184
22.6	128
22.9	23, 128
22.12	24, 221
22.18	24
23	154
23.2	212
23.3	212
23.4	128, 169, 182, 183,

1QM		3.19	15, 195,	10.9-17	50
1.1	197		222	10.20	202
1.4-7	201	3.20	195	10.21	199
1.8-14	197	3.21	195	11.9	74
7.6	209	3.22	195	11.11	214
10.8–12.16	51, 65	3.24	195		
12.2	221	3.25	195	*1QSb*	
12.8	209	3.26	195	4.25	221
13.2-4	198	4.1	195		
13.7–14.1	51, 65	4.2-11	224	*1QpHab*	
13.9-11	197, 202	4.2	195	7	25
13.10	198	4.5	195, 196		
13.12	198, 222	4.6	195	*11QPs*	
16.11	209	4.7-8	201, 223	26.4	223
18.1	209	4.7	196, 219	26.9	130
		4.9	195, 196		
1QS		4.10	196	*CD*	
1.1-20	25	4.11	195	2.2-13	197, 202
1.9-11	196	4.12	196, 222	2.5	202
1.9	218, 224	4.13	196	2.6	198, 222
1.10	195	4.14	196, 201,	2.7-8	202
1.16–2.25	32, 199		223	2.11-13	202
1.18	199	4.17	195, 223	4.13	198
1.24	199	4.19	195	4.15	198
2.5	199	4.20	195, 196	5.17-19	197
2.19	199	4.21	195	5.18	198, 199
3.7	195	4.22	195	13.14-15	197
3.13–4.26	24, 194,	4.23	195, 196,		
	196, 202		222	*Thanksgiving Hymns*	
3.13–4.14	196, 201	4.24	195	3.19	62
3.13	195, 213	8.8	221	5.3	142
3.15	195, 202,	9.3-5	228	6.7	142
	221	10–11	51	9.13	142
3.18-19	195-97	10	65	11.32	142
3.18	222	10.6-8	228	16.17	142

OTHER ANCIENT REFERENCES

Targums		*Ber.*		Talmuds	
Targ. Isa.		1.1–3.5	44	*b. Šab.*	
6.9-10	128	2.4–5.5	46	115	53
28.5-6	125	3.4	45		
28.5	125	4.4	48, 50	Christian Authors	
		6.5	45	*Apos. Const.*	
Mishnah				1–6	75
Ab.		*Tam.*		7	37
2.13	29, 48	5.1	45	7–8	52, 67
				7.1-32	75

JOURNAL FOR THE STUDY OF THE PSEUDEPIGRAPHA
SUPPLEMENT SERIES